New Orleans

"All you've got to do is decide to go and the hardest part is over.

So go!"

TONY WHEELER, COFOUNDER – LONELY PLANET

THIS EDITION WRITTEN AND RESEARCHED BY

Amy C Balfour & Adam Karlin

Contents

Plan Your Trip 4

Welcome to New Orleans 4
New Orleans' Top 10 6
What's New 13
Need to Know 14
First Time New Orleans 16
Top Itineraries 18
If You Like 20
Month by Month 22
With Kids 26
Like a Local 28
Eating 30
Drinking & Nightlife 34
Entertainment.............39
Shopping...................... 42
Gay & Lesbian 44

Explore New Orleans 46

French Quarter 58
Faubourg Marigny & Bywater 85
CBD & Warehouse District 100
Garden, Lower Garden & Central City..................115
Uptown & Riverbend...130
Mid-City & the Tremé 144
Day Trips from New Orleans.......................159
Sleeping 172

Understand New Orleans 187

New Orleans Today 188
History..........................190
People of New Orleans 202
Architecture................ 205
Music 210
Environment 213

Survival Guide 215

Transportation 216
Directory A–Z 220
Glossary........................226
Index 229

New Orleans Maps 236

JOHN COLETTI/GETTY IMAGES ©

FOTOLUMINATE LLC/SHUTTERSTOCK ©

(left) **City Park p146**

(above) **St Louis Cathedral p61**

(right) **George 'Buddy' Guy performing at the Jazz Fest p50**

JOSH BRASTED/GETTY IMAGES ©

Mid-City & the Tremé p144

Faubourg Marigny & Bywater p85

French Quarter p58

CBD & Warehouse District p100

Garden, Lower Garden & Central City p115

Uptown & Riverbend p130

Welcome to New Orleans

The things that make life worth living – eating, drinking and the making of merriment – are the air that New Orleans breathes.

Epicurean Appetite

When it comes to food, New Orleans does not fool around. Well, OK, it does: its playful attitude to ingredients and recipes mixes (for example) alligator sausage and cheesecake into a dessert fit for the gods. But it creates this mind-bendingly rich food with enterprise, innovation and a dedication to perfecting one of the USA's great indigenous cuisines; it's a culinary aesthetic that will have you snoring in the happiest of food comas afterwards.

Celebration Seasons

We're not exaggerating when we say there is either a festival or a parade every week of the year in New Orleans. Sometimes, such as during Mardi Gras or Jazz Fest, it feels like there's a new party for every hour of the day. At almost any celebration in town, people engage in masking – donning a new appearance via some form of costuming – while acting out the satyric side of human behavior. But the celebrations and rituals of New Orleans are as much about history as hedonism, and every dance is as much an expression of tradition and community spirit as it is of joy.

Unceasing Song

New Orleans is the hometown of jazz, but neither the city nor the genre she birthed are musical museum pieces. Jazz is the root of American popular music, the daddy of rock, brother of the blues and not-too-distant ancestor of hip-hop – all styles of music that have defined the beat of global pop for decades. Music – all these varieties plus a few you may never have heard of – are practiced and played here on every corner, in any bar, every night of the week. Live music isn't an event: it's as crucial to the city soundscape as the streetcar bells.

Candid Culture

There aren't many places in the USA that wear their history as openly on their sleeves as New Orleans. This city's very facade is an architectural study par excellence. And while Boston and Charleston can boast beautiful buildings, New Orleans has a lived-in, cozy feeling that's easily accessible. As a result of its visible history you'll find a constant, often painful, dialogue with the past, stretching back hundreds of years. It's a history that for all its controversy has produced a street culture that can be observed and grasped in a very visceral way.

KRIS DAVIDSON/LONELY PLANET ©

Why I Love New Orleans

By Adam Karlin, Author

New Orleans is all about beauty and experiencing the divine through mortal senses. There's joy here, from great food to the best concert of your life, and serenity, found in the shade between live oaks or while watching fireflies on Bayou St John. Whichever way of being I choose for the day, New Orleans indulges me. Basically, I like traveling with soft eyes – eyes that see as a child, with wonder. This town gives me soft eyes the moment I step out the door.

For more about our authors, see p256.

Top: Daniel Farrow performing at Preservation Hall (p81) in the French Quarter

New Orleans' Top 10

Creole Architecture *(p205)*

1 Looks aren't always skin deep. In New Orleans the architectural skin is integral to the city's spirit – and gives an undeniably distinctive sense of place. What immediately sets New Orleans apart from the USA is the architecture of the Creole *faubourgs* (*fo*-burgs), or neighborhoods. This includes the shaded porches of the French Quarter, of course, but also filigreed Marigny homes, candy-colored Bywater cottages and the grand manses of Esplanade Ave.

French Quarter; Faubourg Marigny & Bywater

Mardi Gras *(p50)*

2 Let us start by saying what Mardi Gras is *not:* beads and breasts. With the exception of some rowdy crowds on Canal St, most visitors, and all locals, keep their clothes (or bodypaint) on. And oh, what clothes! You'll see the most fantastic costumes (plus some boring yellow-purple-green rugby shirts Uptown), the weirdest pageantry, West African rituals, Catholic liturgy and massive parade floats, all culminating in the single-most exhausting and exhilarating day of your life. Happy Mardi Gras, baby.

Mardi Gras & Jazz Fest

1

FOTOLUMINATE LLC/SHUTTERSTOCK ©

2
ONE WAY
QUEEN

3

JOSH BRASTED/GETTY IMAGES ©

4

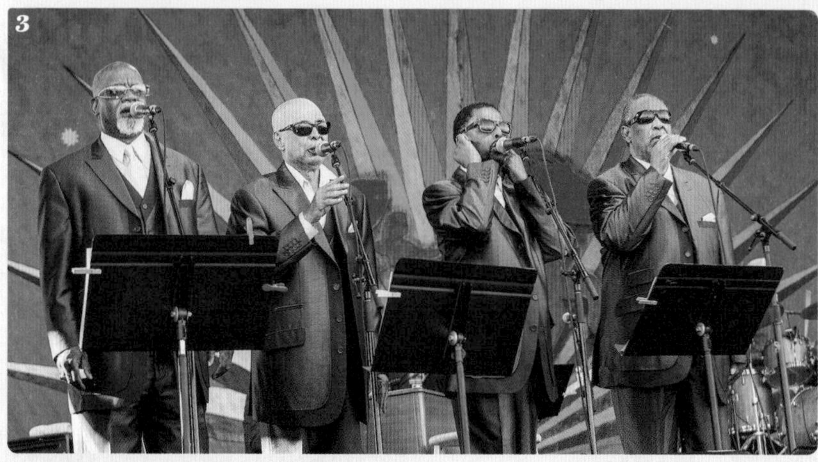

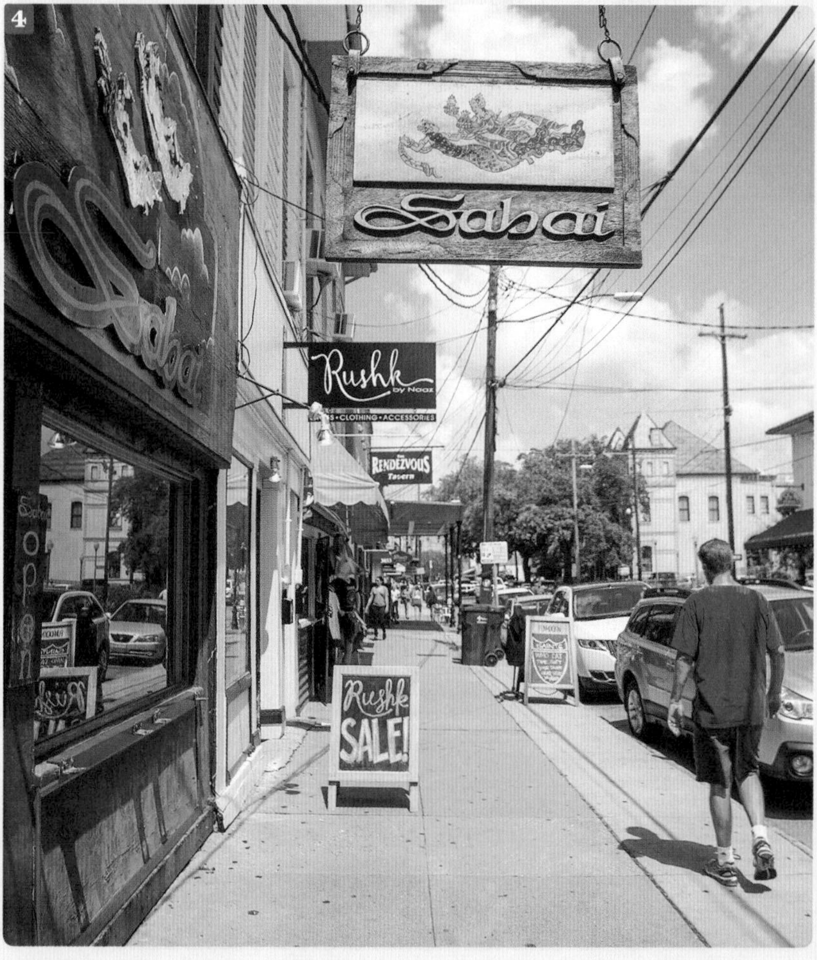

KYLIE MCLAUGHLIN/GETTY IMAGES ©

Jazz Fest *(p50)*

3 You don't have to be a fan of big music festivals to enjoy Jazz Fest. Why? It's about so much more than just stage shows; it's the energy that infuses the city for the last week of April and the first week of May. True lovers of the city return to New Orleans; music proliferates on the streets even more than usual; block parties kick off; and the weather is damn near perfect. The city, in short, struts its stuff, and it's hard not to revel with it during the celebration. TOP LEFT: THE BLIND BOYS OF ALABAMA PLAYING AT JAZZ FEST

Mardi Gras & Jazz Fest

Shopping on Magazine Street *(p142)*

4 Forget Fifth Ave. Erase Oxford St. So long, Rue Saint-Honoré. Magazine St – specifically the 3-mile stretch of it that smiles along the bottom bend of New Orleans' Uptown – may be the world's best shopping street. Sure, there's an absence of big names in large spaces with thumping house music, but you'll uncover a glut of indie boutiques; tons of vintage; po'boys for the hungry; antique warehouses galore; art galleries in profusion; big shady trees; and architecture that will charm your toes off. All this, and dive bars like Ms Mae's.

Uptown & Riverbend

City Park *(p146)*

5 City Park is larger than Central Park and it has alligators, so really, what are you waiting for? If alligators aren't your thing, it is also home to long lines of live oaks and weeping willows; a botanical garden that contains New Orleans in miniature; ice cream; Greek columns; a sculpture garden that surrounds the New Orleans Museum of Art; and a singing tree, festooned with wind chimes and romance – the sort of space where love and music slowly infuse the air with giddiness.

Mid-City & the Tremé

St Charles Avenue Streetcar *(p128)*

6 Some of the grandest homes in the USA line St Charles Ave, shaded by enormous live oak trees that glitter with the tossed beads of hundreds of Mardi Gras floats. Underneath in the shade, joggers pace themselves along the grassy 'neutral ground' (median) while Tulane girls flirt with Loyola boys. Clanging through this bucolic corridor comes the St Charles streetcar, a mobile bit of urban transportation history, bearing tourists and commuters along a street as important to American architecture as Frank Lloyd Wright.

Uptown & Riverbend

Eating a Po'boy *(p31)*

7 If by 'sandwich' we mean a portable meal that contains vegetable and meat enclosed by starch, the po'boy is perfection, the Platonic ideal of sandwiches. But let's get to the detail: it's fresh filling (roast beef or fried seafood are the most common, but the possibilities are endless), tomatoes, lettuce, onion, mayo, pickles and a perfect loaf of not-quite-French bread. The ideal po'boy is elusive: try Mahony's on Magazine St, Domilise's Po-boys Uptown or Parkway in Mid-City.

Eating

6

DARRYL BROOKS/SHUTTERSTOCK ©

KRIS DAVIDSON/LONELY PLANET©

Love Live Music

(p210)

8 Music flows deep in the soul of New Orleans. Every beat, be it Cajun fiddle or brass-band drumline, measures out the rhythm of the cultures that came together to create this startlingly unique city. Frenchmen St is packed with joints playing rock, metal, hip-hop, folk and, of course, jazz. If you can walk its few small blocks without hearing something you like, you may as well keep walking out of New Orleans, because the sound and the soul of this city are inextricably married.

☆ ***Entertainment***

Drinking Classic Cocktails *(p35)*

9 A significant case could be made that the cocktail, a blend of spirits mixed into something delicious and dangerous, was invented in New Orleans. Bitters, long considered a crucial component of any cocktail, is the homegrown creation of a French Quarter pharmacy. When someone calls a drink a 'classic cocktail,' it's because local bartenders have been making it here for centuries. The ultimate New Orleans drink is the Sazerac; it can be enjoyed at any time of day, but always adds a touch of class.

Drinking & Nightlife

9

THE WASHINGTON POST/GETTY IMAGES ©

10

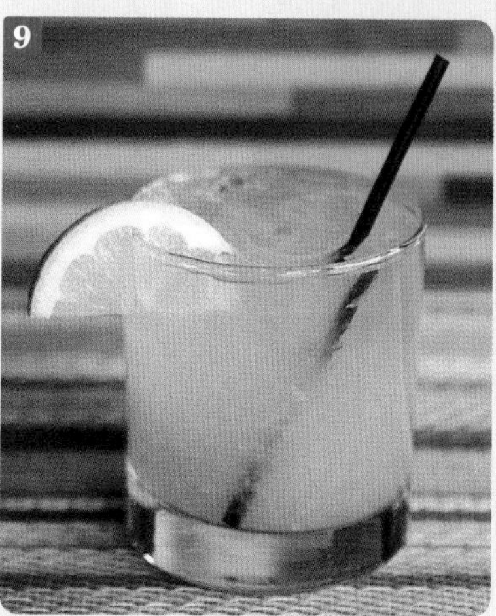

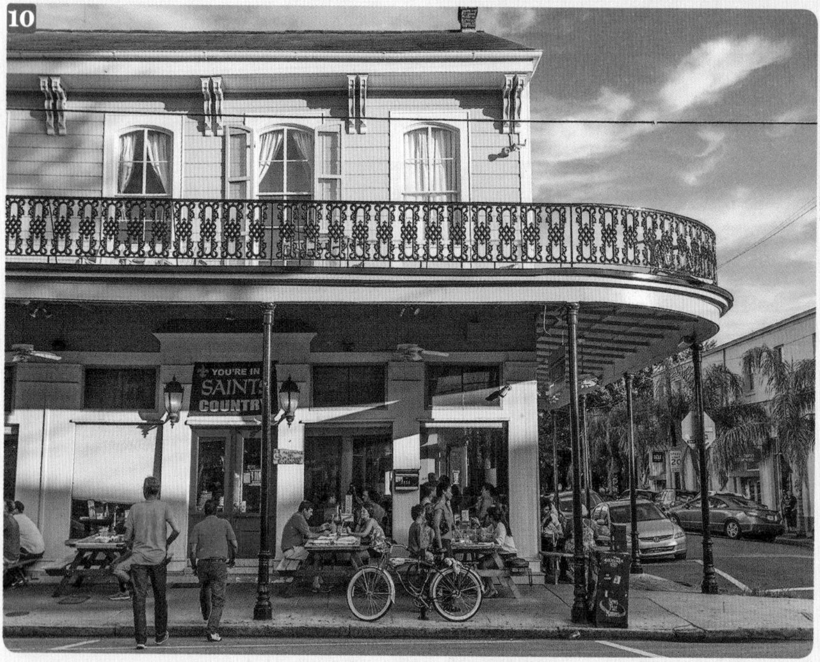

KYLIE MCLAUGHLIN/GETTY IMAGES ©

Garden District Stroll *(p115)*

10 After the Louisiana Purchase, thousands of Americans began moving to New Orleans, until then an entirely French city. Said Yankees decided to show the Europeans they could build homes as pretty as any continental-Caribbean town house, and so constructed enormous, plantation-ready mansions in the area now known as the Garden District. Soaking up architecture is simply magical out here; stroll under live oaks, past fine restaurants and bumping bars – and don't forget to pay a visit to the cemetery too...

Garden, Lower Garden & Central City

What's New

Pop (Dining) Culture

New Orleans has always attracted young, talented chefs. In the past, cooks often had to put in years at a kitchen, and pray for a financial windfall, before opening their own restaurant. Now, a surge in pop-up dining options (restaurants that operate out of a space for a limited time each week) are giving some of the city's most impressive kitchens and chefs room to flex their culinary muscles.

Road to Berlin

Trudge through the closing days of the European theater at the National WWII Museum, a tribute to the efforts of the Western Allied forces. (p102)

SoBou

The name means 'South of Bourbon,' but more pertinent is the food; to say duck beignets with a chicory-coffee sauce is over-the-top would, ironically, be an understatement. (p76)

Latitude 29

Fall in love with this bar, dedicated to the legacy of the Tiki lounge, as you wash your Hawaiian meat pie down with a fine rum cocktail. (p75)

Ba Chi Canteen

Vietnamese classics and cutting-edge cuisine – ever had a rice-flour 'baco'? – all served on the cheap, in a hip, student-centric slice of town. (p135)

Fifi Mahony's

Fifi's is more than a wig shop; it's our preferred stop for when you need to kit yourself out for the celebration of fantasy and revelry in which this city excels. (p80)

Pizza Delicious

'Pizza D' has upped the pie game in New Orleans, bringing excellent New York–style thin-crust goodness to the streets of the Bywater. (p88)

Crescent Park

This lovely stretch of landscaping will one day connect the city's 'downriver' neighborhoods to the Quarter. In the meantime, it makes for a wonderful ramble along the river. (p87)

Peche Seafood Grill

This oh-so-hot venture from local restaurant mogul Donald Link impresses with simple yet savory coastal seafood cooked in an open hearth. (p111)

Southern Food & Beverage Museum

Revamped displays and the open-kitchen restaurant Purloo are the draw at this ode to southern cooking, which moved from the riverfront to Central City. (p119)

NOLA Brewing

Thirsty crowds descend on Tchoupitoulas St for the Friday-afternoon brewery tour and its generous samples – all free. Sixteen taps keep the taproom busy. (p124)

For more recommendations and reviews, see **lonelyplanet.com/usa/new-orleans**

Need to Know

For more information, see Survival Guide (p215)

Currency
US dollars ($)

Language
English

Visas
Required for most foreign visitors unless eligible for the Visa Waiver Program.

Money
ATMs widely available. Credit cards accepted in all accommodations and many, but not all, restaurants.

Cell Phones
Local SIM cards can be used in European and Australian phones. Other phones must be set to roaming.

Time
Central Time (GMT/UTC minus six hours)

Tourist Information
New Orleans Convention Center & Visitors Bureau (☎504-566-5011; www.neworleanscvb.com; 2020 St Charles Ave; ⏲8:30am-5pm Mon-Fri) Plenty of free maps and helpful information.

Daily Costs

Budget: Less than $150
- Dorm bed $30
- Self-cater or cheap takeout $5–10
- Free music shows
- Bicycle rental ($20) or streetcar tickets ($3)

Midrange: $150–$250
- Guesthouse or B&B double room $100–120
- Neighborhood restaurant for two $50–70
- Bicycle rental or split taxi fares ($20–40)

Top End: More than $250
- Fine dining for two, plus wine $150
- Four-star double hotel rooms from $200
- Taxis or car rental ($40–60)

Advance Planning

Three months before Check if any festivals are going down; book hotel rooms if you're arriving during Mardi Gras or Jazz Fest.

One month before Organize car rental. Make bookings at high-end restaurants you don't want to miss.

One week before Read the Gambit (www.bestofneworleans.com) and check www.neworleansonline.com to see what's going on in the way of live music during your visit.

Useful Websites

Gambit (www.bestofneworleans.com) Arts and entertainment listings.

New Orleans Online (www.neworleansonline.com) Official tourism website.

New Orleans CVB (www.neworleanscvb.com) Convention Center & Visitor Bureau.

WWOZ radio (www.wwoz.org) Firm finger on the cultural pulse.

Times-Picayune (www.nola.com) Three times a week.

Lonely Planet (www.lonelyplanet.com/usa/new-orleans) Your trusted traveler website.

New Orleans Hotels (www.neworleanshotels.com) A good database of lodging options.

WHEN TO GO

From mid-March to late May you may have to endure some hot days but in general the weather is pleasant for shorts and shirt sleeves.

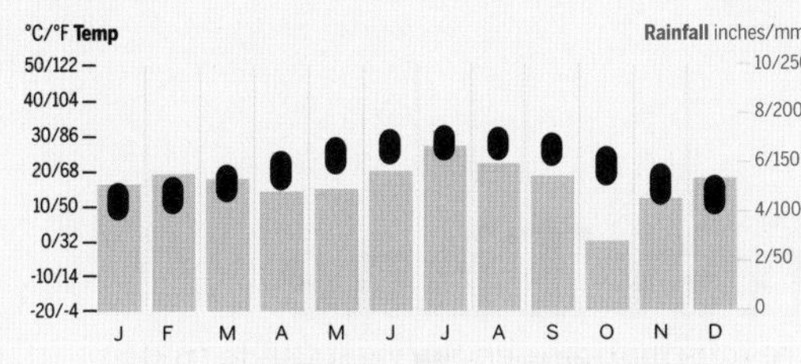

Arriving in New Orleans

Louis Armstrong International Airport (MSY) Located 13 miles west of New Orleans. A taxi to the CBD costs $33, or $14 per passenger for three or more passengers. Shuttles to the CBD cost one way/round-trip $20/38 per person. The E2 bus takes you to Carrollton and Tulane Ave in Mid-City for $2.

Amtrak & Greyhound Located adjacent to each other downtown. You can walk to the CBD or French Quarter, but don't do so at night, or with heavy luggage. A taxi from here to the French Quarter should cost around $10; further afield you'll be pressed to spend more than $20.

For much more on **arrival** see p216

Getting Around

➡ **Streetcar** Service on the charming streetcars is limited. One-way fares cost $1.25, and multi-trip passes are available.

➡ **Bus** Bus services are OK, but try not to time your trip around them. Fares won't run more than $2.

➡ **Walk** If you're just exploring the French Quarter, your feet will serve fine.

➡ **Bicycle** Flat New Orleans is easy to cycle – you can cross the entirety of town in 45 minutes.

➡ **Car** The easiest way to access outer neighborhoods such as Mid-City. Parking is problematic in the French Quarter and CBD.

For much more on **getting around** see p217

Sleeping

Because the bedrock of the local economy is tourism, accommodations are generally of a high standard. Hotels are found in the French Quarter and CBD. These are large, multistory affairs kitted out with amenities; hotels in the French Quarter tend to have a more boutique, historical feel, while CBD properties are more modern. More intimate (and quirky) guesthouses and B&Bs are the norm in the Garden District, Uptown, Faubourg Marigny and the Bywater. There is one hostel in Mid-City.

New Orleans Online (www.neworleansonline.com/book)

Louisiana Bed & Breakfast Association (www.louisianabandb.com)

New Orleans Hotels (www.bestneworleanshotels.com)

Lonely Planet (www.lonelyplanet.com/usa/new-orleans/hotels)

For much more on **sleeping** see p172

THE NEW ORLEANS COMPASS

North, south, east and west? Not in New Orleans. This city's directions are determined by bodies of water and how they flow, not by a compass. Here folks say Lake, River, Up and Down. 'Lake' is Lake Pontchartrain, north of the city. 'River,' of course, is the Mississippi. 'Up' and 'down' refer to the flow of the river, which heads 'down' towards the Gulf of Mexico. So 'Down' basically means 'east,' and 'Up' basically means west. Confused? It makes more sense when you're here, honest.

First Time New Orleans

For more information, see Survival Guide (p215)

Checklist

- Make sure your passport is valid for at least six months past your arrival date
- Check the airline baggage restrictions
- Inform your debit-/credit-card company
- Arrange for appropriate travel insurance
- Have your rental car (p218) organized if you're self-driving
- Confirm dates with your lodging

What to Pack

- Rain gear
- Comfortable walking shoes or sandals
- A nice shirt or dress for a potential night out
- Something that could work as a costume – a feather boa, silly hat etc
- A form of identification besides your passport; New Orleans bouncers are getting strict about IDs

Top Tips for Your Trip

- The French Quarter is one of the most beautiful slices of preserved architecture in North America, and it's home to many of the city's great restaurants, bars and music venues. With that said, many tourists never leave the Quarter. That's a shame, as much of the city's local life occurs outside of its confines.
- From May until as late as October, New Orleans can be hot. Face melting hot. Make sure to hydrate often.
- If you're going to be driving, avoid trying to park in the French Quarter and the CBD, unless you're OK with paying a lot fee. Street parking is tight and subject to residential restrictions.

What to Wear

New Orleanians are pretty casual about fashion, but some of the city's nicer restaurants have a jackets-only policy for men. Usually a jacket will be provided by the restaurant in question (call ahead to check), but gents will still want to bring a collared shirt and slacks. Ladies can get by with a dress or nice set of slacks and shirt.

New Orleanians are always looking for an excuse to wear a costume, and if you stroll down the street in a crazy get up, most folks won't bat an eye. Consider bringing something that can double as funny and/or fancy dress.

Be Forewarned

New Orleans suffers from a high crime rate. Keep your wits about you when taking money out of an ATM, and try to either travel in a group at night, or take a taxi or pedi-cab (great for short-hop trips), especially if you're going to an area you haven't explored yet. This is a city where people like to party, and muggers tend to target those who seem obviously drunk.

A Parade for Every Weekend

Second Lines (p158) are neighborhood parades that proceed through the city's African American neighborhoods. They occur every Sunday from roughly September to June, and are a fascinating insight into local life. Visitors are always welcome, but be prepared for a scene that includes a lot of loud music, public drinking and unabashed public dancing. Check out the Takin' It to the Streets section of WWOZ.org for information on when (and if) a Second Line is occurring during your visit.

Taxes

New Orleans is subject to a 9% sales tax, and hotels are subject to a 14.75% hotel tax. We incorporate this pricing into our reviews.

Tipping

- **Hotels** A dollar or two per bag carried to your room.
- **Restaurants** Not optional! Standard 18% for good service, 20% for exceptional service.
- **Music** It's good manners to kick in a few bucks when the band passes around a bucket or hat.
- **Bars** Leave a dollar every time you order – more if it's a complicated drink or large round.
- **Taxi** Tip 10% or round up the fare.

RAY LASKOWITZ/GETTY IMAGES ©

Jazz musicians celebrating the beginning of Mardi Gras (p50)

Etiquette

New Orleanians tend to be a casual bunch, but good manners go a long way here, as is the case in much of the rest of the American South.

- **Greetings** It's bad form to just dive into the business at hand in New Orleans. Greet someone, ask how they're doing, and expect an honest answer in return; this city has a good attitude, but it also has an honest one.
- **Conversation** In a similar vein: New Orleanians like to chat. Be it small talk or rambling on a topic at hand, the citizens of this city are not, on balance, a reserved people. Don't be surprised if you hear a few uncomfortably long anecdotes or life stories within minutes of meeting someone.

Katrina

Hurricane Katrina irrevocably changed New Orleans, and discussions about it can be charged. If you deem it a natural disaster, realize many people here consider it (with some justification) more of a failure of human-made institutions. Some New Orleanians didn't even live here during the storm; some did and want to forget about it; and some will open their hearts to you. Judge your conversation carefully.

Top Itineraries

Day One

French Quarter (p58)

Wake up and smell the coffee (and enjoy a croissant) at Croissant D'Or (p73). Afterwards sign up for the Friends of the Cabildo walking tour (p66), our favorite introduction to the architectural wonders of the French Quarter.

Lunch Mister Gregory's (p74) Baguettes with innovative sandwich fillings.

French Quarter (p58)

Wander through Jackson Square (p60), the green heart of the neighborhood, and explore the Quarter's museums, such as the Cabildo (p62) and Presbytère (p63). Afterwards, enjoy a free afternoon concert at the Old US Mint (p65).

Dinner Bayona (p76) Base of hometown legend Susan Spicer.

French Quarter (p58)

Relax with a drink at Tonique (p77) or French 75 (p78), two of the finest cocktail bars in a city that invented the cocktail. Take in a show at Preservation Hall (p81) or One Eyed Jacks (p80), and when the music is over have a 3am breakfast at the Clover Grill (p72).

Day Two

CBD & Warehouse District (p100)

Spend a morning visiting the Ogden Museum of Southern Art (p103). Once you've immersed yourself in the aesthetics of the region, consider perusing some history at the National WWII Museum (p102).

Lunch Cochon Butcher (p111) Artisan meats with a Cajun twist.

Garden, Lower Garden & Central City (p115)

Stroll along pretty Magazine St in a state of shopping nirvana. Then walk north, pop into Lafayette Cemetery No 1 (p117) and hop onto the St Charles Avenue Streetcar (p135), heading west toward Audubon Park (p131). Afterwards, take the streetcar towards the Riverbend.

Dinner Ba Chi Canteen (p135) Vietnamese cooked with New Orleans indulgence.

Uptown & Riverbend (p130)

Have a boozy night perusing the excellent beer menu at Cooter Brown's Tavern & Oyster Bar (p139) and consider having an oyster or ten on the side. Then finish it off by heading to the Maple Leaf Bar (p141) or Tipitina's (p141) and rocking out to whoever is playing.

Day Three

Faubourg Marigny & Bywater (p85)

Get the day going with oysters and grits at Cake Café & Bakery (p90). Eat early so you can join the morning Creole Neighborhoods cycle tour with Confederacy of Cruisers (p93). If you don't fancy traveling on two wheels, walk past Washington Square Park (p88) and Elysian Fields Ave into the residential portion of the Marigny.

Lunch Lost Love (p89) dive bar has a surprise Vietnamese kitchen.

Faubourg Marigny & Bywater (p85)

Walk east (or 'down' in New Orleans directional-speak) along Royal or Congress Sts and check out the riot of colorful houses. Once you pass Press St, you're in the Bywater; look for Dr Bob's Studio (p97). Then take a walk into the Crescent Park (p87), where you can enjoy great views of the Mississippi.

Dinner Bacchanal (p89) for wine and cheese in a musical garden.

Faubourg Marigny & Bywater (p85)

Stay in the neighborhood to listen to live music on St Claude Ave or on Frenchmen St (p87).

Day Four

Mid-City & the Tremé (p144)

Consider renting a bicycle and riding around the Tremé; Governor Nicholls St is particularly attractive. Driving is also an option. While in the neighborhood, don't miss the Backstreet Cultural Museum (p151); from here, it's an easy walk into Louis Armstrong Park. (p152)

Lunch Dooky Chase (p155) is the queen of local soul food.

Mid-City & the Tremé (p144)

Head up Esplanade Avenue (p149) and gawk at all the gorgeous Creole mansions sitting prettily under live oaks. Take Esplanade Ave all the way to City Park (p146) and wander around the New Orleans Museum of Art (p146). Afterwards, you can relax for a spell under the trees or along the banks of bucolic Bayou St John.

Dinner Café Degas (p154) for fabulously romantic French fine dining.

Mid-City & the Tremé (p144)

Have a well-mixed drink at friendly Twelve Mile Limit (p156); it also serves barbecue, in case you feel peckish again. End the night at Mid-City Rock & Bowl (p157), a mix of bowling alley and concert hall.

If You Like...

Live Music

Candlelight Lounge Wednesday night with the Tremé Brass Band is one of the most soulful shows in town. (p157)

Tipitina's Legendary live music in Uptown for heaps of character and atmosphere. (p141)

d.b.a. Hosts local legends and international acts of acclaim throughout the week. (p94)

Mid-City Rock & Bowl Zydeco Thursday is as close as you'll come to Cajun country within New Orleans. (p157)

Spotted Cat One of the great smoky jazz bars of New Orleans. (p94)

Snug Harbor This attractive lounge is the classiest jazz establishment in town. (p95)

Hi Ho Lounge Shows range from bluegrass to punk at this eclectic venue. (p94)

Maison Attracts a younger crowd; showcases everything from hip-hop to indie rock. (p95)

AllWays Lounge Come for frontier-pushing music, experimental stuff and damn good dance parties. (p95)

One Eyed Jacks One of the French Quarter's best bars, showcasing genres spanning rap to indie to hard metal. (p80)

Creole Cuisine

Bayona One of the first, and still best, innovators in New Orleans haute cuisine. (p76)

JUDY BELLAH/GETTY IMAGES ©

A display at the Butterfly Garden & Insectarium (p104) in the Warehouse District

Gautreau's Consistently amazing, with a kitchen fronted by Sue Zemanick, one of the brightest rising stars in American gastronomy. (p137)

Dooky Chase The grand dame of African American New Orleans Creole cooking. (p155)

Commander's Palace One of New Orleans' most legendary restaurants, a proving ground for many a young local chef. (p124)

Lilette One of the most promising kitchens in town, Lilette combines great food with a cozy atmosphere. (p137)

Patois Excellent French cuisine given a New Orleans twist, housed in a wonderfully atmospheric historic home. (p137)

Galatoire's Where the New Orleans elite still gathers every Friday; a restaurant and experience of another era. (p72)

Green Spaces

City Park The largest and prettiest green space in the city of New Orleans. (p146)

Bayou St John (p152) This coffee-black waterway is one of the nicest places for a stroll in the city. (p152)

Barataria Preserve See the swamps that define southern Louisiana mere minutes from the state's largest city. (p170)

Alcee Fortier Park A tiny but wonderfully landscaped park on lovely Esplanade Ave. (p150)

Audubon Zoo Located in lush Audubon Park, the zoo is both park area and animal encounter space. (p132)

The Arts

Marigny Opera House Performance art and dance go off in this converted church space. (p94)

Contemporary Arts Center Regular rotating installations feature at this excellent arts museum. (p106)

AllWays Lounge Weird and wonderful performances regularly take the stage here. (p95)

Royal Street Packed with galleries that showcase the many iterations of local art. (p64)

Frenchmen Art Market A regular showcasing of some the city's most creative minds. (p87)

Architecture

Royal Street This is quintessential French Quarter: stroll past fine Creole town houses and wonderful iron balconies. (p64)

St Charles Avenue Live oak trees shade some of the most beautiful plantation-style mansions in the South, best viewed by streetcar. (p135)

Esplanade Avenue Another shady street where the villas are French Caribbean inspired; Degas once lived here. (p149)

Faubourg Marigny & Bywater (p86) Lovely, colorful Creole cottages are scattered over this area like candy. (p86)

For more top New Orleans spots, see the following:

- Eating (p30)
- Drinking & Nightlife (p34)
- Entertainment (p39)
- Shopping (p42)

Museums

National WWII Museum Excellent, comprehensive museum that provides fascinating insights into the largest conflict in history. (p102)

New Orleans Museum of Art Features both contemporary work and a large archaeological section, plus a gorgeous sculpture garden. (p146)

Ogden Museum of Southern Art A mesmerizing peek into the aesthetic of America's most distinctive geographic region. (p103)

Backstreet Cultural Museum Enthralling journey into the street culture of African American New Orleans. (p151)

Butterfly Garden & Insectarium Bugs! Fun for kids, but also accessible to adults, especially those with an interest in the animal kingdom. (p104)

Month by Month

TOP EVENTS

Mardi Gras February/March

Jazz Fest April/May

Super Sunday March

French Quarter Festival April

Fringe Festival November

January

Contrary to popular belief, New Orleans gets cold, and January is pretty nippy. Sports events and tourism-oriented New Year's debauchery give way to the professional partying of Carnival Season by month's end.

Joan of Arc Parade

On January 6, New Orleans celebrates the birthday of the Maid of Orleans – Joan of Arc – with a family-friendly parade (www.joanofarc-parade.com) that runs through the French Quarter. Parade-goers dress in meticulously detailed historical costume.

Martin Luther King Jr Day

On the third Monday in January a charming mid-day parade, replete with brass bands, makes its way from the Bywater to the Tremé, down St Claude Ave.

February

It's Carnival time! In the weeks preceding Mardi Gras the madness in the city builds to a fever pitch, culminating in the main event, the party to end all parties.

Tet

Folks of all backgrounds like to show up at Mary Queen of Vietnam Church (www.mqvncdc.org) in New Orleans East for firecrackers, loud music and great food during the Vietnamese New Year (Tet).

Carnival Season

During the three weeks before Mardi Gras, parades kick off with more frequency each day. Large krewes stage massive affairs, with elaborate floats and marching bands, that run along St Charles Ave and Canal St.

Mardi Gras Day

In February or early March, the outrageous Carnival activity reaches a crescendo as the city nearly bursts with costumed celebrants on Mardis Gras (www.mardigrasneworleans.com). It all ends at midnight with the beginning of Lent.

March

The city has barely nursed its Mardi Gras hangover when the fun starts again. New Orleanians call this Festival Season, as small concerts and free music events kick off every weekend.

St Patrick's Day

The party picks up the weekend of Paddy's Day (www.stpatricks-dayneworleans.com) with the Jim Monaghan/Molly's at the Market parade, which rolls through the French Quarter; and the Uptown/Irish Channel parade, where the float riders toss cabbages and potatoes.

Super Sunday

St Joseph's Night, March 19, is a big masking event for black Indian gangs, who march after sunset around St Claude Ave and LaSalle St. The following Sunday (known as Super Sunday; www.mardigrasneworleans.com/supersunday.html), tribes gather at AL Davis park (Washington & LaSalle St) for a huge procession of the city's Mardi Gras Indian tribes.

Tennessee Williams Literary Festival

The last weekend of March features a four-day fete (www.tennesseewilliams.net) in honor of Tennessee Williams. The playwright called New Orleans his 'spiritual home.' There's a 'Stell-a-a-a!' shouting contest, walking tours, theater events, film screenings, readings and the usual food and alcohol.

Louisiana Crawfish Festival

This huge crawfish feed (www.louisianacrawfishfestival.com) qualifies as the epitome of southern Louisiana culture. It's fun for the family, with rides, games and Cajun music. Held in nearby Chalmette in late March/early April.

Congo Square New World Rhythms Festival

This huge world-music festival (www.jazzandheritage.org/congo-square) rocks into Congo Sq in mid- to late March; expect drumming, dancing, indigenous crafts and delicious food.

April

Festival season continues. Concerts and crawfish boils pick up in frequency as the weather turns a balmy shade of amazing.

Gay Easter Parade

On Easter Sunday the GBLT population of New Orleans (and their straight friends) dress up in their hyperbolic, frilliest Sunday best, then march or ride in horse-drawn carriages past the gay bars of the French Quarter. Fabulous fun.

French Quarter Festival

One of New Orleans' finest events, the French Quarter Festival (www.fqfi.org) rocks the Vieux Carre in mid-April with stages featuring jazz, funk, Latin rhythms, Cajun, brass bands and R&B, plus food stalls operated by the city's most popular restaurants.

Jazz Fest

The Fair Grounds Race Course – and, at night, the whole town – reverberates with good sounds, plus food and crafts, over the last weekend in April and first weekend of May for Jazz Fest (www.nojazzfest.com).

May

There's another month or two before the weather starts to get soupy and, to be honest, the days are already fairly hot. So too is the ongoing music, food and parties.

Bayou Boogaloo

Mid-City gets to shine with this wonderful outdoor festival (www.thebayouboogaloo.com), held on the banks of pretty Bayou St John in mid-May. Expect the usual: food stalls, lots of bands and general good times.

New Orleans Wine & Food Experience

This being a culinary town, the local food and wine fest (www.nowfe.com) is quite the affair. Join to attend various tastings, seminars and meal 'experiences' that push the gastronomic frontiers. Late May.

July

There's a sultry romance to summer that makes you want to sit in a sweat-stained tank top or summer dress and do nothing but drink iced tea. Don't rest. The New Orleans calendar doesn't let up.

Essence Music Festival

Essence magazine sponsors a star-studded lineup of R&B, hip-hop, jazz and blues performances at the Superdome around the July 4 weekend (www.essence.com/festivals).

Running of the Bulls

In mid-July the Big Easy Rollergirls dress up as bulls and chase crowds dressed in Pamplona-style white outfits with red scarves (www.nolabulls.com). The 'bulls' run through the French Quarter – trust us, this one's lots of fun.

Tales of the Cocktail

Sure, New Orleans is a 24/7 festival, but this three-day event (www.talesofthecocktail.com) sets its sights high. Appreciating the art of 'mixology' is the main point, and getting lit up is only an incidental part of the fun.

August

Damn. It's hot. So very, very hot. And there may be hurricanes on the horizon. Who cares? The eating, drinking and merry-making continue, and hotel rates are bottoming out.

Satchmo SummerFest

Louis Armstrong's birthday (August 4) is celebrated with four days of music and food in the French Quarter (http://fqfi.org/satchmo). Three stages present local talents in 'trad' jazz, contemporary jazz and brass bands.

Southern Decadence

Billing itself as 'Gay Mardi Gras,' this five-day Labor Day weekend festival (www.southerndecadence.com) kicks off in the Lower Quarter. Expect music, masking, cross-dressing, dancing in the streets and a Sunday parade that's everything you'd expect from a city with a vital gay community.

White Linen Night

Get decked out in your coolest white duds and wander about the Warehouse District on the first Saturday in August. Galleries throw open their doors to art appreciators and there are lots of free-flowing drinks.

Red Dress Run

The Nola Hash House Harriers lead this charity run (www.nolareddress.tumblr.com) through the Quarter and Downtown. It's a 3- to

(Top) A woman dressed as a skeleton at Mardi Gras (p50)
(Bottom) The Preservation Hall Jazz Band performs at Jazz Fest (p50)

KRISTA ROSSOW/GETTY IMAGES ©

JOSH BRASTED/GETTY IMAGES ©

4-mile run with one rule: Wear a red dress. Or less. Open to both men and women, so there's lots of crimson cross-dressing afoot.

Mid-Summer Mardi Gras

The Uptown Krewe of OAK (Outrageous and Kinky) holds this mini–Mardi Gras every year around the last weekend in August. Revelers parade around the Riverbend, with the party kicking off at the Maple Leaf Bar (p141).

September

The heat doesn't let up and the threat of hurricanes gets even worse, but the music certainly doesn't take a break.

Ponderosa Stomp

Billed as the greatest celebration of American roots music in the world, the Stomp (www.ponderosastomp.com) takes over Howlin' Wolf downtown in mid-September. Lots of blues, rock, folk, jazz, country and soul.

October

Locals love dressing up, costumes, ghost stories and the supernatural, so October is a pretty big month in these parts.

Crescent City Blues & BBQ Festival

Doesn't the name alone make you want to visit? At this mid-October festival (www.jazzandheritage.org/blues-fest), there's barbecue, there are blues and there are good times in Lafayette Park on St Charles Ave.

New Orleans Film Festival

Theaters around the city screen the work of both local and internationally renowned filmmakers for one week in mid-October (www.neworleansfilmsociety.org).

Halloween

Halloween is not taken lightly here. Most fun is to be found in the giant costume party throughout the French Quarter. It's a big holiday for gay locals and tourists, with a lot of action centering on the Lower Quarter.

Voodoo Music Experience

If you thought New Orleans was all jazz and no rock, visit during Halloween weekend. Past acts at Voodoo (http://worshipthemusic.com) have included the Foo Fighters, the Flaming Lips, Queens of the Stone Age, Billy Idol and Ryan Adams (all in one year!).

November

The weather is cooling down and winter is arriving. Arts and entertainment events, plus some of the best sandwiches you'll ever eat, fill up the calendar.

All Saints Day

Cemeteries fill with crowds who pay their respects to ancestors on November 1. It is by no means morbid or sad, as many people have picnics and parties. It wouldn't be out of line for families to serve gumbo beside the family crypt.

Celebration in the Oaks

This City Park celebration is New Orleans' take on Christmas in America, with 2 miles of oak trees providing the lit-up superstructure (www.celebrationintheoaks.com). You can view it in its entirety from your car or in a horse-drawn carriage.

Fringe Festival

Dramatic boundaries are pushed throughout the city, but particularly in the Marigny and Bywater, at this festival (www.nofringe.org) of experimental theater, held around the second weekend of the month.

Po-Boy Festival

Fifty thousand sandwich-lovers descend on Riverbend in November to sample po'boys from New Orleans' best restaurants (www.poboyfest.com).

December

Christmas brings flickering torch lights, chilly winds, gray skies and a festive atmosphere to this city of festivals.

Feux de Joie

'Fires of joy' light the way along the Mississippi River levees above Orleans Parish and below Baton Rouge in December and on Christmas Eve (December 24).

New Year's Eve

Revelers – mostly drunk tourists – pack around Jackson Brewery in the French Quarter, where Baby New Year is dropped from the roof at midnight.

With Kids

New Orleans is a fairy-tale city, with its colorful beads, weekly costume parties and daily music wafting through the air. The same flights of fancy and whimsy that give this city such appeal for poets and artists also make it an imaginative wonderland for children, especially creative ones.

JUDY BELLAH/GETTY IMAGES ©

A carousel at Audubon Zoo (p132)

Best Animal Encounters

Exploring the Audubon Zoo

There's wildlife from around the world in this attractive zoo (p132), but the main attraction is the excellent showcasing of local critters in the form of the Louisiana Swamp. Out in this cleverly landscaped wetland, your kids will get a chance to mug next to a genuine albino alligator, as pretty as freshly fallen snow in a bayou.

Undersea Adventures at Aquarium of the Americas

Dip a toe into the waters of marine biology at this excellent aquarium (p105), where the aquatic habitats range from the Mississippi delta to the Amazon River Basin. Kids and adults will marvel at rainbow clouds of tropical fish, and guess what? There's a white alligator – 'Spots' – living here, too.

Bug Out in the Insectarium

You've got to love a museum (p104) dedicated to New Orleans' insects, where one display focuses on cockroaches, and another is sponsored by the pest-control business. Yet this isn't a museum that focuses on the' 'ick' factor. Rather, you'll get a sense of the beauty and diversity of the entomological world, from gem-colored beetle displays to the serenity of the Butterfly Garden.

Outdoor Adventures

Wander Through City Park

The largest green space in New Orleans is undoubtedly also its most attractive. City Park (p146) has plenty of big trees for shade, lazy waterways filled with fish (and sometimes small alligators!), a model train diagram of the city built entirely of biological materials, and a wonderful carousel and sculpture garden that will be of interest to older kids. Plus Storyland – a nostalgic minipark with more than two-dozen storybook scenes reproduced on a life-size scale.

Barataria Preserve

This green gem (p170) in the national-park crown is located just south of the city. Toddlers to teenagers will enjoy walking along the flat boardwalk, which traverses the gamut of Louisiana wetlands, from bayous to marsh prairie.

Let's Go Ride a Bike

Cycling in New Orleans is pretty easy for fit kids. Younger ones can be taken on short rides through the French Quarter or the Garden District. Older kids should be able to swing bike tours like the ones offered by Confederacy of Cruisers (p93), which take in the city's older Creole neighborhoods on big, tough, comfortable cruiser-style bicycles. Avoid riding through the traffic-congested CBD.

Alcee Fortier Park

By day, this little park (p150), located on shady Esplanade Ave, is a nice spot to stop for a lemonade in the sun and chill out on funky furniture. At night, in warm weather, outdoor movies are sometimes shown, generally in the early part of the evening.

Jackson Square & the River

Jackson Sq (p60) is essentially a constant carnival. Any time of day you may encounter street artists, fortune-tellers, buskers, brass bands and similar folks all engaged in producing the sensory overload New Orleans is famous for (and kids go crazy over). The square is framed by a fairytale cathedral and two excellent museums, and nearby are steps leading up to the Mississippi River, where long barges evoke *Huckleberry Finn* and the Mississippi of Mark Twain. Drop by Café du Monde (p76) for some powdered-sugar treats.

History & Culture for Kids

Under the City's Skin

The Louisiana Children's Museum (p107) is a good intro to the region for toddlers, while older children and teenagers may appreciate the Ogden Museum (p103), Cabildo (p62) and Presbytère (p63). Little ones often take a shine to the candy-colored houses in the French Quarter, Faubourg Marigny and Uptown. The Latter Library (p133) on St Charles Ave has a good selection of children's literature and is located in a pretty historical mansion. The city's cemeteries, especially Lafayette Cemetery No 1 (p117) in the Garden District, are authentic slices of the past and enjoyably spooky to boot.

Festival Fun

The many street parties and outdoor festivals of New Orleans bring food stalls and, of course, great music. Children will love dancing to the beat. Seek out festivals held during the day, such as Bayou Boogaloo (www.thebayouboogaloo.com).

Mardi Gras for Families

Mardi Gras and the Carnival Season are surprisingly family-friendly affairs outside of the well-known boozy debauch in the French Quarter. St Charles Ave hosts many day parades where lots of krewes roll and families set up grilling posts and tents – drinking revelers aren't welcome. Kids are set up on 'ladder seats' (www.momsminivan.com/extras/ladderseat.html) so they can get an adult-height view of the proceedings and catch throws from the floats. The crazy costumes add to the child-friendly feel of the whole affair. See www.neworleansonline.com/neworleans/mardigras/mgfamilies.html.

NEED TO KNOW

When traveling with kids in New Orleans, it helps to be aware of a few lessons.

Pack From April until October it can be oppressively hot and humid. Bring cool, airy clothes and, if you have young ones susceptible to rashes, pack Gold Bond powder or topical creams. Whenever you head outside, take liquid for hydration.

Stroller stress New Orleans' ill-maintained sidewalks are often horrible for strollers – you'll want to bring one that is both maneuverable and durable.

High chairs Most restaurants have high chairs and booster seats and are happy to accommodate kids. Call ahead to make sure, as some places with liquor licenses cannot have patrons under 21.

Like a Local

New Orleans is friendly to visitors, but rewards those who learn the secrets and hangouts integral to its cultural fabric. Local New Orleanians, as eccentric a cast of characters as you'll find, are an invaluable tool for navigating the city's complex social and physical geography.

KRIS DAVIDSON/LONELY PLANET ©

Street performers in the French Quarter (p58)

'Be Nice or Leave'

The 'Be Nice or Leave' sign and slogan can be found throughout the city of New Orleans. It seems like pretty self-explanatory advice, but there's a deeper attitude at work here.

New Orleans tends to operate on tropical time. This isn't just a marketing slogan for the tourists; it really takes a little more time for things to get done here. Sometimes that's because people here have a laid-back attitude; sometimes it's because poor infrastructure has gummed up the wheels of civil society. Often, both of these elements are at work.

The point is, it pays to be patient in New Orleans, and nothing will upset an otherwise friendly New Orleanian more than a pushy visitor telling them the right or more efficient way to do something. Take it easy when you visit. Be nice. Always tip, including when a band passes around a bucket. Locals have learnt that niceness helps them navigate the pitfalls of living in Louisiana. And they're likely to return the attitude tenfold once you've displayed it.

What's Up with Go Cups

One thing that visitors to New Orleans always marvel at, and that locals love as a prime signifier of unique civic identity, is the go cup. You can drink outdoors here! It's the rare New Orleanian who feels the need to down their beer or cocktail with a needlessly huge gulp. They simply ask the bartender for a plastic cup, and on they proceed to the next establishment.

Follow the native example: don't rush to finish your drink; imbibe it as you stroll to your next destination. Always throw your empty cup into the trash. And don't try to enter a new bar with an unfinished go cup. It's kind of rude, and you'll usually get yelled at by a bouncer or bartender.

Neutral Ground

In the rest of the USA, the area that divides two lanes of traffic or two sides of a street is known as a median. In New Orleans it's called a Neutral Ground. Why does the city assign to a strip of curb or grass a title worthy of Switzerland? Following the Louisiana Purchase, when Americans settled in what was then a French-Creole city, the division between Anglos and Francophiles was designated a Neutral Ground.

Here's a practical tip: many intersections in New Orleans run through Neutral Grounds with their own set of traffic lights. Pay attention to how other drivers go through these intersections. Usually, locals will drive through a red lit intersection (assuming there is no oncoming traffic of course) if it is a small intersection, but they'll often wait at the light if it's a large intersection. Rule of thumb: follow the local example.

Pothole Plotting

The streets of New Orleans are infamous for potholes. In certain neighborhoods you'll see chunks taken out of the street that could swallow a car. Some potholes have been around for so long they've been given affectionate nicknames.

You'll often see locals veering around residential streets as if they were driving drunk. Au contraire: they're being particularly vigilant and aware, because they know if they drive in a straight line, they'll destroy their car's undercarriage upon hitting a Grand Canyon–sized pothole. When you're in the neighborhoods, particularly Uptown, Mid-City and the Bywater, drive carefully or risk the sickening crunch of your rental car scraping pavement.

Throw Me Something, Mister!

During Mardi Gras, enormous floats crowded with riders representing the city's Carnival 'krewes' proceed up and down thoroughfares such as St Charles Ave and Canal St. The float riders toss 'throws' to the waiting crowds; throws range from strings of beads to plastic cups, blinking baubles and stuffed animals.

Here are some locally recognized rules for throw-catching. First: locals never bare their breasts for beads. Most find it crude, and there are kids around. Second: if there's a young kid near you, move, or be prepared to give the kid whatever you catch. Third: if a throw hits the ground...well, opinions are split on this. Many locals will say they'd never touch a throw that hit the street, but we've seen more than a few sneakily bend over to scoop up a cup or a unique string of beads. Rest assured it's not the done thing – even if it is occasionally, well, done.

Ain't No Place to Pee...

The Benny Grunch song 'Ain't No Place to Pee on Mardi Gras Day' speaks to a deep-seated sentiment of the New Orleans population. In short: Benny is right. And it's not just on Mardi Gras. This city is rife with parades, processions and festivals, and it's always an effort to find a spot to get back in touch with nature.

The NOPD will bust you for peeing outdoors if they catch you, and cops in the French Quarter are eagle-eyed about that sort of thing. That warning isn't just for men, by the way. Locals get around this issue by plotting a night wherein the next bar is never more than a nervous rush to a stall away. If you find yourself in need of a bathroom, head for a bar, do your business and order a quick drink (or a soft drink if you're not imbibing) – New Orleans has go cups, so you don't have to down the thing before you leave!

Jambalaya, one of New Orleans' signature dishes

Eating

In what other American city do people celebrate the harvest season of sewage-dwelling crustaceans? We're describing a crawfish boil, by the way, which exemplifies New Orleans' relationship with food: unconditional love. This city finds itself in its food; meals are both expressions of identity and bridges between the city's many divisions.

The Native Example

Settlers who arrived in Louisiana had to work with the ingredients of the bayous, woods and prairie, and so developed one of America's only true native-born cuisines. As a result, some say the New Orleans palette is limited to its own specialties, that this is a town of 'a thousand restaurants and three dishes.'

That cliché is a bit tired. First, lots of restaurants are serving what we would deem Nouveau New Orleans cuisine – native classics influenced by global flavors and techniques. And second, international options are popping up more frequently in this town.

Still, this is a place where the homegrown recipes are the best stuff on the menu. As such, we present a rundown of New Orleans and Louisiana specialties.

ROUX

Very few meals begin life in Louisiana without a roux (pronounced 'roo'): flour slowly cooked with oil or butter. Over time, the product evolves from a light-colored 'white' roux into a smokier 'dark' roux. The final product is used as a thickening and flavoring agent. While deceptively simple, local cooks insist their dishes live or die based on the foundation roux.

GUMBO

No cook is without a personal recipe for this spicy, full-bodied soup or stew, which is a bit like Louisiana itself, food-ified. Ingredients vary from chef to chef, but gumbo is almost always served over starchy steamed rice. Coastal gumbo teems with oysters, jumbo shrimp and crabs, while prairie-bred Cajuns turn to their barnyards and smokehouses.

PO'BOY

Maybe you call it a submarine, a grinder or a hoagie. You are wrong. Simply put, a po'boy is an overstuffed sandwich served on local French bread (more chewy, less crispy) and dripping with fillings; the most popular are roast beef, fried shrimp and/or fried oysters, and 'debris' (the bits of roast beef that fall into the gravy). When you order, your server will ask if you want it 'dressed,' meaning with mayonnaise, shredded lettuce and tomato. Say yes.

RED BEANS & RICE

A poor man's meal rich in flavor, this is a lunch custom associated with Mondays. Monday was traditionally wash day and, in the past, a pot of red beans would go on the stove along with the ham bone from Sunday dinner. By the time the washing was finished, supper was ready.

JAMBALAYA

Hearty, rice-based jambalaya (johm-buh-*lie*-uh) can include just about any combination of fowl, shellfish or meat, but usually includes ham, hence the name (derived from the French *jambon* or the Spanish *jamón*). The meaty ingredients are sautéed with onions, pepper and celery, and cooked with raw rice and water into a flavorful mix of textures.

MUFFULETTAS

It's only a slight exaggeration to say that New Orleans *muffulettas* are the size of manhole covers. Named for a round sesame-crusted loaf, *muffulettas* are layered with various selections from the local Sicilian deli tradition, including Genoa salami, shaved ham, mortadella and sliced provolone cheese. The signature spread – a salty olive salad with pickled vegetables, herbs, garlic and olive oil – is what defines the sandwich.

TASSO

This highly prized butcher-shop specialty is basically a lean chunk of ham, cured with filé (crushed sassafras leaves) and other

NEED TO KNOW

Price Ranges

In our listings we use the following price ranges to indicate the cost of a main course.

$ less than $15
$$ $15 to $25
$$$ more than $25

Opening Hours

- Restaurants generally open from 11am to 11pm, with last seatings around 10:30pm.
- Breakfast usually starts around 7am.
- Many restaurants close Sunday, Monday or both.

Reservations

- Where reservations are necessary, we say so in our reviews. But many restaurants have no-booking policies; Galatoire's (p72) and K-Paul's (p76) are two notable examples. Instead of calling ahead, you can expect to wait out on the sidewalk for a table to open.
- There are lots of small, family-run places in New Orleans. Call ahead to these places if you're in a large group.

Tipping

Tipping is not optional. A good tip is 18%, but folks tend to be munificent here; 20% is almost standard. If service is only adequate, 15% is fine. Some places will charge an automatic 18% gratuity for large groups (usually six or more people).

Courses

The **New Orleans School of Cooking** (Map p238; ☎800-237-4841; www.neworleansschoolofcooking.com; 524 St Louis St; courses $24-29) is a popular and pretty awesome way to learn the ins and outs of one of this city's great exports – its culinary tradition. Both open demonstrations and-hands on cooking courses are available.

Eating by Neighborhood

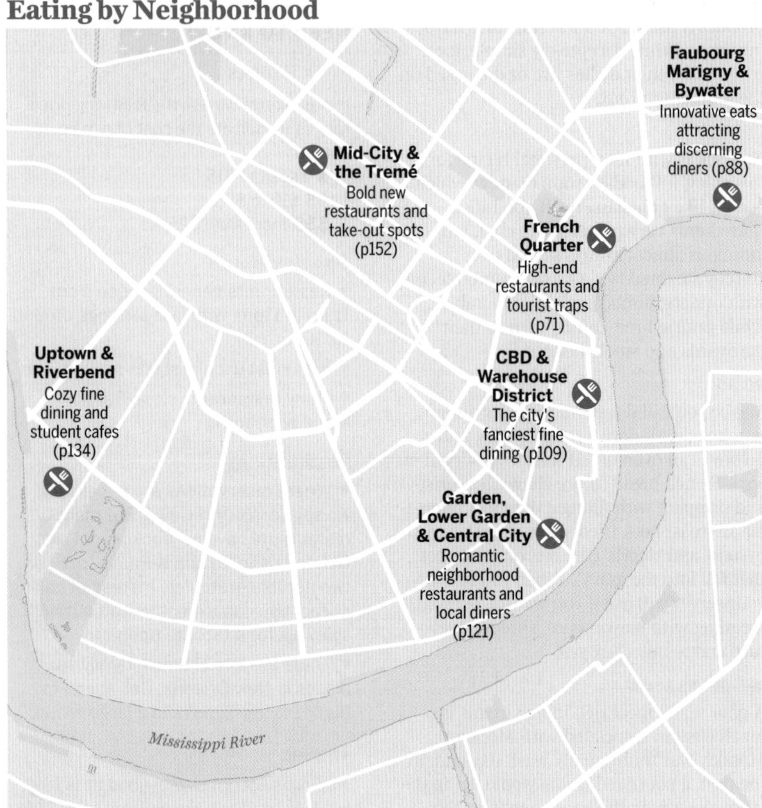

seasonings, and then smoked until it reaches the tough consistency of beef jerky.

BOUDIN

A tasty Cajun sausage made with pork, pork liver, cooked rice and spices. A popular quick bite, especially in Cajun country.

SNOWBALLS

Shaved ice in a paper cup doused liberally with flavored syrup, snowballs are blasts of winter on a steamy midsummer's afternoon.

BEIGNETS

Not so much a dessert as a round-the-clock breakfast specialty akin to the common doughnut, beignets are flat squares of dough flash-fried to a golden, puffy glory, dusted liberally with powdered (confectioner's or icing) sugar, and served scorching hot.

BREAD PUDDING

A specialty in New Orleans and Acadiana, this custardy creation is a good use for leftover bread. Local variations involve copious amounts of butter, eggs and cream, and will usually come topped with a bourbon-spiked sugar sauce.

Lonely Planet's Top Choices

Bacchanal (p89) Wine, cheese, bread and a magically lit garden.

Restaurant August (p110) Fine Creole dining in a 19th-century warehouse.

Cochon Butcher (p111) The pinnacle of Cajun – and carnivorous – cuisine.

Dooky Chase (p155) A lunch buffet sent down by the Creole gastronomy gods.

Surrey's Juice Bar (p121) Best breakfast in the city.

Best for Romantic Meals

Café Degas (p154) Candlelight and French cuisine on a beautiful stretch of Esplanade Ave.

Adolfo's (p92) An intimate Italian eatery sitting over a live-music mecca.

Bacchanal (p89) Outdoor dining, plentiful wine, good cheese and a band on the side.

Lilette (p137) Take your date out for French fare at this lovely, porch-fronted bistro.

Patois (p137) Elegant and filling fare served with wine in a cozy Uptown residence.

Best for Late Nights

Clover Grill (p72) Classic American diner serves the party people in the French Quarter.

Camellia Grill (p134) Butter, grease, fried food and a cast of late-night characters.

Coop's Place (p71) The service is a little surly, but the Cajun cuisine is divine.

Delachaise (p136) Fine wine and stinky cheese served to a crowd of beautiful people.

Best for Po'boys

Mahony's Po-Boy Shop (p136) A perennial po'boy favorite with innovative sandwiches and awesome ingredients.

Domilise's Po-Boys (p134) This down-home shack is the Platonic ideal of a New Orleans sandwich shop.

Parkway Tavern (p152) Grab a po'boy and enjoy a picnic on the banks of Bayou St John.

Guy's (p135) Uptown joint where the sandwiches are made to order every time.

Rampart Food Store (p89) This barren shop has perfected the recipe for a shrimp sandwich.

Best for Classic Creole Cuisine

Commander's Palace (p124) This Garden District institution is the grande dame of classic Creole cuisine.

Dooky Chase (p124) One of the city's iconic restaurants, where Creole cooking is a beloved heritage.

Gautreau's (p137) A lovely Uptown establishment that nails the New Orleans approach to food.

Clancy's (p137) This neighborhood splurge is a romantic option for Creole cookery.

Restaurant August (p110) An elegant setting and presentation belies a gorgeous tableau of New Orleans dishes.

Best for 'Nouveau' New Orleans Cuisine

Peche Seafood Grill (p111) One of the most highly regarded seafood restaurants in the USA.

SoBou (p76) Funky French Quarter restaurant that's decadent and playful with New Orleans recipes.

Bayona (p76) Local ingredients are buttressed by an international approach to cooking techniques.

Herbsaint (p111) Old-school New Orleans food gets a dash of haute technique and execution.

Mat & Naddie's (p139) A locals' spot that likes to experiment, often with delicious results.

Best for Vegetarians

Sneaky Pickle (p90) A no-frills yet delicious vegan diner located in bohemian Bywater.

Seed (p122) Comfort food, contemporary design and vegan cuisine come together here.

Carmo (p111) Creative cuisine and innovative recipes shine at this CBD restaurant.

Green Goddess (p74) International influence, decadent portions and a playful approach to food.

Best for Dessert

Sucré (p121) Pushes the decadence envelope with an enormous catalogue of silly-good chocolates.

Boucherie (p137) There's simply no better dessert in New Orleans than the Krispy Kreme bread pudding.

Green Goddess (p74) A creative and cosmopolitan approach to cuisine yields phenomenal, funky desserts.

Hansen's Sno-Bliz (p136) When it's hot outside, sample the favored icy treat of generations of New Orleanians.

A Sazerac cocktail

Drinking & Nightlife

New Orleans doesn't rest for much. But the city isn't just an alcoholic lush. A typical New Orleans night out features just as much food and music as booze. Here, all your senses are appealed to: your ear for a brass band, your taste for rich food, your sensing of heat on your skin, your observing the visual composition of a streetcar line running past historic homes, as well as your whetted thirst for another beer or shot...

Classic New Orleans Cocktails

The argument can well be made that New Orleans invented the cocktail, and while mixing spirits properly was once a lost art, today a generation of dedicated mixers are out there prepping some mean classics.

➡ **Sazerac** A potent whiskey drink that uses either rye or bourbon as its primary ingredient, with aromatic bitters (including the locally produced Peychaud's), a bit of sugar and a swish of Herbsaint.

➡ **Ramos Gin Fizz** Named for 19th-century New Orleans bartender Henry Ramos, this is a rich, frothy blend of gin, cream, egg whites, extra-fine sugar, fizzy water and a splash of orange-flower water.

➡ **Aviation** Try it on a hot day: gin, maraschino liqueur and lemon juice, plus some other trade secrets depending on which bar is mixing it. Very refreshing.

➡ **Pimm's Cup** A summer tipple traditionally associated with the infamous French Quarter bar Napoleon House. It's a simple mix of the British gin-based liqueur Pimm's No 1, topped with soda or ginger ale.

Beer

Nola Brewing Co (motto: *Laissez la bonne bière verser!* – Let the good beer pour!) is the only brewery based in Orleans Parish. It makes some great brews, ranging from light to dark to intensely hoppy.

That said, Abita, based in St Tammany Parish, is the most popular local brewery. All of its beers are winners, especially the seasonal varietals. Bayou Teche Brewery, based in Arnaudville, is an exciting newcomer to the local brewery scene.

Founded in 1907, Dixie Beer used to be the beer everyone associated with New Orleans, but since Katrina operations have been shipped north to Wisconsin. You can still get a Dixie here, but it's no longer a locally produced drink.

Wine

Wine is and ever has been popular in Louisiana thanks to a strong French cultural influence, but the homegrown industry is small; this state is too humid for viticulture.

Tourist Drinks

The bars on Bourbon St feature neon, sugary beverages that will melt your face and give you an awful hangover. Still interested? OK. The Hurricane, made famous by Pat O'Brien's, is a towering rum drink that gets its bright-pink hue from the healthy portion of passion-fruit juice. The Hand Grenade, sold at Tropical Isle, is a mix of melon liqueur, grain alcohol, rum, vodka and who knows what else. Frozen daiquiris, by New Orleans' definition, are a class of alcoholic Slurpees that come in all the brightest colors of the rainbow. You can pick them up, sometimes by the gallon from, yes, drive-through takeouts.

NEED TO KNOW

Opening Hours

Most dedicated bars open around 5pm, although some places serve drinks during lunch, and some are open 24 hours. Closing time is an ill-defined thing; officially it's around 2am or 3am, but sometimes it's whenever the last customer stumbles out the door. Cafes open early and closing times vary from lunch to late evening (around 9pm).

Prices

This is a cheap town for nighthawks. You'll rarely pay more than $5 for a beer. Sometimes domestics will go for under $3. Cocktails rarely top $6 (unless you're at a higher-end lounge); shots of hard spirits go for around $3 to $5 (more for top-shelf stuff); and everything is cheaper during happy hour. Wine can be expensive at wine bars, but is generally of very high quality. The only time prices go up to annoyingly high levels is during big events such as Mardi Gras and Jazz Fest.

Tipping

It's common to leave a dollar or more for your bartender, even if they just pop the cap off a bottle of beer. You don't have to tip for every drink, but the general rule is to leave a couple of bucks extra for every hour spent at the bar.

Bars vs Lounges vs Clubs

Many bars in New Orleans pull triple duty as live-music venues and restaurants. In our reviews, we try to categorize places based on their primary 'function' – eating, drinking or music.

Top: The New Orleans cityscape at dusk
Left: Bartender at Cure bar (p139)

Drinking by Neighborhood

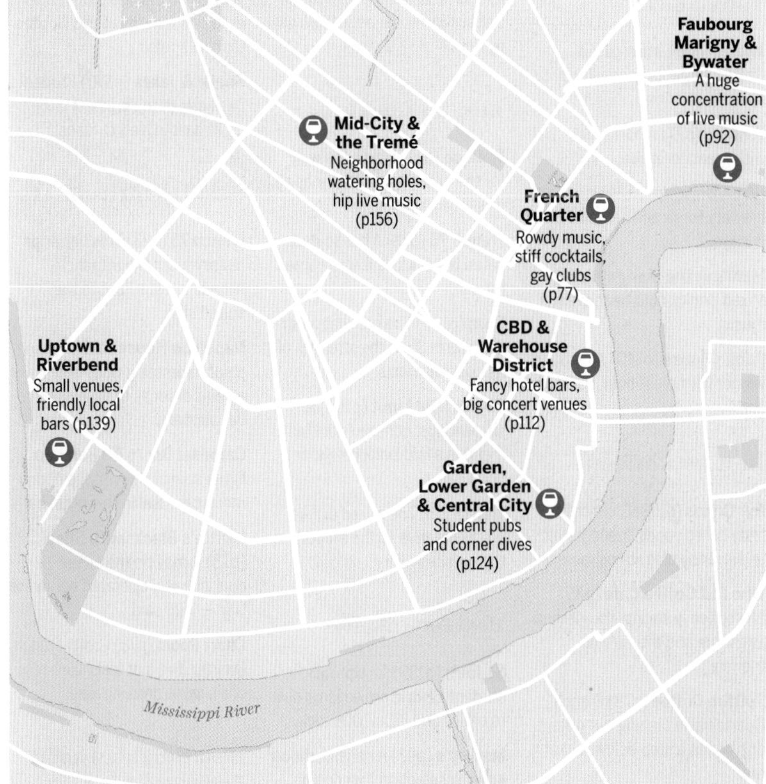

Nonalcoholic Drinks

COFFEE & CHICORY

Coffee here is traditionally mixed with chicory, a roasted herb root. Originally used to 'extend' scarce coffee beans during hard times, chicory continues to be added for its full-bodied flavor, which gives local coffee a slightly bitter twist. We like it served best as café au lait..

ICED TEA

In hot and humid Louisiana, iced tea is more than just a drink – it's a form of air con in a tall, sweaty glass. 'Sweet Tea' is served with enough sugar to keep an army of dentists employed. If you want a proper English cuppa, specify 'hot tea.'

Bars

In general, bars in New Orleans would often be considered 'dives' elsewhere. That's not to say bars here are grotty (although some certainly are); rather, there are many neighborhood joints in New Orleans that are unpretentious spots catering to those looking to drink, as opposed to those who want to meet and chat someone up. If you're in the latter category, head to lounges, which tend to be newer, more brightly lit and possessed of a general modern sensibility.

Clubs

New Orleans isn't much of a nightclub city. There's a general lack of the large spaces nightclubs like to use, particularly in tourist-magnets neighborhoods that have lots of historical housing. And nightclubs aren't really to most folks' speed. If people want to drink, they head to bars; if they want to dance, they opt for live music, and in general locals reject the whole red rope concept. The closest thing the city has to a clubbing scene takes up parts of the Warehouse District, CBD and some of the lounges in swisher hotels.

Lonely Planet's Top Choices

Twelve Mile Limit (p156) Casual neighborhood vibe, great spirits and drinks.

Tonique (p77) A bartenders' bar with great cocktails.

NOLA Brewing (p124) Free brewery tours and samples on Fridays.

Mimi's in the Marigny (p92) Mixed drinks, cold beer, great music.

Publiq House (p140) All around winner with great beer, cocktails and live music.

Best for Coffee

Fair Grinds (p156) Great coffee, tasty baked goods, friendly staff and an artsy cafe atmosphere.

Who Dat Coffee Cafe (p89) The coffee is strong, the kitchen awesome and the service friendly.

Spitfire Coffee (p78) French Quarter cafe dishing out potent drip coffee a step below rocket fuel.

Solo Espresso (p93) Artsy little Bywater cafe that sources coffee from around the world.

Best for Beer

Avenue Pub (p124) A balcony tops a carefully curated beer menu and talented pub-grub kitchen.

Publiq House (p140) This Freret St mainstay maintains an excellent stable of domestics and imports.

NOLA Brewing (p124) The only brewery in Orleans Parish has its own very fine bar and tasting room.

Bulldog (p125) How much do they love beer? Check out the outdoor keg-handle fountain.

Cooter Brown's (p139) Nothing makes an extensive beer menu better than some affordable raw oysters.

Best for Cocktails

Tonique (p77) Worth the wait for the expertly mixed drinks at this little bar.

French 75 (p78) A bar so dedicated to cocktails it was named for one.

Cure (p139) The bar that gentrified Freret St on the strength of its cocktail menu.

Twelve Mile Limit (p156) A stupendous, complex cocktail menu in a laid-back neighborhood bar.

Treo (p156) The mixed drinks are as creative as the artwork in the on-site gallery.

Best for Jukebox

St Joe's (p139) An Uptown, student-centric crowd jams out to oldies and '90s/'00s rock.

Markey's (p93) A neighborhood jukebox selection that could have been plucked from the 1960s.

Pal's (p156) Music flits between eclectic quirks and classical soul.

Twelve Mile Limit (p156) Great bars deserves great music, in the form of oldies, newbies and everything between.

Best for Students

F&M's Patio Bar (p140) Watch the collective tuition of hundreds of students get blown on cheap beer.

Boot (p141) A bar that's so student-centric it's basically part of the Tulane campus.

Bulldog (p125) Med students, young lawyers and older undergrads clink mugs at this Garden District spot.

Snake & Jakes (p140) Students pack one of the craziest late-night bars in New Orleans.

Best Historical Bars

French 75 (p78) This bar drips history, from the attached Arnaud's restaurant to the suited staff.

Napoleon House (p79) Peeling paint, crumbling walls and a general sense of timeless debauchery.

Carousel Bar (p78) Baroque lights spin at the vintage eponymous carousel in this hotel bar.

Lafitte's Blacksmith Shop (p78) It may be the oldest contiguously operated bar in the USA – 'nuff said.

Chart Room (p78) Grotty French Quarter dive that feels like a relic of a bygone drinking age.

Best Neighborhood Bars

Pal's (p156) No trip to Bayou St John is complete without a gingerita at Pal's.

Twelve Mile Limit (p156) Great drinks, good pub food and a local vibe that can't be beat.

BJ's (p92) The epitome of a dirty, dingy and utterly irreplaceable Bywater dive.

Finn McCool's (p156) Mid-City residents cluster at this fantastic sports bar seven nights a week.

Mimi's in the Marigny (p92) Good music, creative cuisine and laid-back music at marvelous Mimi's.

The Golden Eagles Mardi Gras Indians perform at the French Quarter Festival (p23)

Entertainment

Be it live music, the visual arts, dance, film or theater, New Orleans knows how to entertain guests. We would go so far as to say the city is one great stage, and that visitors need not just watch the show, but are welcome to participate as costumed players.

Live Music

There is great live music happening every night of the week in New Orleans, which makes a strong claim to being the best live-music city in the nation. Jazz is definitely not the only genre on offer: R&B, rock, country, Cajun, zydeco, funk, soul, hip-hop and genre-defying experimentation are all the norm.

The Arts

The city of New Orleans has been actively using the arts as a means of revitalizing neighborhoods and building cachet with 'creative class' travelers – the ones who come looking for a local aesthetic and take on beauty. The city has always been a bit of an arts colony, and creativity comes naturally to its citizens.

Many New Orleanians are aspiring and established artists, drawn by conditions that make New Orleans an almost ideal city for the aesthetically inclined. Rents and competition, especially when compared with cities such as New York, Miami, Los Angeles and San Francisco, are relatively low, although there is a corresponding downgrade in exposure.

NEED TO KNOW

Price Ranges

- Standard cover for shows is $5 to $10; the latter price raises an eyebrow.
- During events such as Jazz Fest, however, seeing local celebrities like Kermit Ruffins may run to $15.

Weekly Gigs

Some musicians in New Orleans are regular as clockwork, showing up same time, same place, every week. There's a great vibe at these shows, where it feels like they're entertaining friends. Note the following gigs are not set in stone – bands tour, after all.

- **Sunday** Bruce Daigrepont and the Cajun Fais Do Do at Tipitina's.
- **Monday** King James & the Special Men at BJ's; bluegrass open jam at Hi Ho Lounge; Charmaine Neville at Snug Harbor; Alexis & the Samurai at Chickie Wah Wah.
- **Tuesday** Rebirth Brass Band at Maple Leaf Bar; Wasted Lives at AllWays Lounge; Kermit Ruffins at Bullets.
- **Wednesday** Tin Men with Washboard Chaz, and Walter 'Wolfman' Washington, both at d.b.a., Tremé Brass Band at Candlelight Lounge.
- **Thursday** Corey Henry & the Tremé Funktet at Vaughan's; Zydeco night at Mid-City Rock & Bowl.
- **Friday** Ellis Marsalis at Snug Harbor.
- **Saturday** John Boutté at d.b.a.

THEATER

New Orleans has a strong theatrical bent; numerous local theater companies and a few large theatrical venues for touring productions frequently stage shows. Broadway blockbusters cross the boards at the Mahalia Jackson Theater. Student plays are often performed at the **University of New Orleans** (☎504-280-6317; www.uno.edu; 2000 Lakeshore Dr) and Tulane University's **Lupin Theatre** (Map p250; ☎504-865-5106; Newcombe Circle, Dixon annex). There's also the Freda Lupin Memorial Theatre at the New Orleans Center for Creative Arts (Nocca; p94).

In Faubourg Marigny, improv comedy can be found at the New Movement Theater, while the Shadowbox Theatre and Healing Center host performances ranging from indie to classics. The Mudlark Theatre in the Bywater hosts performance art, fringe shows and, occasionally, giant puppet extravaganzas.

FILM

New Orleans has a few quality cinemas scattered about; our favorites are Prytania Theatre and Zeitgeist. Indie films are sporadically screened in some bars and clubs; check www.bestofneworleans.com for the latest events. Hollywood fare is screened at the Shops at Canal Place.

CLASSICAL MUSIC

The **Louisiana Philharmonic Orchestra** (☎504-523-6530; www.lpomusic.com) is the only musician-owned and -managed professional symphony in the USA. It performs in various churches and concert halls around town; check the website or call for details.

DANCE

The **New Orleans Ballet Association** (NOBA; ☎504-522-0996; www.nobadance.com; tickets $30-75) usually runs a few productions annually. The season is short, fleshed out with visiting dance companies from around the world. Performances are primarily held at the Mahalia Jackson Theater and Nocca. For contemporary dance, see what's on at Nocca..

OPERA

The **New Orleans Opera** (☎504-529-2278; www.neworleansopera.org; tickets $30-125) rarely causes much of a stir, but remains an important part of the local culture. Productions are held at the Mahalia Jackson Theater.

Entertainment by Neighborhood

- **French Quarter** Tourist-oriented entertainment, with a smattering of venues that have genuine local flavor.
- **Faubourg Marigny & Bywater** Fantastic concentration of live music, plus avant-garde galleries and theater.
- **CBD & Warehouse District** A few large concert halls and mid- or small-sized gig spots.
- **Garden, Lower Garden & Central City** Neighborhood bars and corner dives occasionally feature live music acts.
- **Uptown & Riverbend** University-oriented arts scene and a few music spots and bars-cum-venues, many with a student vibe.
- **Mid-City & the Tremé** Locals-oriented theater options and several bars that feature live music and dancing.

Lonely Planet's Top Choices

d.b.a. (p94) Consistently great live music nightly.

Hi Ho Lounge (p94) Eclectic schedule, funky shows.

Maple Leaf Bar (p141) Student-y spot for Uptown's best shows.

Mid-City Rock & Bowl (p157) Live music *and* bowling.

Snug Harbor (p95) Elegant jazz club.

Marigny Opera House (p94) Live dance and eclectic performance art.

Best for Live Music

d.b.a. (p94) Live music pops off all the time, and the beer menu is extensive to boot.

Spotted Cat (p94) A fantastically dingy Frenchmen St dive for the quintessential New Orleans jazz show.

Tipitina's (p141) One of the city's most storied concert halls.

Hi Ho Lounge (p94) An edgy little spot for a wide variety of music.

AllWays Lounge (p95) The place to go for an eclectic mix of genres and dance parties.

Best for Theater

Marigny Opera House (p94) This beautifully restored church hosts a huge variety of theater and dance.

Old Marquer Theatre (p96) A good variety of theater and live performance on artsy St Claude Ave.

New Movement Theater (p94) The easiest access point into the local comedy and improv theater scene.

Mahalia Jackson Theater (p152) Large venue that hosts big theater, music and comedy stage shows.

Best for Jazz

Spotted Cat (p94) A cozy dive bar that hosts some of the funkiest jazz acts in the city.

Snug Harbor (p95) Elegant bar with cocktail-attire-style service and classy acts.

Three Muses (p96) Dinner and jazz come together at this intimate Frenchmen St venue.

Palm Court (p80) Enjoy your jazz with a bit of fresh air and some fine dining.

Chickie Wah Wah (p157) A locals' spot that features great music in the heart of Mid-City.

Best for Rock Music

Siberia (p95) Heavy metal, punk and singer-songwriter nights keep Siberia red hot.

One Eyed Jacks (p80) One of the best live performance venues in the French Quarter.

Checkpoint Charlie (p95) A little bar that hosts some big noise on its dark, intimate stage.

Saturn Bar (p95) Wild acts tear down the roof in this oddball, artsy venue.

Banks Street Bar (p157) A neighborhood bar that isn't afraid to bring the rock.

Best for Hip-Hop & Bounce

Blue Nile (p96) Hip-hop and dancehall acts regularly take the stage at the Nile.

Siberia (p95) Bounce shows and serious booty-shaking are a regular occurrence.

Maison (p95) Younger hip-hop acts attract the college crowd at this Frenchmen venue.

Dragon's Den (p96) A wide mix of genres and talent, but hip-hop often features.

Best for Free Entertainment

Mardi Gras (p53) The party more than earns its reputation as the best free show on Earth.

Frenchmen St (p87) The city's most concentrated live-music strip is a show unto itself.

Bayou Boogaloo (p23) A bucolic Bayou St John setting girded by a fantastic music lineup.

Barkus Parade (p55) It's a parade of dogs in cute costumes! What more do you need?

Second Lines (p158) These brass-band-led neighborhood parades are a peek into New Orleans backstreet culture.

Best for Zydeco

Mid-City Rock & Bowl (p157) A zydeco dance party tears up this bowling alley on Thursday nights.

Jazz Fest (p56) Hit up the *fais-do-do* tent for a foot stomping Cajun dance party.

French Quarter Festival (p23) Zydeco acts are a regular feature of this free music festival.

Bayou Boogaloo (p23) Nothing like some Cajun dance tunes to accompany a perfect day on the water.

Maple Leaf Bar (p141) Get funky with the student crowd at the Leaf's famous zydeco parties.

Shopping

Too many travelers assume shopping in New Orleans equals unspeakable T-shirts from the French Quarter. Wrong! New Orleans is a creative town that attracts innovative entrepreneurs and, as such, features all sorts of lovely vintage antiques, cutting-edge boutiques, functional art and amusing kitsch – and generally lacks the worst chain-store blah.

Souvenirs

There are some really great awful souvenirs out there: T-shirts, foodstuffs (you're in hot-sauce heaven, here), Mardi Gras masks, stripper outfits, voodoo paraphernalia, French Quarter-style street signs and, of course, beads, beads, beads. Besides the unintentional kitsch there's quite a bit of intentional tackiness – this city seems to know how to mock itself.

Arts

Music makes New Orleans go round, and this is a fantastic town for buying original CDs, vinyl and the like, plus very high-quality instruments. A large literary scene has resulted in a good number of independent bookshops, some of which have evolved into unofficial anchors of their respective communities. And visual artists will find no shortage of stores selling supplies for their work.

Antiques

Antiques are big business here, and sometimes it feels like you can't walk past parts of Royal, Chartres, lower Decatur and Magazine Sts without tripping on some backyard, warehouse or studio space exhibiting beautiful examples of found furniture. Pieces tend to be relatively cheap compared to the antiques action in similarly sized metropolises, and the genre goes beyond chairs and armoires to lots of old maps, watches, prints, books and similar doodads.

Fashion

This isn't a city that has a lot of time for the cold, modern school of design or fashion. Locals have opted to live in a place that drips history, and when it comes to personal style, they like to reference older eras while offsetting with their own individualistic accents.

Probably the most distinct face of the local shopping scene is the innumerable boutiques and vintage shops that are sprouting up all along Magazine St and in the vicinity of Riverbend. The post-Katrina arrival of artists, students and save-the-city types added a lot of funky sprinkles to an already hip fashion sundae.

Shopping by Neighborhood

- **French Quarter** Antiques shops, souvenir stalls and art galleries.
- **Faubourg Marigny & Bywater** Arty, eclectic emporiums and vintage.
- **CBD & Warehouse District** Art galleries, clothing and shopping malls.
- **Garden, Lower Garden & Central City** Boutiques, antiques and vintage.
- **Uptown & Riverbend** More boutiques, plus student stores.

Lonely Planet's Top Choices

Maple Street Book Shop (p142) Best bookstore in town.

Crescent City Comics (p142) A great comic and graphic-novel shop.

Euclid Records (p97) Awesome vinyl and old posters; knowledgeable staff.

Tubby & Coos (p158) Lovely bookshop dedicated to sci-fi and kids' lit.

Fifi Mahony's (p80) Crazy wigs and costuming craziness.

Hazelnut (p142) Gifts and elegant home accoutrements.

Best for Souvenirs

Frenchmen Art Market (p87) A boutique art market for those seeking a unique gift from New Orleans.

Simon of New Orleans (p126) Bright and beautiful hand-painted signs with cheeky messages.

Louisiana Music Factory (p97) If you need some local music, you've come to the right store.

Faulkner House Books (p83) A lovely bookshop for picking up works by regional writers.

Dirty Coast (p142) Sweet T-shirts emblazoned with clever, hyper-local jokes and slogans.

I.J. Reilly's (p97) Awesome gifts and objects d'art with an identifiable New Orleans flavor.

Best Vintage Stores

Funky Monkey (p126) Cool, college-age-oriented clothing in the heart of Magazine St.

Trashy Diva (p126) Vintage dresses with a '40s and '50s feel and lots of attitude.

Bloomin' Deals (p143) This store, run by the Junior League, offers genuine cut-rate prices for used clothes.

Magazine Street (p142) The entire street is packed on either end with shops selling vintage clothes.

Best Women's Fashion

Trashy Diva (p126) Lives up to its name, with playful clothes that tap into your inner glamour.

C Collection (p143) A boutique that dresses up the fashionistas of the city's university scene.

Feet First (p143) Head here for the perfect pair of kicks to complete your outfit.

Exodus (p80) A hidden-in-plain-sight boutique that blends urban style with bohemian aesthetic.

SoPo (p158) Southern style gets a stylish makeover at this ultralocal fashion outpost.

Best Men's Fashion

Aidan Gill for Men (p126) For the stylish man in need of a classic shave and a haircut.

Funky Monkey (p126) Vintage and quirky clothes with an eclectic twist and carefree attitude.

Meyer the Hatter (p114) Need to crown your dome? Head to this iconic local hat shop.

Dirty Coast (p142) Local T-shirt shop that sells clothes with a distinct New Orleans twist.

Best for Antiques

Bywater Bargain Center (p97) An endless emporium of found treasures and bric-a-brac from around the world.

Greg's Antiques (p82) French Quarter antique furniture shop that brokers some fantastic deals on historic treasures.

James H Cohen & Sons (p81) Holds an enormous vault of coins, swords, maps and other objects culled from the past.

Moss Antiques (p81) Decorative arts, historic furniture and other home accoutrement.

Magazine Antique Mall (p127) Never-ending rows of trinkets that seem to have been culled from a collective city attic.

NEED TO KNOW

Opening Hours

Hours vary, but as a rule of thumb, shops are open from 9am or 10am to 7pm Monday to Friday, and 10am to 2pm Saturday and Sunday. Some stores are shut on Sunday or Monday, and sometimes both.

Buy Local

Even before Hurricane Katrina, and particularly after the storm, there was a big push in the city to promote local businesses and commerce in New Orleans. To keep abreast of the 'Buy Local' movement, visit http://staylocal.org.

Best Music Stores

Euclid Records (p97) This Bywater shop is one of the iconic local record shops of the South.

Louisiana Music Factory (p97) The shop that sets the standard in collecting and selling local music.

New Orleans Music Exchange (p127) If you're after an instrument to take home, you've come to the right spot.

Peaches Records & Tapes (p81) A French Quarter record shop that loves to introduce tourists to local artists.

Gay & Lesbian

Louisiana is a culturally conservative state, but its largest city bucks that trend. New Orleans has always had a reputation for tolerance and it remains one of the oldest gay-friendly cities in the Western hemisphere, marketing itself as the 'Gay Capitol of the South.' Neighborhoods such as the French Quarter and Marigny are major destinations on the LGBTIQ travel circuit.

The Vibe

New Orleans is a pretty integrated city. Except for the lower part of Bourbon St, few areas or businesses feel exclusively gay. Rather, the queer vibe in the city seems to be strongest during major festivals such as the Gay Easter Parade and Southern Decadence.

History

New Orleans has always had a reputation as a city for outcasts, which for much of history has included the gay and lesbian population. Even today, in conservative states such as Alabama and Mississippi, gay and lesbian youth feel the pull of the Big Easy, where acceptance of their sexuality isn't hard to find.

Artists such as Tennessee Williams, Truman Capote and Lyle Saxon, among many others, found acceptance and purpose here; Williams went so far as to dub New Orleans his 'spiritual home.' Gay Civil Rights battles were fought in New Orleans by groups such as the Gertrude Stein Society. In 1997 Mayor Marc Morial extended domestic-partner benefits to gay and lesbian couples who were city employees; in the same year, Louisiana became the first state in the Deep South to pass hate crimes legislation that covered sexual orientation. One year later, New Orleans pushed new boundaries by being one of the first American cities to list gender identity as protected from discrimination.

Sissy Culture

The civic life of New Orleans is largely split along racial lines, and just as there is a white New Orleans and an African American New Orleans, so too is there an African American queer scene. 'Sissy' is local slang for gay black men – specifically gay black men who grew up in New Orleans' poorer black neighborhoods. A middle-class, queer African American could potentially be as foreign to this culture as a white American. Sissy culture references the language and folk ways of the African American ghetto; its most visible element to visitors is the bounce music of artists such as Big Freedia and Katy Red. While those artists themselves would claim their work is not limited to the LGBTIQ experience, songs like 'Peanut Butter' (a collaboration between Ru Paul and Big Freedia) certainly speak to that community.

Gay & Lesbian by Neighborhood

- **French Quarter** The Lower Quarter, from St Philips St to Esplandde Ave, is a lively gay party.
- **Faubourg Marigny & Bywater** Quieter gay scene largely made up of established couples.
- **Uptown** An out student scene concentrated near Tulane and Loyola.

Lonely Planet's Top Choices

Faubourg Marigny Book Store (p97) This bookstore is also a cornerstone of the gay community.

Country Club (p93) Clothing-optional heated pool? Sounds good.

Café Lafitte in Exile (p78) Oldest gay bar in the South.

Washington Square Park (p88) Notable for a touching HIV/AIDS memorial.

Southern Decadence (p24) One of the craziest parties in town.

Bourbon Pub & Parade (p79) It's 24-hour madness on Bourbon St.

Best Gay & Lesbian Bars

Country Club (p93) Good drinks and food, and a pool in a tropical courtyard.

Bourbon Pub & Parade (p79) A big, over-the-top gay bar that anchors the Quarter's LGBTIQ scene.

Big Daddy's Bar (p94) Laid-back 'gayborhood' bar with a down-to-earth vibe.

Café Lafitte in Exile (p78) Six decades running and going strong; this is a bedrock of the Quarter gay scene.

Best Gay Dance Floors

Oz (p79) A nonstop dance floor that brings out all of the beautiful boys.

Bourbon Pub & Parade (p79) Throws big parties that cater to an all-ages crowd of travelers and locals.

Café Lafitte in Exile (p78) Has been hosting awesome dance parties for years,and shows no signs of stopping.

Best Gay Festivals

Southern Decadence (p24) The biggest LGBT event in New Orleans is always a party for the record books.

Gay Easter Parade (p23) Bunny costumes, tea parties, dainty dresses and lots of fun.

Mardi Gras (p53) Carnival's enormous arts and DIY scene features a strong LGBTIQ presence.

Halloween (p25) Many of the city's best costuming and masking events have overlap with the gay community.

Best Gay Stays

Bywater Bed & Breakfast (p179) Folk art, funky decor and friendly hosts feature heavily at this Bywater establishment.

Green House Inn (p185) An adults-only accommodation that's close to a glut of fine bars and restaurants.

Bourbon Orleans Hotel (p176) In the heart of the French Quarter, within easy distance of the LGBTIQ bar scene.

Lions Inn B&B (p179) Located in the cozy center of the Marigny; a locus for the gay community.

W French Quarter (p178) Hip decor, fantastic on-site eating and the nightlife of the Quarter at your fingertips.

NEED TO KNOW

Gay Bars Never Close

OK, that's not entirely true, but it's safe to say that if you want a 24-hour party, the gay bars on Bourbon St (especially Bourbon Pub) are the place to be. Even the bars that aren't technically open 24 hours are often still kicking around 5am, so it's not like they attract the shrinking violet crowd.

Best Online Resources

Check out these websites for information on queer travel in New Orleans.

Gay New Orleans Online (www.neworleansonline.com/neworleans/lgbt) Probably the most comprehensive collection of queer listings online.

Gay New Orleans (www.gayneworleans.com) Full of information.

Gay Cities (http://neworleans.gaycities.com) Listings, user reviews and LGBTIQ-related content.

Ambush Magazine (www.ambushmag.com) Local take on queer news and issues.

Purple Roofs (www.purpleroofs.com/usa/louisiana.html) Reliable gay travel resource.

KYLIE MCLAUGHLIN/GETTY IMAGES ©

Explore New Orleans

Neighborhoods at a Glance 48

French Quarter 58
Top Sights 60
Sights.................... 65
Eating.....................71
Drinking & Nightlife....... 77
Entertainment 80
Shopping................. 80

Faubourg Marigny & Bywater 85
Sights.................... 87
Eating.................... 88
Drinking & Nightlife....... 92
Entertainment 94
Shopping................ 97

CBD & Warehouse District.............100
Top Sights 102
Sights.................. 104
Eating.................. 109
Drinking & Nightlife.......112
Entertainment 113
Shopping................114

Garden, Lower Garden & Central City...... 115
Top Sights 117
Sights...................118
Eating...................121
Drinking & Nightlife...... 124
Entertainment 126
Shopping............... 126

Uptown & Riverbend 130
Top Sights 132
Sights.................. 133
Eating.................. 134
Drinking & Nightlife...... 139
Entertainment 141
Shopping............... 142

Mid-City & the Tremé..........144
Top Sights 146
Sights.................. 149
Eating.................. 152
Drinking & Nightlife...... 156
Entertainment 157
Shopping............... 158

Day Trips from New Orleans 159
River Road Plantations 160
St Francisville........... 161
Lafayette & Breaux Bridge..................163
Cajun Prairie............167
Down the Bayou.........169

Sleeping...........172

NEW ORLEAN'S TOP SIGHTS

Jackson Square 60

St Louis Cathedral 61

Cabildo 62

Presbytère 63

Royal Street 64

National WWII Museum 102

Ogden Museum of Southern Art 103

Lafayette Cemetery No 1 117

Audubon Zoo 132

City Park 146

St Louis Cemetery No 1 148

Neighborhoods at a Glance

1 French Quarter p58

Also known as Vieux Carré (voo car-*ray;* Old Quarter) and 'the Quarter,' the French Quarter is the original city as planned by the French in the early 18th century. Here lies the infamous Bourbon St, but of more interest is an elegantly aged grid of shop fronts, iron lamps and courtyard gardens. Most visitors begin exploring the city in the French Quarter; some, sadly, never leave it. That's not to say the Quarter isn't lovely, but it's a bit like Disney World, heavy on tourist traffic and light on locals (unless you count your bartender or waiter).

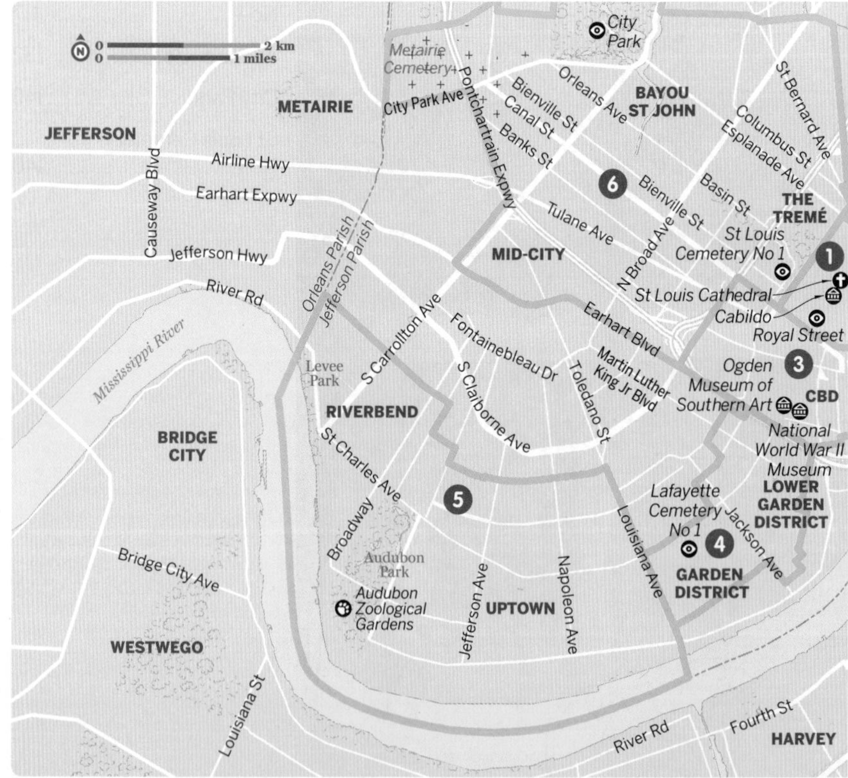

❷ Faubourg Marigny & Bywater p85

North of the Quarter are the Creole *faubourgs* (literally, 'suburbs,' although 'neighborhood' is more accurate in spirit, as these areas are still very much within the city). For visitors, the Marigny and Bywater are fascinating, constituting several interesting slices of the urban landscape: an established area for gays, lesbians and successful creative-class types (artists, graphic designers etc); the edge of gentrification, where exciting new bars and restaurants are opening; and areas that have already been gentrified, evidenced by flash venues with creative cuisine and hip live music.

❸ CBD & Warehouse District p100

Canal St is the 'great divide' that splits the French Quarter from the Central Business District (CBD) and Warehouse District. Between offices and forgettable municipal buildings lie some of the city's best museums, many posh restaurants, an eyesore of a casino, art galleries and excellent arts walks. That said, this area, with its high-rise buildings and converted condos, is the least 'New Orleans' neighborhood in New Orleans.

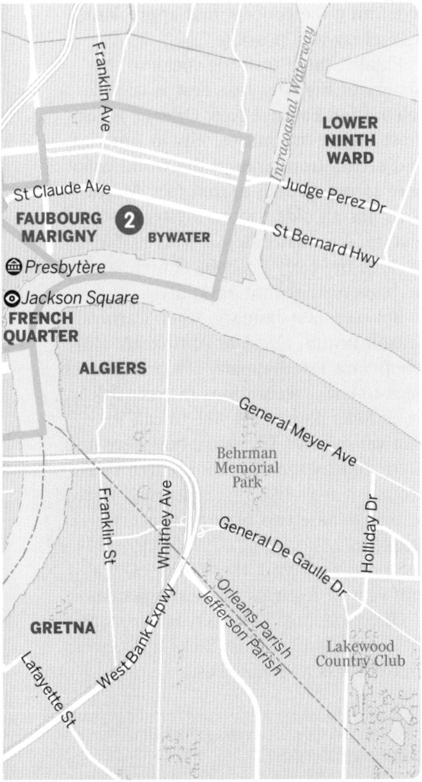

❹ Garden, Lower Garden & Central City p115

Proceeding south along the Mississippi, following the curve of the river's 'U,' the streets become tree-lined and the houses considerably grander; this is the Garden and Lower Garden Districts, the beginning of New Orleans' 'American Sector' (so named because it was settled after the Louisiana Purchase). This area is home to recent graduates and young professionals, and the hip shops and bars that cater to them.

❺ Uptown & Riverbend p130

Uptown is the area where American settlers decided to prove to the original French inhabitants that they could be as tasteful and wealthy as any old-world aristocrat. Magazine St is one of the coolest strips of restaurants and shopping outlets in town. Eventually the 'U' curves north again along the river's bend into Riverbend, popular with the university crowd.

❻ Mid-City & the Tremé p144

The Tremé is the oldest African American neighborhood in the country, characterized by low-slung architecture and residential blocks, some middle class, some rotted by poverty, some gentrifying. This area runs on its west side into Mid-City, a semi-amorphous district that includes long lanes of shotgun houses, poor projects, the gorgeous green spaces of City Park, the elegant mansions of Esplanade Ave and the slow, lovely laze of Bayou St John.

Mardi Gras & Jazz Fest

No two events encapsulate New Orleans like Mardi Gras and Jazz Fest. These festivals are more than celebrations: they contain within themselves every thread of the colorful, complicated New Orleans tapestry.

Festival Season in New Orleans

'Stop exaggerating,' you may say, to which we reply: 'There's no need to exaggerate.' These festivals are incredible. Imagine a bunch of grown men and women riding giant neon shoes and plaster dinosaurs through the street; or Bruce Springsteen, Al Green, Dr John, Tom Petty, Cee-lo, Feist and the Carolina Chocolate Drops playing in the same venue in one weekend; or that you slip through the looking-glass into MOM's Ball and see a band of zombies playing for naked folks in body paint and a cast of costumes that appear to be lifted from Jim Henson's most lurid fantasies.

During Mardi Gras and Jazz Fest, all this happens. The city's flights of fancy and indulgence are realized like at no other time. And everything that makes New Orleans...well...New Orleans becomes a lot more...*New Orleansy*. Let's take the food. The best eats in the city turn up as booth fare in Jazz Fest. Restaurants throw open their doors during Mardi Gras to folks dressed as goblins and fairies. This all speaks to the creativity of the city, expressed in a multitude of ways, from music to visual arts, crafts and theater (as exemplified by Mardi Gras floats and costumes). These festivals reveal the soul of a city that is obsessed with beauty, while both redefining the concept and appreciating it in every way possible.

Finally, these festivals speak to the history of the city. Jazz Fest is such a celebration because New Orleans is the most important musical city in America, and artists from around the world come here to pay tribute to that fact. Mardi Gras has an older, more mysterious history, one that dates at least as far back as the early Catholic church, and perhaps further into antiquity.

Between late January, when Carnival Season begins, and late April/early May, when Jazz Fest happens, it's pretty much back-to-back celebrations in New Orleans, or as folks down here like to call it: 'festival season.' There are lulls here and there, but by the time mid-March rolls around it feels like there's a small festival bridging these two big events every weekend.

So are we saying there's basically a half-year of festivals in New Orleans?

Of course not. The party *never* stops in New Orleans. It just picks up between Mardi Grass and Jazz Fest.

1. Black Mohawk Mardi Gras Indians **2.** The Krewe of Bachus Parade, during Mardi Gras

1

Saga of a Celebration

Pagan Rites

Carnival's pagan origins are deep. Pre-spring festivals of unabashed sexuality and indulgence of appetite are not a rarity around the world. Neither is the concept of denying these appetites as a means of reasserting human forbearance in the face of animalistic cravings.

The early Catholic Church failed to appreciate these traditions, but after trying unsuccessfully to suppress them, the Church co-opted the spring rite and slotted it into the Christian calendar. Shakespeare gave Carnival celebrations his literary interpretation as far back as 1601 with *Twelfth Night;* the play is named for the holiday that traditionally begins the Carnival Season, a day marked by the ascendance of the Lord of Misrule. It's no coincidence that *Twelfth Night* the play, like Twelfth Night the Carnival kick-off, is rife with costuming, cross-dressing, mistaken identities and satirical, often crude pokes at people in power. This attitude persists into Fat Tuesday (Mardi Gras); nothing is sacred on this sacred day, which was celebrated in France and spread to French outposts in the New World.

The Creole Connection

Early generations of Creoles loved to dance and mask. On Mardi Gras people would wear grotesque disguises and attend balls, concerts and theater. From the beginning Carnival crossed race lines. Creoles of color held Carnival balls to which slaves were sometimes invited. Several times, masking was altogether outlawed by authorities who distrusted the way costumes undermined the established social order. The citizenry tended to blend into an unruly, desegregated mob during Mardi Gras. The situation hasn't entirely changed.

Following the Louisiana Purchase, Mardi Gras faded for a while, until a secretive group of wealthy Anglos who called themselves the Mistick Krewe of Comus made their first public appearance in spectacular horse-drawn

1. Mardi Gras beads **2.** A colorful Mardi Gras float

floats illuminated by *flambeaux* (torches) in 1857. New clubs modeled themselves on the Comus, calling themselves 'krewes' (a deliberately quirky spelling of 'crews').

Modern Mardi Gras

During the mid-19th century, a growing number of krewes gave Mardi Gras both structure and spectacle; the former made the celebration easily accessible, while the latter gave it popularity and notoriety outside of New Orleans. Rex first appeared in 1872, Momus a year later and Proteus in 1882. Mythological and sometimes satirical themes defined the parades, making these processions coherent theatrical works on wheels. These old-line krewes were (and for the most part remain) highly secretive societies comprising the city's wealthiest, most powerful men.

Many enduring black traditions emerged around the turn of the 20th century. The spectacular Mardi Gras Indians began to appear in 1885; today their elaborate feathered costumes, sewn as a tribute to Native American warriors, are recognized as pieces of folk art. The black krewe of Zulu appeared in 1909, with members initially calling themselves the Tramps and parading on foot. By 1916, when the Zulu Social Aid & Pleasure Club was incorporated, the krewe brought floats, and its antics deliberately spoofed the pomposity of elite white krewes. Ironically, today's Zulu's members include some of the city's more prominent black citizens, and their annual ball is as full of pomp and posturing as Comus'.

Today's 'superkrewes' began forming in the 1960s. Endymion debuted as a modest neighborhood parade in 1967; now its parades and floats are the largest around: it has nearly 2000 riders and one of its immense floats measures 240ft in length.

All on a Mardi Gras Day

The parade season is a 12-day period beginning two Fridays before Fat Tuesday. Early parades are charming, neighborly processions that whet your

OUR FAVORITE BIG PARADES

Krewe de Vieux Old-school walking parade with sharply satirical floats.

Muses All-female krewe with creative floats.

Zulu Traditionally African American krewe that throws coconuts to the crowd.

Rex Old-line royalty of Mardi Gras.

Thoth Family-friendly Uptown day parade.

appetite for the later parades, which increase in size and grandeur until the spectacles of the superkrewes emerge during the final weekend.

A popular preseason night procession, usually held three Saturdays before Fat Tuesday, is Krewe du Vieux. By parading before the official parade season and marching on foot, Krewe du Vieux is permitted to pass through the French Quarter. The themes of this notoriously bawdy and satirical krewe clearly aim to offend puritanical types.

Watch for Le Krewe d'Etat, whose name is a clever, satirical pun: d'Etat is ruled by a dictator rather than a king. Another favorite is Muses, an all-women's krewe that parades down St Charles Ave with thousands of members and some imaginative, innovative floats; their throws include coveted hand-decorated shoes.

Mardi Gras weekend is lit up by the entrance of the superkrewes, who arrive with their monstrous floats and endless processions of celebrities, as flashy as a Vegas revue. On Saturday night the megakrewe Endymion stages its spectacular parade and Extravaganza, as it calls its ball in the Superdome. On Sunday night the Bacchus superkrewe wows an enraptured crowd along St Charles Ave with its celebrity monarch and a gorgeous fleet of crowd-pleasing floats.

On Mardi Gras morning Zulu rolls along Jackson Ave, where folks set up barbecues on the sidewalk and krewe members distribute their prized hand-painted coconuts. The 'King of Carnival,' Rex, waits further Uptown; it's a much more restrained affair, with the monarch himself looking like he's been plucked from a deck of cards.

Costume Contests

Mardi Gras is a citywide costume party, and many locals take a dim view of visitors who crash the party without one. For truly fantastic outfits, march with the Society of St Ann on Mardi Gras morning. This collection of artists and misfits prides itself on its DIY outfits, which seem to have marched out of a collision between a David Bowie video and a '60s acid trip. The creativity and pageantry on display really needs to be seen to be believed. Other parades that feature great homemade costumes include the Box of Wine parade, the Chewbacchus parade and the Red Beans & Rice procession.

EDU HAWKINS/GETTY IMAGES ©

1. Terence Blanchard performs at Jazz Fest

Information

Gambit Weekly (www.bestofneworleans.com) publishes a Carnival edition during February or March, depending on the date of Mardi Gras. Mardi Gras New Orleans (www.mardigrasneworleans.com) is an excellent website for details of the festivities.

New Orleans Jazz & Heritage Festival

Jazz Fest sums up everything that would be lost if the world were to lose New Orleans. Much more than Mardi Gras, with its secret balls and sparkly trinkets, Jazz Fest reflects the generosity of New Orleans, its unstoppable urge to share its most precious resource – its culture – with the rest of the world. Of course the Fest is first and foremost about music, but it isn't just about jazz. It's jazz *and* heritage, which means any music that jazz came from, and any music that jazz inspired. The multitude of stages and tents feature everything that pours in and out of jazz – blues, gospel, Afro-Caribbean, folk, country, zydeco, Cajun, funky brass, and on and on.

WALKING KREWE REVIEW

Some of the best parades of Carnival Season are put on by DIY bohemian walking krewes, groups of friends who create a grassroots show. Casual observers are always welcome to participate. Just bring a costume!

Barkus Dress up your furry friends for this all-pet parade (www.barkus.org).

Box of Wine Crazily costumed revelers march up St Charles Ave ahead of the Bacchus (God of wine) parade, distributing free wine from boxes along the way.

Intergalactic Krewe of Chewbacchus Dress up as your favorite sci-fi character at this wonderful parade for geeks, nerds and other people we might hang out with on weekends (http://chewbacchus.org).

Red Beans & Rice On Lundi Gras, folks dress up in costumes made from dry beans or as Louisiana food items.

Society of St Anne Traditionally made up of artists and bohemians, St Anne marches on Mardi Gras morning from the Bywater to the Mississippi and features the best costumes of Carnival Season.

Roots of Roots Music

Jazz Fest began in 1970, when the idea of staging a big music festival in New Orleans couldn't have been more natural. The first festival, held in Louis Armstrong Park, featured a remarkable lineup of legendary artists, including Duke Ellington, Mahalia Jackson, Clifton Chenier, Fats Domino and the Meters. Mardi Gras Indians performed, and every now and then a second-line parade (p158) swept through the audience. The ingredients were already in place for a major cultural event with a genuine regional significance. Outside talent, such as Ellington, complemented the local talent and beefed up the event's exposure.

Only 350 people attended that first Jazz Fest. Most likely, the low numbers were due to poor promotion outside New Orleans. Out-of-towners arrived in much greater numbers for the '71 Fest, and with them came a far stronger local response. To accommodate another anticipated jump in attendance, the Fest was moved to the far larger Fair Grounds Race Course a year later, and Jazz Fest really hasn't looked back since. By the late 1970s the festival had grown from one weekend to two, with many legendary moments already solidifying the event's cultural importance.

Mesmerizing performances by the likes of James Booker, the Neville Brothers and Professor Longhair have been recorded for posterity. The musical lineup soon expanded to include big-time national acts, such as Lenny Kravitz, Bruce Springsteen and Bon Jovi, as well as international acts from South America, the Caribbean and Africa.

Experiencing Jazz Fest

Some people choose to do Jazz Fest (www.nojazzfest.com) over and over again, year after year, so obviously there's something addictive about the experience. It doesn't hurt that there are umpteen ways to approach this gargantuan feast of music, food and culture, which takes place over the last weekend of April and the first weekend of May.

Setting the Stage

The first thing to decide is: one weekend of Jazz Fest or two? And if one's enough, then which one?

No one will laugh if you choose one weekend. The drawback is you may have to pick your dates before the Fest schedule is announced. The schedule isn't announced until early February at the earliest. Still, there's statistical logic to making blindfolded decisions this way, as both weekends are always equally packed with big-name show-stoppers and unheard-of talents. Sometimes you'll miss out on a personal favorite if you're not attending every day of the Fest, but in the end something along the way will make up for the loss.

For those who make their Jazz Fest plans late – that's to say, after February – there's the advantage of knowing the schedule. Free-spenders are still likely to find a pricey suite of rooms in the French Quarter at this point, but thrifty types might be frustrated with finding accommodations. If you decide to do both weekends, you'll have four days for bopping around town, or maybe driving out to Cajun Country for Festival International de Louisiane (www.festivalinternational.com) in Lafayette. 'Festival' is the largest free francophone music festival in North America, and is held during the end of April.

At the Fair Grounds

It takes a well-bred racehorse about two minutes to circumnavigate the Fair Grounds track, but the average human will require up to 10 minutes to get from one stage to the next. The only way to get from stage to stage is to walk or half-jog

SCOTT LEGATO/GETTY IMAGES ©

FANFO/SHUTTERSTOCK ©

1. Vintage Trouble perform at Jazz Fest **2.** Traditional Creole dish of grillades and grits

through dense crowds and all kinds of tempting food stalls and vendors. Jazz Fest consists of a dozen performance tents:

Gospel Tent A cherished chapel of earth-shaking live gospel music.

Jazz Tent The lineup here leans more toward the contemporary side of things: Irvin Mayfield, Terence Blanchard, Ellis Marsalis and the like.

Jazz & Heritage Stage Smaller stage where brass bands and the Mardi Gras Indians perform.

Economy Hall Tent Stomp your feet to New Orleans 'trad' jazz with the likes of the Preservation Hall Jazz Band, Walter Payton and the Tremé Brass Band.

Lagniappe Stage Varied entertainment. The stage's isolation from the rest of the Fair Grounds makes it ideal for intimate performances.

Blues Tent Blues, R&B, funk and, occasionally, some rock.

Fais-Do-Do Stage Cajun and zydeco music is the emphasis at this always-hopping stage.

Congo Square This stage has become the venue for world acts from Africa and Latin America.

Acura Stage Main stage where the biggest names appear.

Gentilly Stage Secondary main stage.

Kids Tent Children's music and family-friendly activities.

Food Demonstration Stage Local live cooking lessons.

Food, Glorious Food

In addition to the obvious musical draw, Jazz Fest is justifiably famous for its food stalls, many of which have cult followings. Some of the more popular Fest foods include fried soft-shell crab, Crawfish Monica (cream crawfish sauce over fusilli pasta), crawfish bread, *cochon de lait* (roast suckling pig), po'boys, spinach and artichoke casserole, Cuban sandwiches and Jamaican chicken. Of course, you'll also find jambalaya, red beans and fried catfish.

French Quarter

LOWER QUARTER | UPPER QUARTER

Neighborhood Top Five

❶ Walking up and down the Mississippi River along the **Riverfront** (p69), stopping to watch crowds disembarking from ferries, and listening to music and street performers along the way, before wandering into Jackson Square for, well, even more street performers.

❷ Catching a concert and living local culture at the **Old US Mint** (p65).

❸ Slow-sipping a marvelous cocktail at **Tonique** (p77).

❹ Fitting oneself out for the perfect wig at **Fifi Mahony's** (p80).

❺ Exploring the **Cabildo** (p62) and grounding yourself in the history of Louisiana.

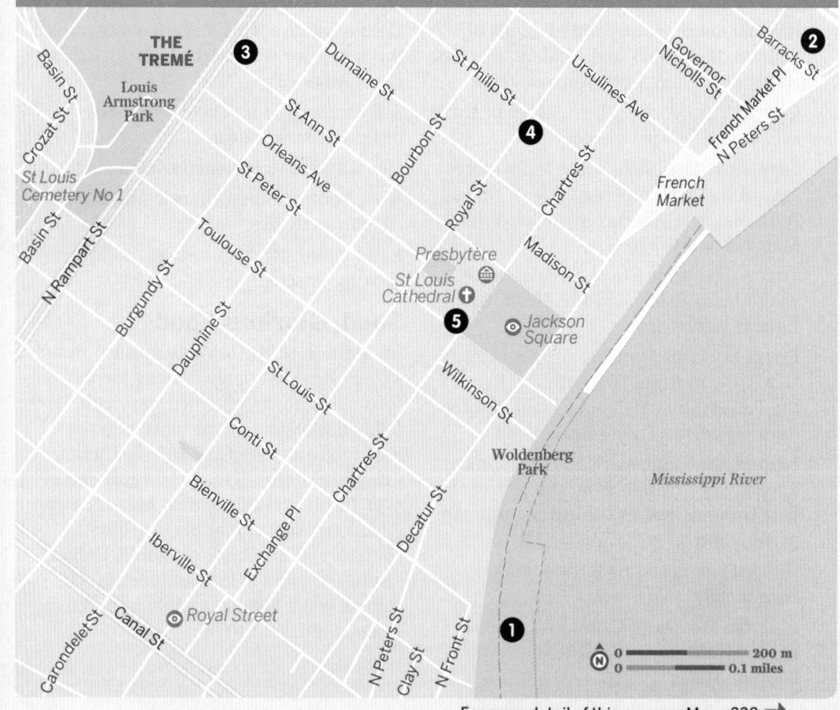

For more detail of this area see Map p238

Explore the French Quarter

Many visitors treat the French Quarter as a sort of adult Disney World, with Bourbon St serving as a neon (lights and drinks) heart of bad behavior. Past this activity, you'll find a compact 'hood where historical preservation, fine dining and great nightlife intersect like nowhere else in the USA.

We would recommend exploring on your first day with the morning walking tour run by Friends of the Cabildo. It's an excellent introduction to both the architecture and history of the area. After the tour, take a walk along the river and consider catching a concert sponsored by the National Park Service at the Old US Mint. Finish the evening with dinner at either Bayona or Sobou, and drinks at French 75 or Tonique.

Next day, walk up and down Royal St and lounge alongside the river. If you feel inclined, rent a bicycle; you can cover lots more ground that way. Go shopping for local music at Peaches or peruse some galleries, and get yourself to Preservation Hall early enough in the evening to see the show. As night well and truly falls, have dinner at Sylvain, and drinks at Lafitte's Blacksmith Shop or Latitude 29.

Local Life

- **History** History seeps though the brick walls of the French Quarter. Locals love the concentration of museums, historical homes and tours that take in this city's colorful (and often criminal) past.
- **Music** While residents tend to skirt the Quarter, many locals love to wander down Royal St (p64) and listen to the buskers doing their musical thing.
- **Food** Some of the best restaurants in the city are in the French Quarter, and many New Orleanians splurge on a romantic night out here.

Getting There & Away

- **Streetcar** The Canal and Riverfront streetcars both skirt the edges of the French Quarter.
- **Bus** The 91 bus runs up Rampart St and Esplanade Ave, which are both boundary roads of the French Quarter.
- **Car** Parking is a hassle in the Quarter; if you're going to drive here, either be prepared to park in a garage or bring lots of quarters for meters.

Lonely Planet's Top Tip

We know your friends told you to go to Bourbon St. Go ahead, but perhaps hold off until you've visited some other neighborhoods.The tackiness of Bourbon is obvious after you've experienced the magic of the rest of New Orleans.

There have been frequent muggings in the Quarter near Esplanade Ave and Louis Armstrong Park. When you walk at night, do so with a friend, or take a bicycle rickshaw.

Best Places to Eat

- Bayona (p76)
- SoBou (p76)
- Coop's Place (p71)
- Eat New Orleans (p73)
- Port of Call (p71)

For reviews, see p71

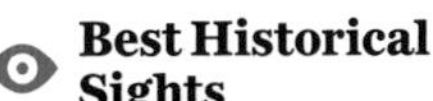

Best Historical Sights

- Cabildo (p62)
- Presbytère (p63)
- Ursuline Convent (p66)
- Historic New Orleans Collection (p65)

For reviews, see p62 

Best Nightlife

- Tonique (p77)
- Cosimo's (p78)
- Molly's at the Market (p77)
- Erin Rose (p78)
- Latitude 29 (p75)

For reviews, see p77 

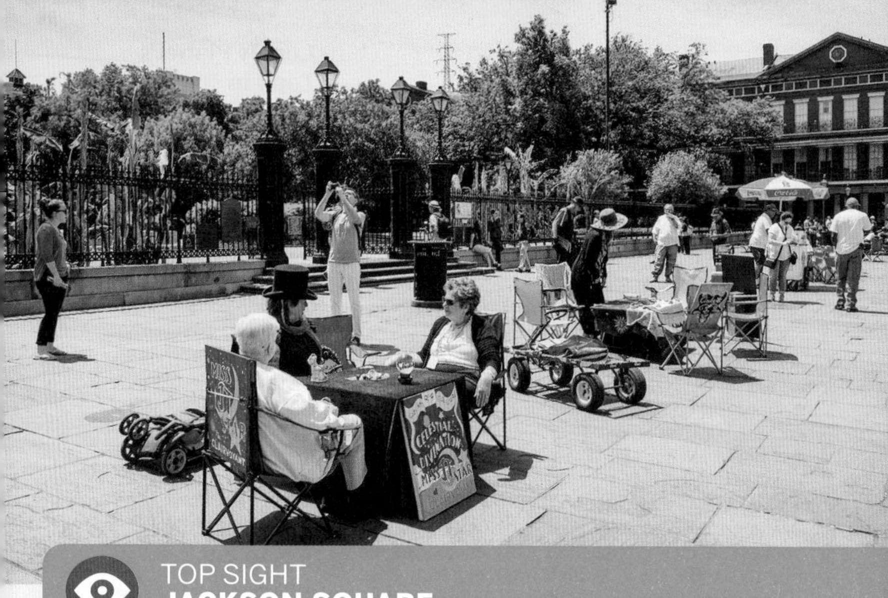

TOP SIGHT
JACKSON SQUARE

Sprinkled with lazing loungers, surrounded by fortune-tellers, sketch artists and traveling performers, and overlooked by cathedrals, offices and shops plucked from a Paris-meets-the-Caribbean fantasy, Jackson Square is one of America's great town squares. It both anchors the French Quarter and is the beating heart of this corner of town.

Whatever happens in the Quarter usually begins here. The identical, block-long Pontalba Buildings overlook the square, and the near-identical Cabildo and Presbytère structures flank St Louis Cathedral, the square's centerpiece.

The square was part of Adrien de Pauger's original city plan and began life as a military parade ground called Place d'Armes (Place of Weapons). Madame Micaëla Pontalba transformed the muddy marching grounds into a trimmed garden and renamed the square to honor Andrew Jackson, the president who saved New Orleans from the British during the War of 1812. Along the edges of that garden you'll see street performers, artists, bands and tourists taking in the atmosphere. It's a gentle, carnival-esque scene, invariably lovely at sunset, which belies a bloody history: during the 1811 German Coast Slave Uprising, three leaders of the rebellion were hung here.

In the middle of the park stands the monument to Andrew Jackson – Clark Mills' bronze equestrian statue of the man, unveiled in 1856. The inscription, 'The Union Must and Shall be Preserved', was added by General Benjamin Butler, Union military governor of New Orleans during the Civil War, ostensibly to rub it into the occupied city's face. The gesture worked. Butler was dubbed 'Beast Butler' by locals, and eventually his face was stamped on the bottom of city chamber pots. Butler deserves some credit too, however: during his tenure as military governor of New Orleans, he instituted health quarantines that drastically reduced yellow fever outbreaks.

DON'T MISS

- Street performers
- Artists
- The Andrew Jackson statue

PRACTICALITIES

- Map p238
- Decatur & St Peter Sts

JORG HACKEMANN/SHUTTERSTOCK ©

TOP SIGHT
ST LOUIS CATHEDRAL

One of the best examples of French architecture in the country is the triple-spire cathedral of St Louis, King of France. It's an innocuous bit of Gallic heritage in the heart of old New Orleans. Still used for services, the structure gets packed out on Christmas Eve at midnight Mass and is one of the most important (and beautiful) churches serving Catholics in the USA today.

Besides hosting black, white and Creole congregants, St Louis has attracted those who, in the best New Orleanian tradition, mix their influences; this includes voodoo queen Marie Laveau, who worshiped here during the height of her influence in the mid-19th century. The interior stained glass and French wall inscriptions offer a peek into New Orleans' Catholic heritage.

In 1722 a hurricane destroyed the first of three churches built here by the St Louis Parish. Architect Don Gilberto Guillemard dedicated the present cathedral on Christmas Eve in 1794. Pope Paul VI awarded it the rank of minor basilica in 1964. St Louis is a working cathedral, so be respectful when you visit. Loud noises and obtrusive picture-taking are frowned upon.

Throughout the year, St Louis hosts events that are at the core of New Orleans' Catholic community. If you're in town during any of the following holidays, try to visit. Christmas services include 5pm vigil on December 24 and midnight Mass on December 25; doors open at 11:15pm. On Palm Sunday (the Sunday before Easter), the transfixing ceremony of the Blessing of the Palms begins at 10:50am. If you can beat your hangover, come on Ash Wednesday (the day after Mardi Gras); ashes, a symbol of mourning and penitence, are distributed at 7:30am, noon and 5pm.

DON'T MISS

- Morning Mass
- Christmas services
- Ash Wednesday

PRACTICALITIES

- Map p238
- ☎504-525-9585
- www.stlouiscathedral.org
- Jackson Sq
- donations accepted, self-guided tour $1
- 8am-4pm

CHUCK WAGNER/SHUTTERSTOCK ©

TOP SIGHT
CABILDO

The former seat of power in Colonial Louisiana serves as the gateway for exploring the history of the state, and New Orleans in particular. It's also a magnificent building on its own merits. The Cabildo, a Spanish term for a city council, leads visitors into airy halls reminiscent of Spanish Colonial design, and features a mansard roof (the narrow, steep-sided roofs commonly found in Europe) added in the French style.

The exhibits, from Native American tools on the 1st floor to 'Wanted' posters for escaped slaves on the 3rd, do a good job of reaffirming the role the building and surrounding region has played in history. Highlights include an entire section dedicated to the Battle of New Orleans, anchored by an enormous oil painting by 19th-century French artist Eugene Louis Lami; a historical *Plan de la Nouvelle Orléans* from 1744 showing a four-block-deep city; and the death mask of Napoleon Bonaparte. Give yourself at least two hours to explore.

American author William Faulkner said, 'The past is never dead. It's not even past.' That quote only begins to hint at the troubled history of race relations in the South. The wing of the Cabildo dedicated to post–Civil War Reconstruction is as even-handed and thorough an attempt at explaining this difficult period as we've seen, and should be of interest to both history enthusiasts and casual visitors alike.

The magnificent Sala Capitular (Capitol Room), a council room fronted by enormous windows giving sweeping views onto Jackson Sq, was the most important room in Louisiana for decades. Civic function and legal action were conducted here; this was the courtroom where *Plessy v Ferguson*, the 1896 case that legalized segregation under the 'separate but equal' doctrine, was tried. The Sala now includes a comprehensive exhibition dedicated to the Louisiana Purchase.

DON'T MISS

- Native American exhibition hall
- Reconstruction exhibits
- Death mask of Napoleon
- Sala Capitular

PRACTICALITIES

- Map p238
- ☎800-568-6968, 504-568-6968
- http://louisianastate-museum.org/museums/the-cabildo
- 701 Chartres St
- adult/child under 12yr/student $6/free/5
- ⏲10am-4:30pm Tue-Sun, closed Mon
- 👪

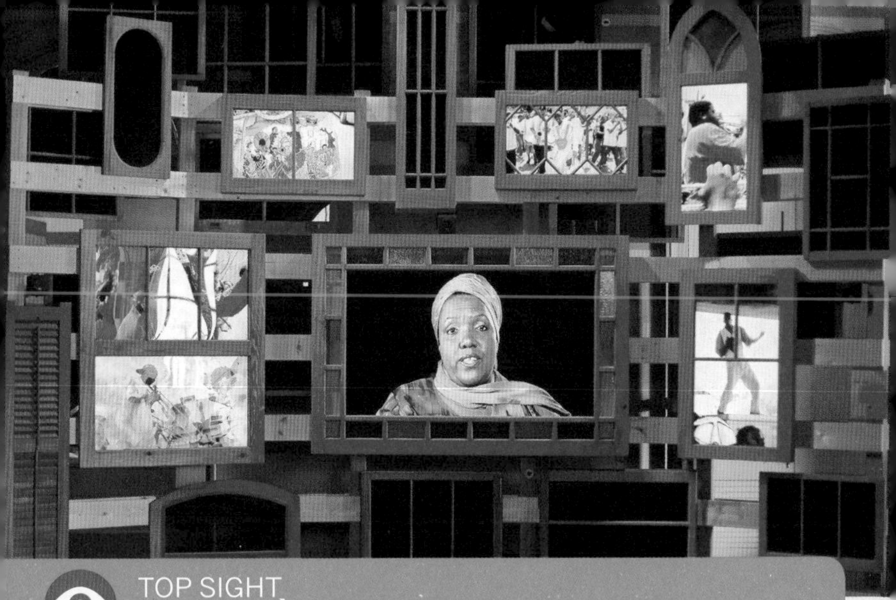

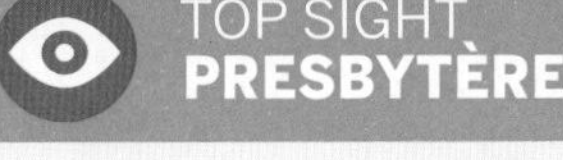

TOP SIGHT
PRESBYTÈRE

MARK J. SINDLER/IMAGE COURTESY OF LOUISIANA STATE MUSEUM ©

Pay a visit to the Presbytère, a museum dedicated to contemporary Louisiana, to learn about the state's present as one of the most dynamic regional cultures in the USA. The structure is as elegantly crafted as the Cabildo, the Presbytère's twin building dedicated to the history of the state; the siblings are separated by St Louis Cathedral overlooking Jackson Sq.

The Presbytère was originally designed in 1791 as a place of residence (also known as a rectory, or *presbytère*) for Capuchin monks. That function never panned out, and the building switched from commercial to civic use for decades, finally becoming a museum in 1911. Today the museum features rotating special exhibits on local life, documenting everything from fashion to art to music, plus two noteworthy permanent exhibitions.

The wonderful permanent exhibit on Mardi Gras exhaustively explores the city's most famous holiday. Here you'll find there's more to Fat Tuesday than wanton debauchery – or at least you'll learn the meaning behind the debauchery. There's an encyclopedia's worth of material inside on the krewes, secret societies, costumes and racial histories that are the threads of the complex Mardi Gras tapestry. We particularly like the exhibit on the 'Courir' Cajun Mardi Gras, held in rural Louisiana, and the bathrooms, which are modeled after the port-a-potties that are as rare as spun gold on Mardi Gras day.

The 'Living with Hurricanes: Katrina & Beyond' exhibit (pictured above) is the best of the many spaces in New Orleans dedicated to explaining the impact of Katrina. It tackles the issue of how the city survives (and thrives) within the hurricane zone. Multimedia displays, stark photography, several attics (literally) worth of found objects and a thoughtful layout combine into a powerful experience.

DON'T MISS

- Special exhibits
- 'Mardi Gras: It's Carnival Time in Louisiana' exhibit
- 'Living With Hurricanes: Katrina & Beyond' exhibit

PRACTICALITIES

- Map p238
- ☎800-568-6968, 504-568-6968
- http://louisianastatemuseum.org/museums/the-presbytere
- 751 Chartres St
- adult/student $6/5
- 10am-4:30pm Tue-Sun, closed Mon
- 👪

TOP SIGHT

ROYAL STREET

Royal St, with its rows of high-end antiques shops, block after block of galleries and potted ferns hanging from cast-iron balconies, is the elegant yin to well-known Bourbon St's Sodom-and-Gomorrah yang. Head here to engage in the acceptable vacation behavior of culinary and consumer indulgence rather than party-till-unconscious excess.

Stroll or bicycle past its patina beauty and fading grace, chat with locals as they lounge on their porches, and get a sense of the fun – with a dash of elegance – that was once the soul of the Vieux Carré.

Outdoor Arcade

Royal St is one of the places where soul still exists in New Orleans. Blocks and blocks of the strip are dedicated to antiques stores and art galleries, making Royal a sort of elegant 19th-century (and very long) outdoor shopping arcade. But there's no getting around the fact that far more visitors have heard of, and spend time on, Bourbon St than Royal St. And to be fair, Royal St is, in a sense, as artificial and manufactured as Bourbon.

Few people actually live on the 13 blocks that constitute the French Quarter stretch of Royal St, although they once did, as attested by rows of wrought-iron balconies and closely packed Creole town houses. You may not be able to tell from the street, but behind many of these buildings lie enormous gardens and leafy courtyards, once spaces of escape from the street scene, now often utilized as dining spaces by restaurants.

Pedestrian Performances

The blocks of Royal St between St Ann and St Louis St are closed to vehicle traffic during the afternoon. Musicians, performers and other buskers set up shop; you may see some teenage runaways shill for pennies, or accomplished blues musicians jam on their Fenders. Either way, the show is almost always entertaining.

DON'T MISS

- Pedestrian section
- Antiques stores
- Architecture
- Art galleries
- Restaurants
- Our stroll in the Vieux Carré (p70)

PRACTICALITIES

- Map p238
- Royal St

Lower Quarter

The Lower Quarter is actually the French Quarter's northern end: in New Orleans, 'up' and 'down' are determined by the flow of the Mississippi rather than the cardinal compass points. This is the quieter, more residential end of the Vieux Carré, filled with museums and historical houses.

FRENCH MARKET MARKET

Map p238 (504-522-2621; www.frenchmarket.org; 1100 N Peters St; vary by vendor) Within its shopping arcades of forgettable souvenirs, it's easy to forget that for centuries this was the great bazaar and pulsing commercial heart for much of New Orleans. Today the French Market is a bit sanitized, a tourist jungle of curios, flea markets and harmless tat that all equals family-friendly fun. Occasionally you'll spot genuinely fascinating and/or unique arts and craftwork.

Following cycles of fire and storm, the market has been built and rebuilt by the Spanish, French and Works Progress Administration (WPA).

OLD US MINT MUSEUM

Map p238 (800-568-6868, 504-568-6993; http://louisianastatemuseum.org/museums/the-old-us-mint; 400 Esplanade Ave; adult/child $6/5; 10am-4:30pm Tue-Sun) The Mint, housed in a blocky Greek-revival structure, is the only building of its kind to have printed both US and Confederate currency. Today it's a museum showcasing rotating exhibits on local history and culture, and contains the Louisiana Historical Center, an archive of manuscripts, microfiche and records related to the state. The Jazz National Historic Park hosts concerts here on weekday afternoons; check in at its office to see who is playing or visit http://musicatthemint.org.

NEW ORLEANS JAZZ NATIONAL HISTORIC PARK CULTURAL CENTER

Map p238 (877-520-0677, 504-589-4841; www.nps.gov/jazz; 916 N Peters St; 9am-5pm Tue-Sat) FREE The headquarters of the Jazz National Historic Park has educational music programs on most days. Many rangers are musicians and knowledgeable lecturers, and their presentations discuss musical developments, cultural changes and musical techniques in relation to the broad subject of jazz. Live music kicks off on Wednesdays and Saturdays. You can pick up a self-guided

THE HISTORIC NEW ORLEANS COLLECTION

The **Historic New Orleans Collection** (Map p238; THNOC; 504-523-4662; www.hnoc.org; 533 Royal St; admission free, tours $5; 9:30am-4:30pm Tue-Sat, from 10:30am Sun) sells itself to visitors as the best introduction to the history of Nola (New Orleans, Louisiana) available. That's slightly hyperbolic, but we do like THNOC for its combination of preserved buildings, museums and research centers all rolled into one. The complex is anchored by **Merieult House** and a series of regularly rotating exhibits in the **Williams Gallery** (Map p238; www.hnoc.org; 533 Royal St; 9:30am-4:30pm Tue-Sat) FREE. The Merieult History Tour dives into 11 galleries' worth of New Orleans' history. It's slightly overwhelming – it presents an original Jazz Fest poster, transfer documents of the Louisiana Purchase, and an 1849 broadside advertising '24 Head of Slaves' (individual children for $500 or entire families for $2400) – but imminently rewarding. The building itself has served as private residence, storehouse and hotel, and is a rare survivor of the 1794 fire that gutted the French Quarter.

The Williams family was always considered eccentric, and their residence, purchased in 1938 in what was then considered a dowdy neighborhood, is stuffed full of art and furniture collected in their world travels. Tours are given from Tuesday to Saturday at 10am, 11am, 2pm and 3pm for $5. As entertaining as the tour is, even better is the intro video, which glosses over the source of their fortune (that is, harvesting out the old-growth cypress of the Louisiana wetlands).

Dedicated travelers and history heads should pop into the **Williams Research Center** (Map p238; 504-523-4662; 410 Chartres St; 10am-4:30pm Tue-Sat); if you have specific queries about almost anything to do with New Orleans, the staff here can help. The archives contain more than 350,000 images and some 2 miles of manuscripts.

GUIDED TOURS IN THE FRENCH QUARTER

The French Quarter is packed with stuff to see; if you have a limited amount of time, you may want to try a guided tour. Tours depart from the addresses listed, and the hours provided are either tour times or times when you can stop by to organise one.

Friends of the Cabildo (Map p238; ☎504-523-3939; www.friendsofthecabildo.org; 523 St Ann St; adult/student $20/15; ⏰10am & 1:30pm Tue-Sun) These excellent walking tours are led by knowledgeable (and often funny) docents who will give you a great primer on the history of the French Quarter, the stories behind some of the most-famous streets and details of the area's many architectural styles.

Soul of Nola (☎504-905-4999; www.soulofnola.com; from $100/hr) Tour guide Cassandra Snyder grew up a nomad, fell in love with New Orleans and now leads highly personalized tours of the culture and hidden spaces of New Orleans. Tours receive rave reviews from travelers. If you're looking to break under the city's skin and want an individualized experience, this is the tour for you. Spanish-language tours available.

Royal Carriage Tours (☎504-943-8820; www.neworleanscarriages.com; cnr Decatur St & Jackson Sq; private tour up to 4 people per 30/60min $90/180, shared carriage per 30/60 min $18/36; ⏰8:30am-midnight) The conductors of these mule-drawn carriage tours know their stuff, revealing the locations of celebrity homes and sites of historic minutiae that constantly impress. Royal Carriages has a good animal welfare track record; it's licensed by the city and doesn't conduct tours if the weather is more than 95°F (35°C).

Haunted History Tours (☎888-644-6787, 504-861-2727; www.hauntedhistorytours.com; 723 St Peter St; adult/child/student & senior $25/14/18; ⏰6pm & 8pm year-round, 3pm 26 Dec-31 July & 1 Oct-30 Nov) Sure, these tours are a little cheesy, but they're fun too, and you'll learn a bit about the shady side of city history.

Tours By Judy (☎504-416-6666; www.toursbyjudy.com; tours from $15) Judy Bajoie, a local scholar and historian, leads well-crafted tours of the city she loves. Contact her for departure information.

New Orleans Culinary History Tours (☎877-278-8240; http://noculinarytours.com; tours from $46; ⏰call ahead) It's hard to beat a tour that is delicious and intellectually stimulating. That's what Kelly Hamilton, a history instructor at Xavier University, offers with these tours that plumb both the past and local pantries.

Magic Tours (☎504-588-9693; www.magictoursnola.com; 441 Royal St; adult/student & senior $25/20; ⏰call ahead) Led by local teachers, historians, preservationists and journalists, Magic Tours admirably gets under the skin of the city.

American Photo Safari (☎504-298-8876; www.americanphotosafari.com; Jackson Sq, by St Louis Cathedral; tours $69; ⏰call ahead) A cleverly focused tour: the photo safari docents don't just show you the sights, they give you lessons in how to take pictures of them as well.

audio walking tour of jazz sites from this office – the tour can be downloaded as an MP3 or listened to by dialing ☎504-613-4062.

URSULINE CONVENT HISTORIC BUILDING

Map p238 (☎504-529-3040; www.stlouiscathedral.org; 1112 Chartres St; adult/student/senior $5/3/4; ⏰10am-4pm Mon-Sat) One of the few surviving French Colonial buildings in New Orleans, this lovely convent is worth a tour for its architectural virtues and its small museum of Catholic bric-a-brac. After a five-month voyage from Rouen, France, 12 Ursuline nuns arrived in New Orleans in 1727. The Ursuline had a missionary bent, but achieved their goals through advancing the literacy rate of women of all races and social levels; their school admitted French, Native American and African American girls.

GALLIER HOUSE MUSEUM HISTORIC BUILDING

Map p238 (☎504-274-0746; www.hgghh.org; 1132 Royal St; adult/student & senior $12/10, combined with Hermann-Grima House $20/18; ⏰tours hourly 10am-2pm Mon, Tue, Thu & Fri, noon-3pm

FRENCH QUARTER GALLERIES

Royal and Chartres Sts are packed with art galleries that showcase the creativity of artists from across the Gulf South.

A Gallery for Fine Photography (Map 238; ☎504-568-1313; www.agallery.com; 241 Chartres St; ⊙10:30am-5:30pm Thu-Mon, by appointment Tue & Wed) This impressive gallery usually has prints such as William Henry Jackson's early-20th-century views of New Orleans and EJ Bellocq's rare images of Storyville prostitutes, made from the photographers' original glass plates. The gallery also regularly features Herman Leonard's shots of Duke Ellington and other jazz legends, as well as the occasional Cartier-Bresson enlargement (available at second-mortgage prices).

Harouni Gallery (Map p238; ☎504-299-4393; www.harouni.com; 933 Royal St; ⊙11am-5pm) Artist David Harouni, a native of Iran, has lived and worked in New Orleans for several decades. He creates works of absorbing depth by painting and scraping multiple layers of medium; the finished product has a surreal, eerie beauty.

Lucky Rose (Map p238; ☎504-309-8000; http://cathyrose.com; 840 Royal St; ⊙10am-6pm Mon-Sat) Cathy Rose blends wonder, whimsy and ethereal aesthetics; her art has whiffs of Chagall – had the painter relocated onto the Mississippi and decided to switch into mixed media and sculpture.

Hemmerling Gallery of Southern Art (Map p238; ☎504-524-0909; www.hemmerlingart.com; 733 Royal St; ⊙11am-6pm Mon-Sat, noon-5pm Sun) William 'Bill' Hemmerling was a self-taught folk artist who incorporated wood, debris and found objects into a powerfully vital body of work. This gallery displays his originals, as well as art by other folk painters and sculptors whose work demonstrates much of the same raw energy.

Gallery Burguieres (Map p238; ☎504-301-1119; www.galleryburguieres.com; 736 Royal St; ⊙10am-7pm) Ally Burguieres' artwork demonstrates plenty of technical skill, but there's also a lot of heart in her paintings and sketches, which focus on animals and fairy-tale scenes. There are lots of prints available if you're looking for affordable artwork for your home.

Michalopoulos Gallery (Map p238; ☎504-558-0505; www.michalopoulos.com; 617 Bienville St; ⊙10am-6pm Mon-Sat, from 11am Sun) Michalopoulos has become one of New Orleans' most popular painters in recent years, in part on the strength of his best-selling Jazz Fest posters. His shop showcases his colorful and expressive architectural studies and paintings that look like van Gogh meets the Vieux Carré. The gallery holds frequent openings on Friday nights. Check the website or call ahead for opening hours and to check on specific events.

Rodrigue Studio (Map p238; ☎504-581-4244; www.georgerodrigue.com; 730 Royal St; ⊙10am-6pm Mon-Sat, noon-5pm Sun) Cajun artist George Rodrigue's gallery is the place to go to see examples of his unbelievably popular 'Blue Dog' paintings. He just keeps painting and painting that darn dog. Look for topical works, in which the dog quietly comments on post-Katrina issues.

Sat, by appointment Wed) Many New Orleans buildings owe their existence, either directly or by design, to James Gallier Sr and Jr, who added Greek-revivalist, British and American accents to the Quarter's French, Spanish and Creole architectural mélange. In 1857 Gallier Jr began work on this town house, which incorporates all of the above elements. The period furniture is lovely; not so much are the intact slave quarters out back – once you see these, you'll recognize them throughout the French Quarter.

BEAUREGARD-KEYES HOUSE HISTORIC BUILDING

Map p238 (☎504-523-7257; www.bkhouse.org; 1113 Chartres St; tours adult/child/student $10/4/9; ⊙tours hourly 10am-3pm Mon-Sat) This 1826 Greek-revival house is named for its two most famous former inhabitants. Confederate General Pierre Gustave Toutant Beauregard commanded the artillery battery that fired the first shots at Fort Sumter in Charleston, SC, starting the Civil War. Francis Parkinson Keyes wrote 51 novels,

MISSISSIPPI RIVERBOATS

New Orleans' current fleet of steamboats are theme-park copies of the old glories that plied the Mississippi River in Mark Twain's day. Gone are the hoop-skirted ladies, wax-mustachioed gents, round-the-clock crap games and the bawdy tinkling on off-tune pianos. Instead, the steamboats offer urbane (but sterile) evening jazz cruises, and while the calliope organ survives, even this unique musical instrument loses some of its panache when applied to modern schmaltz such as 'Tie a Yellow Ribbon on the Old Oak Tree.' Alas.

Still, few visitors to New Orleans can resist the opportunity to get out on the Mississippi and watch the old paddle wheel propel them up the river and back down again for a spell. It's a relaxing pastime that the entire family can enjoy. All tours leave from the riverfront area near Jackson Sq.

Creole Queen (Map p244; ☎504-587-1719, 504-529-4567; www.creolequeen.com) Runs a two-hour dinner-and-jazz cruise (adult/3-5yr/6-12yr $77/12/34, without dinner $44/free/20), featuring a live Dixieland jazz combo, boarding nightly at 6:30pm from the Riverwalk (p217) on Canal St. A historical river cruise leaves from the Chalmette Battlefield at 1:30pm daily (adult/under 6yr/child 6-12yr $28/free/13).

Steamboat Natchez (Map p238; ☎800-233-2628, 504-586-8777; www.steamboatnatchez.com; 400 Toulouse St) The closest thing to an authentic steamboat running out of New Orleans today, the Natchez is steam-powered and has a bona fide calliope on board. The evening dinner-and-jazz cruise (adult/child/teen $77/14/34, without dinner adult/child/teen $46/free/21.50) takes off at 7pm nightly. There are also daytime jazz cruises at 11:30am and 2:30pm with a brunch option (adult/child/teen $40.50/8/20.25, without brunch adult/child/teen $29.50/free/12.25).

many of which were set in New Orleans – and one, *Madame Castel's Lodger* (1962), set in this house. Her collection of some 200 dolls and folk costumes are on display.

1850 HOUSE MUSEUM — HISTORIC BUILDING

Map p238 (☎504-568-6968; http://louisianastatemuseum.org/museums/1850-house; 523 St Ann St; adult/child/senior & student $3/free/2; ⏲10am-4:30pm Tue-Sun) The 1850 House is one of the apartments in the lower Pontalba Building. Madame Micaëla Pontalba, daughter of Don Andrés Almonaster y Roxas, built the long rows of red-brick apartments flanking the upper and lower portions of Jackson Sq. Today, volunteers from the Friends of the Cabildo give tours of the apartment (every 45 minutes or so), which includes the central court and servants' quarters. There are period furnishings throughout.

HISTORIC VOODOO MUSEUM — MUSEUM

Map p238 (☎504-680-0128; 724 Dumaine St; admission $5; ⏲10am-6pm) Of the (many) voodoo museums in the French Quarter, this one is probably our favorite. The narrow corridors and dark rooms, stuffed with statues, dolls and paintings, are something approaching spooky, and the information placards (seemingly written by anthropology dissertation candidates with too much time on their hands) are genuinely informative, if a little dry.

VOODOO SPIRITUAL TEMPLE — MUSEUM

Map p238 (☎504-522-9627; www.voodoospiritualtemple.org; 828 N Rampart St; donations accepted; ⏲10:30am-6pm Mon-Sat, noon-2pm Sun) Mexican crucifix? Check. Tibetan mandala? Ditto. Balinese Garuda? Why not? Miriam William's temple feels more like a mash-up of global religions and New Age mysticism than voodoo, but maybe that's just her interpretation of voodoo. The temple is big on the tour-group circuit and it can be entertaining to watch Miriam give her lectures on life, the universe and everything else. An adjacent gift shop does a brisk trade in candles, cards and *gris-gris* (amulets or spell bags).

LOWER BOURBON STREET — STREET

Map p238 (Bourbon St, btwn St Philip St & Esplanade Ave) At St Philip St, Bourbon shifts from a Dante's *Inferno*-style circle of neon-lit hell into an altogether more agreeable stretch of historical houses, diners and bars, many of which cater to the gay community. In fact, said gay bars are the loudest residents on this, the quieter, more classically New Orleans end of the street.

Upper Quarter

South of Jackson Square is where you'll find most of the booziness and souvenir stands that the majority of tourists associate with the Old Quarter.

JACKSON SQUARE SQUARE, PLAZA

See p60.

ST LOUIS CATHEDRAL CATHEDRAL

See p61.

CABILDO MUSEUM

See p62.

PRESBYTÈRE MUSEUM

See p63.

ROYAL STREET LANDMARK

See p64.

RIVERFRONT PARK

Map p238 (from Bienville to St Philip St) It's supremely pleasant to stroll up to the Mississippi River as it runs by the Quarter. The entire riverfront area has been landscaped with pedestrian paths, public arts projects and small green spaces such as the **Woldenberg Park**. Sunset is the best time to come up here; couples walk around in love; container ships and ferries ply the water; and all feels bucolic. Nearby is the **Jackson (Jax) Brewery**, a mediocre shopping mall that *does* have free public restrooms.

JEAN LAFITTE NATIONAL HISTORIC PARK VISITOR CENTER

Map p238 (504-589-2636; www.nps.gov/jela; 419 Decatur St; 9am-4:30pm Tue-Sat;) FREE This small center serves as a primary visitor center for the six statewide sites of Jean Lafitte National Historic Park. Helpful rangers and a series of interactive, interpretative exhibits provide lots of insight into the history and culture of Louisiana.

CASKET GIRLS & WORKING GIRLS

During the early days of their work, the Ursuline nuns (p66), who arrived in New Orleans in 1727, quickly observed that an unusually high proportion of the colony's women were working in the world's oldest profession, so they decided to call in marriageable teenage girls from France (generally recruited from orphanages or convents). The girls arrived in New Orleans, Biloxi and Mobile with their clothes packed in coffin-like trunks, and thus became known as the 'casket girls.' Educated by the nuns, the girls were brought up to make proper wives for the French men of New Orleans. Over the centuries, the casket-girl legacy became more sensational as some in New Orleans surmised the wood boxes may have contained French vampires.

Of course, prostitution never lost its luster in this steamy port. New Orleans' fabled bordellos are one of the earliest foundations upon which the city's reputation as a spot for sin and fun are built. The most famous 'sporting' houses were elegant mansions, reputedly decorated with some of the finest art and furnishings of their era and staffed with a multiracial cast of employees ranging from white to Creole to black. Around the turn of the 20th century, famously puritan city alderman (councillor) Sidney Story wrote an ordinance that moved the bordellos out of the city's posh residential neighborhoods and into the side of the French Quarter that borders the Tremé. Never ones to miss an opportunity for irony, New Orleanians dubbed their red-light district 'Storyville' in honor of Sidney.

Although there were no Lonely Planet books around at the time, visitors could explore Storyville with the help of the 'Blue Book,' a guide to the area's...attractions. Each book was imprinted with the passage: 'Order of the Garter: *Honi Soit Qui Mal Y Pense*' (Shame to Him Who Evil Thinks). Jazz was largely popularized by visitors listening to music in Storyville's storied pleasure houses. One of the most famous houses, the Arlington, operated at 225 North Basin St (look for the onion-domed cupola, all that's left of the demolished bordello).

Storyville was shut down in 1917 by the federal government. At the time Mayor Martin Behrman lamented that while authorities could make prostitution illegal, 'you can't make it unpopular.'

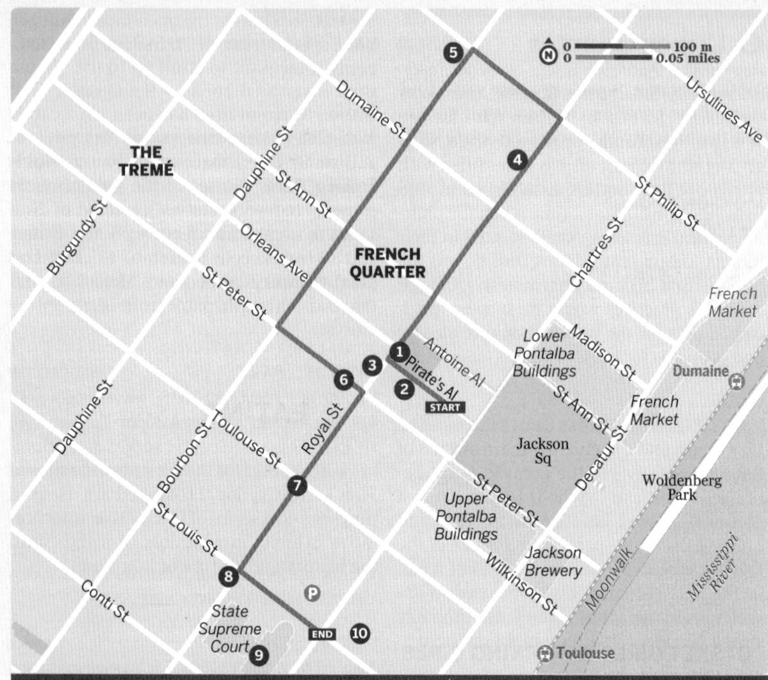

Neighborhood Walk
A Stroll in the Vieux Carré

START PIRATE'S ALLEY
END NAPOLEON HOUSE
LENGTH 1 MILE; 45 MINUTES

This walk explores the French Quarter's two main drags: Bourbon and Royal Sts. Goofus and Gallant, if you will. Think of this as a quick introduction to the Quarter.

Begin at Pirate's Alley, an inviting walkway that cuts through the shadow of St Louis Cathedral. To the right is gated **1 St Anthony's Garden**, a peaceful pocket in the bustling Quarter.

Halfway up the alley, stop in at **2 Faulkner House Books** (p83), which opened in 1990 and quickly became a focal point for New Orleans literary circles. Much of the alley is occupied by the **3 Labranche buildings** (built by Jean Baptiste Labranche, a Creole sugar planter), which wrap around Royal St to St Peter St. Turn right at Royal St, which takes the cake for classic New Orleans postcard images.

Walk to the **4 Cornstalk Hotel** (p177), standing behind a frequently photographed fence. Turn left at St Philip St and head towards Bourbon. On the corner, **5 Lafitte's Blacksmith Shop** (p78) is supposedly where pirate Jean Lafitte ran a blacksmith shop as a front. Have a drink here to brace yourself for a walk along Bourbon St.

Reaching St Peter St, turn left and head to **6 Pat O'Brien's** (p79). Have a look in Pat's courtyard and then continue south to Royal St (you can also walk through Pat's and emerge on Bourbon St, then head back to Royal via Toulouse St).

Go down Royal St past the **7 Historic New Orleans Collection** (p65) and continue on to St Louis St. On this corner, in what is now **8 James H Cohen & Sons** (p81) antique gun shop, the cocktail was supposedly invented. The premises were occupied at the beginning of the 19th century by Pey-chaud's Apothecary.

Turn left and walk a block of St Louis St, back to Chartres. It's impossible not to notice the **9 State Supreme Court Building**. Nearby is **10 Napoleon House** (p79), where we'll end our tour over a bowl of gumbo and a beer in the courtyard.

NEW ORLEANS PHARMACY MUSEUM MUSEUM

Map p238 (☎504-565-8027; www.pharmacymuseum.org; 514 Chartres St; adult/child under 6yr/student $5/free/4; ⏰10am-4pm Tue-Sat) This beautifully preserved little shop groans with ancient display cases filled with intriguing little bottles. Established in 1816 by Louis J Dufilho, at a time when the pharmaceutical arts were – shall we say – in their infancy, the museum claims Dufilho was the nation's first licensed pharmacist, although today his practices would be suspect (gold-coated pills for the wealthy; opium, alcohol and cannabis for those with less cash).

UPPER BOURBON STREET STREET

Map p238 (Bourbon St, btwn Canal & Dumaine Sts) Like Vegas and Cancun, the main stretch of Bourbon St is where the great id of the repressed American psyche is let loose into a seething mass of karaoke, strip clubs and every bachelorette party ever. It's one of the tackiest experiences in the world, but it can be fun for an evening. Everyone needs more skeletons in their closet, and you'll probably stuff a few more in after a night out here.

MUSÉE CONTI HISTORICAL WAX MUSEUM MUSEUM

Map p238 (☎504-525-2605; www.neworleanswaxmuseum.com; 917 Conti St; adult/child/senior $8/7/7.25; ⏰10am-4pm Mon, Fri & Sat) This place sells itself as one of New Orleans' 'best kept secrets,' which is like saying po'boys are undiscovered culinary gems. It's a wax museum that's kitschy and entertaining in the way wax museums should be: local historical figures include Andrew Jackson, Huey Long, Louis Armstrong and Napoleon Bonaparte (caught in the bathtub for some reason), then Frankenstein's monster (chained, for your protection) and Swamp Thing (unchained!).

HERMANN-GRIMA HOUSE HISTORIC BUILDING

Map p238 (☎504-525-5661; www.hgghh.org; 820 St Louis St; tours adult/student & senior $12/10, combined with Gallier House Museum $20/18; ⏰tours hourly 10am-2pm Mon, Tue, Thu & Fri, noon-3pm Sat, by appointment Wed) Samuel Hermann, a Jewish merchant who married a Catholic woman, introduced the American-style Federal design to the Quarter in 1831. Hermann sold the house in 1844 to slaveholder Judge Grima after Hermann reportedly lost $2 million during the national financial panic of 1837. Cooking demonstrations ($15) in the open-hearth kitchen are a special treat on Thursdays from October to May.

MUSICAL LEGENDS PARK PARK

Map p238 (www.neworleansmusicallegends.com; 311 Bourbon St; ⏰8am-10pm Sun-Thu, to midnight Fri & Sat) This pleasant little public square is peppered with statues of some of New Orleans' great musical heroes: Louis Prima, Chris Owens, Pete Fountain, Al Hirt, Fats Domino and Ronnie Kole. Musicians play live jazz within the park from 10am until it closes.

EATING

Lower Quarter

The Lower Quarter features the best cheap eating options around, but there are a few decent high-end places here as well.

★COOP'S PLACE CAJUN $

Map p238 (☎504-525-9053; www.coopsplace.net; 1109 Decatur St; mains $8-17.50; ⏰11am-3am) Coop's is an authentic Cajun dive, but more rocked out. Make no mistake: it's a grotty chaotic place, the servers have attitude and the layout is annoying. But it's worth it for the food: rabbit jambalaya, chicken with shrimp and *tasso* (smoked ham) in a cream sauce – there's no such thing as 'too heavy' here. No patrons under 21.

PORT OF CALL BURGERS $

Map p238 (☎504-523-0120; http://portofcallnola.com; 838 Esplanade Ave; mains $7-21; ⏰11am-midnight, to 1am Fri & Sat) The Port of Call burger is legendary. The meat is unadulterated and, well, meaty, like umami condensed into a patty. Then there's the baked potato on the side, buckling under the weight of sour cream, butter and bacon bits, all served in a 1960s-ish Polynesian tiki bar setting. Be prepared to wait outside in long lines for a seat (no reservations).

FIORELLA'S ITALIAN, LOUISIANAN $

Map p238 (☎504-553-2155; 1136 Decatur St; mains $7-15; ⏰11am-10pm Mon-Wed, to midnight Thu & Sun, to 2am Fri & Sat) Fiorella's is a Sicilian cafe run through a punk-rock wringer, similar to nearby Coop's Cajun Country hipster shack. It's bright and cozy, more a

GALATOIRE'S: THE UNENDING LUNCH

Friday morning is the best time to come to **Galatoire's** (Map p238; 504-525-2021; 209 Bourbon St; mains $17-38; 11:30am-10pm Tue-Sat, noon-10pm Sun), a revered institution of the New Orleans upper crust. That's when the local ladies in big hats and gloves and the men who wear bowties (without irony) buy copious bottles of champagne, gossip to high hell and have eight-hour boozy lunches that, in their way, have been going on forever. Dress the part; jackets are a must for men.

Galatoire's is a special place. Its interior has been frozen in time for over a century, and despite being a top-end joint, the restaurant only recently started taking credit cards. That's not to say you couldn't get meals on credit; some families run tabs at Galatoire's, a sure sign that your name rings out in the right New Orleanian social circles.

There are new stories and new scandals, but they're all told by a relatively stable cast of larger-than-life characters. Some folks act the absolute merry fool at the Galatoire's lunch, proving the old saying: 'What's the difference between crazy and eccentric? Money.' If you can't make it on a Friday – and the lines do sometimes stretch around the block – that's OK. Show up whenever and ask a tuxedo-clad waiter what's fresh. Expect to dine on old-line masterpieces and mainstays: *pompano meunière* (liver with bacon and onions), and the signature *chicken clemenceau* (chicken with fried potatoes, peas, garlic and mushrooms).

neighborhood spot than tourist trap. Said 'hood is the slightly grungy northern end of Decatur St. Expect pastas, pizzas, veal cutlets and an unexpected treat in the form of salty, tasty fried chicken.

BENNACHIN AFRICAN $

Map p238 (504-522-1230; www.bennachinrestaurant.com; 1212 Royal; St; mains $8-16; 11am-9pm, to 10pm Fri & Sat;) West African cuisine (specifically Cameroonian and Gambian) doesn't pose too many challenges to the conservative palette. It's basically meat and potatoes, with a main, such as beef in peanut stew or spinach and plantains, served with some kind of starch used as a scooping accompaniment. The heavy use of okra reminds you how much this cuisine has influenced Louisiana.

CLOVER GRILL DINER $

Map p238 (504-598-1010; 900 Bourbon St; mains $3-8; 24hr) This popular spot near the gay end of Bourbon St resembles an Edward Hopper painting, in which the clientele consists of an out-of-makeup drag queen and a drunk club kid arguing against a backdrop of blaring disco. The food is dependable diner fare: good for a hangover, or for those who can see the hangover approaching.

MONA LISA ITALIAN $

Map p238 (504-522-6746; 1212 Royal St; mains $9-18; 5-10pm Mon-Thu, to 11pm Fri-Sun) An informal and quiet local spot in the Lower Quarter, Mona Lisa is dim, dark and candlelight romantic in its own quirky way. Kooky renditions of da Vinci's familiar subject hang on the walls. Wearing hair curlers, looking 50lb heavier or appearing in the form of a cow, she stares impassively at diners munching on pizzas, pastas and spinach salads.

CENTRAL GROCERY DELI $

Map p238 (504-523-1620; 923 Decatur St; sandwiches $7-10; 9am-5pm Tue-Sun) There are a few New Orleans names inextricably linked to a certain dish, and Central Grocery is the word-association winner for the muffuletta. That's pronounced 'muffalotta,' and the name about sums it up: your mouth will be muffled by a hell of a lotta sandwich, stuffed with meat, cheese and sharp olive salad.

This is a real grocery by the way, one of the last neighborhood vestiges of the New Orleans Sicilian community, and the fresh Italian produce is a draw on its own.

VERTI MARTE DELI $

Map p238 (504-525-4767; 1201 Royal St; meals $4-9; 24hr) Sometimes you just wanna wander the Quarter with a tasty sandwich in hand. If that's the case, get to Verti, a reliable deli with a take-out stand that's got a menu as long as a hot New Orleans summer day. Try the 'All That Jazz,' a ridiculous blend of turkey, shrimp, 'wow sauce,' ham, cheese and who knows what else.

ANGELI ON DECATUR DINER $

Map p238 (☎504-566-0077; www.angelineworleans.com; 1141 Decatur St; mains $6-18; ⏰11am-midnight Mon-Wed, to 2am Thu & Sun, to 4am Fri & Sat;) Great philosophers have long debated one of the most pressing of human questions: what makes a late-night place great? We humbly submit: the food tastes as good when you're sober as when you're trashed at 3am. Enter Angeli – decked out with hipster art and patrons. The burger, pasta and pizza fare here is good no matter your state of mind/inebriation/whatever.

CROISSANT D'OR PATISSERIE BAKERY $

Map p238 (☎504-524-4663; www.croissantdornola.com; 617 Ursulines Ave; meals $3-5; ⏰6am-3pm Wed-Mon) On the quieter side of the French Quarter, this spotlessly clean pastry shop is where many locals start their day. Bring a paper, order coffee and a croissant – or a tart, a quiche or a sandwich topped with béchamel sauce – and bliss out. Check out the tiled sign on the threshold that says 'ladies entrance' – a holdover from earlier days.

EAT NEW ORLEANS CREOLE $$

Map p238 (☎504-522-7222; eatnola.com; 900 Dumaine St; mains $13-27; ⏰11am-2pm Tue-Fri, 5:30-10pm Tue-Sat, brunch 9am-2pm Sat & Sun;) Eat dishes out neo-Creole cuisine served in an airy setting that has become immensely popular with locals; when a New Orleanian is willing to brave French Quarter parking for pork and mustard greens or stuffed peppers, you know there's something good going on. Brunch is something special, with highlights such as fried chicken and gravy with eggs.

IRENE'S CUISINE ITALIAN $$

Map p238 (☎504-529-8811; 539 St Philip St; mains $16-23; ⏰5:30-10pm Mon-Sat) Irene's is a romantic gem, tucked in a corner that's generally missed by travelers. Not that it's easy to miss, given the overwhelming (and overwhelmingly good) scent of garlic emanating from this intimate Italian cavern. Irene's is Italian–French, really: pick from rosemary chicken, seared chops, pan-sautéed fish fillets and great pasta. Reservations aren't accepted and long waits are the norm.

MEAUXBAR MODERN FRENCH $$

Map p238 (☎504-569-9979; www.meauxbar.com; 942 N Rampart St; mains $17-28; ⏰5-11pm Mon-Thu, to midnight Sat, to 10pm Sun) We describe Meauxbar as modern French, but there's a strong Louisiana influence running through the kitchen, as is good and proper. Local pan-roasted oysters are served in a dijon-endive cream sauce, while French onion soup is flipped into a grilled cheese sandwich, complete with brioche and braised beef. The dark setting is romantic; dress smart casual.

CAFÉ AMELIE FRENCH $$

Map p238 (☎504-412-8965; www.cafeamelie.com; 912 Royal St; mains $15-29; ⏰11am-3pm Wed-Sun, 5-9pm Wed, Thu & Sun, to 10pm Fri & Sat) We wax rhapsodic over the Quarter's

FRENCH MARKET

Back in the day, the French Market (p65) was a vital part of French Quarter commercial life: a source of food, gossip and fellowship. Groceries, produce, fresh fish, people screaming prices and deals: it was the sort of open-air bazaar that sets the backdrop of an adventure novel or an Indiana Jones movie.

Today, the market caters largely to tourists, but it's still a lively place, especially on weekends. Currently, it is split into two sections – the farmers market and the flea market. The latter carries a motley assortment of T-shirt and sunglasses vendors, as well as African art (mass-produced), inexpensive silver jewelry, chintzy Mardi Gras masks and dolls, and enough preserved alligator heads to populate a polyurethane swamp. Most prices at the flea market are negotiable. Officially the flea market is open 24 hours, but most vendors keep their own hours and are open from 9am to 5pm.

Only a vestige of former market activity remains at the farmers market. Largely, this has become a pavilion for local food purveyors selling deli sandwiches, po'boys and other foodstuffs; you can also find some locally made arts and crafts here if the souvenirs at the flea market aren't your thing. Hours vary by vendor, but most spots open around 9am and shut around 6pm. Note that an actual farmers market with fresh produce and meats is open on Wednesday from 2pm to 6pm and Saturday from 10am to 2pm.

beautiful backyard gardens, and Amelie's, much beloved by locals, takes the cake. An alfresco restaurant tucked behind an old carriage house and surrounded by high brick walls and shade trees, this is a supremely romantic dining spot. Fresh seafood and local produce are the basis of a modest, ever-changing menu.

Upper Quarter

MISTER GREGORY'S FRENCH $

Map p238 (504-407-3780; www.mistergregorys.com; 806 N Rampart St; mains $5-13; 9am-4pm;) That the French expat community of New Orleans regularly makes its way to Mister Gregory's should tell you something about the quality of this bistro's baguettes and sandwiches. This simple lunch and breakfast spot specializes in deli baguettes, and it does a mean line of *croque*-style sandwiches (with melted cheese and béchamel on top), salads and waffles.

LA DIVINA GELATERIA ICE CREAM $

Map p238 (504-302-2692; http://ladivinagelateria.com; 621 St Peter St; gelato $2.25-8.50, sandwiches $6.50-9.50; 11am-10pm Mon-Wed, 8:30am-10pm Thu, 8:30am-11pm Fri & Sat) When it feels like the street is about to melt under your feet, or you just need a sweet treat that isn't a powdered beignet, head to this Italian-style ice-cream shop. There's a ton of flavors of sweet gelato and sorbet that ought to lower your body temperature. A small selection of sandwiches rounds out the menu.

YO MAMA'S AMERICAN $

Map p238 (504-522-1125; www.yo-mamas.com; 727 St Peter St; mains $7-14; 11am-close, from 10am Sat & Sun) 'Where we eatin' tonight?' 'Yo Mama's.' Chortle, chortle, chortle. Now that *that's* out of the way, let's lay it on the line: peanut butter and bacon burger. Yep, it looks like a cheeseburger, but that ain't melted cheddar on top – it's peanut butter, and honestly, it's great. Yo Mama's stays open until the bartenders feel like closing.

CAFÉ BEIGNET CAFE $

Map p238 (504-524-5530; www.cafebeignet.com; 334 Royal St; meals $6-8; 7am-5pm) In a shaded patio setting with a view of Royal St, this intimate cafe serves omelets, Belgian waffles, quiche and beignets. There's a low-level war among foodies over who does the better beignet – this place or iconic Café du Monde – with the general consensus being this spot uses less powdered sugar. Also located at **Musical Legends Park** (311 Bourbon St, Musical Legends Park; 8am-10pm Sun-Thu, to midnight Fri & Sat).

JOHNNY'S PO-BOYS SANDWICHES $

Map p238 (504-524-8129; http://johnnyspoboys.com; 511 St Louis St; dishes $4-10; 8am-4:30pm) We generally prefer not to grab our po'boys in the touristy Quarter, but we make an exception for Johnny's. A local favorite since 1950, it's the only traditional po'boy joint around. It's all checkered tablecloths, hustle, bustle and good food served by good folks. Breakfast is simple and delicious.

STANLEY CREOLE $

Map p238 (504-587-0093; www.stanleyrestaurant.com; 547 St Ann St; mains $10-16; 7am-7pm) While sandwiches and other lunch-y things are available at Stanley, we're all about the breakfast. Banana French toast and fluffy pancakes provide the sweet, while a Breaux Bridge Benedict with boudin and local hollandaise does up the savory side. Either option is delicious.

SALT N PEPPER INDIAN $

Map p238 (504-561-6070; 201 N Peters St; mains $5-10; 11am-11pm, to midnight Fri & Sat) First: early '90s hip-hop fans beware, this spot won't 'Push It' to new levels of culinary achievement (boo). Second: yup, looks like a dingy dive bar. But Salt N Pepper serves pretty good Indian food, including goat curry and palak paneer. It may not be spicy enough, but if you want cheap and ethnic in the Quarter, this is your option.

SYLVAIN LOUISIANAN $$

Map p238 (504-265-8123; www.sylvainnola.com; 625 Chartres St; mains $12.50-25; 5:30-11pm Mon-Thu, to midnight Fri & Sat, to 10pm Sun, 11:30am-2:30pm Fri & Sat, 10:30am-2:30pm Sun) This rustic yet elegant gastropub draws inspiration from the dedication to local ingredients demonstrated by chefs such as Thomas Keller. The focus is Southern haute cuisine and excellent cocktails; the duck confit served on a bed of black-eyed peas is indicative of the gastronomic experience: rich, refined and delicious.

GREEN GODDESS FUSION $$

Map p238 (504-301-3347; www.greengoddessnola.com; 307 Exchange Pl; mains $12-20; 11am-9pm Wed-Sun;) Who serves lemongrass

THE BIG MUDDY: MISSISSIPPI RIVER

The Mississippi River is more than the defining geographical landmark of New Orleans. It is its soul, its center and its reason for being. 'Why was New Orleans built below sea level?' folks ask. First off, only half the city is below sea level, but the reason is that this spot commands the entrance to the most important river in North America. All the trade, conquest and exploration of this continent is wrapped up in the Mississippi and her moods. It would be criminal to come here and not catch a glimpse of the Mother of Waters.

It can be difficult to appreciate just where the river runs from the streets. Some of our favorite spots for river-watching include numerous benches along the levee opposite Jackson Sq and the Moon Walk, a boardwalk (not the dance) built by and named for former mayor Moon Landrieu.

The Mississippi is no lazy river. It flows through New Orleans at an average depth of about 200ft. Its immense volume of water and sand roils with tremendous, turbulent force, whirling and eddying and scouring at the snakelike curves of its banks. It runs some 2400 miles from Minnesota to the Gulf of Mexico, and its drainage basin extends from the Rockies to the Alleghenies, covering 40% of continental USA. The rain that falls in this vast area ultimately ends up in the Gulf, and most of it is carried there by the Mississippi. The Platte, the Missouri, the Ohio, the Cumberland and the Arkansas – mighty rivers themselves – all feed into the Mississippi, which carries their waters past New Orleans. It drains more water than the Nile, and only the Amazon and the Congo carry a greater volume of water to the sea.

It also moves up to several million tons of sediment into the Gulf every day. Thus, the river has shifted more than 1000 cubic miles of earth from north to south, depositing soil into the Gulf and spreading it to the east and west as the river changed its course. The land that is Louisiana as well as much of the states of Mississippi and Alabama were created by the river.

The river's name is a corruption of the old Ojibwe *Misi-ziibi* (great river). For early European settlers to the Mississippi Valley, the river proved too unruly to serve as a viable route inland until the advent of the steamboat in 1807. During the early part of the 19th century New Orleans' population mushroomed, largely as a result of river traffic and trade.

It is natural for deltaic rivers to flood regularly and to periodically change their course; preventing the Mississippi from flooding is no simple engineering feat. The river has broken its levees on several occasions, most notoriously in 1927, when the river breached in 145 places. That spring, some 27,000 sq miles of farmland, from Illinois to southern Louisiana, turned into a raging sea (up to 30ft deep in places) that flowed steadily down to the Gulf. Entire towns were washed away and a million people were driven from their homes. It took several months for the flooding to recede back to within the river's banks. New Orleans, however, remained high and dry, as north of the city the floodwaters chose the Atchafalaya River's shorter path to the Gulf.

tofu over wasabi brûlée? Or South Indian pancakes and tamarind shrimp? Alongside smoked duck and (oh, man) truffle grits? Green Goddess, that's who. The Goddess combines a playful attitude to preparation with a world traveler's perspective on ingredient sourcing and a workman's ethic when it comes to actually cooking the stuff.

LATITUDE 29 ASIAN **$$**

Map p238 (☎504-609-3811; http://latitude29nola.com; 321 N Peter St; mains $10-24; ⏰3-11pm Sun-Thu, 11am-11pm Fri & Sat) At a bar (p78) dedicated to all things Tiki, of course you find a restaurant that specializes in pan-Asian, vaguely tropical grub. Latitude 29's food is more than a gimmick; the meat pies are hearty and tasty, while *loco moco* (two burgers and an egg served over rice with gravy) will satisfy the nostalgia of expat Hawaiians.

ACME OYSTER & SEAFOOD HOUSE SEAFOOD **$$**

Map p238 (☎504-522-5973; www.acmeoyster.com; 724 Iberville St; mains $11-24; ⏰11am-10pm

Sun-Thu, to 11pm Fri & Sat) They still shuck oysters to order here, which is a beautiful thing, but they also serve gumbo in a bread bowl – nice if you're from the West Coast, but pure madness to local food purists. Ah well, it's a good spot for fresh oysters close to the Bourbon St craziness, and for that we salute Acme with a half shell.

★BAYONA LOUISIANAN $$$

Map p238 (☎504-525-4455; www.bayona.com; 430 Dauphine St; mains $29-38; ⏰11:30am-1:30pm Wed-Sun, 6-9:30pm Mon-Thu, 5:30-10pm Fri & Sat) Bayona is, for our money, the best splurge in the Quarter. It's rich but not overwhelming, classy but unpretentious, innovative without being precocious, and just an all-round very fine spot for a meal. The menu changes regularly, but expect fresh fish, fowl and game prepared in a way that comes off as both elegant and deeply cozy at the same time.

SOBOU MODERN AMERICAN $$$

Map p238 (☎504-552-4095; www.sobounola.com; 310 Chartres St; mains $24-38; ⏰7am-10pm daily) The name means 'South of Bourbon.' The food? Hard to pin, but uniformly excellent. The chefs play with a concept that mixes Louisiana indulgence with eccentricities: sweet-potato beignets slathered with duck gravy and chicory coffee glaze, and the infamous, decadent foie gras burger. The on-site bar mixes mean drinks, and there are tables with beer taps built in!

COURT OF TWO SISTERS CREOLE $$$

Map p238 (☎504-522-7261; www.courtoftwosisters.com; 613 Royal St; mains $18-37; ⏰9am-3pm & 5:30-10pm) The court regularly ranks in 'Best place for brunch in New Orleans' lists, a standing that can be attributed to its setting as much as its food. The latter is a circus of Creole omelets, Cajun pasta salads, grillades, fresh fruits, carved meats and fruity cocktails; the former is a simply enchanting Creole garden filled with sugar-scented warm air against a soft jazz backdrop.

K-PAUL'S LOUISIANA KITCHEN CAJUN $$$

Map p238 (☎504-596-2530; www.kpauls.com; 416 Chartres St; mains $32-44; ⏰5:30-10pm Mon-Sat, 11am-2pm Thu-Sat) This is the home base of chef Paul Prudhomme, who is essentially responsible for putting modern Louisiana cooking on the map. The kitchen's still cranking out quality: blackened twin beef tenders, a signature dish, come with an incredibly rich 'debris' gravy that's been slowly cooked over a two-day period.

BRENNAN'S RESTAURANT CREOLE $$$

Map p238 (☎504-525-9711; www.brennansneworleans.com; 417 Royal St; mains $23-39; ⏰9am-1pm Mon-Fri, 8am-2:30pm Sat & Sun, 6-9pm daily) One of the grande dames of Creole dining, Brennan's has undergone an enormous overhaul. It still offers decadent breakfasts and cocktail 'eye-openers' to start the day. But the cuisine has gotten a little more international, even as it remains old-school rich: bacon-roasted venison is served with chestnut butter, while beef fillet comes with caramelized bananas.

DICKIE BRENNAN'S STEAK $$$

Map p238 (☎504-522-2467; www.dickiebrennanssteakhouse.com; 716 Iberville St; mains $23-44; ⏰5:30-10pm daily, 11:30am-2:30pm Fri) New Orleans, a city of seafood and swamp ingredients, isn't known as a steak town. Yet this steakhouse is considered one of the greatest in the South. There's not a lot we can say about Dickie Brennan's; it does steak, and it does it right. For a side, try the Pontalba potatoes, done up with garlic, mushrooms and ham.

THE BEST BEIGNET IN TOWN?

Café du Monde (Map p238; ☎800-772-2927; www.cafedumonde.com; 800 Decatur St; beignets $2; ⏰24hr) is an iconic fixture in the New Orleans scene and you'll probably want to try it for a beignet fix. But fair warning: it's crowded and hardly romantic (unless you arrive late at night – it's open 24 hours). The beignets are very good, while the coffee is inconsistent. The other option in town for coffee and beignets is (surprise) Café Beignet (p74). We find the coffee is usually better at Cafe du Monde, where the beignets also tend to be a little denser and topped with more sugar – which may or may not be to your liking. A beignet or two probably won't break the bank, though, so why not try both for yourself?

ARNAUD'S CREOLE $$$

Map p238 (☎504-523-5433; www.arnauds.com; 813 Bienville St; mains $27-40; ⊙6-10pm Mon-Sat, 10am-2:30pm & 6-10pm Sun) Back in 1918, 'Count' Arnaud Cazenave turned roughly a whole city block into a restaurant that's served upscale Creole cuisine ever since. The menu includes shrimp Arnaud (shrimp in a rémoulade sauce), and oysters Bienville (an original dish with mushrooms and a white-wine sauce). Show up early for a French 75 at, hey, French 75 (p78). And men, bring a jacket.

BROUSSARD'S CREOLE $$$

Map p238 (☎504-581-3866; www.broussards.com; 819 Conti St; mains $18-40; ⊙5:30-10pm) Broussard's has been around since 1920, buoyed by uncommonly good executions of Creole standbys such as veal and crawfish in a béchamel sauce and redfish stuffed with shrimp, crabmeat and oysters. The on-site Empire Bar does for classic cocktails what this spot does for old-line Creole cuisine. No T-shirts or shorts, gentlemen.

ANTOINE'S CREOLE $$$

Map p238 (☎504-581-4422; www.antoines.com; 713 St Louis St; dinner mains $27-48; ⊙11:30am-2pm & 5:30-9pm Mon-Sat, 11am-2pm Sun) Established in 1840, Antoine's is the oldest of old-line New Orleans restaurants. The dining rooms look like first-class lounges on the *Orient Express* and are named for Mardi Gras krewes. This restaurant invented dishes such as oysters Rockefeller, and while their take may not be the best in town, you're eating history in a space that feels like it should host Jay Gatsby.

NOLA MODERN AMERICAN $$$

Map p238 (☎504-522-6652; www.emerilsrestaurants.com/nola-restaurant; 534 St Louis St; mains $27-38; ⊙11:30am-2pm Thu-Mon, 6-10pm daily) TV chef Emeril Lagasse's French Quarter outpost is pretty damn good. Emeril himself isn't in the kitchen 'Bam!'-ing up your food, but whoever is does a great job with blackberry-stout-glazed ribs, buttermilk cornbread pudding and other sexed-up contemporary Louisianan dishes.

GW FINS SEAFOOD $$$

Map p238 (☎504-581-3467; www.gwfins.com; 808 Bienville St; mains $21-46; ⊙5-10pm Sun-Thu, to 10:30pm Fri & Sat) Fins focuses, almost entirely, on fish: freshly caught and prepped so that the flavor of the sea is always accented and never overwhelmed. For New Orleans this is light, almost delicate dining – you'll still find crabmeat stuffing and tasso toppings, but Fins also knows how to serve a rare yellowtail with a bit of fine sticky rice.

BOURBON HOUSE CREOLE $$$

Map p238 (☎504-522-0111; 144 Bourbon St; mains $16-35; ⊙6:30am-10pm Mon-Thu, to 11pm Fri & Sat, 10am-10pm Sun) The Bourbon House is an outpost of the extensive Brennan restaurant empire. While you'll find a nice rib-eye steak and pulled pork on the menu, seafood is the specialty here. Catfish is served crusted with pecans in a rich butter sauce, while the barbecue shrimp, heavily laced with rosemary and black pepper, is absolute magic.

DRINKING & NIGHTLIFE

There's a lot going on in the Old Quarter, from boozy Bourbon St to quiet Pirate's Alley. Head down to lower Decatur St for a collection of interesting dives and locals' pubs, which lead in a boozy trail all the way to the fun on Frenchman St. We don't review most of the cheese-ball Bourbon St action – these megabars are a dime a dozen.

★TONIQUE BAR

Map p238 (☎504-324-6045; http://bartonique.com; 820 N Rampart St; ⊙noon-2am) Tonique is a bartender's bar. Seriously, on a Sunday night, when the weekend rush is over, we've seen no less than three of the city's top bartenders arrive here to unwind. Why? Because this gem mixes some of the best drinks in the city, and it has a spirits menu as long as a Tolstoy novel to draw upon.

★MOLLY'S AT THE MARKET PUB

Map p238 (☎504-525-5169; www.mollysatthemarket.net; 1107 Decatur St; ⊙10am-6am) A cop, a reporter and a tourist walk into a bar. That's not a joke, just a good description of the eclectic clientele you get at this excellent neighborhood bar. It's also the home of a fat cat that stares stonily at its booze-sodden kingdom, some kicking Irish coffee and an urn containing the ashes of its founder.

COSIMO'S BAR

Map p238 (☎504-522-9715; 1201 Burgundy St; ⏲4pm-2am Mon & Tue, to 5am Wed-Fri, 2pm-5am Sat, 2pm-2am Sun) There aren't a ton of bars in the Quarter that we'd call neighborhood bars, but Cosimo's fits the bill, and does so superlatively well. Dark wood, big windows, gambling machines, a good jukebox, pool tables and bartenders with the right amount of tender and toughness; this is simply a very fine bar, and it deserves your patronage.

LATITUDE 29 COCKTAIL BAR

Map p238 (☎504-609-3811; http://latitude29nola.com; 321 N Peters St; ⏲3-11pm Sun-Thu, 11am-11pm Fri & Sat) Jeff 'Beachbum Berry' is a tiki-bar scholar. If a drink has rum, is served in a faux-Polynesian cup or comes with an umbrella and some fruit, the man has written on it. Now, he serves said drinks from across the tropics in Latitude 29, a bar devoted to all things tiki.

ERIN ROSE BAR

Map p238 (☎504-522-3573; 811 Conti St; ⏲24hr) The Rose is only a block from Bourbon St, but feels a world away. Few tourists make it in here, but it's the go-to cheap spot for off-shift service folks, who hit it up for a beer, banter and a shot or five. Excellent po'boys served in the back.

CHART ROOM BAR

Map p238 (☎504-522-1708; 300 Chartres St; ⏲11am-4am) The Chart Room is simply a great bar. There's a historical patina on the walls, creaky furniture inside, outdoor seating for people-watching and a cast of characters plucked from a Mickey Spillane novel that passed through a carnival.

FRENCH 75 BAR

Map p238 (☎504-523-5433; www.arnaudsrestaurant.com/bars/french-75/; 813 Bienville St; ⏲5:30-10pm) This spot is all wood and patrician accents, but the staff is friendly and down to earth. They'll mix high-quality drinks that will make you feel (a) like the star of your own Tennessee Williams play about decadent Southern aristocracy and (b) drunk.

LAFITTE'S BLACKSMITH SHOP BAR

Map p238 (☎504-593-9761; www.lafittesblacksmithshop.com; 941 Bourbon St; ⏲10:30am-3am) This gutted brick cottage claims to be the oldest operating bar in the country and is certainly one of the most atmospheric in the Quarter. Rumors suggest this spot was once the workshop of pirate Jean Lafitte and his brother Pierre. Whether true or not (historical records suggest 'not'), the house dates to the 18th century.

CANE & TABLE COCKTAIL BAR

Map p238 (☎504-581-1112; www.caneandtablenola.com; 1113 Decatur St; ⏲5-11pm Mon-Thu, to midnight Fri & Sat) When we heard this place served 'proto-tiki' cocktails, we'll admit our eyes inadvertently rolled. But the setting for Cane & Table – romantically faded interior and Mediterranean-style outdoor courtyard – is so stunning it's hard to knock the spot. And hey, those proto-tiki drinks are good; they mix Caribbean flavors, tropical fruits and plenty of rum.

CAROUSEL BAR BAR

Map p238 (☎504-523-3341; http://hotelmonteleone.com/entertainment/carousel-bar; 214 Royal St; ⏲11am-late) At this smart-looking spot inside the historic Monteleone, you'll find a revolving circular bar, canopied by the top hat of the 1904 World's Fair carousel, adorned with running lights, hand-painted figures and gilded mirrors. It takes 15 minutes for the bar to complete a revolution. If it's spinning too fast for you, ease up, pal. Careful on your way out.

SPITFIRE COFFEE CAFE

Map p238 (www.spitfirecoffee.com; 627 St Peter St; ⏲8am-7pm Sun-Thu, to 9pm Fri & Sat) This spot specializes in pour-over coffee and espresso drinks. It serves some of the strongest coffee in the Quarter, eschewing the usual amounts of milk. It's a take-out spot, so grab that coffee, wander over to Jackson Sq, and fuel yourself up for a caffeine-powered day of sightseeing.

CAFÉ LAFITTE IN EXILE BAR

Map p238 (☎504-522-8397; www.lafittes.com; 901 Bourbon St; ⏲24hr) This spot, with its huge video screens and mood lighting, doesn't exactly feel historical, but it's the oldest dedicated gay bar in the USA; Tennessee Williams and Truman Capote both drank here. What's in a name? The owners once ran Lafitte's Blacksmith Shop; when they lost their lease in 1953, they moved here and opened Lafitte in Exile.

OLD ABSINTHE HOUSE BAR

Map p238 (☎504-524-0113; www.ruebourbon.com/oldabsinthehouse; 240 Bourbon St; ⏲9am-3am) The Old Absinthe House attracts

Bourbon St boozers, but it's also one of the city's fabled bars that served absinthe before it was outlawed in 1914. The mysterious beverage had a psychotropic allure and allegedly drove enthusiasts mad. Today, Herbsaint, a locally produced anisette, is a safe stand-in for old absinthe-based drinks.

NAPOLEON HOUSE BAR

Map p238 (504-524-9752; www.napoleonhouse.com; 500 Chartres St; 11am-late) Napoleon House is a particularly attractive example of what Walker Percy termed 'vital decay.' By all appearances, its stuccoed walls haven't received so much as a dab of paint since the place opened in 1797; the diffuse glow pouring through open doors and windows in the afternoon draws out the room's gorgeous patina.

PAT O'BRIEN'S BAR

Map p238 (504-525-4823; www.patobriens.com; 718 St Peter St; noon-late Mon-Thu, 10am-late Fri-Sun) For a tourist trap, Pat O'Brien's has genuine atmosphere and history. The back courtyard, lit by flaming fountains, is genuinely lovely, but the bar could be in a desert and folks would still pack in for the Hurricane, a lethal blend of rum, juice and grenadine. 'Hey, this doesn't taste strong at all!' Thirty minutes later: 'Whash yer name agin?'

DUNGEON CLUB

Map p238 (504-523-5530; 738 Toulouse St; cover $5; midnight-late Tue-Sun) Yes, some bouncers have filed their teeth, and yes, this is a goth and black-metal club, but having descended into the basement chambers, we still ran into some yuppies. DJs keep things throbbing until dawn's early light (egads! sunlight!) and several barkeeps serve up ghoulish cocktails with creepy names such as Witch's Brew and Dragon's Blood.

BOURBON PUB & PARADE CLUB

Map p238 (504-529-2107; www.bourbonpub.com; 801 Bourbon St; 24hr) The Bourbon is the heart of New Orleans' gay scene, or at least the nightlife and party scene. Many of the events that pepper the city's gay calendar either begin, end or are conducted here; during Southern Decadence, in particular, this is the place to be. Ladies are welcome, but this is pretty much a bar for the boys.

OZ CLUB

Map p238 (504-593-9491; www.ozneworleans.com; 800 Bourbon St; 24hr) Your traditional shirtless, all-night-party, loud-music, lots-of-dancing-boys bar, where there are bowls of condoms set out for the customers.

PIRATE'S ALLEY CAFE BAR

Map p238 (504-524-9332; www.piratesalleycafe.com; 622 Pirate's Alley; noon-midnight Mon-Thu, to 2am Fri-Sun) The narrow pedestrian alley hidden in the shadow of St Louis Cathedral is a natural spot for a tiny bar, and this nook fits the bill perfectly. It has the atmosphere of a little Montparnasse hideaway with no claim to fame. You can snag a stool at the bar and meet the regulars, or claim a table out on the alley and soak up the Quarter.

TROPICAL ISLE BAR

Map p238 (504-529-1702; http://tropicalisle.com; 721 Bourbon St; 24hr) Everyone who drinks here has a Tropical Isle memory; usually, it's pretty fuzzy. This touristy bar serves 'Hand Grenades'; drinking more than two is likely to buy you a ticket to Regret Town, characterized by table dancing, bead tossing, bead receiving, the random mashing of tongues down strangers' throats and the eventual gathering of the limp shreds of your dignity the next day. Woo!

ABBEY BAR

Map p238 (504-523-7177; 1123 Decatur St; 24hr) A lot of roughnecks congregate in this atmospheric Decatur St dive. You needn't be pierced or tattooed to fit in, but a little Joe Strummer swagger won't hurt. The jukebox reflects these sensibilities, but

THE EMPEROR'S ABORTED ALCOHOLIC EXILE

Napoleon House has a colorful connection to its namesake. After Waterloo and the subsequent banishment of the emperor to St Helena, a band of loyal New Orleanians reputedly plotted to snatch Napoleon and set him up in this building's 3rd-floor digs. It didn't happen, but you can easily imagine Bonaparte whiling away his last days in this pleasant spot, telling fishing stories about conquering Europe.

also includes rocking sides by the original Man in Black and Lee Hazelwood.

DOUBLE PLAY LOUNGE

Map p238 (504-523-4517; 439 Dauphine St; 4pm-late) Double Play is technically a bar but this friendly spot is also drag central. You'll likely see a lot of queens here ripping at each other's outfits in a sometimes playful, sometimes not, manner. Drag or no drag, the drinks are delightful.

ENTERTAINMENT

ONE EYED JACKS LIVE MUSIC

Map p238 (504-569-8361; www.oneeyedjacks.net; 615 Toulouse St; cover $5-15) If you've been thinking, 'I could use a night at a bar that feels like a 19th-century bordello managed by Johnny Rotten,' you're in luck. Jacks is a great venue; there's a sense here that dangerous women in corsets, men with Mohawks and an army of bohemians with bottles of absinthe could come charging out at any moment. Musical acts are consistently good.

BALCONY MUSIC CLUB LIVE MUSIC

Map p238 (504-301-5912; 1331 Decatur St; 5pm-2am Mon-Thu, 3pm-4am Fri-Sun) Balcony is all about the acts: if there's a dud band playing, you can walk on by without breaking your stride, but on good nights it forms a very convenient step in the French Quarter–Faubourg Marigny Decatur St stumble o' fun.

A BIT OF BURLESQUE

If you're in the mood for something a bit risqué, we'd recommend catching the burlesque show put on by **Fleur de Tease** (504-319-8917; http://fleurdetease.com). These talented ladies, many of whom claim professional dance backgrounds, manage to blend vintage vibe with a modern, in-your-face post-feminist sexuality that is pretty enticing for men and women. Fleur de Tease perform all over town, but there's a semiregular show at **One Eyed Jacks** (p80) every other Sunday.

HOUSE OF BLUES LIVE MUSIC

Map p238 (504-310-4999; www.houseofblues.com; 225 Decatur St; tickets $7-25) House of Blues has put a lot of admirable work into making their New Orleans outpost distinctive: there's tons of folk art and rustic, voodoo-themed murals and sculptures lying about, and the effect is more powerful than kitschy. A few doors down, HOB's small auxiliary club, the **Parish**, is a great spot; you can get pretty up-close-and-personal with artists during gigs.

PALM COURT JAZZ CAFÉ LIVE MUSIC

Map p238 (504-525-0200; www.palmcourtjazzcafe.com; 1204 Decatur St; cover around $5; 7-11pm Wed-Sun) Fans of trad jazz who want to hang out with a mature crowd should head to this supper-club alternative to Preservation Hall. Palm Court is a roomy venue that has a consistently good lineup of local legends; you really can't go wrong if you're a jazz fan. Shows start at 8pm.

SHOPPING

★**FIFI MAHONY'S** BEAUTY

Map p238 (504-525-4343; 934 Royal St; noon-6pm Sun-Fri, 11am-7pm Sat) New Orleans is the most costume-crazy city in the USA, and Fifi Mahony's is the place to go to don a wig. There's a stunning selection of hairpieces here that runs the gamut from the glittered to the beehived, presented in a veritable rainbow of colors. An on-site beauty salon and sassy staff round out the experience.

QUEORK ACCESSORIES

Map p238 (504-481-4910; www.queork.com; 838 Chartres St; 10am-6pm Thu-Mon) Besides boasting a punny name, Queork has a cool, sustainable gimmick: all of the bags, belts and accessories sold here are made from cork. The products both look and feel cool; a fascinating texture belies some pretty fashionable goods.

EXODUS CLOTHING

Map p238 (504-309-2995; exodusgoods.us; 518 Conti St; noon-7pm Tue-Sat, to 6pm Sun, closed Mon) A small but dedicated group of shoppers knows that Exodus is carrying some of the hippest womenswear and accessories in New Orleans (it helps that one of the shop's creative directors is Beyonce's sister, Solange). The goods all have

PREPARING FOR PRESERVATION HALL

Preservation Hall (Map p238; ☎504-522-2841; www.preservationhall.com; 726 St Peter St; cover $15 Sun-Thu, $20 Fri & Sat; ⊙show times 8pm, 9pm & 10pm), housed in a former art gallery that dates back to 1803, is one of the most storied live-music venues in New Orleans. Barbara Reid and Grayson 'Ken' Mills formed the Society for the Preservation of New Orleans Jazz in 1961, at a time when Louis Armstrong's generation was already getting on in years. The resident performers, the Preservation Hall Jazz Band, are ludicrously talented, and regularly tour around the world. These white-haired musos and their tubas, trombones and cornets raise the roof every night.

With that all said, there are some caveats you should know before seeing a show here. First: the set is only about an hour long, and that seems short for $15 ($20 on weekends). Still, you're paying to see musical history as much as music, so we're OK with that. But if we do pay $15, we want to be able to see the band. The Hall is atmospheric, but it is also small and popular. Sets play on the hour, and you need to show up early – an hour before, folks – to snag a seat. Otherwise you'll be standing and, likely as not, your view will be blocked by people in front of you. When it's warm enough to leave the window shutters open, those not fortunate enough to get inside can join the crowd on the sidewalk to listen to the sets. Also note: no booze or snacks are served in the club, and the bathroom is in next-door Pat O'Brien's. We love the Hall, don't get us wrong. Just be aware of the above before you visit.

an urban bohemian vibe, and the location, tucked into a nondescript brick storefront, has a speakeasy feel to it.

CHIWAWA GAGA — PET SHOP

Map p238 (☎504-581-4242; www.chiwawagaga.com; 511 Dumaine St; ⊙noon-6pm) It's hard not to love a pet shop specifically dedicated to costumes for small dogs. That's a bit of a niche obsession, and the folks who run this store are dedicated to sourcing, and often creating by hand, some fantastically elaborate getups for your little pooch.

GREEN EYED GATOR — ARTS

Map p238 (☎504-535-4507; http://greeneyedgator.com; 901 Chartres St; ⊙11am-6pm) Local artists and artisans have filled this gallery with odds, ends and some truly funky paintings. The prices are grounded compared to some of the fancier galleries on Royal St, and there's a general sense of playful creativity in the air.

PEACHES RECORDS & TAPES — MUSIC

Map p238 (☎504-282-3322; www.peachesrecordsneworleans.com; 408 N Peters St; ⊙9am-8pm Mon-Thu, to 9pm Fri & Sat, 10am-8pm Sun) Peaches has been around since 1975, doing the holy work of promoting, cataloguing and marketing the best in local New Orleans music. This enormous record store dominates its corner of Peters St, and is a must-see for anyone who wants to take home a piece of the city's musical heritage.

JAMES H COHEN & SONS — ANTIQUES, SOUVENIRS

Map p238 (☎504-522-3305; shop.cohenantiques.com; 437 Royal St; ⊙9am-5pm Mon-Sat) From the sidewalk, you might be inclined to pass this one by: it's full of guns, including flintlocks, colts, Winchester '73s and even a French musket or two. Beyond weaponry, however, the place is like a museum, stuffed with relics and historical curiosities, from swords to maps and coins. Try not to break anything; the owners are armed, clearly.

OD AOMO — CLOTHING

Map p238 (☎504-460-5730; www.odaomo.com; 839 Chartres St; ⊙11am-6pm Mon-Sat, to 5pm Sun) Dr Sophia Aomo Omoro has worn many hats in her life: runway model, otolaryngology surgeon (we had to look it up, too), philanthropist, and now, proprietor of a high-end fashion boutique. All of the clothes under her label are made in her native Kenya, where she is dedicated to providing increased employment. Her style sits at a hip intersection of ethnic patterns and contemporary chic.

MOSS ANTIQUES — ANTIQUES

Map p238 (☎504-522-3981; www.mossantiques.com; 411 Royal St; ⊙9am-5pm, by appointment Sun) Watch your head when you enter this

PEDICAB CURE

The French Quarter is a nightmare to drive through and worse to park in, and while it can be nice to walk, the distances can be deceivingly long (especially if it's hot – and it's often hot). The best way around is by bicycle. If you don't have your bearings, are uncomfortable riding a bicycle, or are traveling with small children, a good alternative is a New Orleans bicycle taxi/pedicab. Operated by a slew of cheerful riders, these three-wheeled contrivances can be found throughout the French Quarter, CBD and Marigny, and are a nice way of getting from point A to B while avoiding taxi lines and automobile traffic. You can flag down a pedicab or call the dispatch office; try **New Orleans Bike Taxi** (☎504-891-3441; www.neworleansbiketaxi.com) or **NOLA Pedicabs** (☎504-274-1300; www.nolapedicabs.com). Fares are $1 per passenger, per block traveled.

gallery of low-hanging chandeliers. Oof! Too late! Moss is a Royal St institution in the local antiques trade. Only the finest quality antiques and *objets d'art* are sold here. You'll find the perfect thing for your Garden District mansion.

ARCADIAN BOOKS & ART PRINTS BOOKS
Map p238 (☎504-523-4138; 714 Orleans Ave; ⊙10:30am-6:30pm Mon-Sat, noon-5pm Sun) Arcadian is a small, crowded shop that's filled with Southern literature and history, as well as many volumes written in French. Owner Russell Desmond speaks French fluently and is a wonderful, if cynical, ambassador for New Orleans.

GREG'S ANTIQUES ANTIQUES
Map p238 (☎504-202-8577; www.gregsantiques.net; 1209 Decatur St; ⊙noon-10pm Tue-Sun) Besides having rooms full of salvaged furniture and antiques, Greg's regularly exhibits works by New Orleans underground and outsider artists, whose pieces can also take the form of found and folk art sourced from across the city.

BECKHAM'S BOOKSTORE BOOKS
Map p238 (☎504-522-9875; 228 Decatur St; ⊙10am-5pm) This large, neatly organized store has two floors of used books, and also sells used classical LPs. It's definitely worth a browse. Across the street from House of Blues music venue.

LIBRAIRIE BOOKS BOOKS
Map p238 (☎504-525-4837; 823 Chartres St; ⊙10am-5pm) A jam-packed little shop of delights for the avid bookworm and collector. The emphasis here is squarely on very old (and sometimes dusty) volumes. You might dig up an ancient copy of Herbert Asbury's *The French Quarter,* or other tales of old New Orleans. And there are scholarly texts and ample material of more general interest as well.

CENTURIES ARTS, MAPS
Map p238 (☎504-568-9491; 408 Chartres St; ⊙10:30am-6pm Mon-Sat, 11am-6pm Sun) OK, it's a little on the stodgy side, with its selection of 19th-century lithographs and old maps. But flip through the inventory (all of it well organized by theme, date or locale) and you just might find yourself slowing down to look things over. Particularly interesting are the Civil War and Black History sections.

COLLECTIBLE ANTIQUES ANTIQUES
Map p238 (☎504-566-0399; 1232 Decatur St; ⊙noon-6pm) You never know what you'll find between the piles of old furniture stacked along the walls of this large, garage-like emporium of tantalizing junk. Perhaps you collect old photographic portraits from long defunct studios. Or maybe you're just after an art-deco martini shaker, a dented trumpet, a Pee-wee Herman doll, a heavy army-surplus coat or some silverware.

LUCULLUS ANTIQUES
Map p238 (☎504-528-9620; http://lucullusantiques.com; 610 Chartres St; ⊙9am-5pm Mon-Sat) Peeking in the window, you'll see a battery of ancient copper pots that appear to have generations of dents tinkered out of their bottoms. Owner Patrick Dunne is an advocate of using, not merely collecting, antiques. Follow his advice and add more ritual and elegance to your life with an antique *café au lait* bowl or an absinthe spoon.

MS RAU ANTIQUES ANTIQUES
Map p238 (☎888-557-2406; www.rauantiques.com; 630 Royal St; ⊙9am-5:15pm Mon-Sat) With a massive 30,000-sq-ft showroom, and after nearly a century of doing business, MS Rau ranks among New Orleans'

most venerated dealers of antiques. It's a bit serious – these are the sort of frosty antiques that require their own insurance policies – but it's a family business and the professional salespeople are approachable.

LE GARAGE ANTIQUES

Map p238 (☎504-522-6639; 1234 Decatur St; ⏰10am-6pm) This place lives up to its name: it's a garage loaded with interesting stuff to paw through. Items include odd items of clothing, hats, army surplus, curtains, yellowed pool balls, tattered Mardi Gras costumes from yesteryear, knitted Coors beer-can caps, furniture and oodles of *objects d'art* to ogle or buy. Treasures galore: dive in.

NEW ORLEANS CAJUN STORE FOOD, GIFTS

Map p238 (☎504-539-7900; www.neworleanscajunstore.com; 537 St Ann St; ⏰9am-7pm Sun-Thu, to 8pm Fri & Sat) Bet you thought Tabasco was either red or green and always hot, right? Guess again: here you'll find Tabasco ketchup, mayonnaise, cookbooks, plenty of souvenirs and a fairly incredible range of hot (and not so hot) sauces. Need a 500-count pack of mini-Tabasco bottles? This is the place. Also sells all manner of Cajun- and New Orleans–themed kitsch.

JAVA HOUSE IMPORTS GIFTS

Map p238 (☎504-581-1288; www.javahouseimports.com; 523 Dumaine St; ⏰10am-7pm Mon-Thu, from 9am Fri & Sun, 9am-8pm Sat) Java House Imports does indeed have cool imports and statues from Java, as well as Balinese and West African masks, Indian-style Buddhas, lacquer-work from Lombok, and all the other items to prove what a savvy traveler you are.

BOUTIQUE DU VAMPYRE GIFTS

Map p238 (☎504-561-8267; www.feelthebite.com; 712 Orleans Ave; ⏰10am-9pm) Dark candles and gothic gargoyles look down at you, promising a curse of blood, terror and the undead on those who browse but do not buy! Mwa ha ha! This dungeon-esque store stocks all kinds of vampire-themed gifts; our favorite item is a deck of tarot cards with truly surreal, somewhat disturbing artwork. Also: best website URL ever.

FLORA SAVAGE FLOWERS

Map p238 (☎504-581-4728; http://florasavage.net; 1301 Royal St; ⏰10am-6pm Mon-Sat) In town for an anniversary? Met someone you want to impress in a hurry? Take care of your floral needs here. You'll soon be festooning your hotel room with romantic aromas and colors, and your sweetheart will be swooning. Custom arrangements available.

FLEUR DE PARIS ACCESSORIES, CLOTHING

Map p238 (☎504-525-1899; www.fleurdeparis.net; 712 Royal St; ⏰10am-6pm) Some stores in New Orleans exist to indulge the most eccentric of us. This boutique is a case in point. Did you know millinery shops still exist? The custom hats at Fleur de Paris are bouquets of plumage, felt, lace and, here and there, a snatch of black netting. Evening gowns are devastating showstoppers.

VISITING YOKNAPATAWPHA COUNTY

Like many American authors, William Faulkner did a New Orleans stint, briefly renting an apartment in a town house on Pirate's Alley in 1925. While living in the city – which he described as a 'courtesan, not old and yet no longer young,' – Faulkner worked for the *Times-Picayune*, contributed to literary magazine *Double Dealer* and consorted with local literati. Later in his life, the author would go on to redefine the genre of Southern and, arguably, American literature, setting many of his novels in mythical Yoknapatawpha County.

The flat Faulkner rented in New Orleans is now a business and a bona-fide literary attraction. **Faulkner House Books** (Map p238; ☎504-524-2940; http://faulknerhousebooks.com; 624 Pirate's Alley; ⏰10am-5pm) is an essential stop for any bibliophile. It's a pleasant space, with beautifully crafted shelves packed floor to ceiling, offering the dignified atmosphere of a private library. It's not a large store – more than five or six customers at a time and it starts to feel crowded – but offers a commendable mix of new titles and first editions. The selection of books by local and Southern authors is particularly strong, and naturally William Faulkner is a staple. The shop is something of a literary hub, and local authors (Richard Ford, Andrei Codrescu etc) regularly stop by.

ZOMBIE'S HOUSE OF VOODOO SOUVENIRS

Map p238 (☎504-486-6366; 725 St Peter St; ⏰10am-11:30pm Sun-Thu, to 1:30am Fri & Sat) Step inside and you'll see this is one religious store that's not bent on snuffing out the party. An altar at the entry includes a serious request that you not take photos, but then comes a truly splendiferous display of plaster-of-Paris statuettes imported from the Santeria realms of Brazil. All are fun and charming, many are simply beautiful.

CENTRAL GROCERY FOOD

Map p238 (☎504-523-1620; 923 Decatur St; ⏰9am-5pm Tue-Sat) A hyper-busy store offering many of the cooking ingredients typically found in Louisiana kitchens: Zatarain's Creole Seasoning and Crab Boil, McIlhenny Tabasco and Crystal Hot Sauce, chicory coffee and filé for making gumbo. While you're here, grab a jar of Central Gro Co's famous olive relish, the not-so-secret weapon of the muffuletta sandwich.

MASKARADE GIFTS

Map p238 (☎504-568-1018; www.themaskstore.com; 630 St Ann St; ⏰10am-5pm) This shop deals in high-quality masks by local and international artisans. The selection includes everything from classic commedia dell'arte masks from Venice to more way-out designs for your wigged-out end-of-Mardi-Gras state of mind. If your nose is too small, many of the selections here can correct the problem.

HOVÉ PARFUMEUR BEAUTY

Map p238 (☎504-525-7827; www.hoveparfumeur.com; 434 Chartres St; ⏰10am-6pm Mon-Sat, from 11am Sun) Grassy vetiver, bittersweet orange blossoms, spicy ginger – New Orleans' exotic flora has graciously lent its scents to Hové's house-made perfumes for more than 70 years. A brief sniffing visit will leave your head swirling with images of the Vieux Carré's magnificent past. Thus intoxicated, you can ask staff to custom-mix a fragrance for you.

LEAH'S PRALINES FOOD

Map p238 (☎504-523-5662; www.leahspralines.com; 714 St Louis St; ⏰10am-6pm Mon-Fri, until 5pm Sat, 11am-5pm Sun) In the heart of the French Quarter, this old candy shop specializes in that special Creole confection, the praline. Here you'll get some of the very best in town. If you've already tried pralines elsewhere and decided that you don't care for them, we suggest you try some at Leah's before making up your mind completely.

HUMIDITY SKATE SHOP SPORTING GOODS

Map p238 (☎504-529-6822; http://humidityskateshop.net; 515 Dumaine St; ⏰11am-7pm Mon-Sat, noon-6pm Sun) Graffiti chic, Vans shoes, Element, Darkstar and Organika decks, grip tape, Krux trucks and Zero wheels – if any of that makes sense to you, make your way up to Dumaine St.

SOUTHERN CANDY MAKERS FOOD

Map p238 (☎504-523-5544, 800-344-9773; 334 Decatur St; ⏰10am-7pm) Sweet-smelling confections with a Southern accent are created in this neat little shop. A visit is guaranteed to put a big ol' Dolly Parton smile on your face. The toffee is divine and the pralines are to die for. There are special candies for every holiday and you can have something sent off to loved ones around the country.

MARY JANE'S EMPORIUM GIFTS

Map p238 (☎504-525-8004; www.maryjanesemporium.com; 1229 Decatur St; ⏰10am-midnight) By 'Mary Jane,' they're not referring to shoes. This is an essential stop for smokers of legal tobacco products, including finer brands of cigarettes not sold at your basic corner store. Also stocks a variety of apparatus for the smoking of unsanctioned herbal products and such.

Faubourg Marigny & Bywater

Neighborhood Top Five

❶ Wandering around **Frenchmen Street** (p87) starting at, say, 7pm, having dinner, listening to music, getting drunk, listening to more music, dancing a bit, seeing who's playing on the corner of Chartres, scarfing some late-night tacos, then hey! More music!

❷ Spotting container ships from the banks of the **Crescent Park** (p87) as they meander up the Mississippi.

❸ Catching dance, puppetry and all manner of stage-based art at the **Marigny Opera House** (p94).

❹ Watching music, from punk to bluegrass to hip-hop, on rapidly changing **St Claude Avenue** (p95).

❺ Devouring a family-style spicy Sichuan meal with friends at **Red's Chinese** (p88).

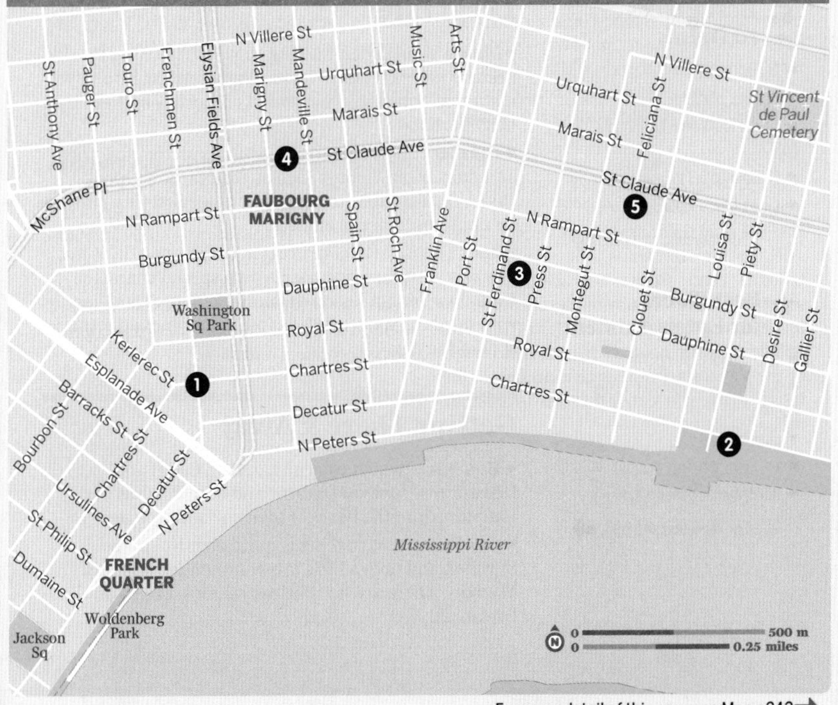

For more detail of this area see Map p242

Lonely Planet's Top Tip

By far the easiest way of exploring these two neighborhoods is by bicycle. On two wheels you're never more than 20 minutes from the edge of the French Quarter and the borders of the Bywater. Be warned that streets are pretty pot-holed; Chartres is reliable past Press St, but also heavily trafficked.

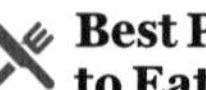

Best Places to Eat

- Bacchanal (p89)
- Elizabeth's (p92)
- Red's Chinese (p88)
- Joint (p89)
- Pizza Delicious (p88)

For reviews, see p88

Best Places to Drink

- BJ's (p92)
- John (p93)
- Mimi's in the Marigny (p92)
- R Bar (p93)
- Lost Love (p93)

For reviews, see p92

Best Places for Entertainment

- Spotted Cat (p94)
- Marigny Opera House (p94)
- d.b.a. (p94)
- Hi Ho Lounge (p94)
- AllWays Lounge (p95)

For reviews, see p94

Explore Faubourg Marigny & Bywater

On your first day, wander around the Marigny by walking up Decatur St and onto Frenchmen St. Then head east along Royal St, taking in the architecture and sampling some of the local cafes and restaurants on the way. Your nighttime activity consists of heading back to Frenchmen St to either party, listen to music or both.

On the second day, either bike or walk out to the Bywater. Again, you'll want to just walk (or bike) around this compact neighborhood, eating, drinking and shopping wherever the spirit moves you. In the evening, head out to catch some shows along St Claude Ave, or see if there's anything interesting showing at one of the local theater companies.

Faubourg Marigny is bounded by Rampart St to the west, the railroad tracks at Press St to the east and Esplanade Ave to the south. The Bywater extends from Press to Poland St. St Claude Ave is, for our purposes, the northern border of both neighborhoods, but as there are more and more places of interest opening north of St Claude, we include some of those spots as well. The southern boundary of the Bywater is easy to spot: it's the Mississippi River.

Local Life

- **Dining** Young chefs and pop-ups (p91) looking to become permanent are increasingly settling into historical homes and renovated properties in these two neighborhoods.
- **Theater** It takes plenty of forms here, from the brick-and-mortar playhouses such as the Marigny Opera House (p94) to the street theater of local artists putting on impromptu performances.
- **Bars** There are a lot of great neighborhood dives out this way, and each one has its own special character. Even if you're not big on drinking, rubbing shoulders with locals at spots like BJ's (p92) gets you under the skin of the city.

Getting There & Away

- **Bus** Bus 5, which you can catch on Canal and Decatur Sts, runs up Decatur and onto Poydras and Dauphine into the heart of Marigny and Bywater.
- **Car** Free street parking is quite plentiful in the Bywater, and only a little less common in Faubourg Marigny. There are no time restrictions, except on Esplanade Ave.

SIGHTS

FRENCHMEN STREET STREET

Map p242 (from Esplanade Ave to Royal St) The 'locals' Bourbon St' is how Frenchmen is usually described to those who want to know where New Orleanians listen to music. The predictable result? Frenchmen St is now packed with out-of-towners each weekend. Still, it's a ton of fun, especially on weekdays, when the crowds thin out. Bars and clubs are arrayed back to back for several city blocks in what may well be the best concentration of live-music venues in the country.

CRESCENT PARK PARK

Map p242 (Piety, Chartres & Mazant Sts; 8am-6pm, to 7pm mid-Mar–early Nov; P) This waterfront park is our favorite spot in the city for taking in the Mississippi. Enter over the enormous arch at Piety and Chartres Sts and watch the fog blanket the nearby skyline. A promenade meanders past an angular metal and concrete conceptual 'wharf' (placed next to the burnt remains of the former commercial wharf); one day, said path will extend to a planned performance space at Mandeville St. A dog park is located near the Mazant St entrance, which also gives disabled access.

OLD NEW ORLEANS RUM DISTILLERY DISTILLERY

(504-945-9400; www.oldneworleansrum.com; 2815 Frenchmen St; admission $10; tours noon, 2pm & 4pm Mon-Fri, 2pm & 4pm Sat & Sun) A short drive north of the Marigny is the Old New Orleans Rum distillery. Founded by local artist James Michalopoulos and his artist-musician friends, the distillery makes great spirits that you'll find sold in most local bars. You can sample all of them, including a rare vintage unavailable outside the factory, on an entertaining 45-minute distillery tour. Fair warning: there's a lot of free rum available, so visit on a full stomach.

ST ROCH CEMETERY CEMETERY

(cnr St Roch Ave & N Roman St; 9am-3pm Mon-Sat, to noon Sun) FREE One of New Orleans' more interesting cemeteries is a few blocks from Faubourg Marigny (driving is recommended). Named for St Roch, a semi-legendary figure whose prayers supposedly averted the Black Death, the site became popular with Catholics during yellow-fever outbreaks. Walk through the necropolis to the 'relic room,' which is filled with ceramic body parts, prosthetics and false teeth; these are ex-votos, testaments to the healing power of St Roch. Marble floor tiles are inscribed with the words 'thanks' and '*merci.*'

FRENCHMEN ART MARKET MARKET

Map p242 (www.facebook.com/frenchmenartmarket; 619 Frenchmen St; 7pm-1am Thu-Sun) Independent artists and artisans line this alleyway market, which has built a reputation as one of the finest spots in town to find a unique gift to take home as a souvenir. 'Art', in this case, includes clever T-shirts, hand-crafted jewelry, trinkets and, yes, a nice selection of prints and original artwork.

CLOUET GARDENS PARK

Map p242 (www.clouetgardens.org; 707 Clouet St; sunrise-sunset;) This formerly empty lot has been transformed by its Bywater neighbors into a wonderful little park filled with public art projects, murals and generally appealing weirdness. Performances, concerts and neighborhood get-togethers are often held here, and it's a favorite with local families.

LIFE IN THE BIKE LANE

The Marigny and Bywater together contain a large concentration of bicycle riders per capita. Unfortunately, at the time of writing (and for as long as anyone can remember), the roads here run the gamut from smooth to being pockmarked with pot-holes. As such, many riders will end up cycling the wrong way down one-way roads to save the bone-jarring pain of sticking to the correct lane.

The other alternative is using the bicycle lane on St Claude Ave, which is fast and smooth, but also a major traffic thoroughfare. Riding along here, especially at night, can feel pretty harrowing, and there have been a number of fatal accidents when cars or trucks have struck a cyclist.

Hundreds of people use this lane safely on a daily basis, but if the traffic makes you nervous, consider riding residential streets or along Chartres St. The stretch of Chartres between Press St and Poland Ave is quite smooth and relatively un-trafficked.

WORTH A DETOUR

THE LOWER NINTH WARD

The Lower Ninth Ward received the most media attention following Hurricane Katrina, even though neighborhoods such as Lakewood and Gentilly were similarly affected. Parts of the Lower Ninth remain pretty devastated, still more wilderness than ruins. From the Bywater, drive a few minutes across the industrial canal on Claiborne or St Claude St and take your second left on Deslonde; you'll see a mix of empty lots and the architectural wonderland of LEED Green Building–certified homes built by Brad Pitt's **Make It Right Foundation** (http://makeitrightnola.org).

Roland Lewis, a Ninth Ward native and former streetcar worker and union rep, showcases the heritage of his home neighborhood in his actual home, which has been converted into the **House of Dance & Feathers** (504-957-2678; houseofdanceandfeathers.org; 1317 Tupelo St; open by appointment). This museum-turned-community-center brims with exhibits on Mardi Gras Indians, Social Aid and Pleasure Clubs, and is the gestalt of a unique American neighborhood. To get here you'll need a car; call Roland beforehand, as the museum is open by appointment only. Admission is free, but donations are gratefully accepted.

Rather than simply driving through the neighborhood or visiting via a tour bus, make an appointment with **Ninth Ward Rebirth Bike Tours** (504-338-3603; http://ninthwardrebirthbiketours.com; tours $60; tours at 9:30am). These guys work closely with Lower Ninth Ward residents to provide a tour that is a kind of dialogue between visitors and locals. Stops include local businesses and the House of Dance & Feathers.

OLD IRONWORKS MARKET

Map p242 (504-782-2569; www.612piety.com; 612 Piety St; 10am-4pm 2nd Sat of month) The monthly arts market held here gathers some of the most creative individuals in the Bywater and Marigny. There's usually street food on sale and activities for the kids. Other events (live theater, music and the like) kick off here on a regular basis; see the website for details.

MARKEY PARK PARK

Map p242 (700 Piety St; sunrise-sunset;) This small park has a playground and is a popular spot for Bywater families.

WASHINGTON SQUARE PARK PARK

Map p242 (cnr Frenchmen & Royal Sts; sunrise-sunset;) Also known as 'Marigny Green,' this park is a popular spot for locals to play with their dogs, toss Frisbees and, based on the frequent smell, smoke things that aren't cigarettes. There's a touching HIV-AIDS memorial on the northern side of the park. Be aware: the park can be a congregation point for the homeless and those suffering from addiction and mental-health issues.

PLESSY V FERGUSON PLAQUE HISTORIC SITE

Map p242 (cnr Press & Royal Sts) FREE This plaque marks the site where African American Homer Plessy, in a carefully orchestrated act of civil disobedience, tried to board a whites-only train car. That action led to the 1896 *Plessy v Ferguson* trial, which legalized segregation under the 'separate but equal' rationale. The plaque was unveiled by Keith Plessy and Phoebe Ferguson, descendants of the opposing parties in the original trial, now fast friends.

EATING

The food cachet of the Marigny and Bywater is increasing by the month, and there's a general bohemian vibe and plethora of good cheap eats in this part of town.

★PIZZA DELICIOUS ITALIAN $

Map p242 (http://pizzadelicious.com; 617 Piety St; pizza by slice from $2.25, whole pie from $15; Tue-Sun 11am-11pm;) Pizza D's pies are thin-crust, New York–style and *good*. The preparation is pretty simple, but the ingredients are fresh as the morning and consistently top-notch. An easy, family-friendly ambience makes for a lovely spot for casual dinner, and it serves some good beer too, if you're in the mood. Vegan pizza available. The outdoor area is pet-friendly.

★RED'S CHINESE CHINESE $

Map p242 (504-304-6030; www.redschinese.com; 3048 St Claude Ave; mains $8-16; noon-3pm

& 5-11pm) Red's has upped the Chinese cuisine game in New Orleans in a big way. The chefs aren't afraid to add lashings of Louisiana flavor, yet this isn't what we'd call 'fusion' cuisine. The food is grounded deeply in spicy Sichuan flavours, which pairs well with the occasional flash of cayenne. The General Lee's chicken is stupendously good.

★BACCHANAL MODERN AMERICAN $

Map p242 (☎504-948-9111; www.bacchanalwine.com; 600 Poland Ave; mains $8-16, cheese from $5; ⊙11am-midnight) From the outside, Bacchanal looks like a leaning Bywater shack; inside are racks of wine and stinky but sexy cheese. Musicians play in the garden, while cooks dispense delicious meals on paper plates from the kitchen in the back; on any given day you may try chorizo-stuffed dates or seared diver scallops that will blow your gastronomic mind.

JOINT BARBECUE $

Map p242 (☎504-949-3232; http://alwayssmokin.com; 701 Mazant St; mains $7-17; ⊙11:30am-10pm Mon-Sat) The Joint's smoked meat has the olfactory effect of the Sirens' sweet song, pulling you, the proverbial traveling sailor, off course and into savory meat-induced blissful death (classical Greek analogies ending *now*). Knock back some ribs, pulled pork or brisket with some sweet tea in the backyard garden and learn to love life.

MAUREPAS FOODS AMERICAN $

Map p242 (☎504-267-0072; http://maurepasfoods.com; 3200 Burgundy St; mains $7-18; ⊙5pm-midnight Mon-Fri, 10am-midnight Sat & Sun; ☑) Maurepas isn't your typical Bywater spot. It's got high ceilings, minimalist decor, polished floors and metal fixtures. And boy is the food good! Try the organic chicken, market greens, grits and poached egg – all delicious. Vegetarians should snack on the soba noodles, and everyone should get drunk on the craft cocktails.

WHO DAT COFFEE CAFE & CAFE NERO CAFE $

Map p242 (☎504-872-0360; 2401 Burgundy St; coffees & pastries $3-5, mains $7-15; ⊙Who Dat 7am-10pm, Cafe Nero 8am-3pm Mon-Wed, to 10pm Thu-Sun; ☑) A supremely comfortable coffee shop, the Who Dat has good pastries, better sandwiches, lovely coffee and cupcakes, many baked with a bit of booze. The on-site restaurant, Cafe Nero, is a hidden treasure. The breakfast menu, in particular, is excellent; the Not Yo Mama's corn cakes, drowning in a cheesy egg sauce, are ridiculously tasty.

LOST LOVE VIETNAMESE $

Map p242 (☎504-949-2009; http://lostlovelounge.com; 2529 Dauphine St; mains $5-10; ⊙kitchen 11am-5pm Mon-Thu, to 1am Fri & Sat, to midnight Sun) This divey neighborhood bar also has a Vietnamese kitchen in the back serving up great pho, *banh mi* (Vietnamese po'boys) and spring rolls. Just be aware the atmosphere isn't standard Vietnamese American dive (formica, old Republic flag, karaoke); this place is more of a neighborhood bar/inked-up hideaway.

ST ROCH MARKET MARKET $

Map p242 (☎504-609-3813; www.strochmarket.com; 2381 St Claude Ave; mains $9-12; ⊙9am-11pm; ☑) Once, the St Roch Market was the seafood and produce market for a working class neighborhood. After it was nearly destroyed by Hurricane Katrina, it was renovated into a shiny food court. The airy interior space hosts 13 restaurants serving food ranging from New Orleans classics to coffee to Nigerian cuisine.

RAMPART FOOD STORE SANDWICHES $

Map p242 (☎504-944-7777; 1700 N Rampart St; po'boys up to $10; ⊙8am-8pm, closed Sun) This convenience store is so barren you'd think it

COOLING OFF IN THE BYWATER

If you're feeling the heat in New Orleans (and look: it's very easy to feel the heat in New Orleans), two of the finest cold treat spots in the city are in this neighborhood.

Meltdown (Map p242; ☎504-301-0905; www.meltdownpops.com; 4011 St Claude Ave; ⊙noon-6pm Wed-Sun) Meltdown does handmade popsicles with funky flavors such as pineapple basil and salted caramel.

Piety Street Snoballs (Map p242; www.612piety.com/piety-street-snoballs; 612 Piety St; ⊙1:30-7:30pm Wed-Sun) Piety Street Snoballs serves the city's favorite frozen treat, laced with syrups that range from old favorites like strawberry and banana to more groundbreaking stuff, including the delicious Vietnamese iced coffee sno-ball. Note that it's open seasonally – during spring and summer.

LATE-NIGHT NOSH IN THE MARIGNY

This being New Orleans – city of music, 24-hour partying and good food – you would think that there would be some great late-night eating options on the city's major live-music strip, Frenchmen St. But, weirdly, you sometimes need to search for chow after a hard night of imbibing and/or music appreciation.

We list our favourites to help you out. Additionally, it's also worth noting that DIY caterers regularly risk the police and set up shop on Frenchmen St, selling tacos, grilling steak sandwiches, burgers and hot dogs, and providing all those other great, greasy things you need after a night out.

Café Negril (p96) Delicious tacos ($2), tamales ($3) and burritos ($4), which you can take outside and snack on in the street. Serves until closing time, which is flexible and usually late – around 3am.

13 Monaghan (p91) Need 24-hour vegetarian food? Bam! There's meat too, carnivores.

Buffa's (p93) Bit of a walk from Frenchmen St, but it's worth it for the cheeseburgers. Open 24 hours.

Gene's (p91) If you're up on St Claude, hit up this pink palace for a hot sausage po'boy, available 24 hours.

Angeli on Decatur (p73) Pasta, pizza, burgers, salads and sandwiches. In the French Quarter, but just a short walk from Frenchmen St.

Dat Dog (Map p242; ☎504-899-6883; http://datdognola.com; 601 Frenchmen St; mains $5-8; ⏰11am-midnight Sun-Thu, to 3am Fri & Sat) The Frenchmen St outpost of this popular local franchise serves the best hot dogs in town, and has a great balcony for viewing the street scene.

were a front for something shady. It's run by Vietnamese immigrants; their English isn't great, but they know to call you 'baby' and how to make some of the best, most overstuffed shrimp po'boys in New Orleans. Pass on everything else, and be prepared for long lines.

CAKE CAFÉ & BAKERY — BREAKFAST $

Map p242 (☎504-943-0010; www.nolacakes.com; 2440 Chartres St; mains $6-11; ⏰7am-3pm Wed-Mon) On weekend mornings the line is literally out the door here. Biscuits and gravy (topped with andouille), fried oysters and grits (seasonally available) and all the omelets are standouts. Lunch is great, too, as are the cakes (king cake!) whipped up in the back.

KEBAB — MIDDLE EASTERN $

Map p242 (☎504-383-4328; www.kebabnola.com; 2315 St Claude Ave; mains $4-7; ⏰11am-midnight Fri-Mon; 📶) Americans are learning what Europeans and Middle Easterners have long known: when you're drunk (and to be fair, even when sober), shaved meat or falafel served on flat bread with lots of delicious sauce and vegetables is amazing. Kebab has come to preach this gospel in New Orleans, and does so deliciously.

SNEAKY PICKLE — VEGAN $

Map p242 (☎504-218-5651; http://yousneakypickle.com; 4017 St Claude St; mains $4-8; ⏰11am-9pm; 📶) 🌿 This city has been sorely in need of a vegan-friendly spot that can hold its own against the city's famously meat-heavy cuisine. Enter the Sneaky Pickle, a little spot on St Claude that dishes out some special tempeh reubens on sourdough, beet flatbreads and a ton of unexpected, tasty specials.

JUNCTION — AMERICAN $

Map p242 (☎504-272-0205; www.junctionnola.com; 3021 St Claude Ave; mains $7-9; ⏰11am-2am) Junction takes a tight-focused approach to cuisine: it does cheeseburgers, and does them well. Variations include an Iowa burger with corn relish, blue cheese and bacon. The cheeseburgers come with hand-cut fries, and there are fine salads and wings on the menu, too. An enormous beer menu also tempts, but because of that, Junction is a 21-and-over establishment.

ARABELLA CASA DI PASTA — ITALIAN $

Map p242 (☎504-267-6108; www.arabellanola.com; 2258 St Claude Ave; mains $4.50-7; ⏰11am-10pm Mon-Thu, to 11pm Fri & Sat; 📶) This little restaurant, slotted next to the ribald karaoke at Kajun's (p95), pumps out wonderful bowls of pasta. The house-made sauces are creative and tasty, running from pork-neck bolognese to pesto cream pecan with basil and parmesan. Larger portions would be nice, but the price is right.

BAO & NOODLE CHINESE **$**

Map p242 (☎504-272-0004; http://baoandnoodle.com; 2700 Chartres St; mains $5-14; ⌚11:30am-2pm & 5-10pm; 🅰) Owner Doug Crowell left the acclaimed Herbsaint (p111) and took over this historic home to serve proper Chinese cuisine. His menu is small and delicious; elegant steamed *bao* (dumplings) are served alongside savory bowls of spicy pork noodles,

SATSUMA CAFE **$**

Map p242 (☎504-304-5962; http://satsumacafe.com; 3218 Dauphine St; mains $5.50-10.50; ⌚7am-5pm) With its chalkboard menu of organic soups and sandwiches, ginger limeade (seriously, this drink on a hot day – heaven), graphic and pop art–decorated walls and lots of Macbooks, Satsuma's like the cute hipster with thick eyeglass frames you've secretly had a crush on. In fact, members of said subculture are largely the clientele of this place.

13 MONAGHAN DINER **$**

Map p242 (☎504-942-1345; www.13monaghan.com; 517 Frenchmen St; mains $6-9; ⌚11am-4am) As it's usually called, '13' is a diner with a twist: much of its delicious greasy-spoon fare is actually vegetarian. A Philly cheesesteak, for example, comes with portobello mushrooms or tofu instead of beef. There's also a meat version, plus great pizza and other diner classics.

KUKHNYA EASTERN EUROPEAN **$**

(☎504-265-8855; 2227 St Claude Ave; mains $5.50-10; ⌚4pm-midnight; 🅰) This restaurant in Siberia (p95) serves, appropriately enough, Eastern European and Russian grub. The *blinis* (crepes) run the gamut from savory (ham and cheese) to sweet (apple), nicely complimented by some hearty beef stroganoff and delicious mushroom and cabbage rolls.

SEOUL SHACK KOREAN **$**

(☎504-417-6206; www.seoulshack.com; 435 Esplanade Ave; mains $5-10; ⌚5-10pm Mon & Wed, to 10:30pm Thu & Sun, to 11pm Fri & Sat, closed Tue) Korean food served out of a music club? Fermented cabbage and the Dragon's Den (p96) go together surprisingly well. Chicken wings, kim-chi braised pork tacos, and rice bowls served with hot Korean chili slaw make for some delicious post-music noshing.

BOOTY'S INTERNATIONAL **$**

Map p242 (☎504-266-2887; http://bootysnola.com; 800 Louisa St; mains $5-12; ⌚3-11pm daily, lunch 10am-3pm Mon-Fri; 🅰) Booty's brings international street foods to the Bywater, generally served small-plate style. It's popular with the young, hip set, who rave over Cuban sandwiches, bowls of ramen and deep-fried plantains, although we wouldn't mind larger portions. The bar doles out excellent cocktails from 9am to 11pm daily (until midnight Friday and Saturday).

GENE'S SANDWICHES **$**

Map p242 (☎504-943-3861; 1040 Elysian Fields Ave; po'boys $7; ⌚24hr) It's hard to miss Gene's: with its pink-and-yellow exterior, it's

POP-UP CULINARY STARS

Pop-up dining in New Orleans is a thing now. If you're unfamiliar with the concept, pop-ups are essentially temporary restaurants that appear at a regular to semiregular location at regular to semiregular intervals. It's a great way for young chefs to showcase their food without taking the financial risk of purchasing a bricks and mortar space.

Here are three of our favorites.

Laphet (www.facebook.com/lahpet) Burmese food in New Orleans is absolutely unexpected. We're totally down with some pickled tea-leaf salad and hard-boiled egg curry at this pop-up affair. Prices and opening times vary; check the website for the latest.

We've Got Soul (www.wevegotsoul.com) This pop-up serves soul food sexed up: slow-braised turkey necks, blackened catfish and creamy mac 'n' cheese. Prices, menus and times vary; check online before your visit.

Four Calendar Cafe (Map p242; www.facebook.com/fourcalendarcafe) Excellent ingredients are lovingly crafted into Modern American cuisine with French and Mediterranean influences at this pop-up. Check changing menu, prices and times on their Facebook page.

one of the most vividly painted buildings on Elysian Fields Ave. The hot sausage po'boy with cheese, and the fact it is served 24/7 with a free drink, is the reason you come here.

MARDI GRAS ZONE GROCERIES **$**

Map p242 (☎504-947-8787; www.mardigraszone.com; 2706 Royal St; po'boys around $8; ⊙24hr) This unexpectedly huge neighborhood grocery store-cum-emporium of weird stuff – Mardi Gras beads (yes) and camping equipment (?) – has a good hot-food stand that's open until midnight, and high-end groceries for sale all night.

OXALIS AMERICAN **$$**

Map p242 (☎504-267-4776; http://oxalisbywater.com; 3162 Dauphine St; mains $9-20; ⊙5-11pm) Oxalis may well consider itself a bar, specifically a whiskey bar, before it considers itself a restaurant, but we come for the food first. It's meant to be paired with whiskeys (the staff can help you out), but however you eat it, it's tasty: new American, thoughtfully sourced winners such as bourbon-glazed lamb belly and fresh veggies served on a bed of creamy polenta.

ADOLFO'S ITALIAN **$$**

Map p242 (☎504-948-3800; 611 Frenchmen St; mains $8-20; ⊙5:30-10:30pm) If you take a date to this intimate Italian cubby squeezed on top of a jazz club (the Apple Barrel) and get nowhere afterwards, chances are they were simply too hard to please. Adolfo's is as romantic as anything and the food isn't bad either – all working-class Italian Americano fare with some requisite New Orleans zing.

MARIZA ITALIAN **$$**

Map p242 (☎504-598-5700; http://marizaneworleans.com; 2900 Chartres St; mains $16-22; ⊙5-10pm Tue-Thu, to 11pm Fri & Sat, closed Sun & Mon) Mariza proves New Orleans Italian cuisine doesn't have to be served out of a space that looks like someone's house. Not that we're complaining about those spots, but sometimes you want high-end Italian cuisine served in a contemporary space. Settle into the darkened environment, order some wine and enjoy sweetbread risotto and braised lamb belly on polenta.

FATOUSH MEDITERRANEAN **$$**

Map p242 (☎504-371-5074; www.fatoushrestaurantnola.com; 2372 St Claude Ave; mains $10-21; ⊙8am-10pm Mon-Sat, to 5:30pm Sun; 📶✍) Located in a vibrant purple building, Fatoush whips up Mediterranean fare with a focus on Middle Eastern staples: quality falafel, kebabs and fresh salads, plus screamingly good squeezed juices.

FRANKLIN AMERICAN **$$**

Map p242 (☎504-267-0640; www.thefranklinnola.com; 2600 Dauphine St; mains $17-29; ⊙6pm-midnight) The Franklin is as fancy as this area gets: smooth industrial design, low lighting, black-clad waitstaff and hip ambience. Which is all well and good, but how's the food? Quite good, actually: contemporary American with more than a hint of Southern influence – check the redfish with crabmeat, served in a brown rice-leaf wrap.

ELIZABETH'S CAJUN, CREOLE **$$**

Map p242 (☎504-944-9272; www.elizabethsrestaurantnola.com; 601 Gallier St; mains $16-26; ⊙8am-2.30pm & 6-10pm Mon-Sat, 8am-2.30pm Sun) Elizabeth's is deceptively divey, but the food's as good as the best New Orleans chefs can offer. This is a quintessential New Orleans experience: all friendliness, smiling sass, weird artistic edges and over-indulgence on the food front. Brunch and breakfast are top draws – the praline bacon is no doubt sinful but consider us happily banished from the Garden.

DRINKING & NIGHTLIFE

MIMI'S IN THE MARIGNY BAR

Map p242 (☎504-872-9868; 2601 Royal St; ⊙6pm-2am Sun-Thu, to 4am Fri & Sat) The name of this bar could justifiably change to 'Mimi's is the Marigny'; we can't imagine the neighborhood without this institution. Mimi's is as attractively disheveled as Brad Pitt on a good day: all comfy furniture, pool tables, an upstairs dance hall decorated like a Creole mansion gone punk, and dim, brown lighting like a fantasy in sepia.

BJ'S BAR

Map p242 (☎504-945-9256; 4301 Burgundy; ⊙5pm-late) This Bywater dive attracts a neighborhood crowd seeking cheap beers, chilled-out banter and occasional live music, especially the Monday blues-rock show by King James & the Special Men, which starts around 10pm. How great is this place? Robert Plant felt the need to put on an impromptu set here the last time he visited town.

COUNTRY CLUB BAR

Map p242 (☎504-945-0742; www.thecountryclubneworleans.com; 634 Louisa St; ⊙bar 10am-1am, restaurant 11am-9pm Sun-Thu, to 10pm Fri & Sat) From the front, it's a well-decorated Bywater house. Walk inside and there's a restaurant, sauna, leafy patio with bar, heated outdoor pool, 25ft projector screen and a hot tub! There's a $10 towel rental fee if you want to hang in the pool area, which is a popular carousing spot for the gay and lesbian community (all sexualities welcome).

R BAR BAR

Map p242 (☎504-948-7499; 1431 Royal St; ⊙3pm-3am Sun-Thu, to 6am Fri & Sat) This grotty spot is a neighborhood dive that seamlessly blends punk rock sensibility with the occasional confused French Quarter tourist. It's kind of magnificent: a beer and a shot costs a few bucks, the pool tables constantly crack, the jukebox is great and you can get a haircut on Mondays for $10.

JOHN BAR

Map p242 (☎504-942-7159; 2040 Burgundy St; ⊙24hr) The clever name comes courtesy of the toilet bowl seats and tables arrayed around an otherwise pretty open interior space. The (extremely) strong drinks come courtesy of friendly bartenders, who serve them in mason jars – bonus. An excellent dive spot to start a Frenchmen St bar crawl.

LOST LOVE BAR

(☎504-949-2009; http://lostlovelounge.com; 2529 Dauphine St; ⊙6pm-midnight) Dark and sexy, the Lost Love is that vampy Marigny girl or moody artist your momma told you to stay away from, mixed with a bit of blue-collar dive-bar sensibility. Don't listen to her. The drinks are cheap; pours are strong. There's regular karaoke and HBO shows on a projector, and an excellent Vietnamese kitchen in the back.

FAUBOURG WINES WINE BAR

Map p242 (☎504-342-2217; http://faubourgwines.com; 2805 St Claude Ave; ⊙noon-9pm Tue-Thu, to 10pm Fri & Sat, to 7pm Sun) Faubourg (as many call it) is primarily a wine shop but also offers tons of wine classes, and an in-house bar provides a spot for some nice sipping with locals. Pop-up restaurants frequently tromp across the space. The owners make a point of providing affordable bottles, including a rack of under $10 vintages.

CONFEDERACY OF CRUISERS

Our favorite bicycle tours in New Orleans, **Confederacy of Cruisers** (Map p242; ☎504-400-5468; www.confederacyofcruisers.com; tours from $49) set you up on cruiser bikes that come with fat tires and padded seats for Nola's flat, pot-holed roads. The main 'Creole New Orleans' tour takes in the best architecture of the Marigny, Bywater, Esplanade Ave and the Tremé. Confederacy also does a 'History of Drinking' tour ($49, and you have to be 21 or over) and a tasty culinary tour ($89).

MARKEY'S BAR

Map p242 (☎504-943-0785; 640 Louisa St; ⊙2pm-3am Mon-Thu, 11am-3am Fri-Sun) Markey's stands out for two reasons: its barn-red exterior and the fact that it is a straight-up good neighborhood hangout. There's shuffleboard, cheap beer, sports on the TV and an excellent jukebox. Score.

BUFFA'S BAR

Map p242 (☎504-949-0038; www.buffasrestaurant.com; 1001 Esplanade Ave; ⊙24hr) Buffa's wears a lot of hats. First and foremost, it's a neighborhood bar with a back-room stage that hosts the occasional band, quiz night, open mic and TV or movie screening. Second, it's a 24-hour spot that serves one of the best damn cheeseburgers in town. What's not to love?

SOLO ESPRESSO CAFE

(☎504-408-1377; www.soloespressobar.com; 1301 Poland Ave; coffee $3-5; ⊙8am-3pm Mon-Sat) This little shack serves some very fine, strong, small-batch coffee. Graphic novels provide for a bit of reading material.

ORANGE COUCH CAFE

Map p242 (☎504-267-7327; 2339 Royal St; coffees & pastries $3; ⊙7am-10pm;) An icebox-cool cafe, all Ikea-esque furniture, polished stone flooring, local artwork and photography on the walls, graffiti-lined restrooms and, yes, an orange leather couch in the midst of it all. Very Marigny; the sort of place where a tattooed attorney takes out a Mac and a tort law manual and cracks away for hours.

FLORA GALLERY & COFFEE SHOP CAFE
Map p242 (504-947-8358; 2600 Royal St; coffees & pastries $3-5; 6:30am-midnight;) Flora is almost the perfect New Orleans cafe. If you could smoke inside, as in the old days, some might say it'd be 10 out of 10. No offense, nonsmokers, but it's just the sort of place – madcap art, antique-store furniture, lush gardens and a Parisian bohemian atmosphere – that demands the accompaniment of clouds of tobacco smoke.

BIG DADDY'S BAR BAR
Map p242 (504-948-6288; 2513 Royal St; 4pm-2am) If it's too crowded at popular Mimi's bar across the street, or if you're gay and tired of the thumpa-thumpa-bass queer scene on Bourbon, head to this friendly 'gayborhood' bar, a jumping spot where all sexualities are welcome for friendly banter and cheap drinks.

YUKI IZAKAYA LOUNGE
Map p242 (504-943-1122; 525 Frenchmen St; 5pm-3am) If you want a clean feeling in the morning after a night on the town, order off the extensive sake menu at Yuki. As you sip your rice wine, chill out to house-lounge music and achieve hipster Zen, watching subtitled Japanese art-house flicks projected onto the walls.

☆ ENTERTAINMENT

SPOTTED CAT LIVE MUSIC
Map p242 (www.spottedcatmusicclub.com; 623 Frenchmen St; 4pm-2am Mon-Fri, from 3pm Sat & Sun) It's good the Spotted Cat is across the street from Snug Harbor. They're both great jazz clubs, but where the latter is a swish martini sorta spot, the former is a thumping sweatbox where drinks are served in plastic cups – an ideal execution of the tiny New Orleans music club.

MARIGNY OPERA HOUSE PERFORMING ARTS
Map p242 (504-948-9998; www.marignyoperahouse.org; 725 St Ferdinand St) This former church has been remodeled into a performing-arts space that's infused with the sort of romantic dilapidation that very much fits the New Orleans aesthetic. The Opera House gained national prominence when Solange Knowles (Beyonce's sister) got married here; on other days, the venue hosts theater, music and showcases its own dance company.

HI HO LOUNGE LIVE MUSIC
Map p242 (504-945-4446; www.hiholounge.net; 2239 St Claude Ave; 6pm-2am Sun-Thu, to 3am Fri & Sat) Alt-country, folk, rock, punk, brass bands, dance parties and Mardi Gras Indians regularly pop up at the Hi Ho. It can get pretty packed, but this remains one of the best mid-sized venues in town for a live act.

D.B.A. LIVE MUSIC
Map p242 (504-942-3731; www.dbaneworleans.com; 618 Frenchmen St; 5pm-4am Mon-Thu, from 4pm Fri-Sun;) Swank d.b.a. consistently schedules some of the best live music in town. Listening to John Boutté's sweet tenor, which sounds like birds making love on the Mississippi, is one of the best beginnings to a night in New Orleans. Brass bands, rock shows, blues – everything plays here. Plus, there's an amazing beer selection. Seriously d.b.a., you freaking *win*.

NEW MOVEMENT THEATER THEATER
Map p242 (504-302-8264; http://newmovementtheater.com; 2706 St Claude Ave) Improv

THE NEW ORLEANS CENTER FOR CREATIVE ARTS

New Orleans, like few American cities of its size, lives and dies off its arts scene. This is a city unapologetically in love with (and largely built on) the work of its musicians, painters and writers, and many of the next generation of such artists are educated at the **New Orleans Center for Creative Arts** (Map p242; Nocca; 504-940-2787; www.nocca.com; 2800 Chartres St). As it is a school, Nocca understandably isn't open to visitors 24/7, but check the website for details on upcoming public performances, gallery shows and the like.

Admission to this prestigious center, one of the best arts schools in the USA, is by audition only. If accepted, students (who are concurrently enrolled in their normal schools) specialize in fields ranging from the visual arts and creative writing to dance and cooking, instructed by artists at the top of their craft.

LOCAL KNOWLEDGE

THE ST CLAUDE SHUFFLE

St Claude Ave isn't the city's prettiest roadway, to be sure, but the stretch between Touro and Mandeville St is one of the best live-music strips in New Orleans. Just don't expect jazz; the clubs here play hip-hop, rock, punk and all manner of craziness. If you want a night out with locals and good music, head up here to check out the **Hi Ho Lounge** (p94) or any of these other great venues:

AllWays Lounge (Map p242; ☎504-218-5778; http://theallwayslounge.net; 2240 St Claude Ave; ⌚6pm-midnight, to 2am Thu & Fri) In a city full of funky music venues, the AllWays stands out as one of the funkiest. On any given night of the week you may see experimental guitar, local theater, thrash-y rock, live comedy or a '60s-inspired shagadelic dance party. Also: the drinks are supercheap.

Siberia (Map p242; ☎504-265-8855; www.siberianola.com; 2227 St Claude Ave; ⌚4pm-late) There's always an interesting crowd of inked-up punks, sensitive hipsters and hoodie-clad hardcores (or wanna-be hardcores) in Siberia, which hosts everything from punk rock to singer-songwriter nights to heavy metal to bounce shows. An on-site Eastern European–themed restaurant satisfies any cravings you may have for *blinis*.

Kajun's Pub (Map p242; ☎504-947-3735; http://kajunpub.com; 2256 St Claude Ave; ⌚24hr) Kajun's is guaranteed for a good cast of characters. We suppose this bar is technically a live-music venue too...if you count karaoke as live music. Whatever; the karaoke is awesome (sometimes awesomely bad) and the beer flows 24/7.

Sweet Lorraine's (Map p242; ☎504-945-9654; 1931 St Claude Ave; ⌚5pm-late Tue-Sat, 11am-3pm Sun) A neighborhood jazz club where you can hear good 'trad jazz' and contemporary grooves. Thursday night is blues night with Chucky C and Clearly Blue, while on Sundays, Lorraine's hosts a delicious jazz brunch.

theater, by its nature, can be hit or miss. The best sort hits more than half the time; the New Movement, we can happily report, hits well above this average. The company has a cast of regular players from around the way and a stable schedule of classes that train new talent in the art of off-the-cuff comedy.

SNUG HARBOR — JAZZ

Map p242 (☎504-949-0696; www.snugjazz.com; 626 Frenchmen St; ⌚5-11pm) There may be bigger venues but, overall, Snug Harbor is the best jazz club in the city. That's partly because it usually hosts doubleheaders, giving you a good dose of variety, and partly because the talent is kept to an admirable mix of reliable legends and hot up-and-comers; in the course of one night you'll likely witness both.

VAUGHAN'S — LIVE MUSIC

Map p242 (☎504-947-5562; 800 Lesseps St; cover $7-15; ⌚noon-2am) On most nights of the week this is a Bywater dive, but on Thursdays regular live music brings the house down. If Corey Henry and the Treme Funktet are playing, get over here.

SATURN BAR — LIVE MUSIC

Map p242 (☎504-949-7532; http://saturnbar.com; 3067 St Claude Ave; ⌚Mon-Sat 5pm-2am, from 6pm Sun) In the solar system of New Orleans bars, Saturn is planet punk. Originally it was an eclectic neighborhood bar where a crew of regulars appreciated, without irony, the outsider art, leopard-skin furniture and a general, genuinely unique aesthetic. Today the punk scene and hipster enclaves are united by neon-lighting fixtures, flashy gambling machines and great live music.

CHECKPOINT CHARLIE — LIVE MUSIC

Map p242 (☎504-281-4847; 501 Esplanade Ave; ⌚24hr) Charlie's is so grungy it could start a band in early '90s Seattle. Acts you've likely never heard of (plus some you probably know) tromp on the stage, playing a mix of rock, metal and punk, most of it very good.

MAISON — LIVE MUSIC

Map p242 (☎504-371-5543; www.maisonfrenchmen.com; 508 Frenchmen St; ⌚5pm-2am Sun, Tue & Wed, to 2:30am Thu, to 3am Mon & Fri, to 3:30am Sat) With three stages, a kitchen and a decent bar, Maison is one of the more eclectic performance spaces on Frenchmen St.

On any given night you may be hearing Latin rumba in one hour, indie rock in another and Nola brass to round out the evening.

THREE MUSES JAZZ

Map p242 (☎504-252-4801; www.3musesnola.com; 536 Frenchmen St; ⊙5pm-2am) This excellent restaurant hosts jazz every night, and the incomparable Glen David Andrews is a regular performer. It's perfect for when you need to combine good food and music loud enough to enjoy, but soft enough to keep your ears from hurting. The kitchen closes at 10pm on weekdays and 11pm on weekends.

CAFÉ NEGRIL LIVE MUSIC

Map p242 (☎504-944-4744; 606 Frenchmen St; ⊙7pm-1am Mon-Wed, 5pm-2am Thu-Sun) When you spin the Frenchmen St musical wheel, Negril is the reggae-blues-Latin-world music stop. So if you're craving that sort of groove, and the dancing that goes with it (this is definitely one of the 'dancier' clubs on Frenchmen), roll on in.

APPLE BARREL LIVE MUSIC

Map p242 (☎504-949-9399; 609 Frenchmen St; ⊙1pm-3am Sun-Thu, to 5am Fri & Sat) The Barrel is roughly the size of its namesake: you can fit perhaps a dozen customers in here without going elbow to elbow. It fits in musicians, too, who tend to play some very fine jazz, blues and folk.

OLD MARQUER THEATRE THEATER

Map p242 (☎504-298-8676; www.oldmarquer.com; 2400 St Claude Ave) This small theater regularly features plays written and performed by local New Orleanians, as well as established shows from outside the city, and events such as slams. There's an indie flavor to what's on offer, and the cozy atmosphere you get from witnessing a community of like-minded artists perform together.

DRAGON'S DEN LIVE MUSIC

Map p242 (☎504-940-5546; http://dragonsdennola.com; 435 Esplanade Ave; ⊙8pm-2am Mon-Thu, to 5am Fri-Sun) When it comes to rock, ska, punk, drum-and-bass, dubstep and hip-hop, the Den consistently hosts some of the best acts in New Orleans.

BLUE NILE LIVE MUSIC

Map p242 (☎504-948-2583; http://bluenilelive.com; 532 Frenchmen St; ⊙6pm-2am) Hip-hop, reggae, jazz, soul and funk are the live-music staples in the downstairs section of the Nile. Things get pretty sweaty, sensual and meat-markety in the upstairs balcony room, with its dedicated dance floor, as the night goes on.

HEALING CENTRAL

One of the most distinctive buildings lining otherwise ordinary St Claude Ave is the bright orange facade of the **Healing Center** (Map p242; http://neworleanshealingcenter.org; 2372 St Claude Ave), a sort of mall for all things New Age. It's full of shops whose owners would likely harm us for comparing them to a mall – if they weren't all non-violence practitioners.

Sorry, we don't mean to be cute. This is a place in touch with its chakras and proud of it. There's plenty to discover inside, including a cast of alternative-medicine practitioners who rotate in and out of the center's studio spaces. Offices for various New Orleans NGOs can be found on the 2nd floor of the center.

Call ahead for hours if they're not listed.

Artisans' Well (☎504-232-3496; 2372 St Claude Ave; ⊙10am-6pm Mon-Sat) This little shop specializes in indigenous art from Mexico and Central America.

Wild Lotus Yoga (☎504-899-0047; http://wildlotusyoga.com; 2372 St Claude Ave) Widely considered one of the best and friendliest yoga studios in town. Call for class times.

New Orleans Food Co-op (☎504-264-5579; www.nolafood.coop; ⊙7am-10pm) The healthiest store in town, specializing in locavore and organic groceries.

Café Istanbul (☎504-975-0286; www.cafeistanbulnola.com) Multifunctional arts space that regularly hosts musicians, poets, dance recitals and movie screenings.

Island of Salvation Botanica (☎504-948-9961; http://islandofsalvationbotanica.com; ⊙10am-5pm Tue-Sat, 11am-6pm Sun) Run by wonderfully genial owners who sell vodoo spells, cards, spell components and the like for serious practitioners of the faith.

SHOPPING

FAUBOURG MARIGNY BOOK STORE BOOKS

Map p242 (504-947-3700; www.fabonfrenchmen.com; 600 Frenchmen St; noon-10pm) The South's oldest gay bookstore is a ramshackle, intellectual spot, and a good place to pick up local 'zines and catch up on the New Orleans scene, gay or otherwise. Look for the subtle (enormous) rainbow flag.

I.J. REILLY'S HANDICRAFTS

Map p242 (504-304-7928; https://ijreillys.squarespace.com; 632 Elysian Fields; 10am-5pm Wed-Mon) How deeply New Orleans is this store? It's named for Ignatious Reilly, protagonist of *A Confederancy of Dunces,* and located in the Kowalski house from *A Streetcar Named Desire.* Inside, the shop sells all manner of clever New Orleans gifts, from photography books to printed screens and local artwork.

EUCLID RECORDS MUSIC

Map p242 (504-947-4348; www.euclidnola.com; 3301 Chartres St; 11am-7pm daily) New Orleans is the kind of town that deserves really cool record shops, and Euclid is happy to oblige. It's got all the ingredients: racks of rare vinyl, old concert posters, a knowledgeable staff that looks plucked from a Nick Hornby novel (except they're all friendly, eschewing the music-snob stereotype) and a board listing whatever live music you should see while in town.

LOUISIANA MUSIC FACTORY MUSIC

Map p242 (504-586-1094; www.louisianamusicfactory.com; 421 Frenchmen St; 11am-8pm Sun-Thu, to 10pm Fri & Sat) Where else would you find one of the best repositories of New Orleans and Louisiana music than the head of Frenchmen St? The Louisiana Music Factory, besides boasting racks of local music (and staff who love to chat about music), also often hosts concerts on its sales floor.

BYWATER BARGAIN CENTER ANTIQUES

Map p242 (504-948-0007; 3200 Dauphine St; 11am-6pm) This emporium is a treasure trove of, well, treasures, if you follow the old adage that one person's junk is another's... well, you know. There are found objects, old door frames, handmade crafts, plaster alligators playing zydeco and who knows what else. Most impressive is a collection of Mexican folk art, including Oaxacan sculpture and Dia del Muerte paraphernalia.

STELLA!

Tennessee Williams fans, listen up. The home at the center of *A Streetcar Named Desire* is at 632 Elysian Fields. Currently the building houses the shop **I.J. Reilly's** and the bicycle rental outfit **A Bicycle Named Desire** (Map p242; 504-345-8966; http://abicyclenameddesire.com; 632 Elysian Fields; 4/8/24hr rental $20/25/35, per additional day $25; 10am-5pm Wed-Mon), of course. If you're tempted to stand outside in a tank top and yell at the top of your lungs, we suggest saving the 'Stella!' screams for the Tennessee Williams festival in late March.

If you ever wondered where the title for the iconic play comes from, yes, it does allude to the 'desire' that rips apart the lives of the main characters; but it's also a literal reference to the old Desire streetcar line that once ran up Elysian Fields Ave.

DR BOB'S STUDIO ARTS

Map p242 (504-945-2225; http://drbobart.net; 3027 Chartres St; 10am-5pm Mon-Sat, to 4pm Sun) Self-taught outdoors artist Dr Bob is a fixture in the Bywater, and you're sure to recognize his signature work – the 'Be Nice or Leave' signs that appear in restaurants and bars around town. Garbage-can lids, bottle caps, trashed musical instruments and essentially anything that strikes Dr Bob's interest is turned into art.

NEW ORLEANS ART SUPPLY ARTS

Map p242 (504-949-1525; www.art-restoration.com/noas/index.htm; 3041 N Rampart St; 9am-7pm Mon-Fri, to 5pm Sat, 10am-5pm Sun) If you're one who likes to sketch while traveling, here's a good place to go for a fresh supply of pencils, paint and pads. The selection is very high quality. There's an attached pet shop, too, if you're traveling with furry friends.

ELECTRIC LADYLAND TATTOOS

Map p242 (504-947-8286; http://electricladylandtattoo.com; 610 Frenchmen St; noon-midnight, to 10pm Sun) New Orleans is an old port filled with bars, right? Then a tattoo is just about the coolest souvenir you can get. This is a clean, brightly lit spot that also happens to be a bit of an informal community center with the inked crowd.

1
MAISON BOURBON
TRICOU
CIGARS
PIPES & MORE
CIGARETTES

2
TAMA
FENDER
ED WILLS

ROB HAMMER/CORBIS ©

1. Bourbon St in the French Quarter 2. Blues gig at Decatur St in the French Quarter 3. Snug Harbor (p95) on Frenchmen St

Best Neighborhoods for a Night Out

Nightlife is integral to New Orleans. Locals know how to have a good time, and that doesn't just mean boozing on Bourbon St (in fact, locals tend to avoid Bourbon). Here are some of the best areas for living life to the hilt once the sun dips down.

Frenchmen Street

Frenchmen can admittedly get aggressively crowded on weekends. But it still hosts the best concentration of music gigs in the city. Music tends to go off around 6pm, 10pm and 1am; weeknights are a little more casual.

St Claude Avenue

There's great music in St Claude Sq, which encompasses the Hi Ho Lounge, AllWays Lounge, Siberia and Kajun's. These bars host some of the city's most enterprising acts; while you may come across some brass bands, you can also find rock, pink, hip-hop and bounce.

Off Bourbon in the Quarter

Going out in the French Quarter isn't all about neon-colored drinks and bad karaoke. Head to Chartres St and up Decatur St to find bars that cater to both locals and discerning visitors.

Freret Street

If you're looking for a student atmosphere, head Uptown to Freret St. Note: 'student' doesn't mean silly (well, not necessarily); go cups are banned on Freret, and the scene here is more focused on live-music venues, artsy bars and craft cocktails.

Franklin Avenue

Franklin Ave cuts across some fine neighborhood bars in Faubourg Marigny that cater to an GLBT crowd as well the bohemian locals who call the Marigny home.

CBD & Warehouse District

CBD | WAREHOUSE DISTRICT

Neighborhood Top Five

❶ Immersing yourself in the dramatic sights and sounds of WWII at the **National WWII Museum** (p102) with oral histories, wall-sized photos and a multisensory 4D movie.

❷ Appreciating the moody landscapes at the **Ogden Museum of Southern Art** (p103) then strolling gallery-lined Julia St.

❸ Animal-watching at the **Aquarium of the Americas** (p105) and the **Butterfly Garden & Insectarium** (p104).

❹ Living the highlife at the **Roosevelt New Orleans** (p183) hotel with a drink at the Sazerac Bar, dinner at Domenica and jazz at the Fountain Lounge.

❺ Bar- and club-hopping in the **Warehouse District** (p112) between Constance and Fulton Sts.

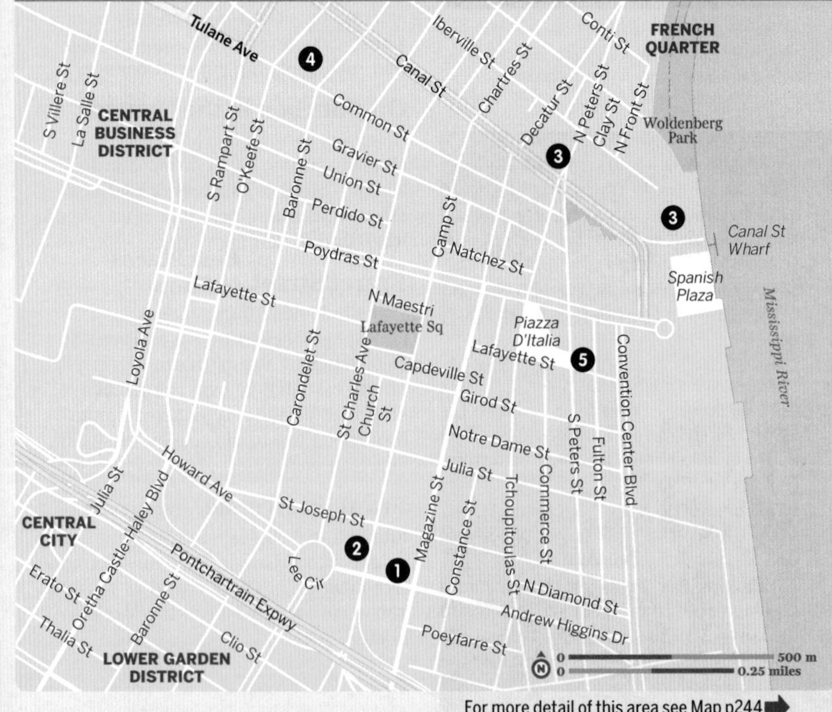

For more detail of this area see Map p244

Explore CBD & Warehouse District

The Central Business District (CBD) and Warehouse District stretch from the I-10 and the Superdome to the river and are bordered by Canal St and the elevated I-90. Poydras St divides the two neighborhoods. City tourism maps muddle the boundaries somewhat, but the Lafayette Square District and the Arts District overlap with the Warehouse District.

The business district is the downtown area that runs from the Superdome to St Charles Ave, with a small sliver that extends beyond St Charles to the river. The neighborhood features posh hotels, the Superdome, the Audubon museums and Harrah's casino, and is easily walkable.

On your first morning, eat breakfast at Ruby Slipper or Le Pavillon downtown before visiting the Aquarium of the Americas and nearby Butterfly Garden & Insectarium. Later, catch a game at the Superdome or take a river cruise on the Mississippi. End with a cocktail at one the CBD's many hotel bars. The French Quarter, just across Canal St, is within easy walking distance, too.

Spend your second day in the Warehouse District, bounded by the I-90, St Charles Ave, Poydras St and the river. The WWII Museum, the Ogden Museum of Southern Art and the Civil War Museum are clustered near Lee Circle. Grab lunch at Peche or Cochon Butcher, then visit the Julia St galleries.

Restaurants, bars and live music are the draw in the evening. Walk along Fulton St, S Peters St or Tchoupitoulas St to find the action.

Local Life

➡ **Walk this way** It's an easy walk from downtown offices and hotels to Warehouse District restaurants.

➡ **Lunch deals** The city's nicest restaurants often serve affordable lunches. Enjoy top chefs at Herbsaint (p111), Drago's (p110) and Emeril's (p112).

➡ **Hangouts** Shoot the breeze at Cochon Butcher (p111) or catch a game and sip brews at Rusty Nail (p113).

Getting There & Away

➡ **Car** From the airport, most hotels are easily accessible off the elevated I-90. Cars coming in from the east should exit off the I-10.

➡ **Taxi or shuttle** A cab from Louis Armstrong Airport to the CBD costs $33 for one or two people. Shuttles cost $20 per person one-way.

➡ **Train/bus** The Amtrak and Greyhound stations border Loyola Ave near the Superdome. A new streetcar route, the Loyola-UPT line, runs from the stations to Canal St.

Lonely Planet's Top Tip

Canal St separates the French Quarter from the CBD. If you want to be near, but not in, the Bourbon St craziness, book a hotel room in the CBD. Walking just two or three extra blocks will bring quieter streets and hotels.

Best Places to Eat

- Cochon Butcher (p111)
- Peche Seafood Grill (p111)
- Restaurant August (p110)
- Domenica (p110)
- Herbsaint (p111)

For reviews, see p109 ➡

Best Places to Drink

- Rusty Nail (p113)
- Lucy's Retired Surfers Bar (p113)
- Swizzle Stick Bar (p112)
- Sazerac Bar (p112)
- Circle Bar (p112)

For reviews, see p112

Best Places to Shop

- Center for Southern Craft & Design (p103)
- Ariodante (p114)
- The Flea Market at the Butterfly Garden & Insectarium (p104)
- Meyer the Hatter (p114)

For reviews, see p114

TOP SIGHT
NATIONAL WWII MUSEUM

The National WWII Museum drops you into the action. Wall-sized photographs capture the confusion of D-Day. Riveting oral histories tell remarkable stories of survival. A stroll through the snowy woods of Ardennes feels eerily cold. Exhibits like these make this grand facility so engaging; artifacts, battles and war strategies are humanized through personal recollections and heat-of-the-action displays.

How did this fascinating place, opened in 2000 as the National D-Day Museum, land in New Orleans? The reconstructed LCVP or 'Higgins boat,' on display in the Louisiana Pavilion, provides the link. Originally designed by local entrepreneur Andrew Jackson Higgins for commercial use on Louisiana's bayous, these flat-bottomed amphibious landing craft moved tens of thousands of soldiers onto Normandy's beaches during the D-Day invasion on June 6, 1944.

The museum continues to open in several stages across three pavilions. The new Campaigns of Courage Pavilion spotlights the European and Pacific theaters. Inside, the Road to Berlin galleries cover European battlefronts. A reconstructed Quonset hut – with a bombed-out roof – brings the air war powerfully close. The Road to Tokyo galleries will highlight the Pacific theater. Visitors can personalize their explorations by registering for a dog tag, which connects them with the same WWII participant at various exhibits.

The Louisiana Memorial Pavilion covers D-Day in four galleries. Don't miss the German Enigma machine. A restored Boeing B-17 bomber is visible from catwalks in the US Freedom Pavilion: The Boeing Center, and you can join an immersive submarine experience inspired by the last patrol of the USS *Tang*.

The film *Beyond all Boundaries* takes a 4D look at America's involvement in the war on a 120ft-wide screen. Get ready for rumbling seats and a dusting of snowflakes!

DON'T MISS

- Louisiana Memorial Pavilion
- Campaigns of Courage Pavilion
- US Freedom Pavilion
- *Beyond All Boundaries*

PRACTICALITIES

- Map p244
- ☎504-528-1944
- www.nationalww2museum.org
- 945 Magazine St
- adult/child/senior $23/14/20, plus 1/2 films $5/10
- 9am-5pm

RICHARD CUMMINS/ALAMY ©

TOP SIGHT
OGDEN MUSEUM OF SOUTHERN ART

Although the Ogden Museum sits just a few steps away from the Civil War Museum and the city's iconic statue of Robert E Lee, this vibrant collection of Southern art is certainly not stuck in the past. It's one of the most engaging museums in New Orleans, managing to be beautiful, educational and unpretentious all at once.

The collection got its start more than 30 years ago when Roger Ogden and his father began purchasing art as gifts for Roger's mother. Ogden soon became a passionate collector and by the 1990s the New Orleans entrepreneur had assembled one of the finest collections of Southern art anywhere – one that was far too large to keep to himself. Today his namesake museum and its galleries hold pieces that range from impressionist landscapes and outsider folk art to contemporary installation work. The Ogden is affiliated with the Smithsonian Institute in Washington, DC, giving it access to that bottomless collection.

The glass-and-stone Stephen Goldring Hall, with its soaring atrium, provides an inspiring welcome to the grounds. The building, which opened in 2003, is home to the museum's 20th- and 21st-century exhibitions as well as the Museum Store and its **Center for Southern Craft & Design**. 'Floating' stairs between floors will lead you to select pieces from regional artists as well as Southern landscapes, ceramics, glasswork and eye-catching works from self-taught artists. The Ogden's 18th-, 19th- and early-20th-century collections will be showcased in the Patrick F Taylor Library and the Clementine Hunter Education Wing, both under renovation.

DON'T MISS

- Southern Landscapes
- Self-Taught, Outsider and Visionary Art
- Museum Store & Center for Southern Craft & Design
- Ogden after Hours

PRACTICALITIES

- Map p244
- ☎504-539-9650
- www.ogdenmuseum.org
- 925 Camp St
- adult/child 5-17yr/student $10/5/8
- ⏲10am-5pm Wed-Mon, plus 5:30-8pm Thu

SIGHTS

CBD

Hotels and skyscrapers fill the CBD, a no-nonsense grid of bland buildings anchored by the hulking Superdome. A few historic buildings add character, particularly in the area surrounding Lafayette Sq, the heart of the former Faubourg St Mary.

MERCEDES-BENZ SUPERDOME STADIUM

Map p244 (☎504-587-3663, box office 504-587-3822; www.superdome.com; Sugar Bowl Dr) The Superdome hovers like a giant bronze hubcap between the elevated I-10 freeway and downtown's skyscrapers. The immense indoor stadium, which seats more than 73,200, has hosted NCAA Final Four basketball games, presidential conventions, the Rolling Stones (largest indoor concert in history), Pope John Paul II and seven Super Bowls. On New Year's Day the college-football Sugar Bowl is played here, and in fall this is the home turf of the New Orleans Saints.

The Superdome gained notoriety in 2005 when it was designated a 'refuge of last resort' during Hurricane Katrina. Some 25,000 to 30,000 people huddled under the dome as Katrina's winds blew off part of the roof. Power went out and food and water supplies were quickly depleted as people lived in squalor and waited nearly a week for buses to carry them out of the flooded city. Initial unconfirmed reports of rape, riot and murder within the Dome have been debunked. In all, six people died inside the Superdome (one apparent suicide, one overdose and the rest from natural causes, mainly elderly or infirm who suffered from pre-existing conditions), plus several more in the immediate vicinity.

In 2011 the facility completed a six-year, $336 million renovation project that modernized the building and ensured occupancy by the Saints through to 2025. The structure was built on top of an ancient burial ground, which some say is the source of the Saints' seemingly cursed 40-year history.

STREET PARKING IN THE CBD

Free parking is nearly impossible to find downtown, and parking meters typically run from 8am to 6pm Monday through Saturday. Sidewalk parking kiosks that accept coins and credit or debit cards are common, but you'll still find plenty of the old coin-gobbling meters. It's handy to know that you can use your credit card in one of the new kiosks even if you are parking in a spot with an old meter that accepts only coins. If using a kiosk, place the receipt on your dashboard when parked at a metered spot. The maximum time allowed for most spots is two hours ($3). Double-check all signs for variances.

GALLIER HALL HISTORIC BUILDING

Map p244 (☎504-658-3627; www.nola.gov; 545 St Charles Ave) Architect James Gallier Sr designed this monumental Greek-revival structure, which was dedicated in 1853. It served as New Orleans' city hall until the 1950s, and far outclasses the city's current one (a few blocks away). Today the building is used for private functions and VIP funerals, and it's a focal point for Mardi Gras parades, most of which promenade past the grandstand erected here on St Charles Ave.

Both Confederate president Jefferson Davis and homegrown R&B legend Ernie K-Doe have lain in state here – only in New Orleans.

Warehouse District

The old warehouses that line most of the streets in this part of town have proved perfectly suitable for the arts district that now thrives here. The museums and galleries are joined by some of the city's finest restaurants.

NATIONAL WWII MUSEUM MUSEUM

See p102.

OGDEN MUSEUM OF SOUTHERN ART MUSEUM

See p103.

BUTTERFLY GARDEN & INSECTARIUM ZOO

Map p244 (☎504-581-4629; www.auduboninstitute.org; US Custom House, 423 Canal St; adult/child/senior $17/12/14; ⊙10am-5pm Tue-Sun, plus Mon Jun-Aug; 👪) We'll be honest: if you're not a fan of bugs and creepy-crawlies, you may be happier elsewhere. Because at

CBD LANDMARKS

Scattered throughout the CBD are historic buildings where some of the city's biggest (and, in some cases, most notorious) wheelers and dealers operated. Keep an eye out for them when wandering through the neighborhood.

New Orleans Cotton Exchange (Map p244; 231 Carondelet St) Some would say New Orleans was built on cotton. In the mid-19th century, when one-third of all cotton produced in the USA was routed through New Orleans, the receiving docks on the levee were perpetually covered by tall stacks of cotton bales ready to be shipped out. The Cotton Exchange was founded in 1871 to regulate trade and prices. The building here, dating from the 1920s, is the third Cotton Exchange to occupy this site.

United Fruit Company (Map p244; 321 St Charles Ave) A cornucopia of tropical produce graces the entrance to this building. The United Fruit Company, infamous for controversial neocolonial practices in Central America, was based here from the 1930s until the 1970s. For many decades, the company held a virtual monopoly on the banana trade throughout much of the world. It's now part of Chiquita Brands International, based in Cincinnati, OH.

this lively museum, you'll do more than stare at insects: you'll listen to them, touch them and, if you dare, even taste them. It's a multisensory adventure that's especially fun for kids. The eight-minute 4D film *Awards Night: The Tiniest Show on Earth* spotlights the world's most amazing insects. Our favorite exhibit? The mesmerizing leaf-cutter ants, working hard!

Adventurous visitors can munch on chocolate chirp cookies (topped with crickets) or mango chutney with waxworms in the Bug Appetit room, or pet an exotic insect, such as the thumb-sized Madagascar roach, in the Metamorphosis Gallery. The Louisiana Swamp Gallery and Insects of New Orleans display highlight regional creepy crawlies. The latter exhibit examines yellow fever, a mosquito-borne virus that killed more than 40,000 people in the city between 1805 and 1905. For a more tranquil setting, wander the butterfly garden, an Asian-themed walk-though exhibit where colorful butterflies flicker past with abandon. The insectarium's retail shop, **The Flea Market**, sells bug-related gifts, from huggable stuffed bumble bees to a start-your-own-ant-colony kit.

The museum is located inside the carriageway of the city's historic US Custom House. Construction of the building began in 1848, but it took 33 years and nine architects to complete it. Confederate soldiers were imprisoned on the site when Union forces occupied New Orleans during the Civil War. Today, because it is a federal building, visitors' bags will be searched.

AQUARIUM OF THE AMERICAS AQUARIUM

Map p244 (☎504-581-4629; www.auduboninstitute.org; 1 Canal St; adult/child/senior $24/18/19, with IMAX $29/23/23; ⊙10am-5pm Tue-Sun; 🚸) Part of the Audubon Institute, the immense Aquarium of the Americas is loosely regional, with exhibits that delve beneath the surface of the Mississippi River, Gulf of Mexico, Caribbean Sea and far-off Amazon rainforest.

The new and impressive **Great Maya Reef** lures visitors into a 30ft-long clear tunnel running through a 'submerged' Mayan city, home to exotic fish. Upstairs, the penguin colony, the sea-horse gallery and **Parakeet Pointe**, where you can feed the colorful birds, are perennially popular. In the **Mississippi River Gallery**, look for the rare white alligator.

Some 10,000 fish were lost when Hurricane Katrina wiped out the aquarium's filtration and temperature-control systems, but the aquarium reopened the following year. Unfortunately, there are no major exhibits spotlighting Hurricane Katrina or the BP oil spill, two of the biggest events to affect southern Louisiana's waterways in the last 15 years. You will find, however, BP's aquarium sponsorship plaque, along with plaques for Shell, Exxon and others, beside the 400,000 gallon Gulf of Mexico tank – home to some intimidating sharks.

The adjacent IMAX theater screens educational and commercial movies throughout the day.

BLAINE KERN'S MARDI GRAS WORLD MUSEUM

(☎504-361-7821; www.mardigrasworld.com; 1380 Port of New Orleans Pl; adult/child 2-11yr/senior $20/13/16; ⏱tours 9:30am-4:30pm; 👪) We dare say Mardi Gras World is one of the happiest places in New Orleans by day – but at night it must turn into one of the most terrifying funhouses this side of Hell. It's all those faces, man, the dragons, clowns, kings and fairies, leering and dead-eyed…

That said, by day we love touring Mardi Gras World – the studio warehouse of Blaine Kern (Mr Mardi Gras) and family, who have been making parade floats since 1947. Tours last 30 to 45 minutes.

Visitors start by watching a 15-minute movie – which is followed by king cake – then continue into the depths of the warehouse, one of 15 storage buildings found across New Orleans. You can see many of the floats up-close, any time of the year. There are never less than 2000 props in the inventory, and the company builds about 50 or 60 new ones each year. Kern learned the trade from his father and passed it down to his sons. You might also see figures built for the studio's other commercial projects, including the ubiquitous cows representing the Chick-Fil-A fast food chain.

If you're staying at a nearby hotel, you may be able to catch the company's free shuttle. Otherwise, parking in the lot beside the entrance costs $10.

CONTEMPORARY ARTS CENTER ARTS CENTER

Map p244 (CAC; ☎504-528-3805; www.cacno.org; 900 Camp St; adult/child/student $10/free/$8; ⏱11am-5pm Wed-Mon) From the outside, the CAC is pretty unassuming. But once inside, the grand modernist entrance, an airy, spacious vault with soaring ceilings and conceptual metal and wooden accents, is impressive. The best reason to visit? A good crop of rotating exhibitions by local as well as international artists, plus a packed events calendar that includes plays, skits, dance and concerts.

Admission for school children (up to 12 years) is free.

CIVIL WAR MUSEUM MUSEUM

Map p244 (☎504-523-4522; www.confederatemuseum.com; 929 Camp St; adult/child 7-14yr & senior $8/5; ⏱10am-4pm Tue-Sat) Tattered gray uniforms, rebel swords, faded diaries and a lock of General Robert E Lee's silver hair. This collection of Civil War memorabilia pays homage to the Confederacy and the local boys who fought for the rebel cause. The museum used to be a center of Confederate apologia. Today it's been largely politically corrected, but it remains a collection of things as opposed to a contemporary, interpretation-driven educational museum.

Once known as the Confederate Museum, this is Louisiana's oldest operating museum. It's a smallish space centered in the Confederate Memorial Hall, a chamber of dark wood and exposed cypress ceiling beams with a decidedly stately vibe. The permanent exhibition is one of the largest compilations of Confederate artifacts in the country and includes lots of swords, guns, flags and uniforms. The most moving exhibits are the handful of displays describing local heroes or spotlighting soldiers who died in battle. There is a lack of material relating to slavery, perhaps because of the paucity of material possessions slaves could have left behind.

ACTIVITIES IN CBD & WAREHOUSE DISTRICT

The **Canal Street Ferry** (www.nolaferries.com; per person $2; ⏱6am-9:45pm Mon-Fri, 10:45am-8pm Sat, 10:45am-6pm Sun) runs from the foot of Canal St to Algiers Point. It's the easiest way to get out on the Mississippi River and admire New Orleans from the traditional river approach (which smells like mud, poo and petroleum). Ride on the deck and you may see the state bird, the brown pelican. On weekdays, the ferry leaves Canal St on the quarter hour and the half hour and returns from Algiers on the hour and half hour. On weekends, the schedule flips, with the ferry leaving Canal St on the hour. On the Algiers side, stretch your legs and learn about Louis Armstrong and other jazz greats on the Jazz Walk of Fame along the levee. Need sustenance after that five-minute ride? Grab a beer at one of the local watering holes just off the ferry or stroll a few blocks to **Toute de Suite Cafe** (www.toutesuitecafe.com; 347 Verret St; pastries under $4, sandwiches $7; ⏱7am-5pm Tue-Sat, to 3pm Sun, to noon Mon) for coffee and cookies.

LOUISIANA CHILDREN'S MUSEUM — MUSEUM

Map p244 (☎504-523-1357; www.lcm.org; 420 Julia St; admission $8.50; ⏲9:30am-4:30pm Tue-Sat, noon-4:30pm Sun mid-Aug–May, 9:30am-5pm Mon-Sat, noon-5pm Sun Jun–mid-Aug) This educational museum is like a high-tech kindergarten where the wee ones can play in interactive bliss till nap time. Lots of corporate sponsorship equals lots of hands-on exhibits. The Little Port of New Orleans gallery spotlights the five types of ships found in the local port. Kids can play in a galley kitchen, or they can load cargo. Elsewhere kids can check out optical illusions, shop in a pretend grocery store or get crafty in an art studio.

Children under 16 years must be accompanied by an adult.

PRESERVATION RESOURCE CENTER — HISTORIC BUILDING

Map p244 (☎504-581-7032; www.prcno.org; 923 Tchoupitoulas St; ⏲9am-5pm Mon-Fri) FREE If you're interested in the architecture of New Orleans or a self-guided walking tour, then start here. The welcoming Preservation Resource Center, located inside the 1853 Leeds-Davis building, offers free pamphlets with walking-tour maps for virtually every part of town. Helpful staff shares information about everything from cycling routes to renovating a historic home. Check the website for details about the Shotgun House tour in March and the popular Holiday Home tour in December. The neighborhood brochures are also available online.

LEE CIRCLE — LANDMARK

Map p244 Called Place du Tivoli until it was renamed to honor Confederate General Robert E Lee after the Civil War, Lee Circle is a tragic example of an urban junction planned badly. The presence of a nearby elevated freeway mars what should be a pleasant roundabout. Oh well; the **Robert E Lee monument** at its center, dedicated in 1884, is attractive, and still refuses to turn its back on the North. It's within two blocks of the Civil War Museum and the National WWII Museum.

SCRAP HOUSE — MONUMENT

Map p244 (Convention Center Blvd, near John Churchill Chase St) Built entirely out of found and recycled material, this eye-catching sculpture, by artist Sally Heller, honors the victims of Hurricane Katrina. A ruined shack that resembles Dorothy's house blown off-track, the sculpture sits in a tree constructed from pieces of oil drums. Inside, a light shines for those seeking to return home. It's a powerful piece of work in an appropriate setting – across from the Convention Center, where so many refugees were displaced in the aftermath of the storm.

HARRAH'S CASINO — CASINO

Map p244 (☎504-533-6000; www.harrahsneworleans.com; 8 Canal St; ⏲24hr) You'd think all manner of vice would be welcome in the Big Easy, but Harrah's, near the foot of Canal St, doesn't get much local love. It's a big casino – 115,000 sq ft for gaming – that's part of a national chain, and it pretty much feels exactly like that. Nevertheless, people do trickle in for the casino gambling, buffet dining and hotel discounts. The casino developed a small pedestrian mall, lined with restaurants and watering holes, on nearby Fulton St.

AUDUBON EXPERIENCE

Families and travelers who *really* like animals may want to visit all three of the facilities managed by the Audubon Institute: the **aquarium** (p105) and **insectarium** (p104), in the CBD, and the **zoo** (p132); in Audubon Park in Uptown. If that's the case, buy the **Audubon Experience package** (www.auduboninstitute.org) and see all three, within 30 days, as well as an IMAX movie, at a reduced overall price of $40/30 per adult/concession.

TOP FIVE HOTEL BARS IN THE CBD

Swizzle Stick Bar (p112), Loews Hotel

Sazerac Bar (p112), Roosevelt Hotel

Bellocq (p113), Hotel Modern

Loa (p112), International House

Polo Club Lounge (p112), Windsor Court Hotel

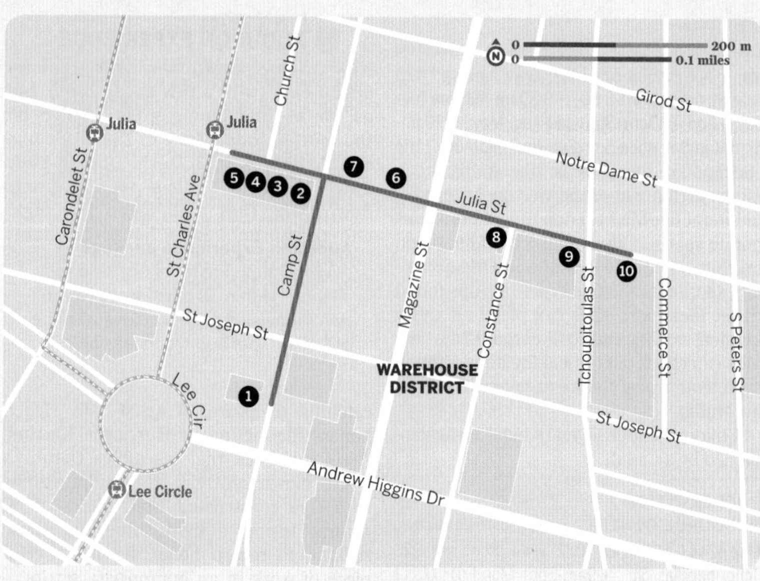

Local Life
A Gallery Walk in the Arts District

The ever-burgeoning Arts District (www.neworleansartsdistrict.com) holds the most impressive concentration of serious galleries in the city. Many are on Julia St. Drop by any of them to pick up a free map and guide to the district's art dealers. The neighborhood Art Walk is held the first Saturday of the month between 6pm and 9pm.

❶ Southern Art

Sleeping late is not a crime in New Orleans, and the Ogden Museum of Southern Art (p103), bless its heart, fully embraces this concept. Doors open 10am. So sleep off last night then head to this airy museum for local and regional art. The Southern Landscapes gallery sets an inspirational tone for a day of exploring.

❷ Art is All Around Us

The 'Food Court' collection, with its small paintings of beignets, shrimp and other Louisiana fare, will make your stomach growl at the jam-packed **Jean Bragg Gallery of Southern Art** (Map p244; ☎504-895-7375; www.jeanbragg.com; 600 Julia St; ⏰10am-5pm Mon-Sat). This welcoming gallery is a good source for the arts-and-crafts–style Newcomb Pottery, which originated at New Orleans' own Newcomb College. Bragg also deals in classic landscapes by Louisiana painters and spotlights a contemporary artist monthly.

❸ Repurpose Your Accessories

Local entrepreneur Traci L Claussen at **REpurposingNOLA Piece by Peace** (Map p244; www.repurposingnola.com; 604 Julia St; ⏰11am-5pm Mon, Thu-Sat) designs eye-catching but functional totes and designer goods from burlap coffee sacks and other found materials, all sown by local seamstresses.

❹ Take a Closer Look

Next door, check out the intriguing drawings and lively paintings of world traveler **Alex Beard** (www.alexbeardstudio.com; 608 Julia St). From puzzles to children's books to fine art, his adventures in 'abstract realism' will pull you in for a closer look.

❺ History with a Twist
New Orleans artist George Schmidt, a member of the New Leviathan Oriental Fox-trot Orchestra and the owner of the **George Schmidt Gallery** (Map p244; ☎504-592-0206; www.georgeschmidt.com; 626 Julia St; ⏲12:30-4:30pm Tue-Sat), describes himself as a 'historical' painter. Indeed, his canvases evoke the city's past, awash in a warm, romantic light. His Mardi Gras paintings are worth a look.

❻ Refuel at Carmo
Seeking healthy fare? New Orleanians praise the salads and sandwiches at tropically infused Carmo (p111), a bustling cafe with plenty of vegetarian and vegan choices. All artfully presented, of course.

❼ Last-Minute Gifts
It's hard to leave Ariodante (p114) empty-handed. This small but well-stocked gallery sells jewelry, glass works, ceramics and fine art by local and regional artists.

❽ Louisiana Landscapes
One of the district's most prominent galleries, **Arthur Roger** (Map p244; ☎504-522-1999; www.arthurrogergallery.com; 432 Julia St; ⏲10am-5pm Mon-Sat) represents several dozen artists, including Simon Gunning, whose landscapes are haunting records of Louisiana's disappearing wetlands.

❾ Going National
The impressive **Soren Christensen Gallery** (Map p244; ☎504-569-9501; www.sorengallery.com; 400 Julia St; ⏲10am-5:30pm Tue-Fri, 11am-5pm Sat) showcases the work of nationally renowned painters and sculptors. The gallery is known for its nontraditional sensibility.

❿ Studying the Coast
Gulf Coast art is the emphasis in nationally recognized **Lemieux Galleries** (Map p244; ☎504-522-5988; www.lemieuxgalleries.com; 332 Julia St; ⏲10am-6pm Mon-Sat), a good place to get a handle on the breadth of the regional arts scene. Works here include Shirley Rabe Masinter's realistic paintings of New Orleans – note the wonderful local signage – and Jon Langford's depictions of local musicians.

EATING

New Orleans' downtown isn't great for cheap eats (with a few exceptions), but as far as fine dining goes, you've hit the mother lode. Many of the city's big-name chefs – John Besh, Donald Link, Emeril LeGasse – have posh outposts downtown. That said, even the high-end restaurants here have affordable lunchtime menus if you want to sample fine food on the cheap.

CBD

RUBY SLIPPER – DOWNTOWN BREAKFAST **$**
Map p244 (www.therubyslippercafe.net; 200 Magazine St; mains $8-14; ⏲7am-2pm Mon-Fri, 8am-2pm Sat, 8am-3pm Sun) This rapidly growing local chain specializes in down-home Southern breakfasts prepared with decadent oomph. How does fried chicken on a biscuit with poached eggs and tasso cream sauce sound? Soon after the doors open in the morning this lively joint is full up with solos, families, college-age kids, renegade convention-goers and folks revving up before the party that is New Orleans.

The name is inspired by *The Wizard of Oz,* giving a nod to the call of home after Hurricane Katrina.

MOTHER'S DELI **$**
Map p244 (☎504-523-9656; www.mothersrestaurant.net; 401 Poydras St; breakfast $3-12, mains lunch & dinner $11-27; ⏲7am-10pm) At lunchtime, expect to see a line out the door. Mother's is a longtime crowd-pleaser that has drawn locals, conventioneers and tourists for years. The quality isn't what it was in its storied past, but the history and come-as-you-are hospitality make up the difference. Mother's invented the 'debris' po'boy and serves the justifiably famous 'Ferdi Special' – a po'boy loaded up with ham, roast beef and debris.

In general, though, its sandwiches don't compare with other city stalwarts. Breakfast is your best bet – it's standard meat-and-eggs stuff, but brilliantly done and served in enormous portions. The turtle soup, available on Saturdays, is also recommended.

DOMENICA ITALIAN $$

Map p244 (☎504-648-6020; 123 Baronne St; mains $13-30; ⊙11am-11pm;) With its wooden refectory tables, white lights and soaring ceiling, Domenica feels like a village trattoria gone posh. The 'rustic' pizza pies at this lively, often-recommended spot are loaded with nontraditional but enticing toppings (clams, prosciutto, smoked pork) and are big enough that solo diners should have a slice or two left over.

Pizzas, beer and wines are half-price during happy hour (from 2pm to 5pm).

More-substantial fare includes creative pastas, smoky meats and an intriguing lineup of soft and hard cheeses. Domenica is run by partners John Besh and Alon Shaya, the latter a Jewish chef who prepares the occasional Passover dinner with an Italian touch.

JOHNNY SANCHEZ MEXICAN $$

Map p244 (☎504-304-6615; www.johnnysanchezrestaurant.com; 930 Poydras St; lunch $8-22, dinner $8-28; ⊙11am-10pm Sun-Thu, to midnight Fri, 5-11pm Sat) Day of the Dead meets vintage New Orleans at this stylish new venture that has people chattering, and chowing down with gusto. A modern taqueria from chefs Aaron Sanchez and John Besh, the restaurant serves traditional Mexican dishes with innovative flavors, sourced from local fishers and farms. Highlights include crispy brussels sprouts, lamb enchiladas and tacos.

And oh, those tacos, lined with savory fillings ranging from *carne asada* to pork belly, goat and shrimp. Most dishes are easily shared, making this lively place a great option for small groups.

LE PAVILLON BREAKFAST BUFFET

Business folk know that one of the best breakfasts downtown is the hearty buffet at **Le Pavillon** (Map p244; www.lepavillon.com; 833 Poydras Ave; breakfast buffet $20; ⊙6:30-10am Mon-Fri, to 11:30am Sat). Stroll past the man in the top hat, walk straight through the opulent lobby and glide into the Crystal Room where omelets, apple-smoked bacon, biscuits and gravy, and Bananas Foster waffles stand ready to shred your diet.

DRAGO'S SEAFOOD RESTAURANT SEAFOOD $$

Map p244 (☎504-584-3911; www.dragosrestaurant.com; 2 Poydras St; lunch mains $12-20, dinner $18-52; ⊙11am-10pm) Charbroiled oysters at Drago's? Heaven on the half shell. This sprawling restaurant in the downtown Riverside Hilton is loaded with tourists, but oyster creations are the real deal thanks to Drago Cvitanovich, a Croatian immigrant who brought a heady knowledge of shellfish from the Dalmatian Coast to the Gulf. Oysters drip with butter, garlic, parmesan and their own juices after kissing an open fire.

The surf-and-turf menu is alright (we like the 'Shuckee Duckee' – a duck breast topped with oysters and cream sauce), but the oysters are the real draw here.

CAFÉ ADELAIDE CREOLE $$

Map p244 (☎504-595-3305; www.cafeadelaide.com; 300 Poydras St; lunch mains $14-18, dinner $24-30; ⊙breakfast & lunch Mon-Fri, brunch Sat & Sun, dinner 5:30-9pm Sun-Thu, to 10pm Fri & Sat) This jazzy restaurant is a Brennan family tribute to their endearingly eccentric aunt Adelaide. We love the pop-art portraits of her that hang above the dining room. The motto here is the namesake's own, 'Eat, drink and carry on,' a philosophy realized by haute Creole cuisine – shrimp and tasso corndogs, cast-iron Louisiana blue crab with gnocchi, and double pork chop with an absinthe bbq sauce.

It's all as good as it sounds, and the attached Swizzle Stick is one of downtown's better bars.

★RESTAURANT AUGUST CREOLE $$$

Map p244 (☎504-299-9777; www.restaurantaugust.com; 301 Tchoupitoulas St; lunch $23-36, dinner $33-42; ⊙5-10pm daily, 11am-2pm Fri & Sun;) For a little romance, reserve a table at Restaurant August, the flagship of chef John Besh's nine-restaurant empire. This converted 19th-century tobacco warehouse, with its flickering candles and warm, soft shades, earns a nod for most aristocratic dining room in New Orleans, but somehow manages to be both intimate and lively. Delicious meals take you to another level of gastronomic perception.

The signature speckled trout Pontchartrain is layered with lump crabmeat, wild mushrooms and hollandaise. The five-course, two-hour tasting menu ($97 per person, with wine pairings $147) makes local foodies weep. There's also a prix-fixe lunch ($20.15) with various options. Solo diners do just fine at the easygoing but professional bar.

BON TON CAFÉ CAJUN $$$

Map p244 (☎504-524-3386; www.thebontoncafe.com; 401 Magazine St; mains $17-45; ⏰11am-2pm & 5-9pm Mon-Fri) Whoa, where did all these people come from? Bon Ton looks low-key and stuffy beneath its Magazine St awnings, but step through the door at lunchtime and you'd think half of downtown is here. This classy but sassy joint, an old-style Cajun restaurant that's been open for half a century, maintains an old-school menu of redfish, rice, steak and lots of butter.

Don't pass on the rum-soaked bread pudding.

Warehouse District

★COCHON BUTCHER SANDWICHES $

Map p244 (www.cochonbutcher.com; 930 Tchoupitoulas St; mains $10-12; ⏰10am-10pm Mon-Thu, to 11pm Fri & Sat, to 4pm Sun) Tucked behind the slightly more formal Cochon, this newly expanded sandwich and meat shop calls itself a 'swine bar & deli.' We call it our favorite sandwich shop in the city, if not the entire South. From the convivial lunch crowds to the savory sandwiches to the fun-loving cocktails, this welcoming place from local restaurant maestro Donald Link encapsulates the best of New Orleans.

The sandwiches – pork belly, bacon melt, smoked turkey – are stuffed with abandon and best enjoyed with one of the palate-pleasing sides. Easygoing but efficient staff and wallet-friendly prices round out this gastronomic holiday. The North Carolina–style barbecue is succulent but messy, and the cold roast beef is oh-so tender.

★PECHE SEAFOOD GRILL SEAFOOD $

Map p244 (☎504-522-1744; www.pecherestaurant.com; 800 Magazine St; small plates $9-14, mains $14-27; ⏰11am-10pm Mon-Thu, to 11pm Fri & Sat) We're not sure why, but there is a split opinion locally about this latest venture from Donald Link. Put us firmly in the lick-the-plate and order-more category. Coastal seafood dishes are prepared simply here, but unexpected flourishes – whether from salt, spices or magic – sear the deliciousness onto your tastebuds. The vibe is convivial, with a happy, stylish crowd sipping and savoring among the exposed-brick walls and wooden beams.

A large whole fish, made for sharing, is a signature preparation, but we recommend starting with the smoked tuna dip and the fried bread with sea salt. No reservations? Try one of the two bars – but arrive early.

CARMO HEALTH FOOD, SANDWICHES $

Map p244 (☎504-875-4132; www.cafecarmo.com; 527 Julia St; lunch $9-12, dinner $9-15; ⏰11am-3pm Mon, to 10pm Tue & Wed, to 11pm Thu-Sat; 🅥) Need a break from boudin balls, red beans and rice, and heavy cream sauces? Step into this no-fuss cafe for creative salads, sandwiches, raw fish creations, and vegetarian and vegan dishes – most with a tropical spin. The popular Rico comes as a salad or sandwich with pulled pork or vegan 'meat' plus cheese, avocado, salsa and a kicky sauce. Numerous fruit juices are available, too. Order at the counter.

COCHON CAJUN $$

Map p244 (☎504-588-2123; www.cochonrestaurant.com; 930 Tchoupitoulas St; small plates $8-14, mains $19-26; ⏰11am-10pm Mon-Thu, to 11pm Sat & Sun) The phrase 'everything but the squeal' springs to mind when perusing the menu at Cochon, regularly named one of New Orleans' best restaurants. At this bustling eatery Donald Link pays homage to his Cajun culinary roots, and the menu revels in most parts of the pig, including pork cheeks with creole cream cheese and fried boudin. Other meats include rabbit, alligator and oysters.

The food could be overly rich but ends up being hearty and smoky without inducing a food coma.

HERBSAINT MODERN LOUISIANAN $$

Map p244 (☎504-524-4114; www.herbsaint.com; 701 St Charles Ave; lunch mains $14-20, dinner $27-30; ⏰11:30am-10pm Mon-Fri, from 5:30pm Sat) Herbsaint's duck and andouille gumbo might be the best restaurant gumbo in town. The rest of the food ain't too bad either – it's very much modern bistro fare with dibs and dabs of Louisiana influence, courtesy of owner Donald Link. Currently, the fried catfish comes with green rice and chilies, while the shrimp and grits are joined with tasso-stewed collard greens.

The dining room, warmly lit by windows, is especially pleasant for lunch. For a salad, try the poached farms chicken over greens with almond-picada vinaigrette – tasty! There's also a limited bistro menu available from 1:30pm to 5pm. Reservations are a good idea for dinner.

ROCK-N-SAKE SUSHI $$

Map p244 (www.rocknsake.com; 823 Fulton St; sushi $2-20, mains $16-28; ⌚5-10pm Tue, Wed & Sun, to 11pm Thu, 11am-2:30pm & 5:30pm-midnight Fri, 5pm-midnight Sat) Rock-n-Sake can be off-putting, especially on weekend nights: it's perhaps a little too hip; the sushi chefs can look sullen; and the music can be too rockin' if you're in the mood for relaxing. In other words, it's a scene. But this shouldn't detract from the fact that Rock-n-Sake serves some of the best sushi around. To enjoy it, pop in early.

The popular New Orleans roll pays homage to the city with spicy crawfish, spicy tuna and chili-mayo sauce. And those sullen sushi chefs? They open up pretty quickly if you ask about the rolls.

EMERIL'S CREOLE $$$

Map p244 (☎504-528-9393; www.emerils.com; 800 Tchoupitoulas St; lunch mains $12-25, dinner $24-38; ⌚6-10pm daily, 11:30am-2pm Mon-Fri) The noise level can be deafening, but Emeril's remains one of New Orleans' finest dining establishments. The kitchen's strengths are best appreciated by ordering the daily specials. The full-on Emeril experience includes partaking of the cheese board with a selection from the restaurant's eclectic wine list. The bar is a favorite with visiting celebrities and is a fun see-and-be-scene local spot.

DRINKING & NIGHTLIFE

Downtown may look like a nightlife wasteland, but there's some great live music peppered about the office blocks. More pertinently, New Orleans, while home to many great dives, can lack in the hip lounge stakes; the CBD works to remedy this situation.

CBD

SWIZZLE STICK BAR BAR

Map p244 (☎504-595-3305; www.cafeadelaide.com; 300 Poydras St; ⌚11am-11pm) This swell bar is the tipsy companion to Café Adelaide, and its good-time vibe seems poised to spill into the lobby of the adjoining Loews Hotel. A dash of adult fun massaged with heavy levels of quirkiness, it's a snazzy spot for an after-work drink or pre- or post-convention tipple.

Cocktail names reflect the bar's sense of fun: Wild Magnolia, Bitter Kitten, A Little Soused on the Prairie. Happy hour is from 3pm to 6pm daily. Depending on the crowd, the Swizzle Stick may stay open until 1am or 2am.

SAZERAC BAR BAR

Map p244 (☎504-636-1891; http://therooseveltneworleans.com; 523 Gravier St; ⌚5pm-late Tue-Fri, from 9pm Sat) Walking through Hotel Roosevelt's chandeliered lobby and into the polished glow of the Sazerac Bar, you feel as if you've stepped back into a well-heeled era of hushed wheeling and dealing and high-society drinking. With its art-deco murals, subdued lighting and plush couches, the Sazerac Bar is an inviting alternative to rowdy French Quarter bars nearby.

So sidle up to the bar, order a sazerac (created in New Orleans) and gossip like it's 1929.

POLO CLUB LOUNGE BAR

Map p244 (☎504-523-6000; 300 Gravier St; ⌚11:30am-midnight Mon-Thu, to 1am Fri & Sat, 11am-midnight Sun) Need to prep for the fox hunt? Try this bar in the Windsor Court Hotel. The overstuffed chairs, tweedy bookshelves, nightly jazz and soft clink of hushed merry-making are meant to evoke aristocratic old England. A wine cobbler or port, anyone? Those looking for trendier libations can check out the latest in mixology at the Cocktail Bar off the 1st-floor lobby.

Live jazz happens Tuesdays through Saturdays from 6pm.

CIRCLE BAR BAR

Map p244 (☎504-588-2616; 1032 St Charles Ave; ⌚4pm-late, shows 10pm) Picture a grand Victorian mansion, all disheveled and punk, and you've caught the essence of this strangely inviting place to drink. Live acts of varying quality – folk, rock and indie – occupy the central space, where a little fireplace and lots of grime speak to the coziness of one of New Orleans' great dives. The house teeters on Lee Circle, across from a somber statue of General Lee.

LOA LOUNGE

Map p244 (☎504-553-9550; www.ihhotel.com/bar.html; 221 Camp St; ⌚5pm-late) Off the lobby of the fashionable International House hotel, Loa is a stylish place to sip a well-crafted cocktail. Everyone looks good bathed in candlelight. If you practice voodoo, or you're after a full-coverage religious plan, you can leave an offering at the voodoo altar on your way out. Loa, if you're wondering, are voodoo spirits.

Warehouse District

RUSTY NAIL BAR

Map p244 (☎504-525-5515; www.therustynail.biz; 1100 Constance St; ⊙4pm-1am Mon-Thu, 2pm-3am Fri, noon-3am Sat, to 1am Sun) The Rusty Nail is a dive bar for newbies. Yeah, it lurks in a dark spot under the I-90 overpass, but it's also flanked by loft complexes that look downright trendy. The twinkling white lights are kinda cute, too and, heck, on Thursdays they host a trivia night. Come on in, have a beer or a scotch (there's a long list) and kick back.

Inside, it's dark and small; Zeppelin's probably playing; a couple of guys are watching the game, and maybe a couple of other guys are setting up to play music in the corner. Outside, look for food trucks Wednesday through Saturday nights.

LUCY'S RETIRED SURFERS BAR BAR

Map p244 (☎504-523-8995; www.lucysretiredsurfers.com; 701 Tchoupitoulas St; ⊙11am-late Mon-Fri, 10am-late Sat & Sun) There's always somebody sipping a drink at one of the sidewalk tables at Lucy's, a beach-bum kinda spot oddly plopped in the middle of downtown. It draws the 20- and 30-something crowd, but it's also decent for an after-work drink. Have something colorful and cold, and we'll see you at the next bar. Closing time varies.

BELLOCQ COCKTAIL BAR

Map p244 (www.thehotelmodern.com/bellocq; 936 St Charles Ave; ⊙5pm-midnight Mon-Thu, 4pm-2am Fri & Sat, to 10pm Sun) White candles, plush Victorian chairs, intimate nooks, deep purples and blacks – Bellocq has a boudoir style well-suited to upscale vampires in the mood for brooding. Named for a pre-prohibition maritime photographer who secretly snapped photos of local madams, Bellocq pays homage to the golden age of drink with 'cobblers' and other 1800s-inspired cocktails.

On Lee Circle, the bar is part of the trendy Hotel Modern.

IN WINO VERITAS

Topping our list of New Orleans acronyms, the **Wine Institute of New Orleans** (WINO; Map p244; www.winoschool.com; 610 Tchoupitoulas St; ⊙2-10pm Sun-Tue, to midnight Wed-Sat) is the place to spend an evening wine tasting or learning more about a certain varietal or wine region ($40). But we're going to assume you're simply keen to try some very good wines. Lucky you. Pop by to sample 120 different types of vino on tap, plus a fair amount of pâté and cheese.

CAPDEVILLE BAR

Map p244 (www.capdevillenola.com; 520 Capdeville St; ⊙11am-2:30pm & 5-11pm Mon-Thu, 11am-midnight Fri & Sat) The compact Capdeville is an upscale pub with retro roots – check out that jukebox and the album covers – on the 1st floor of the Intellectual Property building just off Lafayette Sq. After a stroll past the Julia St galleries or a date in the Federal District Court, pop in for a whiskey or Guinness at the elevated bar.

BARCADIA BAR

Map p244 (www.barcadianeworleans.com; 601 Tchoupitoulas St; ⊙11am-2am) This sprawling, high-energy bar celebrates the games of your youth in a big and flashy way. There's life-size Jenga, towering Connect Four, air hockey, pop-a-shot and loads of '80s arcade games. Nope, it's not relaxing, but it is a potentially fun way to mingle.

☆ ENTERTAINMENT

The following venues are on S Peters St, within walking distance of several good restaurants, hotels and bars. To make a night of it, grab dinner before a show then see what's happening later on.

HOWLIN' WOLF LIVE MUSIC

Map p244 (☎504-522-9653; www.thehowlinwolf.com; 907 S Peters St; cover free-$35; ⊙hours vary) One of New Orleans' best venues for live blues, alt-rock, jazz and roots music, the Howlin' Wolf draws a lively crowd. It started out booking local progressive bands, but has become a stop for bigger-name touring acts such as Hank Williams III and Allison

Krauss. The club is now offering comedy acts on Tuesdays and Thursdays.

REPUBLIC NEW ORLEANS LIVE MUSIC

Map p244 (☎504-528-8282; www.republicnola.com; 828 S Peters St; cover $10-50; ⊙hours vary) Republic showcases some pretty awesome live acts, including George Clinton and other good funk and blues talent, but it's also a place where teenagers from the 'burbs come to behave very badly. There's your conundrum: your night may consist of a potentially great show, but there's a good chance it will also include screeching, jostling teens. Most shows start at 10pm.

FOUNTAIN LOUNGE LIVE MUSIC

Map p244 (☎504-648-5486; www.therooseveltneworleans.com; 130 Roosevelt Way; ⊙4-10pm Tue-Thu & Sun, to midnight Fri & Sat) Recently revamped and now ever so chic, the Fountain Lounge inside the Roosevelt Hotel is an upscale place to listen to live music, from modern jazz to cool lounge classics. Performances Wednesday through Saturday. Check online for times.

SHOPPING

This part of town is chiefly concerned with business and art. It's not good for window shopping, but if you know what you're looking for, you may find yourself zeroing in on that perfect little specialty shop. Our gallery walking tour (p108) recommends art galleries and indie shops in the Arts District.

ARIODANTE CRAFTS

Map p244 (www.ariodantegallery.com; 535 Julia St; ⊙10am-5pm Mon-Sat) On Julia St for 25 years in 2015, this small but well-stocked gallery sells jewelry, glass works, ceramics and fine art by local and regional artists. It's a fun place to browse.

MEYER THE HATTER ACCESSORIES

Map p244 (☎504-525-1048; www.meyerthehatter.com; 120 St Charles Ave; ⊙10am-5:45pm Mon-Sat) This cluttered shop, a half-block from Canal St, has a truly astounding inventory of world-class hats. Biltmore, Dobbs, and Stetson are just a few of the milliners represented. Fur felts dominate in fall and winter, and flimsy straw hats take over in spring and summer. The selection of lids for the ladies seemed a wee bit skimpy on our last visit.

SHOPS AT CANAL PLACE MALL

Map p244 (☎504-522 9200; www.theshopsatcanalplace.com; 333 Canal St; ⊙10am-7pm Mon-Sat, noon-7pm Sun) No, you didn't come to New Orleans to shop at Ann Taylor, Brooks Brothers, J Crew or Saks Fifth Avenue, but if someone spills a hurricane over your last white shirt or you forgot to pack your heels, this glossy mall will be a blessing.

OUTLET COLLECTION AT RIVERWALK MALL

Map p244 (☎504-522-1555; www.riverwalkmarketplace.com; 500 Port of New Orleans Pl; ⊙10am-9pm Mon-Sat, to 7pm Sun) After an $82 million renovation, the Riverwalk re-opened in 2014 as a collection of outlet stores. Got your walking shoes? The mall is half a mile long, stretching from Poydras to Julia St along the river. Retailers include Coach, Forever 21, the Guess Factory Store and Neiman Marcus Last Call Studio.

Garden, Lower Garden & Central City

GARDEN & LOWER GARDEN DISTRICTS | CENTRAL CITY | GARDEN & LOWER GARDEN

Neighborhood Top Five

❶ Sipping 25¢ martinis and savoring bread pudding soufflé at ever-stylish **Commander's Palace** (p124) is one of the most enjoyable ways to live like a local. Walk off the meal with a sidewalk stroll past lush lawns and stately mansions.

❷ Learning about the past at **Lafayette Cemetery No 1** (p117), where crypts hold tragic tales.

❸ Studying BBQ, hot sauce and absinthe at the **Southern Food & Beverage Museum** (p119), followed by a meal at adjoining Purloo or **Cafe Reconcile** (p124).

❹ Wandering past paintings of local musicians and Mardi Gras festivities at the **McKenna Museum of African American Art** (p121).

❺ Popping into clothing boutiques, art galleries, music shops and day spas on **Magazine Street** (p126).

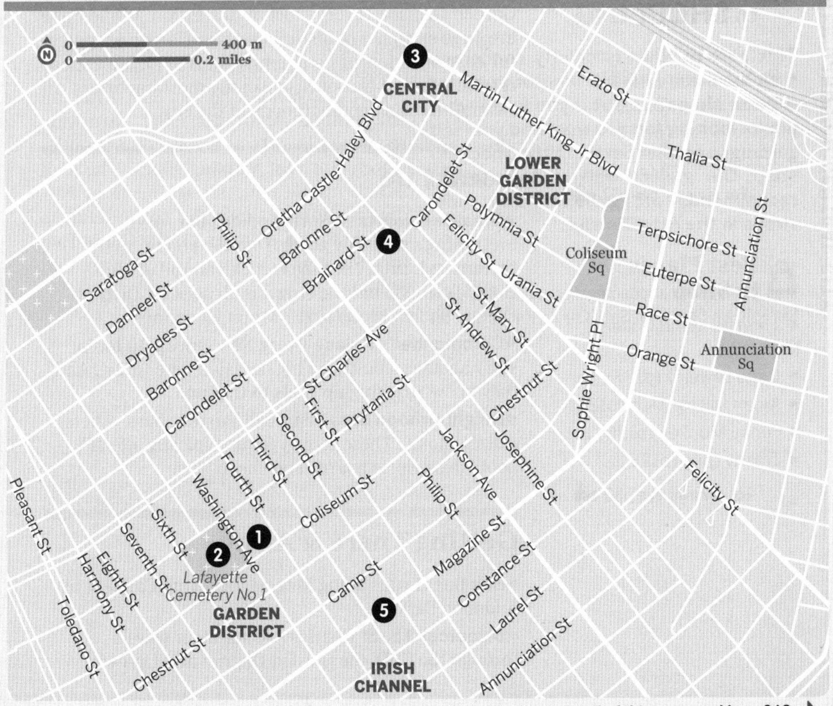

For more detail of this area see Map p248

Lonely Planet's Top Tip

Avoid parking hassles on Magazine St by using public transportation. From the French Quarter and CBD, hop on the St Charles Ave streetcar at Canal St in the morning, then catch bus 11 on Magazine St to return to your hotel in the afternoon.

Best Places to Eat

- Commander's Palace (p124)
- Coquette (p123)
- Surrey's Juice Bar (p121)
- District: Donuts Sliders Brew (p121)
- Sucré (p121)

For reviews, see p71

Best Places to Drink

- Bulldog (p125)
- Root Squared (p125)
- Rendezvous (p125)
- Balcony Bar (p125)
- Tracey's (p122)

For reviews, see p77

Best Places to Shop

- Thomas Mann Gallery I/O (p127)
- Gogo Jewelry (p127)
- Aidan Gill for Men (p126)
- Funky Monkey (p126)
- Trashy Diva (p126)

For reviews, see p80

Explore Garden, Lower Garden & Central City

The Garden District, Lower Garden District and Central City are three distinct neighborhoods, each offering a different experience. Two days is enough time to explore all three.

The Garden District exudes Old Southern excess with its historic mansions, lush greenery, chichi bistros and upscale boutiques. Your first morning, soak up the mixture of tropical fecund beauty and white-columned old-money elegance on a walking tour where stately homes and colorful gardens shimmer beside sidewalks bursting with roots. The Garden District is a rectangular grid bounded by St Charles Ave, Jackson Ave, Magazine St and Louisiana Ave. Magazine St and St Charles Ave are the main commercial thoroughfares; Prytania St is the most scenic (and the quickest).

Between the CBD and the Garden District, the Lower Garden District is somewhat like the Garden District but not quite as posh. Here the houses are pleasant, not palatial. There's a studenty vibe about, and plenty of bars and restaurants for those with university-stunted wallets and university-sized appetites for fun. The Lower Garden District is upriver (in this case, south) from the CBD. Magazine St is the main thoroughfare.

Central City, which lies between the CBD and Lower Garden District, is very much in transition. While there are large stretches of blight here, there is also a wonderful concentration of community activist organizations rebuilding what was once one of the most important African American neighborhoods in the city.

Local Life

- **Breakfast joints** At Surrey's Juice Bar (p121), everything's seriously good, from the boudin to the shrimp and grits. The vibe is rock and roll at Slim Goodie's (p123), but the crowd is all ages. At District: Donuts Sliders Brew (p121)? Mmm, doughnuts.
- **Commander's Palace** Every New Orleanian has a story about celebrating a big occasion here (p124). And they know 'dressing up' adds to the fun.
- **Neighborhood bars** Some call 'em dive bars, others call 'em home. These scruffy joints typically offer TV, pool tables, darts boards and cheap beer.

Getting There & Away

- **Bus** Bus 11 runs along Magazine St from Canal St to Audubon Park.
- **Streetcar** The St Charles Ave streetcar travels through the CBD, the Garden District and Uptown.

JORG HACKEMANN/SHUTTERSTOCK ©

TOP SIGHT
LAFAYETTE CEMETERY NO 1

A thick wall surrounds a battalion of gray crypts at this moody place, a tiny bastion of history, tragedy and Southern gothic charm in the heart of the Garden District. It's a place filled with stories – of German and Irish immigrants, deaths by yellow fever, social societies doing right by their dead – that pulls the living into New Orleans' long, troubled past.

Established in 1833 by the former City of Lafayette, the cemetery is divided by two intersecting footpaths that form a cross. Look out for the structures built by fraternal organizations such as the Jefferson Fire Company No 22, which took care of its members and their families in large shared crypts. Some of the wealthier family tombs were built of marble, with elaborate detail rivaling the finest architecture in the district, but most tombs were constructed simply of inexpensive plastered brick. You'll notice many German and Irish names on the above-ground graves, testifying that immigrants were devastated by 19th-century yellow-fever epidemics.

The cemetery filled to capacity within decades of its opening (more than 10,000 people are buried here), and before the surrounding neighborhood reached its greatest affluence. By 1872 the prestigious Metairie Cemetery had opened and its opulent grounds began to appeal to those with truly extravagant and flamboyant tastes.

In July 1995 author Anne Rice staged her own funeral here. She hired a horse-drawn hearse and a brass band to play dirges, and wore an antique wedding dress as she lay down in a coffin. The event coincided with the release of one of her novels.

The spell here is broken the moment a black-and-white-clad waiter strides past the cemetery's grated gates, hurrying to his shift at Commander's Palace restaurant next door. He's a vivid reminder that time marches on and that, yes, perhaps you are ready for lunch and a 25¢ martini. This is New Orleans after all.

DON'T MISS

- ➡ Social society crypts
- ➡ Cemetery tour (p119)

PRACTICALITIES

- ➡ Map p248
- ➡ Washington Ave, at Prytania St
- ➡ 7am-2:30pm Mon-Fri, to 2pm Sun

SIGHTS

Garden & Lower Garden Districts

Leafy, lovely and very walkable, the Garden and Lower Garden Districts are good places to soak up 19th-century architecture, bright flowers and the haunting trees that give this city its distinctive, subtropical character. Magazine St is great for window-shopping and restaurant- and bar-hopping.

LAFAYETTE CEMETERY NO 1 CEMETERY
See p117.

IRISH CHANNEL NEIGHBORHOOD
Map p248 The name Irish Channel is a bit of a misnomer. Although this historic neighborhood, which borders the Garden Districts, was settled by poor Irish immigrants fleeing the 1840s potato famine, many German and black residents have coexisted here in a truly multicultural gumbo. This is still a working-class cluster of shotgun houses and you may not want to walk around alone at night, but in general it's pleasant for ambling. Come St Patty's Day, a big block party takes over Constance St in front of Parasol's.

On a historical note, wage-earning Irish were widely regarded as more economical than slaves, particularly for dangerous assignments, since it cost nothing to replace an Irish laborer who died on the job.

HOUSE OF BROEL HISTORIC BUILDING
Map p248 (☎504-522-2220; www.houseofbroel.com; 2220 St Charles Ave; adult/child under 12yr $10/5; ⌚tours 11am-3pm Mon-Fri) The House of Broel, built in the 1850s, is a bit of a funhouse. The entire two-story building was elevated in 1884 to allow for the construction of a new 1st floor. This was done so that the new owner could throw elaborate parties for his three daughters in a more spa-

LOCAL KNOWLEDGE

TOP HISTORIC SITES & SPORTS BARS

Melissa Smith, author of *Historic Photos of New Orleans*, archivist at Amistad Research Center and cowriter on the fan site www.chicksinthehuddle.com, shares local favorites.

Top Historic Sites

Bayou St John It's a great area to visit. Not only is there NOMA (p146) and the Gardens (p146), but you also have a lot of great history. Before it was filled in, it was an outlet between the lake and the river. Prior to the Colonial period, the bayou was used heavily by American Indians for trading, and some of our oldest structures are actually in that part of town. It's where the Pitot House is, as well as Ursuline High School. I find it one of the most beautiful areas of town.

Cemeteries So much of the area's history is in its cemeteries. They speak to you in many ways – more, at times, than the written word can say. Some of the groups I've studied over time are benevolent societies. Their crypts tend to be in the Mid-City cemeteries (p148), where you have wonderful names like Oddfellows Rest and the Katrina Memorial.

Cabildo (p62) It's one of the oldest buildings in the city. It was also the seat of government. The upstairs promenade is just breathtaking when you can see the whole city. It feels like history comes alive when you walk in there – not because it's a museum but because of what it represents across the board. It's also just a beautiful, beautiful building.

Best Bars for Watching the Saints

Cooter Brown's (p139) It has so many televisions and really good bar food. It's a great atmosphere, and is one of the few bars in town that attracts a cross-section of society, whether it's student, local or tourist.

Lucy's Retired Surfers Bar (p113) A lot of Saints players hang out there, so that tends to be a hot spot as well to watch Saints games.

cious setting. Current owner Bonnie Broel, a long-time New Orleans dress designer and fashion maven, displays some of her ballgowns as well as her astounding collection of themed, highly detailed dollhouses.

On the tour, note the home's black marble fireplace and the original mirror framed by carved tobacco leaves. As for the dollhouses, the Best Little Whorehouse in Texas includes a lady of the night on a teeny tiny bed.

The house also hosts weddings and other events.

ST VINCENT'S INFANT ASYLUM — HISTORIC BUILDING

Map p248 (1507 Magazine St) This large red-brick orphanage was built in 1864 with assistance from federal troops occupying the city. It helped relieve the overcrowded orphanages filled with youngsters of all races who had lost their parents to epidemics and the Civil War. The orphanage is now a budget guesthouse, but is not otherwise open to the public.

GOODRICH-STANLEY HOUSE — HISTORIC BUILDING

Map p248 (1729 Coliseum St) This historic home was built in 1837 by jeweler William M Goodrich. Goodrich sold the house to the British-born merchant Henry Hope Stanley, whose adopted son, Henry Morton Stanley, went on to gain fame for finding the missing Scottish missionary, Dr David Livingstone, and uttering the legendary question, 'Dr Livingstone, I presume?' He was subsequently knighted and founded the Congo Free States. The house originally stood a few blocks away and was moved to its current spot in 1981. Not open to the public.

GRACE KING HOUSE — HISTORIC BUILDING

Map p248 (1749 Coliseum St) Behind a handsome wrought-iron fence, this papaya-hued house was named for the Louisiana historian and author who lived here from 1905 to 1932. It was built in 1847 by banker Frederick Rodewald and features Greek Ionic columns on the lower floor as well as Corinthian columns above. Not open to the public.

⊙ Central City

Some areas here can get dodgy after dark. At night, park close to your destination on a well-traveled street.

ACTIVITIES IN GARDEN, LOWER GARDEN & CENTRAL CITY

After a few hard days of getting stuffed with rich Creole food and sloshed on pints of NOLA Blonde, it's time to treat yourself to a little cleansing experience at the **Belladonna Day Spa** (Map p248; ☎504-891-4393; www.belladonnadayspa.com; 2900 Magazine St; ⌚9am-6pm Mon & Tue, Fri & Sat, to 8pm Wed & Thu, to 5pm Sun). When you're done spoiling yourself, take home fragrant lotions and colorful cleansers for some home-grown renewal.

The nonprofit **Save Our Cemeteries** (☎504-525-3377; www.saveourcemeteries.org; tours $15-20 per person) leads daily tours of Lafayette Cemetery No 1 daily at 10:30am. The entire proceeds are used for cemetery restoration and documentation. Reservations are recommended because spots are limited. Tours meet at the Washington Ave entrance. Children under 12 years enter for free.

SOUTHERN FOOD & BEVERAGE MUSEUM — MUSEUM

Map p248 (☎504-569-0405; www.southernfood.org; 1504 Oretha Castle Haley Blvd; adult/child under 12yr $10/free; ⌚11am-5:30pm Thu-Mon) You don't have to be a gourmet or mixologist to enjoy this made-from-scratch museum, which celebrates Southern cooking and cocktails with exhibits sourced from every state south of the Mason-Dixon. The well-stocked **Museum of the American Cocktail** displays old elixir bottles, cocktail-making tools, tiki glasses and a picture of an impressively mustachioed bartender. In the back corner, the **La Galerie Absinthe** recreates the 1895 Old Absinthe House, with artifacts spotlighting the mysterious spirit. Check the website for details about cooking classes in the demo kitchen.

In 2014 the museum moved to the former Dryades Market, which was built in 1849. The market was part of a bustling commercial hub catering to African Americans, and Jewish, German and Italian immigrants.

The attached pan-Southern restaurant, Purloo (p124), plans to offer made-to-order food to visitors, who may want to sample regional specialties as they explore the museum.

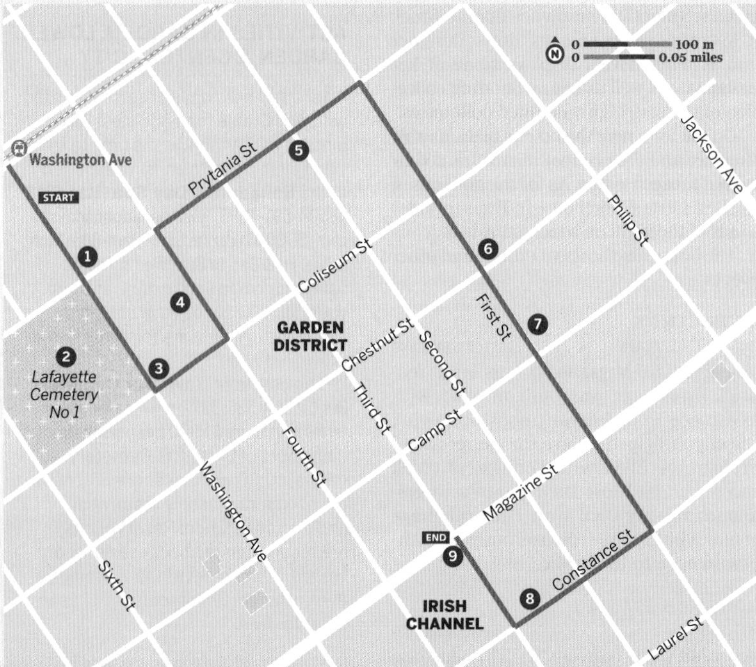

Neighborhood Walk
Green, Green New Orleans

START THE RINK
FINISH TRACEY'S
LENGTH 1 MILE; TWO TO THREE HOURS

Soak up the 'green' of New Orleans from the historic, magnolia-shaded streets of the Garden District to the Emerald Island heritage of the Irish Channel.

From the CBD, take the St Charles Ave streetcar (p135) to Washington Ave. Walk one block south to **1 The Rink**, an 1880s skating rink turned 21st-century mini-mall. **2 Lafayette Cemetery No 1** (p117), one of the city's oldest cemeteries, stands across Prytania St, as does the dapper **3 Commander's Palace** (p124), the elegant crown jewel of the Brennan restaurant empire. Pop in for a 25¢ martini at lunchtime, but remember – no shorts allowed.

Around the corner at 1448 Fourth St is **4 Colonel Robert Short's House**, designed by architect Henry Howard. Once the home of a Confederate officer, it's an exemplary double-gallery home with fine cast-iron details, including a cast-iron cornstalk fence.

Continue to the **5 Women's Guild of the New Orleans Opera Association** at 2504 Prytania, a Greek revival home designed by William Freret in the late 1850s. Turn right onto First St where you'll find **6 Joseph Carroll House** at No 1315, a beautiful center-hall house with double galleries laced with cast iron.

7 Rosegate, at 1239 First St, is the former residence of author Anne Rice. The spinner of vampire tales lived in the 1857 home for many years, and regularly invited fans to tour inside. Which, by the way, is beautiful but disappointingly free of bats, organ music and Tom Cruise mooning about in a frilly jacket. It's no longer open to the public.

South of First St, homes quickly become shotgun shacks. This is the Irish Channel, home to working-class Irish, Germans and African Americans. Head down First St, turn right into Constance and walk along until you come to **8 Parasol's** (p122) on the corner of Third St and **9 Tracey's** (p122), on the corner of Third and Magazine Sts, two quintessential New Orleans neighborhood bars.

MCKENNA MUSEUM OF AFRICAN AMERICAN ART MUSEUM

Map p248 (☎504-586-7432; www.themckenna-museum.com; 2003 Carondelet St; adult/student & senior $5/3; ⊙11am-4pm Thu-Sat, by appointment Tue & Wed) Although the displayed work at this beautiful two-story institution comes from all over the African diaspora, most of it is created by local New Orleans artists. Images of Mardi Gras and the New Orleans music scene are highlights. The artwork is part of a collection amassed during some 30 years of collecting by Dr Dwight McKenna. Real standouts are the temporary exhibitions, such as 2014's *Queens Rule!*, a celebration of Mardi Gras Indian queens. Check the website for details of the packed calendar.

ASHÉ CULTURAL ARTS CENTER ARTS CENTER

Map p248 (☎504-569-9070; www.ashecac.org; 1712 Oretha Castle-Haley Blvd) An important anchor for the local African American community, Ashé (from a Yoruba word that could loosely be translated as 'Amen') regularly showcases performances, art and photography exhibitions, movie screenings and lectures with an African, African American or Caribbean focus, and beyond. Check the online calendar for upcoming events. The on-site **Diaspora Boutique** (☎504-569-9070; www.ashecacboutique.com; 1712 Oretha C Haley Blvd; ⊙10am-6pm Mon-Sat), which stocks clothing, earrings and crafts, is also worth a look.

EATING

Foodies can pick and choose from studenty Mexican burrito shops, old-line Creole cafes, great sandwich shops and some truly excellent breakfast joints. With a high student population, there's a decidedly young, hip and economical bent to the food on offer in the Lower Garden. There's not as much variety in the Garden District – just one of the most storied restaurants in the country.

Garden & Lower Garden

★SURREY'S JUICE BAR AMERICAN $

Map p248 (☎504-524-3828; 1418 Magazine St; breakfast & lunch $6-13; ⊙8am-3pm) Surrey's makes a simple bacon-and-egg sandwich taste – and look – like the most delicious breakfast you've ever been served. And you know what? It probably is the best. There's boudin biscuits; eggs scrambled with salmon; biscuits swimming in salty sausage gravy; and a shrimp, grits and bacon dish that should be illegal. And the juice, as you might guess, is blessedly fresh. Cash only.

★DISTRICT: DONUTS SLIDERS BREW DOUGHNUTS, BURGERS $

Map p248 (www.donutsandsliders.com; 2209 Magazine St; doughnuts & pastries under $6, sliders $4-6; ⊙7am-9pm) District makes us feel naughty – and we like it. In the morning, truly decadent donuts lure from the counter – we enjoyed the piled-high cookies and cream. After 11am fancy sliders step onto the scene, and they are gobsmackingly good. Fortunately they are also small, so the guilt is not overwhelming. Note that the 'brew' here is coffee, not beer.

If the fried oyster slider is available, make sure you get it.

STEIN'S DELI DELI $

Map p248 (☎504-527-0771; www.steinsdeli.net; 2207 Magazine St; sandwiches $7-13; ⊙7am-7pm Tue-Fri, 9am-5pm Sat & Sun) You may get a no-nonsense 'What?' when you step up to the counter, but it's just part of the schtick at this scruffy deli. For quality sandwiches, cheese and cold cuts, this is as good as the city gets. Owner Dan Stein is a fanatic about keeping his deli stocked with great Italian and Jewish meats and cheeses, and some fine boutique beers.

SLICE PIZZA $

Map p248 (☎504-525-7437; www.slicepizzeria.com; 1513 St Charles Ave; mains $8-13, pizzas $13-22; ⊙11am-11pm Mon-Sat, to 10pm Sun) One of those places you'll find yourself returning to again and again if you're staying in the Lower Garden District for more than a few days. Highlights? Nice staff, happy-hour specials (2pm to 6pm) and damn good pizza. Toppings for the thin crust pies can be as artisanal or run-of-the-mill as you like. Slices start at $3. Also serves po'boys, pastas and salads.

SUCRÉ CHOCOLATE $

Map p248 (www.shopsucre.com; 3025 Magazine St; cookies & chocolates $2-7; ⊙8am-10pm Sun-Thu, to midnight Fri & Sat) Willy Wonka's chocolate factory has put away its top hat and

LOCAL KNOWLEDGE

SOUTHERN FOOD & BEVERAGE MUSEUM: COOKING DEMOS & AN INTERACTIVE KITCHEN

Lots of museums brag about their interactive exhibits and multisensory experiences. But very few of these high-tech displays spotlight the sense of taste. Not so at the revamped **Southern Food & Beverage Museum** (p119) and its new in-house restaurant **Purloo** (p124).

The museum and the restaurant, which is named for a low-country, paella-like stew, celebrate food traditions and flavors from across the Southern states. Each state has its own exhibit area, and these exhibits are supplemented by an array of food-centric activities. 'Every month we're going to focus on a different Southern state and bring in chefs, farmers, food producers and writers to do dinners and lectures here,' explains Purloo chef Ryan Hughes.

Before joining forces with the museum, Hughes was the mastermind behind 140 pop-up restaurants across New Orleans, each with a multicourse menu focusing on a different region of the South. Hughes formed relationships with farmers and food producers from across the region while preparing his menus, and he sourced from many of their farms. He plans to share his knowledge with Purloo's diners, who can watch Hughes and his sous chefs in action from one of 30 counter seats wrapped around the open kitchen. Questions about the food and the preparation are encouraged while the cooks prepare your meal.

An upcoming goal for the museum? IPad touch screens at some of the museum displays, where visitors can order one of the Southern specialties described in the exhibit. A fresh sample will be carried over from the restaurant. Now that, we think, is interactive museum-going at its finest.

purple suede coat and gone decidedly upscale. Artisanal chocolates, chocolate bars, toffee, marshmallows, gelato and other confections beckon from behind the glass counter. One macaroon will set you back $2 – but you can gain comfort from the fact that Sucré is widely considered to have the best chocolate in town.

SEED HEALTH FOOD $

Map p248 (www.seedyourhealth.com; 1330 Prytania St; mains $7-14; ⏲11am-10pm Mon-Fri, 10am-10pm Sat & Sun; ☎) Vegetarians and vegans can now nosh with abandon in New Orleans, just like their more carnivorous friends. This spare and boxy addition to the Lower Garden District calls its menu 'garden-based' and whips up delicious salads and sandwiches plus a few heartier mains such as vegetarian spaghetti and pad Thai. Blended juices and cocktails, all made with fresh juice, add to the fun.

PARASOL'S SANDWICHES $

Map p248 (☎504-302-1533; www.parasolsbarandrestaurant.com; 2533 Constance St; po'boys $7-16; ⏲11am-9pm Sun-Thu, to 10pm Fri & Sat) Parasol's isn't just in the Irish Channel; it sort of *is* the Irish Channel, serving as community center, nexus of gossip and, naturally, watering hole. Yes, it's first and foremost a bar, but you can order some of the best po'boys in town from the seating area in the back. That big ol' roast beef is a messy, juice-filled conduit of deliciousness.

There's a mad cast of characters both behind and at the bar, but don't feel threatened; all in all this is one of the friendliest neighborhood spots in New Orleans. This place is also St Paddy's Day headquarters, when a huge block party happens on the street.

TRACEY'S SANDWICHES $

Map p248 (http://traceysnola.com; 2604 Magazine St; mains $5-12; ⏲11am-10pm Sun-Thu, to midnight Fri & Sat, bar 11am-late) This neighborhood bar, known for its roast beef po'boys, is where you go to watch the Saints play on a lazy Sunday afternoon – the joint's got 20 TVs. Order your pub grub at the window, grab a buzzer, then settle in until you're buzzed (in both senses of the word).

The crowd sitting outside can look kind of scruffy, but c'mon in – it's a welcoming place, and the trendy exposed-brick wall will give urban hipsters a modicum of comfort. And parasols hang from the ceiling.

JUAN'S FLYING BURRITO MEXICAN $

Map p248 (☎504-569-0000; www.juansflying-burrito.com; 2018 Magazine St; mains $5-14; ⌚11am-10pm Sun-Thu, to 11pm Fri & Sat) The answer to that perennial question, 'What happens when you cross a bunch of skinny-jeans-clad hipsters with a tortilla?', is (ta da) Juan's. The food is about as authentically Mexican as Ontario, but that doesn't mean it's not good; the hefty burritos pack a satisfying punch. The margaritas are tasty and the quesadilla comes with ground beef, bacon and blue cheese – yes, please.

There's a new downtown location at 515 Barrone St near Poydras St.

SLIM GOODIE'S DINER DINER $

Map p248 (☎504-891-3447; 3322 Magazine St; mains $4-15; ⌚6am-3pm) The grease is as prevalent as the '70s rock in this happenin' place, where hipsters in dirty tennis shoes serve hipsters in wool caps. But hey, Slim Goodie's was among the first restaurants to reopen after Hurricane Katrina, so it deserves a hell of a lot of credit. Burgers, shakes, American breakfasts and other short-order standards anchor the menu. It's good, if not exactly awe-inspiring.

And we jest about the hipsters – they're just the most eye-catching folks in the all-ages, all-fashion crowd.

★COQUETTE MODERN FRENCH $$

Map p248 (☎504-265-0421; www.coquettenola.com; 2800 Magazine St; small lunch plates $11-22, dinner $12-24, lunch mains $16-23, dinner $24-32; ⌚11:30am-2:30pm Fri & Sat, 10:30am-2pm Sun, 5:30-10pm daily) Coquette mixes wine-bar ambience with friendly service and a bit of white linen; the result is a candlelit place where you don't feel bad getting tipsy. Explore beyond the respectable wine menu, though – there's some great Louisiana-sourced food here, often with an innovative global spin. Choices may include crawfish bisque with oyster cream and truffle, or a succulent red snapper with ham hock broth.

The small plates are eclectic and highly recommended. Menus change daily. At the low-key but inviting bar, you might just find yourself seated beside a recognizable TV actor, dining and relaxing after a day on set.

SAKE CAFÉ UPTOWN JAPANESE $$

Map p248 (☎504-894-0033; www.sakecafeup-town.us; 2830 Magazine St; sushi & mains $12-24; ⌚11:30am-10:30pm Mon-Thu, to 11:30pm Fri & Sat,12:30pm-10:30pm Sun) Believe it or not, fish in this town doesn't have to come fried, swimming in a thick sauce or stuffed with bacon/crawfish/crabmeat/whatever. Sake Uptown (the original is in Metairie) serves decent sushi that's popular with the young, yuppie types that populate the Lower Garden District and surrounds.

FROM MYTHS TO THE MOVEMENT

Dryades St, named for legendary Greek tree spirits, is still known as such in much of town, but the official new name of this road is Oretha Castle-Haley Blvd (often shortened to OC Haley). The road is named for a local legend and Civil Rights activist who was a founding member of the Congress of Racial Equality, one of the leading organizations in the 1960s Civil Rights movement. Castle-Haley organized boycotts of segregated businesses and was one of the main leaders of local civil-disobedience and direct-action campaigns. Ironically, Castle-Haley's successful battle for integration helped hasten the decline of the street eventually named for her. When African Americans could shop anywhere they wanted, they began moving away from the traditionally black businesses clustered around Dryades, while simultaneous white flight contributed to an economic downturn across the city.

Central City was once a major center for African American health care. The Keystone Insurance Company (now defunct) was one of the few of its kind that would fund pensions, funerals and, of course, medical treatment for black citizens. Said individuals may have been treated at Flint Goodridge Hospital (at Louisiana and Freret Sts); up until the 1950s, this was the only facility in the city where black doctors could legally practice medicine. The First African Baptist Church of New Orleans, at 2216 Third St, was founded in 1817 and is the oldest continually operating black church in Louisiana.

In testament to this area's contribution to the Civil Rights struggle, there is a statue of Martin Luther King at the corner of Martin Luther King Blvd and S Claiborne Ave.

★**COMMANDER'S PALACE** CREOLE $$$

Map p248 (☎504-899-8221; www.commanderspalace.com; 1403 Washington Ave, Garden District; dinner mains $28-45; ⏰6:30-10:30pm daily, 11:30am-2pm Mon-Fri, to 1pm Sat, 10:30am-1:30pm Sun) Commander's Palace is a dapper host, a seer-suckered bon vivant who wows with white-linen dining rooms, decadent dishes and attentive Southern hospitality. The nouveau Creole menu runs from crispy oysters with brie-cauliflower fondue, to shrimp and grits with goat's cheese and roasted mushrooms. The dress code adds to the charm – no shorts or T-shirts; jackets preferred at dinner. It's a very nice place – but also lots of fun.

Owner Ella Brennan takes pride in her ability to promote her chefs to stardom; Paul Prudhomme and Emeril Lagasse are among her alumni. And note that some of that stiff-upper-lip formality is put on; the lunch special, after all, is the 25¢ martini. Reservations are required.

Central City

CAFÉ RECONCILE DINER $

Map p248 (☎504-568-1157; http://reconcileneworleans.org; 1631 Oretha Castle-Haley Blvd; mains $9-15; ⏰11am-2:30pm Mon-Fri) Café Reconcile fights the good fight by recruiting and training at-risk youth to work as kitchen and floor staff. The food is simple and, frankly, really good. It's very much of the humble New Orleans school of home cookery: red beans and rice, fried chicken, shrimp Creole and the like, with the spotlight on daily specials.

PURLOO SOUTHERN $$

Map p248 (☎504-324-6020; www.nolapurloo.com; 1504 Oretha Castle-Haley Blvd; small plates $7-13, mains $23-26; ⏰11am-3pm Tue-Sat, 5-10:30pm Tue-Thu, to 11pm Fri & Sat) Chef Ryan Hughes, noted for his popular pop-up restaurants, celebrates the South at this new eatery beside the Southern Food & Beverage Museum. Sourced regionally, the menu spotlights specialties from across the South, from Cape Hatteras to the low country to the Delta. The U-shaped bar wraps around the open kitchen, and questions are encouraged as you dine.

The restaurant's 16ft Brunswick bar was salvaged from Lake Pontchartrain after Hurricane Katrina. It once sat inside Bruning's, the third oldest restaurant in New Orleans (opened in 1859), until it was destroyed by the storm. On a budget? A Blue Plate dinner is offered nightly for $15.

DRINKING & NIGHTLIFE

Bars in this part of New Orleans tend to attract a youngish student and post-student crowd. Magazine St is, in its way, as much fun as Bourbon or Frenchmen Sts in the French Quarter and Faubourg Marigny neighborhoods. It's wild without being ridiculous or idiotic (unlike Bourbon St) and while it lacks the live-music scene of Frenchmen, it makes up for that with a better variety of bars. The drinking and entertainment scene in Central City is a little slow, but you can find interesting craft cocktails at Purloo (p124) beside the Southern Food and Beverage Museum.

★**NOLA BREWING** BREWERY

(☎504-301-1117; www.nolabrewing.com; 3001 Tchoupitoulas St; ⏰2-11pm Mon-Thu, 1-11pm Fri, 11am-11:30pm Sat & Sun) Free craft beer at 2pm on Fridays. Yep, you read that right. This cavernous brewery welcomes guests once a week for a free brewery tour that kicks off with sloshy cups of craft brew, and a food truck or two out front. The rest of the week? Stop by the cozy taproom where 16 beers (eight originals and eight seasonals) await.

As for the brewery tour, it's a high-energy gathering of youngish folk and beer enthusiasts who want to get gently buzzed and hang out in a festival-like setting – and maybe learn about beer. Beloved originals include the NOLA Blonde and the Hopitoulas.

In 2015 the brewery plans to open a new taproom, with a rooftop bar, right next door.

AVENUE PUB PUB

Map p248 (www.theavenuepub.com; 1732 St Charles Ave; ⏰24hr) From the street, this scruffy pub looks like a nothing-special neighborhood dive. But with more than 40 beers on tap and another 135-odd in bottles, plus a staff with serious dedication to the taste of their drafts, this two-story beer bar is earning national accolades. The bourbon list is impressive, too. The upstairs patio is a fine place to watch the world go by.

BULLDOG

BAR

Map p248 (☎504-891-1516; www.draftfreak.com; 3236 Magazine St; ⏲11:30-2am Mon-Fri, 11am-2am Sat & Sun) With 40 or so brews on tap and more than 100 by the bottle or can – from Louisiana to Mexico to Italy and points beyond – the Bulldog works hard to keep beer enthusiasts happy. The best place to sink a pint is in the courtyard, which gets packed with the young and beautiful almost every evening when the weather is warm.

ROOT SQUARED

WINE BAR, COCKTAIL BAR

Map p248 (www.facebook.com/RootSquaredNola; 1800 Magazine St; ⏲5pm-midnight Tue-Sat) Perched above Magazine St between two famed dive bars, The Saint and Half Moon, this swanky new wine and cocktail bar seems to have dropped from the sky. Gourmet small plates, attentive service and upscale-but-inviting decor add to the allure. Several cocktails are $5 during happy hour (5pm to 7pm). As for the small plates, the steak tartare is superb.

The bar is upstairs from Square Root, a contemporary restaurant known for its open kitchen and multicourse dining experience.

SAINT BAR & LOUNGE

BAR

Map p248 (☎504-523-0500; www.thesaintneworleans.com; 961 St Mary St; ⏲7pm-late) The Saint? Of what? How about a great backyard beer garden enclosed in duck blinds and filled with tattooed young professionals, Tulane students, good shots, good beers, good times and a photo booth that you will inevitably end up in before the night is through. It's not the cleanest bar (nickname: the Taint), but it sure is a fun one.

As the bartender told us, the worst part of the city's new smoking ban may be that 'people are going to realize what this place really smells like.'

RENDEZVOUS

BAR

Map p248 (☎504-891-1777; www.therendezvoustavern.com; 3101 Magazine St; ⏲3pm-late Mon-Fri, 1pm-late Sat & Sun) Dartboard, pool table, a long and dark bar, old-looking mirrors on the wall and a few video poker machines. And Billy Squier's 'The Stroke' on the speakers. Yup, this place meets all requirements for a legitimate New Orleans dive bar. Very much a locals' hangout, the Rendezvous attracts a mixed bag of college students and yuppies. Plus a few outliers to keep it real.

LOCAL KNOWLEDGE

UNITED CABS

New Orleans may be pretty lax in its drinking laws, but locals know better than to drink and drive. There's no need for you to get behind the wheel after a night of drinking, either. Just ask a New Orleans native, or those who frequent the dive bars of the Garden District and Uptown; they've memorized the phone number for **United Cabs** (☎504-522-9771; www.unitedcabs.com; ⏲24hr), a company that has been around since 1938, and they'll repeat it by rote.

United's available 24/7, and with more than 400 cars in their fleet, you probably won't be waiting long.

BALCONY BAR

BAR

Map p248 (☎504-894-8888; 3201 Magazine St; ⏲4:30pm-late) This student-centric neighborhood bar is a good place for pizza, carousing and sitting on the eponymous balcony while watching the Magazine St parade march by on balmy nights. The kitchen is open late.

HALF MOON

BAR

Map p248 (☎504-522-7313; www.halfmoongrillnola,com; 1125 St Mary St; ⏲5pm-2am) On an interesting corner, just half a block from Magazine St, the Half Moon beckons with a cool neighborhood vibe. This dive is good for a beer, short-order meal or an evening shooting stick. The kitchen is open till 2am. Look for the sweet neon sign.

IGOR'S LOUNGE

BAR

Map p248 (☎504-568-9811; 2133 St Charles Ave; ⏲24hr) Play pool, lose money on the slots, tap your foot to Old Crow Medicine Show on the speakers and do your laundry? Yep, and you know it's time to leave this dive if the sinuous bar starts looking straight. Igor's constant rotation of characters makes it a good place to drop into, or make it your terminus if staying nearby.

KREWE DU BREW

COFFEE

Map p248 (www.krewedubrewnola.com; 1610 St Charles; pastries $3; ⏲7am-6pm) We like the Mardi Gras–themed name as well as the saucy chalkboard sign that sits on the sidewalk outside this indie coffee shop. It's a good place to grab a coffee and pastry before a stroll through the Garden District.

STILL PERKIN' CAFE

Map p248 (http://neworleanscoffeeshop.com; 2727 Prytania St; mains $2-7; ⏲7am-6pm Mon-Fri, 8am-6pm Sat, to 5pm Sun; 📶) Perched on the corner of Prytania St and Washington Ave, this bright coffee shop is a great place to start or finish a Garden District walking tour or a visit to Lafayette Cemetery. In addition to lattes and iced coffees, there's a decadent selection of scones and other treats plus a few sandwiches and wraps. It's in the 1880s Rink mini-mall.

ENTERTAINMENT

ZEITGEIST CINEMA

Map p248 (☎504-352-1150; www.zeitgeistnola.org; 1618 Oretha Castle-Haley Blvd; adult/concession $8/7) This old movie house has been around since the 1920s. It screens independent and art films.

SHOPPING

Magazine St is by far New Orleans' best shopping strip, and as a center for commercial activity it begins in the Lower Garden District, near its intersection with Felicity St. From here you can follow Magazine west all the way to Audubon Park and essentially shop or window browse in antiques stores and boutiques almost the entire way.

★**AIDAN GILL FOR MEN** BARBER, ACCESSORIES

Map p248 (☎504-587-9090; www.aidangillformen.com; 2026 Magazine St; ⏲10am-6pm Mon-Fri, 9am-5pm Sat, noon-6pm Sun) Shave and a haircut…40 bits. Or $40. Apiece. But who's counting at this suave barbershop, where smartly dressed mobsters of the Prohibition era would surely have felt comfortable? It's all about looking neat and stylish, in a well-heeled, masculine sort of way. High-end shaving gear and smart gifts for men are sold in front, and the barber shop is in back.

TRASHY DIVA CLOTHING

Map p248 (☎504-299-8777; www.trashydiva.com; 2048 Magazine St; ⏲noon-6pm Mon-Fri, 11am-6pm Sat, 1-5pm Sun) It isn't really as scandalous as the name suggests, except by Victorian standards. Diva's specialty is sassy 1940s- and '50s-style cinched, hourglass dresses and belle epoque undergarments – lots of corsets, lace and such. The shop also features Kabuki-inspired dresses with embroidered dragons, and retro tops, skirts and shawls reflecting styles plucked from just about every era.

FUNKY MONKEY VINTAGE

Map p248 (☎504-899-5587; www.facebook.com/funkymonkeyneworleans; 3127 Magazine St; ⏲11am-6pm Mon-Wed, to 7pm Thu-Sat, noon-6pm Sun) You'll find wigs in every color at Funky Monkey, which sells vintage attire for club-hopping men and women. This funhouse of frippery is also a good spot for Mardi Gras costumes. It's tiny, though, and can get jam-packed with customers. In addition to wigs, look for jeans, jewelry, tops, sunglasses, hats and boots.

Annoyingly, it's turned into one of those vintage shops where the secondhand stuff is as expensive as new clothes from a big brand name, but the clothes are admittedly very hip-to-trip. The welcoming staff is a bonus.

SIMON OF NEW ORLEANS ARTS, ANTIQUES

Map p248 (☎504-524-8201; 1028 Jackson Ave; ⏲10am-5pm Mon-Sat) Local artist Simon Hardeveld has made a name for himself by painting groovy signs that hang like artwork in restaurants all over New Orleans.

GARDENS OUTSIDE THE GARDENS

New Orleans has always been a green city, at least in terms of color and hue. The climate and the Caribbean Colonial planning philosophy of the city is behind a lush overgrowth effect that is noticeable even in poorer parts of the city. The trick of many New Orleanian plant lovers is channeling this awesome fecundity into plots that are both attractive and utilitarian. Enter **Parkway Partners** (☎504-620-2224; www.parkwaypartnersnola.org; 1137 Baronne St; ⏲office 8:30am-4pm Mon-Fri), which funds urban tree-planting projects and similar programs. At the time of writing there were 42 such gardens scattered across the city, plus three orchards, each one a lovely example of community partnerships and grass-roots beautification efforts, which also help to leech lead out of the local soil (New Orleans has unusually high levels of lead contamination).

You'll probably recognize the distinctive stars, dots and sparkles that fill the spaces between letters on colorfully painted signs such as 'Who Died & Made You Elvis?' The gallery is part of Antiques on Jackson, which Hardeveld owns with his wife Maria.

GARDEN DISTRICT BOOKSHOP BOOKS

Map p248 (☎504-895-2266; www.gardendistrict-bookshop.com; 2727 Prytania St; ⊙10am-6pm Mon-Sat, to 5pm Sun) Want a book about New Orleans history or a coffee table tome about Mardi Gras? Then stop by this well-stocked indie bookstore inside the Rink mini-mall. The store also sells travel guides, bestsellers, cookbooks, postcards and a select collection of first-edition works. Check the online calendar for book signings with local authors, who drop in every now and then.

THOMAS MANN GALLERY I/O JEWELRY

Map p248 (☎504-581-2111; www.thomasmann.com; 1810 Magazine St; ⊙11am-5pm Mon-Sat) A giant crawfish. A robot made of wood. Jewelry. Baskets. Candle holders. If you need a funky but finely designed gift, pop in here. The 'I/O' in the name stands for 'insight-full objects.' Local craftsman Thomas Mann specializes in jewelry and sculpture, and his gallery is a smorgasbord of glass and metal.

GOGO JEWELRY JEWELRY

Map p248 (www.ilovegogojewelry.com; 2036 Magazine St; ⊙11am-5pm Mon-Sat) Ladies, if you're looking for stylish, one-of-a-kind jewelry – rings, necklaces, cuffs – with a bit of sass, GoGo is a good place to start.

FLEURTY GIRL CLOTHING

Map p248 (www.fleurtygirl.net; 3117 Magazine St; ⊙11am-6pm Mon-Thu, 10am-7pm Fri & Sat, 11am-5pm Sun) Fleurty Girl celebrates New Orleans and the city's unofficial symbol – the fleur-de-lis – with a feminine, cheeky style. T-shirts sporting local and topical messages, often involving football, are its raison d'être.

NEW ORLEANS MUSIC EXCHANGE MUSIC

Map p248 (☎504-891-7670; 3342 Magazine St; ⊙10:30am-6pm Mon-Sat, 1-5pm Sun) Ladies might get a 'Can I help you, baby?' when exploring this large shop, which specializes mostly in secondhand instruments. It's the place to go for a nice used horn. There's an entire room of brass and woodwinds, all priced fairly, and to find it, you must weave through a maze of guitars, bass amps, and lots of other music stuff.

LOCAL KNOWLEDGE

LOCALLY GROWN T-SHIRTS

For your own wearable souvenir, head to Magazine St, where three indie shops sell a breezy mix of locally inspired shirts. **Dirty Coast** (p142) sprang to life after Hurricane Katrina. Its founding slogan? 'Be a New Orleanian. Wherever You Are.' The company's shirts tend to embrace local issues with witty flair. **Fleurty Girl** (p127) sells eye-catching T-shirts for chicks, with a focus on southern hospitality, good times and football. You'll find locally designed shirts at **Storyville** (Map p248; www.storyvilleapparel.com; 3029 Magazine St; ⊙10am-8pm), which holds contests for new material. So yeah, you went to New Orleans and all you got was this awesome T-shirt.

JIM RUSSELL RECORDS MUSIC

Map p248 (☎504-522-2602; www.jimrussell-records.com; 1837 Magazine St; ⊙noon-4:30pm Mon-Sat) A dense emporium of used 45s, with some very rare, collectible and expensive disks featuring all the blues, R&B and soul stars of the past. The used LPs have mostly given way to CDs, and there's an uneven selection available. Russell, a former DJ and concert promoter who opened the store in 1968, died in 2014 at age 94, but the store rocks on.

BIG FISHERMAN SEAFOOD FOOD

Map p248 (☎504-897-9907; www.bigfisherman-seafood.com; 3301 Magazine St; ⊙11am-6pm Mon-Fri, 10am-6pm Sat, 10am-5pm Sun) If you're here in the spring during crawfish season, you may develop a taste for the little mudbugs. But you haven't had the full-on crawfish experience unless you've been invited to a crawfish boil in someone's backyard. This busy little shop will pack some up for you so you can carry 'em back to your own bungalow or someone else's. Prices fluctuate, so call ahead. Also sells sausages.

MAGAZINE ANTIQUE MALL ANTIQUES

Map p248 (☎504-896-9994; www.magazineantiquemall.com; 3017 Magazine St; ⊙10:30am-5:30pm, from noon Sun) Scary baby dolls. Hats. Chandeliers. Coca Cola memorabilia. Inside this overstuffed emporium, rummagers are likely to score items of interest in the dozen or so stalls, where independent dealers peddle an intriguing and varied range of antique bric-a-brac. Bargain hunters aren't likely to have much luck, though.

St Charles Avenue Streetcar

The clang and swoosh of the St Charles Avenue streetcar is as essential to Uptown and the Garden District as live oaks and mansions. New Orleanians are justifiably proud of their moving monument, which began life as the nation's second horse-drawn streetcar line, the New Orleans & Carrollton Railroad, in 1835.

Laying the Line

In 1893 the line was among the first streetcar systems in the country to be electrified. Now it is one of the few streetcars in the USA to have survived the automobile era. Millions of passengers utilize the streetcar every day despite the fact the city's bus service tends to be faster. In many ways, the streetcar is the quintessential vehicle for New Orleans public transportation: slow, pretty, and if not entirely efficient, extremely atmospheric.

Another streetcar line plies Canal St and you should ride it, but if we're honest, the route isn't as pretty as the St Charles line. There are plans to build a new line from Canal St, up Rampart St to Elysian Fields Ave.

Along the Avenue

It's only slightly hyperbolic to claim St Charles Ave is the most beautiful street in the USA. Once you enter the Garden District, the entire street is shaded under a tunnel of big, old live oak trees that look like they could have wiped the floor with an orc army in a Tolkien novel.

KRIS DAVIDSON/LONELY PLANET ©

SIOUXSNAPP/SHUTTERSTOCK ©

DAVID REDFERN/GETTY IMAGES ©

1. The St Charles Avenue streetcar **2.** St Charles Avenue during Carnival season **3.** A jazz musician rides a streetcar in New Orleans

Gorgeous houses, barely concealed behind the trees, house the most aristocratic elite of the city. Those same elite often ride in the floats that proceed along St Charles during Carnival season; look up to the tree branches and you'll see many are laden with shiny beads tossed from Mardi Gras floats. Within the Neutral Ground, or median space that houses the streetcar tracks, you'll often see joggers and families passing through the verdant corridor. By far the best way of experiencing this cityscape is via the slow, antique rumble of the streetcar; free from driving your eyes are free to gaze on all the beauty.

A STREETCAR NAMED DESIRE

Tennessee Williams' play *A Streetcar Named Desire* is the most famous stage (and, arguably, film) depiction of New Orleans. The story follows Blanche Dubois as she moves in with her sister, Stella, and brother-in-law, Stanley Kowalski. In the ensuing drama, everyone gets along and no one suffers crippling emotional trauma. Just kidding! Of course, it's the reverse.

The name of the play derives from both the flawed desire of the characters and the actual streetcar that ran to Desire St. That streetcar has been replaced by the No 80 Desire–Louisa bus line, which sadly lacks Marlon Brando screaming in a tank top.

Uptown & Riverbend

UPTOWN | RIVERBEND

Neighborhood Top Five

❶ Savoring a blue-cheese smothered steak and a slice of alligator-sausage cheese-cake at **Jacques-Imo's Café** (p138) before catching the Rebirth Brass Band next door at the **Maple Leaf Bar** (p141).

❷ Strolling beneath live oaks in Audubon Park then ogling alligators, foxes and swamp monsters in the **Audubon Zoo** (p132).

❸ Shopping for eye-catching pottery, housewares and art on bustling **Magazine Street** (p142).

❹ Dining and imbibing at locally owned eateries on ever-so-hot **Freret Street** (p138).

❺ Learning about art, jazz and African American history on the scenic campus of **Tulane University** (p133).

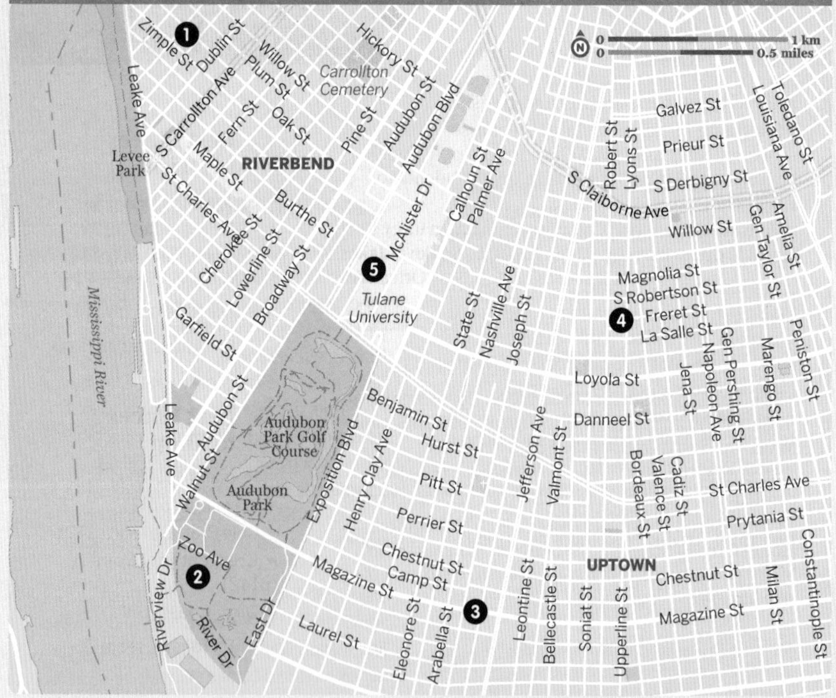

For more detail of this area see Map p250

Explore Uptown & Riverbend

If you've only got one day, check out the Audubon Zoo in the morning. Magazine St runs past the zoo, so after your visit with the elephants and giraffes, spend the rest of the day exploring the shops and art galleries that line this busy thoroughfare. Enjoy dinner on Freret St, located above St Charles, then catch a band or grab drinks at a local dive.

If you've got another day, ride the St Charles Ave streetcar to Tulane for a bit of wandering. Continue into Riverbend to check out the shops and restaurants off S Carrollton Ave, particularly along Maple St and Oak St. For dinner, take your own po'boy challenge, sampling different versions from some of the most famous po'boy shops in the city and finding your favorite.

Maps of New Orleans rarely agree on the area's extents, but we'll say Uptown includes everything west of Louisiana Ave, between Magnolia and the river, including the universities and Audubon Park. St Charles Ave, Magazine and Tchoupitoulas Sts are the main routes that more or less follow the contours of the river. The Riverbend is the area above the campuses and Audubon Park. Where St Charles Ave meets S Carrollton Ave is the nexus of the area.

Local Life

➡ **Exercising** Lush Audubon Park (132), with its 100-year-old live oaks and paved jogging trail, is beloved by runners, walkers and cyclists.

➡ **Shopping** Magazine St lures the masses with indie shops, galleries and, yes, Whole Foods (p136), while boutiques and thrift stores alike draw students to Riverbend.

➡ **Dive bars** Spending a blurry evening at grungy but loveable dives, from Ms Mae's (p140) to Snake & Jakes (p140), is part of what it means to be a New Orleanian.

Getting There & Away

➡ **Bus** Bus 11 runs along Magazine St from Canal St to Audubon Park. Pick it up at the corner of Canal and Magazine Sts in front of the Sheraton Hotel.

➡ **Streetcar** The St Charles Ave streetcar travels through the CBD, the Garden District and into Uptown.

➡ **Car** Metered parking ($1.50 per hour) is required along much of Magazine St between 8am and 6pm Monday through Saturday. Look for free parking on side streets.

Lonely Planet's Top Tip

Magazine St stretches from downtown to Audubon Park, covering 4 miles in the Garden District and Uptown. To get a handle on its shops, galleries and restaurants before your trip, order or download the block-by-block guide published by the **Magazine St Merchants Association** (☎342-4435; www.magazinestreet.com). You can also pick it up at many member stores. Visit the website for a listing of upcoming events.

Best Places to Eat

➡ Jacques-Imo's Café (p138)

➡ Gautreau's (p137)

➡ Clancy's (p137)

➡ Patois (p137)

➡ Boucherie (p137)

➡ Domilise's (p134)

For reviews, see p134 ➡

Best Places to Drink

➡ St Joe's (p139)

➡ Columns Hotel (p139)

➡ Bouligny Tavern (p140)

➡ Delachaise (p136)

➡ Snake & Jakes (p140)

For reviews, see p139 ➡

Best Places to Shop

➡ Potsalot (p142)

➡ Hazelnut (p142)

➡ Cole Pratt Gallery (p142)

➡ Crescent City Comics (p142)

➡ Dirty Coast (p142)

For reviews, see p142 ➡

TOP SIGHT
AUDUBON ZOO

DANE JORGENSEN/SHUTTERSTOCK ©

The gray foxes sleeping on the rocking chairs in the Louisiana Swamp exhibit clearly have this zoo thing figured out. And they don't seem too worried about the alligators loitering around the bend. The Swamp is one of 10 animal exhibit areas at the Audubon Zoo, which is home to an excellent array of international animals, from Asian elephants to towering giraffes to a poisonous dart frog or two.

The Swamp's Cajun setting is a wonderland of bald cypress and Spanish moss, natural wonders of southern Louisiana bayou country. Bobcats and lynx are on view, and you may see a red fox chilling on a log in the swamp scrub. Human intrusions are poignantly represented with several exhibits drawing attention to bayou industries. One of these is a 'Christmas tree' oil-rig cap, so named because its complicated valves and controls look like decorations on a Christmas tree. Step inside to see the famous white alligators and the yellow-eyed Swamp Monster.

The Reptile Encounter displays examples of the largest snakes in the world – from the king cobra that grows to more than 18ft in length to the green anaconda that reaches 38ft. Many local species of snake are also on view. Other memorable sections include the Mayan-style Jaguar Jungle and the South America Pampas with its raised walkway. Poems and quotes dot the walkways, while eco-minded plaques reinforce the precarious position of many of these animals in the wild. The child-focused Watoto Walk, built to resemble Masai villages in Kenya and Tanzania, is a petting zoo. Look for elephant and orangutan enclosures, as well as a Lazy River water feature for kids.

The zoo is inside **Audubon Park**, a lovely riverside spot with 1.8-miles of multi-use paved trail unfurling beneath a shady canopy of live oaks. Behind the zoo is The Fly, the waterfront section where people toss Frisbees and chill out, just beyond the levee.

DON'T MISS

- Louisiana Swamp
- White alligators
- Jaguar Jungle
- Reptile Encounter

PRACTICALITIES

- Map p250
- ☎504-581-4629
- www.auduboninstitute.org
- 6500 Magazine St
- adult/child 2-12yr/senior $19/14/15
- 10am-4pm Tue-Fri, to 5pm Sat & Sun Sep-Feb, 10am-5pm Mon-Fri, to 6pm Sat & Sun Mar-Aug

SIGHTS

AUDUBON ZOO ZOO

See p132.

TULANE UNIVERSITY UNIVERSITY

Map p250 (☎504-865-5000; www.tulane.edu; 6823 St Charles Ave) The campus of Tulane, a premier Southern university, is an attractive tableau of live oaks, red-brick buildings and green quads spread across 110 acres above Audubon Park. This is one of the prettiest colleges in the country, and it's a pleasant place to stop and stretch your legs if you're riding the St Charles Ave streetcar across town.

Tulane has an interesting origin as a yellow-fever buster. In 1834 the Medical College of Louisiana was founded in an attempt to control repeated cholera and yellow-fever epidemics. By 1847 the University of Louisiana merged with the school, and in 1883, Paul Tulane gave the school a $1 million donation that initiated significant expansion and slapped his name on the entire institution.

Tulane boasts around 13,500 students in 10 colleges and schools, including a law school whose entire student body seems to fill up Magazine St cafes during exam time, and the highly regarded medical school, now relocated downtown. Big-name alumni include former French president Jacques Chirac, Republican politician Newt Gingrich, TV presenter Jerry Springer, and a very long list of Louisiana governors, judges and assorted politicos.

The **Amistad Research Center** (Map p250; ☎504-862-3222; www.amistadresearchcenter.org; Tilton Memorial Hall, Tulane University; ⏲8:30am-4:30pm Mon-Fri) FREE, which holds more than 15 million documents, is one of the nation's largest repositories of African American history. Despite the size of the collection, the facility is not a museum. For visitors, there is a small area on the 2nd floor with rotating exhibits that offer insights on ethnic heritage you're not likely to get from any other source. A past exhibit about African Americans in sports included documents and photographs related to the Negro Baseball League. The displayed works of art from the Aaron Douglas Collection are another reason to drop by.

Oral histories are the heart of the music holdings at the **Hogan Jazz Archive** (Map p250; ☎504-865-5688; http://jazz.tulane.edu; 3rd fl, Jones Hall, 6801 Freret St, Tulane University; ⏲8:30am-5:30pm Mon-Fri), a collection of New Orleans jazz artifacts that includes sheet music, photographs, journals and recordings. Most of the archive's great wealth of material is not on exhibit; the helpful staff will retrieve items for you. Treasures include stacks of 78rpm recordings with early sides by the Original Dixieland Jazz Band in 1917. Interested in architecture? Walk down the hall to see what's displayed in the **Southeastern Architectural Archives** (Map p250; 3rd fl, Jones Hall, 6801 Freret St, Tulane University; ⏲9am-noon, 1-5pm Mon-Fri), which recently put the spotlight on Gulf Coast bungalows.

Flanked by beautiful Tiffany stained-glass triptychs, the **Newcomb Art Gallery** (Map p250; ☎504-865-5328; www.newcombartgallery.tulane.edu; 6823 St Charles Ave, Woldenberg Art Center; admission free; ⏲10am-5pm Tue-Fri, 11am-4pm Sat & Sun) FREE is a great spot to soak up some art, typically with a local or regional spin; just outside is a pretty green where students sunbathe, toss Frisbees and generally recede into the happiest rhythms of American higher ed.

TOURO SYNAGOGUE SYNAGOGUE

Map p250 (☎504-895-4843; www.tourosynagogue.com; 4238 St Charles Ave) Despite the fact that Jews were officially banned from New Orleans under the Code Noir (Black Code), which was in effect from 1724 until the Louisiana Purchase in 1803, they have been calling the Crescent City home since the 18th century. Founded in 1828, Touro is the city's oldest synagogue (and the oldest in the country outside of the original 13 colonies) and bears a slight resemblance to a red-brick Byzantine temple, with squat buttresses and bubbly domes. The local congregation began as an amalgamation between local Spanish-descended Jews and German Jewish immigrants, a relatively rare mixed lineage in American Judaism.

MILTON LATTER MEMORIAL LIBRARY BUILDING

Map p250 (☎504-596-2625; www.neworleanspubliclibrary.org; 5120 St Charles Ave; ⏲9am-8pm Mon & Wed, to 6pm Tue & Thu, 10am-5pm Sat, noon-5pm Sun) Poised elegantly above shady stands of palms, the Latter Memorial Library was once a private mansion. The Isaac family (owners from 1907 to 1912) installed Flemish-style carved woodwork, Dutch murals and French frescoed ceilings and passed the property to aviator Harry Williams and his silent-film-star wife, Marguerite Clark (1912–39). The couple was known for throwing grand parties. The next owner was local horse racer Robert S Eddy, followed by Mr and Mrs Harry Latter, who gave the building to the city in 1948.

The bottom floor and the entire exterior facade of the Italianate beaux arts building remain stately if a bit worn.

LEVEE PATH PARK

Map p250 Part of the Mississippi River Trail, this unique public greenway runs atop the levee space that follows the curves of the Mississippi River all the way from the Fly behind Audubon Park to Jefferson Parish and beyond. It's a nice spot for walking, jogging or biking, but views onto the river are occasionally only so-so.

Be aware there aren't enough paths connecting the levee to the street below, so if you try to cross off the path, you may get ankle deep in Mississippi mud. Still, it's a good little green space.

EATING

Uptown and Riverbend are arguably the hottest food corridors in the city. There's no shortage of options, including shotgun shack diners, po'boy-slinging bars and cute garden cottages hiding some of the best Creole fine dining in town. Freret St, which has undergone a remarkable renaissance since Hurricane Katrina, is the latest foodie mecca, where new eateries put a gourmet spin on old favorites such as pizza, hamburgers and hot dogs.

Uptown

★DOMILISE'S PO-BOYS CREOLE $

Map p250 (5240 Annunciation St; po'boys $6-18; ⏲10am-7pm Mon-Wed & Fri, 10:30am-7pm Sat) Domilise's is everything that makes New Orleans great: a dilapidated white shack by the river serving Dixie beer, staffed by long-timers and prepping some of the best po'boys in the city. Locals tell us to opt for the half-and-half (oysters and shrimp) with gravy and cheese, but honestly, we think the oyster, dressed but otherwise on its own, is the height of the po'boy maker's craft.

Order at the front counter, stop by the bar, grab a seat, and welcome home. And oh, they'll tell you if the oysters are juicy, if you wanna know.

ST JAMES CHEESE CO DELI $

Map p250 (☎504-899-4737; www.stjamescheese.com; 5004 Prytania St; mains $9-16; ⏲11am-6pm Mon-Wed, to 8pm Thu-Sat, to 4pm Sun) Founded by an Englishman obsessed with all the right things (namely, meat and fermented milk products), St James is the best cheese shop in the city; there's a veritable atlas of cheese here. From the Gruyère grilled cheese to the French ham with brie, the sandwiches all sound enticing; we like the mozzarella with basil pesto and salami.

Enjoy a three-cheese plate and a glass of wine for $15 during happy hour (from 5pm to 8pm Thursday to Saturday).

SATSUMA MAPLE HEALTH FOOD $

Map p250 (www.satsumacafe.com; 7901 Maple St; breakfast $6-10, lunch $6-11; ⏲7am-5pm; 🖉) A stylish, bright-faced crowd lines up from the counter to the door at this popular health-food cafe beloved for its light and gourmet breakfasts. Choices include house-made granola, a tofu scramble and the 'green' breakfast sandwich with egg, arugula, tomato and avocado mash. Look for salads and sandwiches at lunch. Fresh organic juices sold, too.

DAT DOG AMERICAN $

Map p250 (☎504-899-6883; www.datdognola.com; 5030 Freret St; mains under $8; ⏲11am-10pm Mon-Sat, to 9pm Sun; 👪) Who dat who say Dat Dog? Da whole doggone city, dat's who. Every part of your tasty dog, from the steamed link to the toasted sourdough bun to the flavor-packed toppings, is produced with exuberance. Sausage choices include duck, alligator and crawfish. If you like your dawgs spicy, try the Louisiana hot sausage from nearby Harahan. And grab about 10 napkins for every topping. Several vegetarian dogs are available, too.

CAMELLIA GRILL DINER $

Map p250 (☎504-309-2679; 626 S Carrollton Ave; mains $4-11; ⏲8am-midnight Sun-Thu, to 2am Fri & Sat) Go ahead, accept the straw. You'll see what we mean after grabbing your seat. And the food? We love the burger-chili-Reuben diner fare, and the fact that all of the staff look like 50 Cent or The Ramones. And they all call each other – and you – 'baby.' Plus, they dress in tux shirts and black bow-ties.

One of our favorite New Orleans stories happened here: apparently a woman walked into Camellia and asked if it served low-fat dessert. The line cook's response? To dip a slice of pecan pie in melted butter and throw it on the grill. That's what you get!

CREOLE CREAMERY — ICE CREAM $

Map p250 (www.creolecreamery.com; 4924 Prytania St; 1 scoop $2.75; ⏲noon-10pm Sun-Thu, to 11pm Fri & Sat) Every single flavor at Creole Creamery sounds and is uniquely delicious: Steen's molasses oatmeal cookie; I Scream Fudge!; Bananas Foster; Lavender honey. And the list goes on. The good news? You can't go wrong. Flavors rotate, but you'll always find vanilla and chocolate. You'll earn a spot in the Hall of Fame if you eat eight scoops with eight toppings.

GUY'S — SANDWICHES $

Map p250 (☎504-891-5025; 5259 Magazine St; po'boys $7-13; ⏲11am-4pm Mon-Sat) It's very simple: Guy's is basically a one-man operation that does some of the best po'boys in town. Sandwiches are made fresh and to order, with a level of attention you don't get anywhere else in the city. Even when the line is out the door – and it often is – each po'boy is painstakingly crafted.

So yes, that loaf will take a while, but damn is it worth it.

BA CHI CANTEEN — VIETNAMESE $

Map p250 (www.facebook.com/bachicanteenla; 7900 Maple St; mains $4-15; ⏲11am-2:30pm Mon-Fri, to 3:30pm Sat, 5:30-9pm Mon-Wed, 5:30-10pm Thu-Sat) Do not be skeptical of the bacos. These pillowy bundles of deliciousness – a *banh bao* crossed with a taco – successfully merge the subtle seasonings of Vietnamese fillings with the foldable convenience of a taco-shaped steamed flour bun. Pho and *banh mi* – dubbed po'boys here – round out the menu.

It's a spare, casual spot with white-paper tablecloths and a bottle of Sriracha hot sauce and hoisin on every table.

IL POSTO — CAFE $

Map p250 (www.ilpostocafe-nola.com; 4607 Dryades St; mains less than $11; ⏲7am-5pm Mon, to 9pm Tue-Fri, 8am-9pm Sat, to 5pm Sun) At some point during an extended New Orleans trip, you're going to burn out on eggs Benedict, house-made boudin and bread pudding. Stylish Il Posto will be there for you when that happens. Order scones, croissants and bagels in the morning or stop by at lunch for prosciutto and mozzarella panini or beet and walnut salad with a glass of wine.

And the cookies by the register? Always a good idea.

CASAMENTO'S — SEAFOOD $

Map p250 (☎504-895-9761; www.casamentosrestaurant.com; 4330 Magazine St; mains $5-24; ⏲11am-2pm Tue-Sat, 5:30-9pm Thu-Sat early Sep–mid-May) One word: oysters. That's why you come here. Walk through the 1949 soda-shop-esque interior, across the tiled floors to a marble-top counter; trade a joke with the person shucking shells and get some raw boys with a beer. The thick gumbo with Creole tomatoes and oyster loaf (a sandwich of breaded and fried oysters) is suitably incredible. Cash only.

If the shucker respects the way you down your 'erster,' they might give you a fist bump on your way out the door.

TEE-EVA'S OLD-FASHIONED PIES & PRALINES — CREOLE $

Map p250 (www.tee-evapralines.com; 5201 Magazine St; praline cookie $2, pint of gumbo/jambalaya $5; ⏲11am-6pm Mon-Sat, noon-5pm Sun) It's impossible to nibble a praline from Tee-Eva's over the course of a day. Trust us, after one bite, you're a goner for the whole thing – right then. Tee-Eva once sang backup to the

ST CHARLES AVENUE STREETCAR

A buck twenty-five gets you on the **St Charles Avenue Streetcar** (p128; per ride $1.25; 👪) , which plies the oldest continuously operating street railway system in the world. This moving monument began life as the nation's second horse-drawn streetcar line, the New Orleans & Carrollton Railroad, in 1835. In 1893 the line was among the first systems to be electrified. Now it is one of the few streetcars in the USA to have survived the automobile era.

The fleet of antique cars survived the hurricanes of 2005 and today full service has been restored all the way to South Carrollton Ave. In recent times the line has carried more than 3 million passengers a year.

late, great local legend Ernie K-Doe; now she whips up snowballs and pralines, some fine hot lunches and some very fine Louisiana sweet and savory pies.

As you're heading toward Audubon Park from the Garden District, look for a red-and-yellow sign on your right.

HANSEN'S SNO-BLIZ DESSERTS $

Map p250 (☎504-891-9788; www.facebook.com/snobliz; 4801 Tchoupitoulas St; snowballs $3-7; ⊙1-7pm Tue-Sun Mar-Sep) The humble snowball (shaved ice with flavored syrup) is New Orleans' favorite dessert. Citywide consensus is that Hansen's, in business since 1939, does the best ball in town. Founder Ernest Hansen actually patented the shaved-ice machine. Now his granddaughter, Ashley, runs the family business, doling out shaved ice under everything from root-beer syrup to cream of nectar. Call or check the Facebook page before your visit to make sure it's open for the season.

MAHONY'S PO-BOY SHOP SANDWICHES $

Map p250 (www.mahonyspoboys.com; 3454 Magazine St; po'boys $9-22; ⊙11am-9pm) A convenient po'boy place with a fun atmosphere, Mahony's is a welcome if sometimes expensive choice. Digs are a converted Magazine St house with a tiny front porch. The Peacemaker with fried oysters, bacon and cheddar is a crowd-pleaser as is the grilled shrimp and fried green tomatoes, although we found the latter, at $14.95, lacking in oomph.

Take note that a new chef has recently taken the helm, and we hear menu changes are afoot.

KYOTO JAPANESE $

Map p250 (☎504-891-3644; www.kyotonola.com; 4920 Prytania St; mains $8-14, sushi & rolls $3-25; ⊙11am-2:30pm & 5-10pm Mon-Thu, to 10:30pm Fri, noon-3pm & 5-10:30pm Sat) Sporting a blond-wood interior, friendly hipster staff and chefs who care about creating fine raw-fish dishes, Kyoto is our favorite sushi bet in the city. The menu offers all your tuna, eel and yellowtail favorites plus local specialties such as crawfish rolls. It's popular with students, young families and Japanese expats (which may be the highest praise of all).

WHOLE FOODS MARKET $

Map p250 (www.wholefoodsmarket.com/stores/arabellastation; 5600 Magazine St; ⊙8am-9pm) What's that monstrosity? I hate it! Wait, it's Whole Foods? I love it! Yep, the gleaming organic market on Magazine St triggers mixed feelings. It sells organic foods and fills a neighborhood niche, but its opening in 2002 signaled a change in the character of Magazine St, which was largely composed of indie stores. Come here to meet your self-catering needs.

DELACHAISE INTERNATIONAL $$

Map p250 (☎504-895-0858; www.thedelachaise.com; 3442 St Charles Ave; small plates $8-28, cheese plates $13-28; ⊙5pm-late Mon-Thu, 3pm-late Fri-Sun) If you're looking for a place to relax, sip wine and watch the world go by,

LOCAL KNOWLEDGE

FOODIE FAVORITES GO UPTOWN

Three of New Orleans' most beloved restaurants – Willie Mae's Scotch House (p155), Domenica (p110) and Satsuma Cafe (p91) – have recently opened outposts in Uptown. So if you're looking for a reason to step off the St Charles Ave streetcar, why not try one of these fresh spins on old favorites?

Satsuma Maple (p134) For a fresh and healthy breakfast or lunch, join the stylish crowds at a spin-off of the popular Satsuma in the Bywater.

Willie Mae's Grocery & Deli (May p250; 7457 St Charles Ave; mains $10-16; ⊙11am-9pm) For fried chicken and comfort food, it's hard to beat Willie Mae's, which opened Willie Mae's Grocery & Deli in 2014.

Pizza Domenica (Map p250; www.pizzadomenica.com; 4933 Magazine St; pizza $11-18; ⊙11am-10pm Mon-Thu, to 11pm Fri & Sat, 10am-10pm Sun) Fans of wood-fired pizza can burn off calories with the short walk between the St Charles Ave streetcar and the much-lauded Pizza Domenica, which opened in 2014 on Magazine St. It's a more casual version of Chef Alon Shaya's Domenica in the Roosevelt Hotel.

Delachaise is a great choice. It's just steps from the St Charles streetcar line. The small plates are wonderful in their indulgent way, especially the ridiculously over-the-top grilled cheese sandwich with house-made apple butter. And everyone lovingly recalls the *pommes frites* – fried in goose fat.

If it's late at night, you're hungry and you need something a little more refined than a burger, head here.

★GAUTREAU'S MODERN AMERICAN **$$$**

Map p250 (☎504-899-7397; www.gautreaus-restaurant.com; 1728 Soniat St; mains $22-42; ⏰6-10pm Mon-Sat) There's no sign outside Gautreau's, just the number 1728 discreetly marking a nondescript house in a residential neighborhood. Cross the threshold to find a refined but welcoming dining room where savvy diners, many of them New Orleanian food aficionados, dine on fresh, modern American fare. Chef Sue Zemanick has won every award a rising young star can garner in American culinary circles.

Entrees range from sautéed cobia with créme fraîche beurre blanc and king trumpet mushrooms to the lauded roasted chicken with garlic mashed potatoes. Zimarek's accolades include 'Top 10 Best New Chefs' in *Food & Wine* magazine and 'Chef of the Year' in *New Orleans* magazine. Call several days in advance for reservations.

★CLANCY'S CREOLE **$$$**

Map p250 (☎504-895-1111; www.clancysrestaurant.com; 6100 Annunciation St; lunch $16-18, dinner $25-35) This white-tablecloth neighborhood restaurant embraces style, the good life and Creole cuisine with a chattering joie de vivre and top-notch service. The city's professional set comes here to gossip and savor the specialties: fried oysters and brie, veal with crabmeat and béarnaise, and lobster and mushroom risotto. Want to go where the locals go? Come here, and dress up a little. Reservations recommended.

PATOIS FRENCH, CREOLE **$$$**

Map p250 (☎504-895-9441; www.patoisnola.com; 6078 Laurel St; lunch $13-21, brunch $13-19, dinner $23-32; ⏰5:30-10pm Wed & Thu, to 10:30pm Fri & Sat, 11:30am-2pm Fri, 10:30am-2pm Sun) The interior of Patois feels like the cozy house of very good friends – who happen to be very good cooks. Head chef Aaron Burgau went through his paces in New Orleans' top restaurants, including Commander's Palace, before opening Patois. The setting has an unaffected rustic romantic vibe, while the menu is French haute with New Orleans accents (or 'patois').

LILETTE FRENCH **$$$**

Map p250 (☎504-895-1636; www.liletterestaurant.com; 3637 Magazine St; lunch mains $11-24, dinner $26-37; ⏰11:30am-2pm Tue-Sat, 5:30-9:30pm Mon-Thu, to 10:30pm Fri & Sat) Where has all the romance gone? To this white-linen bistro that sparkles with a traditional but lively European vibe. Chef John Harris adds an innovative spin to familiar dishes. The white-truffle parmigiana toast with wild mushrooms is a nice start to date night, and a solid lineup of mains, including grilled hanger steak with fries and marrowed bordelaise sauce, ensures a perfect evening.

Lunch is a nice way to pass an afternoon on Magazine St. Harris owns the equally stylish Bouligny Tavern next door.

Riverbend

REFUEL CAFE **$**

Map p250 (☎504-872-0187; www.refuelcafe.com; 8124 Hampson St; mains $7-13; ⏰7am-2pm Mon-Fri, 8:30am-2pm Sat & Sun) Hip Refuel packs 'em in tight on Sunday mornings, but still manages to look cute and breezy. It adds a bit of chic to the local coffee scene, but it's hardly pretentious; service is some of the friendliest in town. Fresh food such as Baja omelets with avocado are served alongside Southern mainstays such as creamy cheese grits with andouille. Order at the counter.

MAGASIN CAFE VIETNAMESE **$**

Map p250 (www.magasincafe.com; 4201 Magazine St; mains $5-13; ⏰11am-3:30pm, 6-9pm Tue-Sat) The food is fresh and light, but deceptively filling, inside this spare and shiny cube. Magasin won't be embraced by those who think pho is only good if it's served in a grubby hovel in a sketchy neighborhood far, far away. But everyone else? Come join the party. The *banh mi* sandwiches are a great deal, starting at $4.50.

One of the best parts of the experience? The service, which is simultaneously thoughtful, efficient and attentive.

★BOUCHERIE SOUTHERN **$$**

Map p250 (☎504-862-5514; www.boucherie-nola.com; 8115 Jeannette St; lunch $10-18, dinner $15-18; ⏰11am-3pm & 5:30-9:30pm Tue-Sat) The

HOT NEIGHBORHOODS: FRERET STREET

The revitalization of decaying Freret St into a much-lauded dining destination is one of New Orleans' biggest post-Katrina success stories. The eight-block strip, which stretches from Jefferson Ave to Napoleon Ave, had been in a state of serious decline for decades. Named for 19th-century mayor and cotton baron William Freret, the street was a prosperous business corridor in the 1920s and 1930s. The neighborhood lost families to white flight from the 1950s into the 1970s, and the fatal shooting of a popular business owner in front of his store in the mid-1980s hastened the slide. Mother Nature seemed to deal the final blow in 2005 when the levee broke and several feet of water doused the neighborhood.

A few community stalwarts started the **Freret Street Market** (Map p250; www.freretmarket.org; cnr Freret St & Napoleon Ave; ⏲noon-5pm 1st Sat of month Sep-Jun) in 2007, but the revitalization really began after Neal Bodenheimer and Matthew Kohnke transformed a 100-year-old former firehouse into craft cocktail bar **Cure**. City council member Stacy Head, who represents the district, helped the neighborhood win a more development-friendly zoning designation, and new eateries began trickling onto the strip. That trickle has become a storm; by 2011 there were 11 new restaurants on Freret St and today there are 16. The 2014 PBS documentary *Getting Back to Abnormal* examines the Freret district's 2010 city council race, spotlighting Head, her opponent, race relations and post-Katrina politics.

This new dining and drinking destination presents a bedeviling dilemma for gourmands who are only in town for a short time – how do you decide where to go? Truthfully? It's hard to go wrong. You'll find topping-slathered hot dogs and sausages at **Dat Dog** (p134), gourmet deep-dish pies at **Midway Pizza** (Map p250; ☎504-322-2815; www.midwaypizzanola.com; 4725 Freret St; pizzas $14-20; ⏲11:30am-11pm Sun-Wed, to midnight Thu-Sat), natural burgers at **The Company Burger** (Map p250; http://thecompanyburger.com; 4600 Freret St) and comfort food from the bayou and the delta at **High Hat Cafe** (Map p250; ☎504-754-1336; www.highhatcafe.com; 4500 Freret St; mains $11-20; ⏲11am-9pm Sun-Thu, to 10pm Fri & Sat). For craft beer and cocktails try the new **Freret Street Publiq House** (p140). For a list of the 20 or so eateries and bars in the neighborhood, visit www.thenewfreret.com. Bon appetit!

thick, glistening cuts of bacon on the BLT can only be the work of the devil – or chef Nathanial Zimet, whose house-cured meats and succulent Southern dishes are lauded citywide. Savor boudin balls with garlic aioli, blackened shrimp in bacon vinaigrette, and smoked Wagyu brisket with gloriously stinky garlic-parmesan fries. The Krispy Kreme bread pudding with rum syrup is a wonder.

Boucherie is the Cajun word for a celebratory community pig-pickin'. The food here captures that down-home exuberance. As the motto says, 'It's fine dining for the people.'

★JACQUES-IMO'S CAFÉ — LOUISIANAN $$

Map p250 (☎504-861-0886; www.jacquesimoscafe.com; 8324 Oak St; mains $20-32; ⏲5-10pm Mon-Thu, to 10:30pm Fri & Sat) Ask locals for restaurant recommendations in New Orleans, and almost everybody mentions Jacques-Imo's. We understand why: cornbread muffins swimming in butter, steak smothered in blue-cheese sauce, and the insane yet wickedly brilliant shrimp and alligator-sausage cheesecake. That's the attitude at Jack Leonardi's exceedingly popular restaurant: die, happily, with butter and heavy sauces sweating out of your pores.

Jacques is a few doors from the famous Maple Leaf Bar, and many people make an evening out of these two spots. But you don't need an excuse to dine at this dive-cum-haute-cuisine outpost. On busy nights expect long waits.

COWBELL — BURGERS $$

Map p250 (www.cowbell-nola.com; 8801 Oak St; mains $12-28; ⏲11:30am-9pm Tue-Thu, to 10pm Fri & Sat) Cowbell has a scruffy charm – scuffed wooden floors, Elvis on the ceiling – that makes you want to stay awhile. Its riverside perch by the levee is appealing too, but it's the juicy grass-fed beef burgers that seal the deal. Nonbeef options include grilled Gulf fish tacos and lime-grilled organic chicken. We hear the mac 'n' cheese is divine.

Solos will do just fine at the efficient but friendly bar, and carnivores who like their burgers medium rare will get 'em that way.

LA PETITE GROCERY FRENCH **$$**

Map p250 (☎504-891-3377; www.lapetitegrocery.com; 4238 Magazine St; mains $16-34; ⏰11:30am-2:30pm Tue-Sat, 10:30am-2:30pm Sun, 5:30-9:30pm Sun-Thu, to 10:30pm Fri & Sat) Petite is one of the many cozy and popular bistros squeezed into the crowded Uptown dining scene. We like the lunches, which consist of some very fine sandwiches and salads. The dinners are good but not great for the price, and include bistro mainstays such as Gulf shrimp and grits. Chef Justin Devillier is three-time James Beard nominee for Best Chef: South. Look for Beard's latest venture, Balise, in the CBD.

MAT & NADDIE'S CREOLE **$$$**

Map p250 (☎504-861-9600; www.matandnaddies.com; 937 Leonidas St; mains $22-29; ⏰5:30-9:30pm Mon, Tue & Thu-Sat) Set in a beautiful riverfront shotgun house with a Christmas-lights-bedecked patio in the back, Mat & Naddie's offers rich, innovative, even amusing food – such as Gulf fish quenelles with crawfish sauce, chocolate peanut-butter gooey butter cake – and a friendly staff. It's high quality topped with quirkiness and, honestly, it's one of our favorite splurges in the city.

DRINKING & NIGHTLIFE

There's not much difference between this drinking scene and the fun going on in the Lower Garden District; Magazine St maintains a generally young, hip, neighborhoody vibe throughout. Bars in Riverbend attract more of a student crowd.

Uptown

CURE BAR

Map p250 (☎504-302-2357; www.curenola.com; 4905 Freret St; ⏰5pm-midnight Sun-Thu, to 2am Fri & Sat) This stylish purveyor of cocktails and spirits flickers like an ultramodern apothecary shop, a place where mysterious elixirs are expertly mixed to soothe whatever ails you. A smooth and polished space of modern banquettes, anatomic art and a Zen-garden outdoor area, Cure is where you come for a well-mixed drink, period. It's drinks for adults in a stylish setting.

The premise here is that a good cocktail is the height of a bartender's craft. Classics like the sidecar and the Rob Roy are given an innovative spin with spices, citrusy additions and, occasionally, chocolate. On Friday and Saturday evenings men will be asked to remove their baseball caps – a tactic intended to filter out rowdy undergrads.

ST JOE'S BAR

Map p250 (www.stjoesbar.com; 5535 Magazine St; ⏰4pm-3am Mon-Fri, noon-3am Sat, to 1am Sun) The bartender might make a face when you order a blueberry mojito – mojitos are hard to make. But dang, dude, you make 'em so good. They've been voted the best in town by New Orleanians several times. Patrons at this dark-but-inviting place are in their 20s and 30s, and friendly and chatty, as are the staff.

The layout is also a draw – the narrow front leads past a series of faux-Catholic shrines into a spacious backyard that feels like a cross between an Indonesian island and a Thai temple. And the jukebox? Well stocked with jazz, rock and blues.

COLUMNS HOTEL BAR

Map p250 (www.thecolumns.com; 3811 St Charles Ave; ⏰2pm-midnight Mon-Thu, 11am-2am Fri & Sat, to midnight Sun) With its antebellum trappings – a raised front porch, white Doric columns, a flanking live oak – the Columns Hotel harks back to a simpler era. Oh yes, we're going to party like it's 1859. But truthfully, it's not as aristocratic as all that; it's more a place where college students and just-graduates act the part of the Southern upper-crust.

This hotel bar is a great place to sit back with a cool glass of gin while fanning yourself and watching the St Charles streetcar crank past.

COOTER BROWN'S TAVERN & OYSTER BAR BAR

Map p250 (☎504-866-9104; www.cooterbrowns.com; 509 S Carrollton Ave; ⏰11am-late; 📶) Cooter's scores points with locals because it served as a community gathering place in the aftermath of Katrina. College kids, local characters and Uptown swells drop in for brews and freshly shucked oysters, or to shoot pool or watch sports on TV. It also takes beer seriously, with 84 taps. The Snooty Cooter beer bar in back spotlights craft brews.

Pause to appreciate the tavern's 'Celebrity Hall of Foam and Beersoleum' – a gallery of more than 100 plaster bas-relief statuettes of everybody from Liberace to Chairman Mao, each holding a bottle of beer. This curious, still-growing exhibit is the work of the uniquely talented Scott Conary.

FRERET STREET PUBLIQ HOUSE BAR

Map p250 (☎504-826-9912; www.publiqhouse.com; 4528 Freret St; ⏲4pm-midnight Mon-Thu, to 2am Fri, 2pm-2am Sat, to midnight Sun; 🐾) Hello Publiq House. Welcome to Freret St. So glad you're here. Let's call this place an uber-neighborhood bar – it goes above and beyond your typical corner dive. Trivia night. Cornhole night. Burlesque shows. Crawfish boils. More than 90 local and national beers available, plus some fancy cocktails. Live music, on a side-room stage, ranges from jazz to rock to funk.

This place has a welcoming vibe. And your dog is allowed inside, except during shows.

LE BON TEMPS ROULÉ BAR

Map p250 (☎504-897-3448; 4801 Magazine St; ⏲11am-3am) A neighborhood bar – a very good one at that – with a mostly college and postcollege crowd drawn in by two pool tables and a commendable beer selection. Late at night, high-caliber blues, zydeco or jazz rocks the joint's little back room.

It's the sort of bar where a lesbian punches a guy for trying to steal her girlfriend's Abita, and then all three laugh about the incident afterwards.

BOULIGNY TAVERN COCKTAIL BAR, WINE BAR

Map p250 (☎504-891-1810; www.boulignytavern.com; 3641 Magazine St; ⏲4pm-midnight Mon-Thu, to 2am Fri & Sat) You're going to look good in Bouligny Tavern. Sexy lighting, *Mad Men* decor, inventive cocktails and an extensive wine list – it all comes together as a lively, flattering tableau. A fashionable addition to the Magazine St bar scene, Bouligny draws after-work crowds and those prepping their palate before a meal at chef John Harris' companion restaurant Lilette next door.

The small plates are divine, particularly the bruschetta and the gouda beignets. You don't like gin? Try one of their gin cocktails – we're guessing you'll change your mind. This low-key hideaway is in a house fronted by a live oak, and it's easy to miss. Look for the alluringly lit alley-way patio.

SNAKE & JAKES BAR

Map p250 (☎504-861-2802; www.snakeandjakes.com; 7612 Oak St; ⏲from 7pm) Looking like a bayou bait shack tarted up for Christmas, Snake & Jakes is an institution. Some say the place messes with the space-time continuum – enter at 3am and a mere five minutes later you're stumbling outside and the sun's coming up. If this happens to you, pat yourself on the back: you're now a fully fledged honorary New Orleanian.

If you end up here any time before 3am, it's probably too early. When you're out with your buddies and someone says, 'Let's go to Snakes,' that's a sure sign the night is either going to get much better or immeasurably worse.

F&M'S PATIO BAR BAR

Map p250 (☎504-895-6784; www.fandmpatiobar.com; 4841 Tchoupitoulas St; ⏲7pm-4am Sun-Thu, to 5:30am Fri & Sat) If you're old enough to be paying off your student loans, you may want to give F&M a pass on weekends, when every college student in Louisiana tests the structural integrity of the bar's leopard-print pool tables by dancing on them. The rest of the week this is a fine place, with pool, a grill and a semi-outdoor area for a cold beer.

MS MAE'S BAR

Map p250 (☎504-895-9401; 4336 Magazine St; ⏲24hr) The vibe at this famed dive – one of the toughest in the city – isn't exactly warm and fuzzy, especially if you're a solo-traveling chick. But late-night with friends? It's a dark den of all that is sinful and fun. Every thread of the human tapestry gets woven into this great, grotty hole.

Ms Mae sold the bar in 2010, but this legendary place keeps on. Despite its gritty reputation, we hear she always kept the women's bathroom immaculately clean. And it does sit across the street from the police precinct. There's even a website dedicated to the stupid behavior folks inevitably engage in here (http://msmaeswallofshame.blogspot.com).

MONKEY HILL BAR BAR

Map p250 (☎504-899-4800; www.monkeyhillbar.com; 6100 Magazine St; ⏰3pm-2am Mon-Thu, to 3am Fri, 1pm-3am Sat, 2pm-2am Sun) Toward the quiet end of Magazine St, Monkey Hill looks and feels like a neighborhood bar, but it's also one of the best happy-hour spots (3pm to 8pm weeknights) in this part of town and hosts some good live music on a monthly basis. If you're near Audubon Park late in the afternoon, it's a fine place to stop.

BOOT BAR

Map p250 (☎504-866-9008; www.thebootneworleans.com; 1039 Broadway St; ⏰11am-5am) Considering the Boot is almost located within Tulane's campus, it's unsurprising this college bar practically doubles as student housing for that university. If you're within the vicinity of 21 years old, this place is a lot of fun; otherwise, you might think you've accidentally stumbled into Athens, what with all the Greek system types (ie frat boys and sorority girls) about.

Riverbend

RUE DE LA COURSE CAFE

Map p250 (www.ruedelacourse.com; 1140 S Carrollton Ave; ⏰6:30am-11pm Mon-Fri, 7am-11pm Sat & Sun; 📶) The setting alone – a cavernous former bank building on the corner of Carrollton Ave and Oak St – is reason enough to step inside for a look-see. Once over the threshold, with a glimpse at the pastries and list of hot and cold javas, you'll surely be tempted to settle in and soak up the atmosphere. Cash only.

OAK WINE BAR WINE BAR

Map p250 (www.oaknola.com; 8118 Oak St; ⏰5-11pm Tue-Thu, to midnight Fri & Sat) With a both swanky and spare setting, the vibe is a little off-kilter, but if you'd like a glass of wine or a specialty cocktail in a nondivey setting, this is a nice choice. You can catch live jazz and acoustic folk here on Friday and Saturday nights at 9pm. Offers 30 wines by the glass.

☆ ENTERTAINMENT

Many bars in Uptown and Riverbend offer live music. We list venues that do it particularly well and are worth a special trip.

★MAPLE LEAF BAR LIVE MUSIC

Map p250 (☎504-866-9359; www.mapleleafbar.com; 8316 Oak St; cover $10, Mon free; ⏰3pm-late) The premier nighttime destination in the Riverbend area, the legendary Maple Leaf's dimly lit, pressed-tin caverns are the kind of environs you'd expect from a New Orleans juke joint. Work up a sweat on the small dance floor directly in front of the stage or relax at the bar in the next room. The funky Rebirth Brass Band ($15) plays Tuesdays, starting between 10pm and 11pm.

Scenes from the film *Angel Heart* (1987), in which the late, great blues man Brownie McGhee starred, were shot here. There's also a nice back patio on which to cool your heels.

TIPITINA'S LIVE MUSIC

Map p250 (☎504-895-8477; www.tipitinas.com; 501 Napoleon Ave) 'Tips,' as locals call it, is one of New Orleans' great musical meccas. The legendary Uptown nightclub, which takes its name from Professor Longhair's 1953 hit single, is the site of some of the city's most memorable shows, particularly when big names such as Dr John come home to roost. Outstanding music from local talent packs 'em in year-round.

This is one of the few non–French Quarter bars regularly drawing tourists. The joint really jumps in the weeks prior to Mardi Gras and during Jazz Fest.

GASA GASA LIVE MUSIC

Map p250 (☎504-304-7110; www.gasagasa.com; 4920 Freret St) We're unsure what is most interesting at this newish performance and drinking space inside an art gallery: the art, the music or the patrons. The name means 'easily distracted' or 'doing too many things at once' in Japanese – but we can't confirm that because, well, all of the above. Come for an eclectic array of live music, from jazz to folk to indie.

Big Freedia was on the lineup for the first anniversary celebrations.

PRYTANIA THEATRE CINEMA

Map p250 (☎504-891-2787; www.prytaniatheatreneworleans.com; 5339 Prytania St; tickets adult/child under 12yr/senior $11.50/9.50/9.50, matinee $5.75) This old movie-house has been around since the 1920s, and screens independent and art films as well as classics. Our favorite theater in the city.

SHOPPING

Magazine St is the city's best shopping strip. You can take a good multi-mile window-shopping hike stretching from Audubon Park to Louisiana Ave. The area around Maple St in Riverbend is another hopping carnival of consumption. Fashionable shops and restaurants front a small square on Dublin St near S Carrollton Ave, where it meets St Charles Ave. To get here, take the St Charles Ave streetcar (or bus 11 to bus 32) to the Riverbend near Camellia Grill. On the river side of S Carrollton, Oak St is an older neighborhood commercial zone intersecting with the streetcar line. It's reasonably compact for strolling and offers a few interesting businesses, along with restaurants and the stellar Maple Leaf Bar.

DIRTY COAST — CLOTHING

Map p250 (☎504-324-3745; www.dirtycoast.com; 5631 Magazine St; ⏰11am-6pm Mon-Fri, 10am-6pm Sat & Sun) You're not a cool new New Orleanian if you haven't picked up one of the clever T-shirts or bumper stickers (eg Make Wetlands, Not War), all related to local issues, inside jokes and neighborhood happenings, in this ridiculously cool store. Staying in the Warehouse District? Check out its new location at 329 Julia St.

POTSALOT — ARTS, CRAFTS

Map p250 (www.potsalot.com; 3818 Magazine St; ⏰10am-5pm Tue-Sat) Owners Alex and Cindy Williams, who have made and sold pottery from their Magazine St shop since 1993, call their exquisite creations functional art. Their unique, personally tested pieces are made for use in the kitchen, bathroom and den, and include everything from bowls and platters to lamps and vases and, yes, lotsa pots. Their eye-catching sinks – with scallops, dimples and rolled lips – are particularly cool.

> ### MAGAZINE STREET
>
> For the true-blue shopper, New Orleans doesn't get much better than Magazine St. For some 6 miles the street courses through the Warehouse District and along the riverside edge of the Garden District and Uptown, lined nearly the entire way with small shops selling antiques, art, contemporary fashions, vintage clothing, and other odds and ends. The street hits its peak in the Lower Garden District (near Jackson Ave), the Garden District (between 1st and 7th Sts) and Uptown (from Antonine St to Napoleon Ave). No car? Take bus 11.

HAZELNUT — HOMEWARES

Map p250 (☎504-891-2424; www.hazelnutneworleans.com; 5515 Magazine St; ⏰10am-6pm Mon-Sat) If you accidentally knock over a display of poinsettas after the Christmas holidays, and it starts falling…actor Bryan Batt of *Mad Men* fame (he played art director Salvatore Romano) might just swoop in and save it before it hits the ground. Not that we'd, er, know anything about that. The gracious, unflappable Batt co-owns Hazelnut, an elegant, pleasantly eclectic gift and homewares shop.

In addition to classically cool New Orleans-print toile, the shop also sells gilded glassware, postmodern ceramics and other interior-decor must-haves for the stylishly modern.

CRESCENT CITY COMICS — COMICS

Map p250 (www.crescentcitycomics.com; 4916 Freret St; ⏰11am-7pm Mon-Sat, noon-6pm Sun) Helpful, on-the-ball staff members are what make Crescent City Comics shine. The store is compact but well stocked, with sections dedicated to everything from local comics to underground to graphic reads. Neil Gaiman and sci-fi action figures are also in the stacks. Check it out.

MAPLE STREET BOOK SHOP — BOOKS

Map p250 (www.maplestreetbookshop.com; 7523 Maple St; ⏰10am-6pm Mon-Sat, 11am-5pm Sun) This beloved Uptown shop celebrated its 50th anniversary in 2014. Founded by sisters Mary Kellogg and Rhoda Norman, it is one of the most politically progressive, well-stocked bookshops in the city. The store sells new, used and rare books in an invitingly overstuffed setting.

COLE PRATT GALLERY — ART

Map p250 (www.coleprattgallery.com; 3800 Magazine St; ⏰10am-5pm Tue-Sat) This fine-art gallery showcases the work of 42 contemporary Gulf Coast and Southern artists. Paintings here might include Susan Downing-White's Gulf Coast landscapes or David Armentor's haunting black-and-white photos of sugar farms and mills.

FEET FIRST — SHOES

Map p250 (www.feetfirststores.com; 4122 Magazine St; ⊙10am-6pm Mon-Sat, to 5pm Sun) Feet First has been selling shoes to New Orleans' fashionistas for more than 30 years. Pop into this bright store for sandals, boots and heels as well as jewelry, frocks and T-shirts.

PELICAN COAST CLOTHING CO — CLOTHING

Map p250 (www.pelicancoastclothing.com; 5509 Magazine St; ⊙10am-6pm Mon-Sat, noon-5pm Sun) Dapper dudes and Tulane students get their preppy on at this small and friendly shop. It's packed tight with colorful ties and sports shirts, plus some cool travel bags.

BERTA'S & MINA'S ANTIQUITIES — ART

Map p250 (4138 Magazine St; ⊙10am-6pm Mon-Sat, noon-4pm Sun) This painting-cluttered gallery specializes in regional folk art, especially the works of the late Nilo Lanzas, whose daughter operates the shop. Lanzas began painting at 63 and produced an impressive body of work, most of it of an outsider art or religious bent. Museums and serious collectors have snatched up many of Lanzas' paintings. You'll find dozens of nice pieces, all eye-catching and worthy of homes.

His daughter, Mina, also paints and her works show alongside her father's and a few other artists from the city and its surrounds. The gallery is one of the oldest on Magazine St.

C COLLECTION — FASHION

Map p250 (☎504-861-5002; www.ccollectionnola.com; 8141 Maple St; ⊙10am-6pm Mon-Sat) This boutique, preening fashionably inside a converted house, does its best to keep the female population of Tulane University (and the women of Riverbend region in general) looking smart with its range of short shorts, flowy skirts, cute dresses and silky shirts plus fashionable sunglasses, scarves, jeans and shoes. New outfits are posted at www.facebook.com/ccollection.

BLOOMIN' DEALS — CLOTHING, BOOKS

Map p250 (www.jlno.org; 4645 Freret St; ⊙10am-5pm Tue-Sat, 12:30-4:30pm Sun) OK, so this Junior League–run thrift store isn't exactly Bloomingdales, but some of the donations may have originated there. The women's collection is extensive – there's lots of jeans – and you might just pick up a unique ball gown that's only been worn once at Mardi Gras. There's lots of used books for sale, too (from 25¢).

PIED NU — FASHION, HOMEWARES

Map p250 (☎504-899-4118; www.piednunola.com; 5521 Magazine St; ⊙10am-5pm Mon-Sat) If you need a hand-poured candle that lasts 60 hours, try one of the sweet-smelling Diptyques on sale here. As you soak up that vanilla-scented goodness, browse elephant-printed cotton T-shirt dresses, cinched poet-dresses and low-joe sneakers. Set it all off with tiny leaf earrings – you'll make yourself almost as endearing as this precious luxury shop.

Mid-City & the Tremé

MID-CITY | THE TREMÉ

Neighborhood Top Five

❶ Spending a lazy afternoon at **City Park** (p146), checking out art, outdoor sculptures, gardens and a toy train, then blissing out under an oak tree as the world spins by.

❷ Indulging in a night of good barbecue and better cocktails at **Twelve Mile Limit** (p156).

❸ Hearing stories about New Orleans' most intriguing former citizens on a tour of the crypts at **St Louis Cemetery No 1** (p148).

❹ Seeing the Tremé Brass Band jam at the **Candlelight Lounge** (p157).

❺ Eating a po'boy at **Parkway Tavern** (p152) – you'll never go back to normal sandwiches.

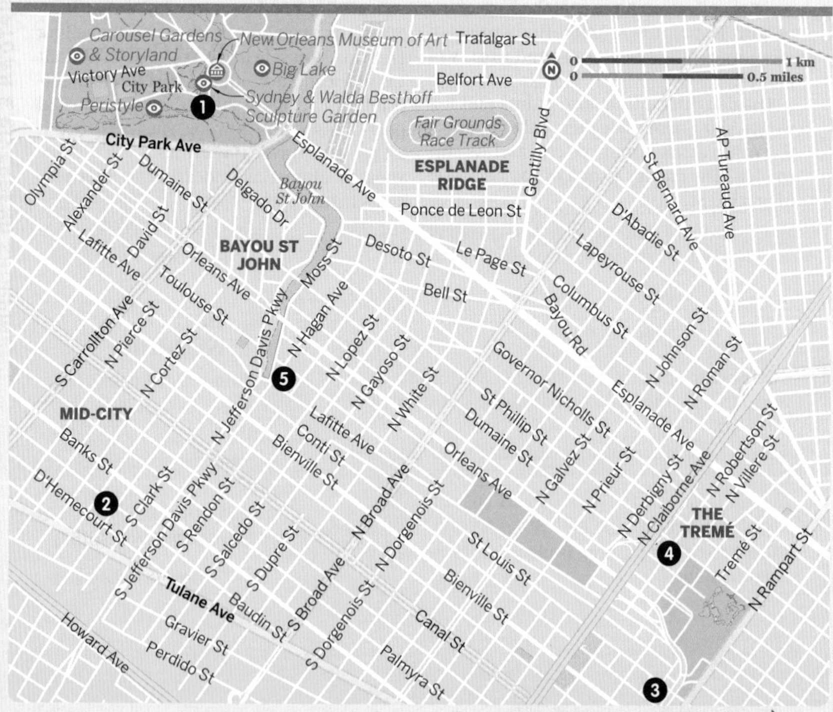

For more detail of this area see Map p254

Explore Mid-City & the Tremé

A bike ride may be the most pleasant way to explore the 'green' sections of these neighborhoods, either on your own or with the folks at Confederacy of Cruisers (p93). If you cycle independently, just roll up attractive Esplanade Ave and take it all the way to City Park, stopping at St Louis Cemetery No 3 along the way. Explore the park and the New Orleans Museum of Art, and afterwards stop in for dinner at Café Degas. In the evening, enjoy a drink at Pal's or Twelve Mile Limit.

On the second day, walk around the Tremé, making sure you stop by the Backstreet Cultural Museum and St Louis Cemetery No 1. Have lunch at Dooky Chase, then drive up to Bayou St John, enjoy the serenity and consider dinner at Parkway Tavern.

Starting from the southwest, near Banks St, Mid-City is a mix of commercial lots and residential blocks. Northeast is Bayou St John, ringed with historic houses, and the great green stretches of City Park. In the southeast, Esplanade Ave runs to the French Quarter. The Tremé is less amorphous, being bound by Rampart St, Louis Armstrong Park, Claiborne Ave (or Broad St, definitions vary) and St Bernard Ave.

Local Life

➡ **Food** These leafy neighborhoods are chock full of unassuming restaurants serving fantastic comfort food. The low-key friendliness of these joints just adds to the allure.

➡ **Green spaces** City Park is the obvious contender for top green space in New Orleans, but there's also Bayou St John, Esplanade Ave and plenty of tree-lined streets.

➡ **Nightlife** As with the food scene, there's a ton of unexpected nightlife gems in this corner of town, from convivial bars to great music venues.

Getting There & Away

➡ **Streetcar** The City Park spur of Canal St hits Carrollton St, then heads up that road all the way to City Park.

➡ **Bus** The 91 runs up Esplanade Ave, turns into Mid-City and drops by City Park. The 27 follows Louisiana Ave, and also hits the park. The 94 bus runs along Broad, cutting through both Mid-City and the Tremé.

➡ **Car** Free street parking is plentiful throughout both neighborhoods.

Lonely Planet's Top Tip

Mid-City & the Tremé are best explored by car. Sights are spread out in small clusters of activity across the cityscape. Walking around parts of the Tremé at night, especially near St Louis Cemetery No 1 and the Iberville projects, is not recommended.

Best Cultural Sights

➡ Backstreet Cultural Museum (p151)

➡ New Orleans Museum of Art (p146)

➡ St Louis Cemetery No 1 (p148)

➡ Besthoff Sculpture Garden (p146)

➡ Le Musée de f.p.c. (p149)

For reviews, see p152 ➡

Best Outdoor Activities

➡ City Park (p146)

➡ Bayou St John (p152)

➡ Botanical Gardens (p146)

➡ Kayakitiyat Tour (p149)

➡ Esplanade Avenue (p149)

For reviews, see p149 ➡

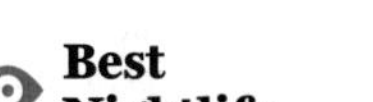

Best Nightlife

➡ Twelve Mile Limit (p156)

➡ Mid-City Rock & Bowl (p157)

➡ Candlelight Lounge (p157)

➡ Pal's (p156)

➡ Chickie Wah Wah (p157)

For reviews, see p156 ➡

ROY LICHTENSTEIN'S "FIVE BRUSHSTROKES"/IMAGE COURTESY OF NEW ORLEANS MUSEUM OF ART. ©

TOP SIGHT
CITY PARK

Live oaks, Spanish moss and lazy bayous frame this masterpiece of urban planning. Three miles long and 1 mile wide, dotted with gardens, waterways, bridges and home to a captivating art museum, City Park is bigger than Central Park in NYC, and it's New Orleans' prettiest green space. It's also a perfect expression of a local 'park,' in the sense that it is an only slightly tamed version of the forest and Louisiana wetlands – Bayou Metairie runs through the grounds – that are the natural backdrop of the city.

Looking like a vague cross between Lenin's tomb and a Greek temple, the **New Orleans Museum of Art** (Map p254; NOMA; ☎504-658-4100; www.noma.org; 1 Collins Diboll Circle; adult/child 7-17yr $10/6; ⏲10am-6pm Tue-Thu, to 9pm Fri, 11am-5pm Sat & Sun) is one of the finest art museums in the South. There's strong representation from regional and American artists, but the work of masters who have passed through the city, such as Edgar Degas, is also prominent. Temporary exhibitions are daring but accessible to the average art-lover. Our favorite section is the top floor, chockablock with fantastic African, Asian, Oceanic, pre-Columbian and Native American art.

DON'T MISS

- Sydney & Walda Besthoff Sculpture Garden
- Botanical Gardens
- New Orleans Museum of Art
- Carousel Gardens
- Storyland
- Singing Oak

PRACTICALITIES

- Map p254
- ☎504-482-4888
- www.neworleanscitypark.com
- Esplanade Ave & City Park Ave

Three of George Rodrigue's Blue Dogs – in red, yellow and blue – await your arrival in the pleasant **Sydney & Walda Besthoff Sculpture Garden** (Map p254; ☎504-488-2631; www.noma.org; 1 Collins Diboll Circle; ⏲10am-6pm Mon-Fri, to 5pm Sat & Sun) FREE, which sits beside the New Orleans Museum of Art. The garden opened in 2003 with pieces from the world-renowned Besthoff collection and today holds more than 60 pieces, dotted across 5 acres. Most are contemporary works by artists such as Antoine Bourdelle, Henry Moore and Louise Bourgeois.

The **Botanical Gardens** (Map p254; ☎504-483-9386; www.neworleanscitypark.com; City Park; adult/child 36in & under $4/free; ⏲10am-4:30pm Tue-Sun) exhibits local and international flora, and there are stirring examples of Works Progress Administration (WPA) workmanship and art-deco design in the form of pavilions and function halls such as the Pavilion of Two Sisters and Lath House. The gardens are delightful year-round, except in humid August. For the best bloom display, visit in March and April. The fascinating Train Garden replicates the city in 1:22 scale miniature size, cut through with 1300ft of rail.

Overlooking Bayou Metairie like a Greek temple is the **Peristyle** (Map p254; City Park), a classical pavilion topped by Ionic columns, built in 1907. Four concrete lions stand watch, while weddings, dances, recitals and curious tourists meander through.

Anyone who doesn't like the charmingly dated **Carousel Gardens** (Map p254; ☎504-483-9402; www.neworleanscitypark.com; 7 Victory Ave, City Park; adult/children 36in & under $4/free, rides $4; ⌚10am-5pm Tue-Thu, 10am-10pm Fri, 11am-10pm Sat, 11am-6pm Sun Jun & July, Sat & Sun only spring & fall) must surely have a heart of stone. This lovingly restored antique carousel is housed in a 1906 structure with a stained-glass cupola. In the 1980s, residents raised $1.2 million to restore the broken animals, fix the squeaky merry-go-round and replace the Wurlitzer organ. The results are spectacular in a tweedy, tinkly kind of way. You can board the tiny City Park Railroad here as well, plus a little Ferris wheel, bumper cars and a tilt-a-whirl.

There are no rides at **Storyland** (www.neworleanscitypark.com; adult/child 36in & under $4/free; ⌚10am-5pm Tue-Fri, until 6pm Sat & Sun), located next to Carousel Gardens, but the fairy-tale statuary provides plenty of fuel for young imaginations. Children can climb upon the Jabberwocky from *Alice in Wonderland*, or enter the mouth of the whale from *Pinocchio*. If these characters seem strangely similar to Mardi Gras floats, it's because they were created by master float-builder Blaine Kern. During the Christmas season it's lit up like a Christmas tree and all very magical.

If you want to potter around Big Lake, which anchors the far southeast corner of the park, there are paddleboats for rent at **Wheel Fun Rentals** (☎504-483-9375; off Friederichs Ave, City Park; per hr from $20; ⌚10am-5pm Thu-Sun). Here you can also rent bicycles ($9/25 per hour/half-day) and pedal around the park. Fancy some putt-putt golf? Try the new 36-hole course at **City Putt** (www.neworleanscitypark.com; City Park; adult/child 4-12yr $8/6; ⌚10am-10pm Sun & Tue-Thu, to midnight Fri & Sat) across from Storyland.

A few steps from the sculpture garden, take a break for coffee, beignets and gumbo at **Morning Call** (Map p254; www.neworleanscitypark.com; Dreyfous Ave, City Park; $2-10; ⌚24hr), conveniently open 24/7.

A TOUCH OF HISTORY

City Park occupies the site of the former Allard Plantation; much of the infrastructure and improvements, including pathways, bridges and the art-deco style Tad Gormley Stadium, were built by the Works Progress Administration (WPA) during the Great Depression. The arboreal life is magnificent, and includes strands of mature live oaks – thousands of them, some as old as 600 years – along with bald cypresses, Southern magnolias and other species. During Hurricane Katrina nearby canals flooded and inundated more than 90% of the park in up to 8ft of saltwater. Though the ground has recovered, many priceless trees were lost. One tree that wasn't was the **Singing Oak** (City Park), also known as the Singing Tree, which stands festooned with chimes, some up to 14ft in length. Standing under the tree during the slightest breeze is pretty magical.

The Popp Fountain is wonderful, and another impressive example from the WPA. Promenades planted with perennials and 26 Corinthian columns surround the centerpiece of water erupting from a bronze base of cavorting dolphins.

TOP SIGHT
ST LOUIS CEMETERY NO 1

New Orleans is a city of cemeteries. Influenced by the massive mausoleum-building cultures of the Spanish and French, large above-ground necropolises were once all the rage here. The most famous example of the genre is St Louis Cemetery No 1, opened in 1789 and today stuffed with tombs, graves and tourists.

Unfortunately, ongoing vandalism and tomb desecration forced the Archdiocese of New Orleans, which oversees the cemetery, to limit visitation to relatives and organized tours.

The supposed crypt of voodoo queen Marie Laveau (p150), where people leave offerings and candles, is the big drawcard – and a source of much of the vandalism. Debates over which Marie Laveau – mother or daughter, if either – was actually buried here will never be resolved; however, what is known is that living members of the Glapion family consider the 'X' marks scratched by visitors to be vandalism. There is no spiritual significance to these chicken scratches, and desecrating tombs is technically illegal. Don't do it.

Civil-rights figure Homer Plessy also rests in the cemetery, as does real-estate speculator Bernard de Marigny and architect Henry Latrobe. The white pyramid-shaped tomb is the future resting place of actor Nicholas Cage.

The Italian Mutual Benevolent Society Tomb is responsible for the tallest monument in the cemetery. Like other immigrant groups in New Orleans, the Italians formed a benevolent association to pool funds and assist in covering burial costs. Its tomb is big enough to hold the remains of thousands. In 1969, to the obvious shock of the families who own tombs here, a demented rape scene in the movie *Easy Rider* was filmed here. Note the headless statue *Charity* on the Italian Society tomb – urban myth maintains actor Dennis Hopper, who starred in the film, was responsible for tearing off the head.

For tours, consider nonprofit Save Our Cemeteries (p119).

DON'T MISS

- ➡ Marie Laveau tomb
- ➡ Italian Mutual Benevolent Society tomb
- ➡ Nicolas Cage's future tomb

PRACTICALITIES

- ➡ Map p254
- ➡ www.noladeadspace.com
- ➡ 1300 St Louis St
- ➡ admission by guided tour
- ➡ 9am-3pm Mon-Sat, to noon Sun
- ➡ 👪

SIGHTS

Mid-City

CITY PARK PARK

See p146.

ESPLANADE AVENUE STREET

Map p254 (btwn Rampart St & City Park) Esplanade is one of the most beautiful streets in New Orleans, yet barely recognized by visitors as such. Because of the abundance of historical homes, Esplanade, which follows the 'high ground' of Esplanade Ridge, is known as the Creole St Charles Ave. Both streets are shaded by rows and rows of leafy live oaks, but whereas St Charles is full of large, plantation-style American villas, Esplanade is framed by columned, French Creole–style mansions.

PITOT HOUSE HISTORIC BUILDING

Map p254 (504-482-0312; www.pitothouse.org; 1440 Moss St; adult/child under 12yr & senior $7/5; 10am-3pm Wed-Sat) The Pitot House, perched prettily beside Bayou St John, is an excellent example of classical French New Orleans architecture. Constructed circa 1799, it's the only Creole Colonial house along the bayou that is open to the public. The shaded verandah served as a living area whenever the weather got too hot. The house is named for resident James Pitot, who served as first mayor of incorporated New Orleans and lived here from 1810 to 1819. Visitation is by guided tour.

LE MUSÉE DE F.P.C. MUSEUM

Map p254 (Free People of Color Museum; 504-914-5401; www.lemuseedefpc.com; 2336 Esplanade Ave; tour adult/student & senior $15/10; noon-4:40pm Sat & Sun) Inside a lovely 1859 Greek revival mansion in the Upper Tremé, this museum showcases a 30-year collection of artifacts, documents, furniture and art. It all tells the story of a forgotten subculture: the 'free people of color' before the Civil War, who played a unique but prominent role in the development of the city. The small but fascinating collection includes original documentation of slaves who became free, either by *coartación* (buying their own freedom) or as a reward for particularly good service.

Rooms spotlight different eras in the city's history, with a focus on physician and newspaper publisher Dr Louis Charles Roudanez, born in 1823. Visitation is by guided tour, which can also be arranged by appointment on days the museum is closed.

ACTIVITIES IN MID-CITY & THE TREMÉ

It's nice to see the Bayou from the shore, but how about on the water? Get in touch with the following if you want to paddle.

Kayakitiyat (http://kayakitiyat.com; tours from $40 per person) Kayakitiyat leads tours on the Bayou seven days a week. The best is the Pontchartrain Paddle ($65), a four-hour tour that traverses the length of the Bayou.

Nola Gondola (985-778-5034; www.nolagondola.com; rides per couple $90; 1-8pm Mar-Jun, Aug-Dec) Look into getting poled around with that special someone on a gondola in City Park with Nola Gondola. Your 50-minute ride comes with crackers, cheese, and croony Italian music. The company will provide champagne or wine glasses, but bring your own bubbly or vino.

ST LOUIS CEMETERY NO 3 CEMETERY

Map p254 (504-482-5065; 3421 Esplanade Ave; 8am-4:30pm Mon-Sat, to 4pm Sun) This long but compact cemetery was established in 1854 at the site of the old Bayou Cemetery and is worth strolling through for a few minutes (longer if you're a cemetery enthusiast). Of particular note is the striking monument James Gallier Jr designed for his mother and father, who were lost at sea. It's a few steps to the right just after you enter from Esplanade Ave. The cemetery's wrought-iron entrance gate is a beauty.

FAIR GROUNDS RACE COURSE LANDMARK

Map p254 (504-944-5515; www.fairgroundsracecourse.com; 1751 Gentilly Blvd) Laid out in 1852, this is the third-oldest race track in the nation. During the Civil War, you could catch bear fights here. Today, besides horse races, the Fair Grounds is the site of the annual Louisiana Derby (in March) and the Jazz Fest. Buried in the infield are derby winners from a past era. The racing season runs from late November through March, Thursday through Sunday, usually with a 1:25pm post time.

ALCEE FORTIER PARK PARK

Map p254 (3100 Esplanade Ave) This pretty park, strung up with lights and lanterns and decked out with funky furniture, sits across the road from one of the most attractive stretches of Esplanade, an area replete with restaurants, shops and a general breezy ambience. Movies are sometimes screened here on evenings, especially for kids.

METAIRIE CEMETERY CEMETERY

(☎504-486-6331; 5100 Pontchartrain Blvd; ⊙until dark) Established in 1872 on a former race track (the grounds, you'll notice, still follow the oval layout), this is the most American of New Orleans' cities of the dead. Highlights include the Brunswig mausoleum, a pyramid guarded by a sphinx statue; the Moriarty monument, reputedly the 'tallest privately owned monument' in the country; and the Estelle Theleman Hyams monument, its stained-glass fixture casting a somber blue light over a slumped, despondent angel. Seeing everything on the 150-acre grounds is most easily accomplished by car.

OUR LADY OF THE ROSARY RECTORY HISTORICAL BUILDING

Map p254 (☎504-488-2659; 1342 Moss St) Built around 1834 as the home of Evariste Blanc, Our Lady of the Rosary Rectory exhibits a combination of styles characteristic of the region. The high-hipped roof and wraparound gallery seem reminiscent of West Indies houses but were actually the preferred styles of French Canadians who originally settled Bayou St John. However, it's the neoclassical details which make it obvious this building is from a later period. Call the church to discuss visitation.

VOODOO QUEEN

Voodoo became wildly popular in New Orleans after it was introduced by black émigrés from St Domingue (now Haiti) at the beginning of the 19th century, but very little is known with certainty about the legendary 19th-century voodoo queen Marie Laveau, who gained fame and fortune by shrewdly exploiting voodoo's mystique. Though details of her life are shrouded in myth and misconception, what has been passed down from generation to generation makes for a fascinating story.

She was born in 1794, a French-speaking Catholic of mixed black and white ancestry. Invariably described as beautiful and charismatic, at age 25 she married a man named Paris. He died a few years later, and Marie became known as the Widow Paris. She had 15 children with another man, Glapion, who is believed to have migrated from St Domingue, and may have been Laveau's first connection to voodoo.

In the 1830s she established herself as the city's preeminent voodoo queen, and her influence crossed racial lines. Mostly she reeled in stray husbands and helped people avenge wrongs done to them. According to legend, she earned her house on St Anne St as payment for ensuring a young man's acquittal in a rape or murder trial.

Marie apparently had some tricks up her sleeve. She is said to have worked as a hairdresser in the homes of upper-class white women, and it was not uncommon for these women to share local society gossip while having their hair done. In this way, Laveau gained a familiarity with the vagaries of the elite, and she astutely perceived the value of such information. At the peak of her reign as voodoo queen, she employed an entire network of spies, most household servants in upper-class homes.

Reports on Laveau's activities suggest there was more to her practice than nonpractitioners were permitted to witness – which makes these reports suspect. Part of the Laveau legend involves rituals she presided over in the countryside around New Orleans. According to sensational accounts, Laveau's followers danced naked around bonfires, drinking blood and slithering on the ground like snakes before engaging in all-out orgies.

Maison Blanche, a brothel by Lake Pontchartrain, was reputedly operated by Marie Laveau, but it is uncertain if this was the same Marie Laveau – there were two people known by the name, the second being the daughter of the original Marie Laveau. The elder Laveau died in 1881 and is believed to be buried in St Louis Cemetery No 1. The younger lived into the early 20th century.

CEMETERY VISITS

In 2015 the Archdiocese of New Orleans decided to limit visitation to St Louis Cemetery No 1 to relatives of those interred in the cemetery and to approved tour groups. The current plan is to extend the ban to other cemeteries overseen by the Archdiocese.

The decision stemmed from ongoing acts of vandalism on cemetery grounds. One of the most notable occurred in 2013 when vandals painted the tomb of voodoo queen Marie Laveau bright pink. Not only did the vandals desecrate the tomb, but they also used moisture-trapping latex paint. Moisture is a key source of damage to brick-and-mortar tombs. Restoring the tomb cost $10,000. There is also a long history of visitors scrawling three X's across Laveau's crypt as part of a wish-fulfillment ritual. Elsewhere in the cemetery vandals have stolen elaborate pieces of fencing and raided tombs.

Another reason for the new rule? By requiring tour companies to obtain a license, there may be more oversight over their quality and behavior. For tours by experienced and knowledgeable guides, consider Save Our Cemeteries (p119).

SANCTUARY HISTORIC BUILDING

Map p254 (924 Moss St) This historic house was built by Evariste Blanc from 1816 to 1822 on land originally granted in 1720–1 to French Canadians. The once-swampy property was later transferred to Don Andrés Almonaster y Roxas, the real-estate speculator who commissioned St Louis Cathedral on Jackson Sq in the French Quarter.

The Tremé

ST LOUIS CEMETERY NO 1 CEMETERY

See p148.

★BACKSTREET CULTURAL MUSEUM MUSEUM

Map p254 (☎504-522-4806; www.backstreet-museum.org; 1116 Henriette Delille St, formerly St Claude Ave; per person $8; ⊙10am-5pm Tue-Sat) Mardi Gras Indian suits grab the spotlight with dazzling flair – and finely crafted detail – in this informative museum, which examines the distinctive elements of African American culture in New Orleans. The museum isn't terribly big – it's the former Blandin's Funeral Home – but if you have any interest in the suits and rituals of Mardi Gras Indians as well as Second Line parades and Social Aid & Pleasure Clubs (the local black community version of civic associations), you need to stop by.

The guided tours are usually great, but sometimes feel rushed, so be sure to ask lots of questions. Ask for information about upcoming Second Lines so you can check one out first hand.

NEW ORLEANS AFRICAN AMERICAN MUSEUM MUSEUM

Map p254 (☎504-566-1136; www.noaam.org; 1418 Governor Nicholls St; adult/student/child $7/5/3; ⊙11am-4pm Wed-Sat) At time of research this small museum was in the midst of a $6 million renovation and closed to visitors. Before closing, the museum displayed an eclectic mix of exhibits mainly dating from slavery and Reconstruction. It's an interesting spot just by dint of its location: the Meilleur-Goldthwaite House, also known as the Tremé Villa. This pretty house was the site of the city's first brick yard and is an exemplar of the Creole architectural style. In the back are restored shotgun houses and slave quarters.

MORTUARY CHAPEL CHURCH

Map p254 (☎504-525-1551; www.judesshrine.com; 411 N Rampart St; donations accepted) A fear of yellow-fever contagion led the city to forbid funerals for fever victims at St Louis Cathedral. Built in 1826 near St Louis Cemetery No 1, the Mortuary Chapel offered services for victims, its bell tolling constantly during epidemics. In 1931 it was renamed Our Lady of Guadeloupe. Inside the chapel is a statue of St Jude, patron saint of impossible cases.

Also of interest is the statue of St Expedite, who may never have existed (legend says his name comes from a box of saint statues stamped with the order 'Expedite').

ST AUGUSTINE'S CHURCH CHURCH

Map p254 (☎504-525-5934; www.staugustine-catholicchurch-neworleans.org; 1210 Governor

Nicholls St) Open since 1841, 'St Aug's' is the second-oldest African American Catholic church in the country, a place where Creoles, émigrés from St Domingue and free persons of color could worship shoulder to shoulder, even as separate pews were designated for slaves. The future of the church remains in question, so try to visit; more visitors increases the chance of this historic landmark being preserved.

Call ahead to see if it's possible to arrange a visit. Don't miss the Tomb of the Unknown Slave, fashioned to resemble a grim cross assembled from chain links.

LOUIS ARMSTRONG PARK PARK

Map p254 (701 N Rampart St; ⏲8am-6pm) The entrance to this massive park has got to be one of the greatest gateways in the USA, a picturesque arch that ought rightfully to be the final set piece in a period drama about Jazz Age New Orleans. The original Congo Sq is here, as well as a **Louis Armstrong statue** and a **bust of Sidney Bechet**. The **Mahalia Jackson Theater** (☎504-525-1052, box office 504-287-0350; www.mahaliajacksontheater.com; 1419 Basin St) hosts opera and Broadway productions.

EATING

Mid-City

★PARKWAY TAVERN SANDWICHES $

Map p254 (☎504-482-3047; www.parkwaypoorboys.com; 538 Hagan Ave; po'boys under $13; ⏲11am-10pm Wed-Mon) Who makes the best po'boy in New Orleans? Honestly, who can say? But tell a local you think the top sandwich comes from Parkway and you will get, at the least, a nod of respect. The roast beef in particular – a craft some would say is dying among the great po'boy makers – is messy as hell and twice as good.

Take one down to nearby Bayou St John, and munch that sandwich in the shade. Louisiana bliss. The homemade bread pudding with rum sauce is also divine – and secretly our top choice at Parkway.

PAGODA CAFE CAFE $

Map p254 (www.pagodacafe.net; 1430 N Dorgenois St; breakfast $3-8, pastries under $5, sandwiches $8-10; ⏲7am-4pm Tue-Sat, 9am-3pm Sun; 📶✍) In a land of dimly lit dive bars and heavy Creole buffets, Pagoda Cafe is

NEW ORLEANS: BORN ON THE BAYOU

Today, Bayou St John is a pleasant backdrop for a stroll or a short paddle in a kayak. But take a closer look. This sometimes smelly creek is the reason this city exists. It was originally used by Native Americans as a wet highway to the relatively high ground of Esplanade Ridge, but then French explorers realized the waterway was the shortest route between the Mississippi River – and by extent the Gulf of Mexico – and Lake Pontchartrain. It was essentially for this reason that New Orleans was built in its commanding position at the mouth of the Mississippi. Eventually a canal built by Governor Carondelet extended the bayou to the edge of the French Quarter, and the bayou acted as the city's chief commercial harbor. Life in the area thrived; beautiful houses lined the bayou (many remain here today), and voodoo queen Marie Laveau and followers supposedly conducted rituals on the waterfront.

The era of steamboats made direct navigation up and down the Mississippi easier, and the bayou began to be eclipsed. Navigation ended with the filling of the canal in 1927, but the bayou remained an important geographic point of reference. Since 2005 it has also become a bone of contention between local residents and the Army Corps of Engineers. The Corps insists St John is a potential source of floodwater and have proposed sealing it off from Pontchartrain. Some residents say opening sector gates on the bayou's pump houses could facilitate the natural flow of water, which would freshen up the bayou (which can grow darkly stagnant), improve water quality and reintroduce important flora and fauna to the bayou bank.

The issue is still being fought. In the meantime, come out here to stroll along the bayou (stagnant or not, it is scenic and supremely serene, especially at sunset), enjoy a po'boy from the **Parkway Tavern**, catch one of the many concerts played on the median that runs through the bayou and gape at the gorgeous residences. You are able to visit **Pitot House** (p149), a restored mansion with a lovely set of gardens in the back.

MEET THE BOYS ON THE BATTLEFRONT

The most significant African American tradition of Carnival began in 1885 when a Mardi Gras Indian gang, calling itself the Creole Wild West, paraded the city's backstreets on Mardi Gras. Their elaborately beaded and feathered suits and headdresses made a huge impression, and many more black Indian gangs soon followed – the Wild Tchoupitoulas, Yellow Pocahontas and Golden Eagles, among many others. The new tradition, some say, signified respect for Native Americans who constantly fought US expansion in the New World. A canon of black Indian songs was passed down from generation to generation, with lyrics often fusing English, Creole French, Choctaw and African words until their meaning was obscure.

From the beginning, 'masking Indian' was a serious proposition. Tribes became organized fighting units headed by a big chief, with spy boys, flag boys and wild men carrying out carefully defined roles. Tremendous pride was evident in the costly and expertly sewn suits, and when two gangs crossed paths, an intense confrontation would ensue as members of each tribe sized each other up. Often violence would break out. As is the case with many of Mardi Gras' strongest traditions, this was no mere amusement.

Big chiefs became pillars of communities, and some became legends – among them Big Chief Jolly of the Wild Tchoupitoulas and Tootie Montana of the Yellow Pocahontas. Chief Jolly, an uncle of the Neville Brothers, made his mark by recording black Indian classics backed by the Meters. The Wild Magnolias, long led by Big Chief Bo Dollis (who died in 2015), is one of the most dynamic Indian groups and appears at clubs in New Orleans and at Jazz Fest.

Over the years, black Indian suits gained recognition as extravagant works of folk art, and they are exhibited as such at the **Backstreet Cultural Museum** (p151), at the **Presbytère** (p63) and at Jazz Fest. Layers of meaningful mosaics are designed and created in patterns of neatly stitched sequins. Multilayered feathered headdresses – particularly those of the big chiefs – are more elaborate and flamboyant than the headgear worn by Las Vegas show performers. The making of a new suit can take the better part of a year.

Visitors not in town for Mardi Gras are likely to have other opportunities to see the Indians at Jazz Fest, or occasionally performing in clubs such as Tipitina's. They also parade annually on St Joseph's Night (roughly midway through the Lenten season) and on Indian Sunday (also known as Super Sunday).

a sprightly diversion. This compact place serves healthy fare with a global spin. In the morning, look for bacon-and-egg tacos, toast with Nutella and bananas, and house-made granola. For lunch to-go, grab a turnover or a sausage pastry, or settle in for a lemongrass tofu *banh mi*.

Also sells coffee and teas. All seating is outdoors.

RUBY SLIPPER BREAKFAST $

Map p254 (☎504-309-5531; www.therubyslippercafe.net; 139 S Cortez St; mains $10-17; ⏰7am-2pm Mon-Fri, 8am-2pm Sat, to 3pm Sun; ✎) Oooh, that migas dish, with its pepper jack, spicy chorizo, avocado and scrambled eggs – it is one hot mess of deliciousness. The Slipper serves some of the best morning food in town. The fare? Let's call it basic American breakfast food prepared with a touch of gourmet flair: the hollandaise has a kick, and a poached egg tops the crispy chicken biscuit. The lunches are lovely, too.

DIS AND DAT BURGERS, AMERICAN $

Map p254 (www.disanddat.com; 2540 Banks St; burgers & hot dogs $7-10; ⏰5:30am-3pm Mon, to 9pm Tue-Thu, to 10pm Fri, 7am-10pm Sat, to 3pm Sun) Brought to you by the folks behind the smack-your-lips-delicious hot dogs at Dat Dog, this new venture adds beef patties to the mix, offering burgers as well as a few choice dogs. The Surf & Turf burger is topped with crawfish étouffée. Also open for breakfast.

Park in front of the warehouse next door on Banks St, enter the shotgun shack and order at the bar. If you're lucky, the Violent Femmes might be adding it up on the sound system.

LIUZZA'S BY THE TRACK DINER $

Map p254 (☎504-218-7888; www.liuzzasnola.com; 1518 N Lopez St; mains $7-16; ⊙11am-7pm Mon-Sat) Mmmm, that gumbo. This quintessential Mid-City neighborhood joint does some of the best in town. The barbecue shrimp po'boy is to die for and the deep-fried garlic oysters are legendary. All that said, the real reason to come is the atmosphere: we've seen a former city judge and a stripper dining together here, which is as 'Only in New Orleans' an experience as you can get. Liuzza's is nearly impossible to squeeze into during Jazz Fest, which is held at the nearby Fair Grounds Race Course.

ANGELO BROCATO ICE CREAM $

Map p254 (☎504-486-1465; www.angelobrocatoicecream.com; 214 N Carrollton Ave; scoop of gelato $3.25, pastries under $4; ⊙11am-5pm Tue-Sat) When an ice-cream parlor passes the 100-year mark, you gotta step back and say, 'Clearly, they're doing something right.' Opened in 1905 by Signor Brocato himself, a Sicilian immigrant who scraped together his savings from working on a sugar plantation, this is the oldest ice-cream shop in New Orleans. Inside, silky gelatos, perfect cannoli and crispy biscotti catch the eye and wow the tastebuds.

TWELVE MILE LIMIT BARBECUE $

Map p254 (☎504-488-8114; 500 S Telemachus St; mains $7-11; ⊙kitchen 5-11pm Tue-Thu, to midnight Fri & Sat, 10am-2pm Sat & Sun) Besides being an excellent bar, Twelve Mile Limit's kitchen cranks out great barbecue; the smell from outside is almost as overpowering as the rich flavor of that sweet, spicy smoked meat. On Mondays, swap out barbecue for a free meal, typically something like red beans and rice.

TOUP'S MEATERY AMERICAN, LOUISIANA $$

Map p254 (☎504-252-4999; www.toupsmeatery.com; 845 N Carrollton Ave; lunch $15-22, small plates $7-21, mains $18-29; ⊙11am-2:30pm Tue-Sat, 5-10pm Tue-Thu, 5-11pm Fri & Sat) Cheese plates. Charcuterie boards. These are standard appetizers at restaurants across the land. But they are nothing compared to the chest-pounding glory that is the Toup's Meatery Board, a Viking-worthy platter of meat. House-made and -cured, this carnivore's feast will harden your arteries in a single glance. But oh, that butter-soft marrow on the bone.

At this Mid-City hot spot, which looks like a hunting lodge dressed up nice, meat includes beef, pork, goat, quail, lamb, chicken and seafood, with boudin balls, cracklin' and hog's head cheese available as sides. New Orleans beers are on tap, and Pimms cups are available by the pitcher.

CAFÉ DEGAS FRENCH $$

Map p254 (☎504-945-5635; www.cafedegas.com; 3127 Esplanade Ave; lunch $11-17, dinner $19-30; ⊙11am-3pm & 6-10pm Wed-Sat, 10:30am-3pm & 6-9:30pm Sun) A pecan tree thrusts through the floor and ceiling of the enclosed deck that serves as Café Degas' congenial dining room. A rustic, romantic little spot, Degas warms the heart with first-rate French fare. Meals that sound familiar on the menu (steak *frites au poivre,* parmesan-crusted veal medallions) are arranged with extraordinary beauty on the plate.

Brunch is gorgeous; the crab crepe with hollandaise is decadent.

LOLA'S SPANISH $$

Map p254 (☎504-488-6946; www.lolasneworleans.com; 3312 Esplanade Ave; mains $13-28; ⊙5:30-9:30pm Sun-Thu, to 10:30pm Fri & Sat)

THE POPULARITY OF POPEYES

Ask a New Orleanian where the best fried chicken in town is and they'll probably tell you to try **Willie Mae's** or **Fiorella's** (p71). Now ask them where *they* eat fried chicken, and they'll very likely reply, 'Popeyes.' Seriously.

Though fried chicken is not as popular here as in the rest of the South, folks still take their fried bird seriously, which is why we find it all the more amusing that so many locals swear by a chain restaurant that markets a caricature of the city outside of its limits.

But hey – we trust any New Orleanian's take on food. The **Popeyes** (www.popeyes.com) here are pretty good (folks say the food tastes better than in other states and, to be honest, it just might). We'll never tell you to pass up a local business in favor of Popeyes, but if there's nothing else around…well, just sayin'. There are numerous locations around town.

Enjoy wine and conversation with crowds of Mid-City locals who swear by Lola's paellas and *fideuas* (an angel-hair pasta variation on the former). Inside, it's all elbows and the buzz of conversation and, incidentally, very good grub. This isn't haute Barcelona cuisine; it's the Spanish peasant fare Hemingway wrote chapters about: rabbit, meats, fresh seafood, olive oil and lots of delicious garlic. Bring cash.

MANDINA'S ITALIAN **$$**

Map p254 (☎504-482-9179; www.mandinasrestaurant.com; 3800 Canal St; mains $12-20; ⏱11am-9:30pm Mon-Thu, to 10pm Fri & Sat, noon-9pm Sun) In the Italian American New Orleans community, funerals were followed by a visit to this institution for turtle soup. The menu may be conservative, but when you've been around for more than 100 years you stick to what you know. In this case that's Sicilian Louisiana food: trout almandine, red beans and veal cutlets, and bell peppers stuffed with macaroni and meat.

The dining room is as historic as any building in the city and just as crucial to its culture.

NONNA MIA CAFÉ & PIZZERIA ITALIAN **$$**

Map p254 (☎504-948-1717; www.nonnamia.net; 3125 Esplanade Ave; pizza $12-20, mains $10-16; ⏱11am-9pm Sun-Thu, to 10pm Fri & Sat; 🌿) Getting tired of heavy, rich Creole cuisine? How about a fresh slice of pizza and some ice tea in Nonna Mia's outdoor courtyard? The caramelized onions, goat's cheese and artichoke hearts are delicious proof that pizza apparently doesn't need pepperoni to be perfect.

MOPHO VIETNAMESE **$$**

Map p254 (☎504-482-6845; www.mophonola.com; 514 City Park Ave; lunch $7-18, dinner $7-28; ⏱11am-10pm Sun-Thu, to 11pm Fri & Sat) You haven't heard about MoPho? Where ya been hiding? This hot-hot-hot new pho joint from former Restaurant August chef Michael Gulotta is on every must-eat list in town. Traditional Vietnamese dishes often come with a Louisiana kick, from Gulf shrimp spring rolls to *banh mi*-style po'boys. We give props for the stylish digs, attentive service and the great name. The pho? Solid, not swoon-inducing.

The Tremé

WILLIE MAE'S SCOTCH HOUSE SOUTHERN **$**

Map p254 (2401 St Ann St; fried chicken $11; ⏱10am-5pm Mon-Sat) Willie Mae's has been dubbed some of the best fried chicken in the world by the James Beard Foundation, the Food Network and other media. It thus sees a steady flow of tourist traffic. The chicken, served in a basket, is pretty damn good, as are the butter beans.

LIL' DIZZY'S LOUISIANAN, CREOLE **$**

Map p254 (☎504-569-8997; www.lildizzyscafe.com; 1500 Esplanade Ave; breakfast $7-14, lunch $10-16, buffet $16-18; ⏱7am-2pm Mon-Sat, 8am-2pm Sun) One of the city's great lunch spots, Dizzy's does mean soul food specials in a historic shack owned by the Baquet family, who have forever been part of the culinary backbone of New Orleans. The fried chicken is excellent, the hot sausages may be better and the bread pudding is divine.

CAJUN SEAFOOD SEAFOOD **$**

Map p254 (☎504-948-6000; 1479 N Claiborne Ave; takeout $5-19; ⏱10:30am-9pm) The name says it all: this is a grocery-store takeout that's one of the best budget options in town for raw seafood and cooked hot plates, such as fried chicken, boudin, fish plates and the like. The boiled shrimp are always freakishly huge, as are the shrimp po'boys.

★**DOOKY CHASE** SOUTHERN, CREOLE **$$**

Map p254 (☎504-821-0600; 2301 Orleans Ave; buffet $20, mains $16-25; ⏱11am-3pm Tue-Thu, 11am-3pm & 5-9pm Fri) Ray Charles wrote 'Early in the Morning' about Dooky's; civil rights leaders used it as informal headquarters in the 1960s; and Barack Obama ate here after his inauguration. Leah Chase's labor of love is the backbone of the Tremé, and her buffets are the stuff of legend. Top-notch gumbo and excellent fried chicken are served in a white-linen dining room to office workers and ladies who lunch.

The vegetarian gumbo z'herbes, served on Thursday during Lent, is the great New Orleans dish done green with mustards, beet tops, spinach, kale, collards and Leah knows what else; committed carnivores should give it a try.

DRINKING & NIGHTLIFE

There are some decent bars out this way, but they tend to be neighborhood places that out-of-towners may not consider worth the drive. But there are a few key exceptions. In general the scene here is lively, local and happy to share a beer and a story with a stranger. Plus, there's a bowling alley, concert hall and a bar that serves free food... just sayin'.

★TWELVE MILE LIMIT — BAR

Map p254 (500 S Telemachus St; ⏲5pm-midnight Mon-Thu, to 2am Fri & Sat, to 11pm Sun) Twelve Mile is simply a great bar. It's staffed by people who have the skill, both behind the bar and in the kitchen, to work in four-star spots, but who chose to set up shop in a neighborhood, for a neighborhood. The mixed drinks are excellent, the match of any mixologist's cocktail in Manhattan, and the vibe is super accepting.

For a twangy drink that might become your new favorite, try the Great Idea, a housemade ginger-beer concoction. Twelve Mile also hosts free (!) dinners on Monday nights, which is just perfect, really.

TREO — COCKTAIL BAR

Map p254 (☎504-304-4878; www.treonola.com; 3835 Tulane Ave; ⏲11:30am-11pm Tue-Thu, to midnight Fri & Sat) Let's Get Figgy With It. Beetin' Down the Block. Rob Ford. The Homewre – wait a minute, did Treo just name one of its drinks after Toronto's hard-partying mayor? We like your saucy style, Treo – and your thoughtfully crafted cocktails. This stylish new spot is luring crowds to a re-energized Tulane Ave. Tipplers have a choice of seasonal drinks and Louisiana-style small plates.

For a touch of culture, check out the art gallery upstairs. And that cool art piece on the ceiling? A wooden map of New Orleans.

PAL'S — BAR

Map p254 (www.palslounge.com; 949 N Rendon St; ⏲3pm-late) This great neighborhood bar is a little more convivial for the older generation, although it's definitely an all-ages crowd. The men's bathroom, wallpapered with vintage pinups, is like a walk through the history of *Playboy* magazine, while the backroom air hockey is always enjoyable. Open until at least 3am Sunday through Thursday, and at least 4am on Friday and Saturday.

FAIR GRINDS — CAFE

Map p254 (☎504-913-9072; 3133 Ponce de Leon St; ⏲6:30am-10pm; 📶) Like many of the best indie coffee shops, Fair Grinds is comfy, hip and unpretentious. And, of course, it serves a good cup of joe. It also showcases local art and generally acts as the beating heart of Mid-City's bohemian scene; plus, it supports community development associations and hosts regular folk-music nights. So grab your laptop and order a coffee.

FINN MCCOOL'S — BAR

Map p254 (☎504-486-9080; www.finnmccools.com; 3701 Banks St; ⏲11am-3am Mon-Fri, 9am-3am Sat, 10am-3am Sun) Want a surreal New Orleans experience? Arrive at 6am when premier league soccer or big international rugby games are playing. You'll see an odd mix of European sports enthusiasts, British expats and local Hispanic packed into this neighborhood bar. Finn's is an excellent spot for a beer any time (especially during St Paddy's Day), but we particularly love it for watching soccer. Check the website or call for game days and hours.

MID-CITY YACHT CLUB — BAR

Map p254 (☎504-483-2517; www.midcityyachtclub.com; 440 S St Patrick St; ⏲11:30am-3pm Mon-Thu, to 3:30am Fri, 10:30am-4am Sat & Sun) The Yacht Club is so much a part of the neighborhood that one of the owners took his boat out to save flooded Katrina victims (hence the name of the bar, which isn't near a lake or ocean). More than this, it is literally a part of the neighborhood: the bar is made from wood salvaged from storm debris.

BAYOU BEER GARDEN — BAR

Map p254 (☎504-302-9357; www.bayoubeergarden.com; 326 N Jefferson Davis Pkwy; ⏲11am-2am Sun-Thu, to 5am Fri & Sat) The Bayou has been sorely needed in New Orleans: a beer bar with an enormous outdoor deck that serves pub grub. Simple, right? Shows lots of sports, and thus attracts an interesting mix of jocks and punky locals on game days.

PEARL WINE CO — WINE BAR

Map p254 (☎504-483-6314; www.pearlwineco.com; 3700 Orleans Ave; ⏲noon-midnight Mon-Sat, to 8pm Sun) On the 1st floor of the American Can Building, this wine shop and lounge is an inviting place to relax and sip wine after a morning exploring City Park or strolling Bayou St John. Free wine tastings on Thursday and Friday nights (5pm to 7pm), and live jazz on Saturday (8pm).

ENTERTAINMENT

★MID-CITY ROCK & BOWL LIVE MUSIC

(☎504-861-1700; www.rockandbowl.com; 3000 S Carrollton Ave; ⏲5pm-late) A night at the Rock & Bowl is a quintessential New Orleans experience. The venue is a strange, wonderful combination of bowling alley, deli and huge live-music and dance venue, where patrons get down to New Orleans roots music while trying to avoid that 7-10 split. The best time and place in the city to experience zydeco is the weekly Thursday-night dance party held here. For a sit-down dinner of Creole and Cajun specialties – inside a restaurant jauntily lit for Christmas – try **Ye Olde College Inn** (www.collegeinn1933.com), which is on the property and shares owners, but is a few steps from the bowling alley complex.

★CANDLELIGHT LOUNGE LIVE MUSIC

Map p254 (☎504-525-4728; 925 N Robertson St; ⏲2pm-late daily) Deep in the Tremé, the Candlelight looks like a bunker on the outside and…a slightly nicer bunker on the inside. Most nights it's a neighborhood bar, but on Wednesday around 10pm (and occasionally other nights) it hosts the Tremé Brass Band ($10 cover), one of the most enjoyable live sets in the city. This is as wonderful as local music gets in this town.

SAENGER THEATRE THEATER

Map p254 (☎504-525-1052; www.saengernola.com; 143 N Rampart St) The Saenger's ornate 1927 facade was designed by noted New Orleans architect Emile Weil. It has been refurbished and renovated into one of the finest indoor venues in the city.

CHICKIE WAH WAH LIVE MUSIC

Map p254 (☎504-304-4714; www.chickiewahwah.com; 2828 Canal St; ⏲shows around 8pm) Despite the fact it lies in Mid-City on one of the most unremarkable stretches of Canal St as you please, Chickie Wah Wah is a great jazz club. Local legends such as the Sweet Olive String Band or Meschya Lake, and plenty of international talent, all make their way across the small stage.

BANKS STREET BAR LIVE MUSIC

Map p254 (☎504-486-0258; www.banksstreetbarandgrill.com; 4401 Banks St; ⏲11am-2am) While Banks Street Bar is a quintessential neighborhood dive, it's also renowned as a good place to catch local music seven nights a week. It's famous for hosting good rock shows, but also hosts jazz, funk, brass and the rest. And maybe even the awesomely named Clockwork Elvis. It gets loud in here, so don't plan on discussing representation and repression in the latter works of Terrence Malick between sets.

BULLETS LIVE MUSIC

Map p254 (☎504-669-4464; 2441 AP Tureaud Ave; ⏲bar 7am-midnight, shows 7:30-8pm) Don't be put off by the name; Bullets is just a sports bar. It's also the home base of trumpeter Kermit Ruffins, who hosts a concert here for his family and friends almost every Tuesday starting (very roughly) around 7:30pm. At press time Ruffins was on a break, but his band was playing, so call first to confirm he'll be there.

CLOSING THE CONGO SQUARE CIRCLE

Near the main entrance to Louis Armstrong Park is **Congo Sq** (Map p254), one of the most important spots, arguably, in the development of modern music. Once known as Place de Negres, this area used to be just outside the city's walls (Rampart St, as the name suggests, was the town limit). Under the French Colonial law, slaves were allowed to gather here on Sundays. The period of rest became one of both celebration and preservation of West African rituals, which largely revolve around song and dance. Sunday became a day of letting off steam and channeling latent discontent, and it must have been, at the time, the largest celebration of traditional African culture in continental North America – slaves were forbidden from practicing traditional culture in the American colonies.

The practice was shut down when US settlers took over New Orleans, but it was alive long enough to imprint its musical stamp on the city's cultural substrate. By the late 19th century, brass bands were blending African rhythms with classical music. These bands played on a weekly basis in Congo Sq, and their sound eventually evolved, especially near the bordellos of nearby Storyville, into jazz – itself a foundation for the variations of pop music (R&B, rock and roll, even hip-hop) the USA would give the world in the 20th century.

SECOND LINE!

Second Lines aren't the alternate queue at the bank window, if you're wondering. No, Second Line specifically refers to parades put on by the city's African American Social Aid & Pleasure (S&P) Clubs. The S&P members deck themselves out in flash suits, hats and shoes and carry decorated umbrellas and fans. This snazzy crowd, accompanied by a hired band, marches through the city pumping music and 'steppin'' – engaging in a kind of syncopated marching dance that looks like a soldier in formation overcome by an uncontrollable need to get fun-*kay*. This is the First Line, and marching behind it is the Second Line: the crowds that gather to celebrate the music. Hundreds, sometimes thousands of people – the majority African American – dance in the Second Line, stopping for drinks and food all along the parade route. Many folks bring along coolers full of beer and soda, plus rolling grills, too.

So what are these S&P clubs? There are theories they have their roots in West African secret societies, cultural institutions that are a big part of the societies slaves were plucked from. If you have been to West Africa and witnessed any kind of secret society activity, it's hard not to detect some similarities with the Second Line. Still, while this theory has an appealing veneer of anthropological allure, the roots of Second Lines may be more based on economics. In the 19th and 20th centuries S&P clubs functioned as insurance agencies for African Americans, as well as brokers who would help arrange the traditional (and expensive) New Orleans jazz funeral procession. The act of the parade, which the S&P helped fund, may have been eventually appended to these brokerage responsibilities.

While that role has faded, the S&P clubs remain important civic institutions. There are a few dozen in the city, and traditionally Second Lines roll every weekend, except for summers, usually in the Tremé or Central City. They're not the easiest thing to find, but keep abreast of 90.7 WWOZ (www.wwoz.org) or stop by the Backstreet Cultural Museum (p151) to ask – and be on the lookout for parades and music if you're driving around on a Sunday.

SHOPPING

★F&F BOTANICA SPIRITUAL SUPPLY — SOUVENIRS

Map p254 (☎504-289-2304; www.orleanscandleco.com; 801 N Broad Ave; ⏰10am-6:30pm Tue-Sat) Hesitant to enter a 'voodoo store'? Don't worry, staff couldn't be more helpful at this jam-packed shop that's lined with colorful candles. Forget all the fake voodoo shops in the French Quarter; this is a genuine Puerto Rican botanica that sells issue-related candles (success, love, etc), *gris-gris* (spell bags or amulets) and spell components for use in voodoo and Santeria (the latter is a Puerto Rican religion related to voodoo).

No tourist-oriented Hollywood-style dolls here; real worshippers drop in to deal with real issues, which, according to the spell lists, seem to mainly related to heartache, immigration and the law. We guarantee you'll walk away with a candle.

MASSEY'S — OUTDOOR EQUIPMENT

Map p254 (☎504-648-0292; 509 N Carrollton Ave; ⏰10am-7pm Mon-Sat, noon-6pm Sun) Massey's is a large, well-stocked chain carrying an excellent selection of camping, hiking and general outdoors gear.

SOPO — CLOTHING, GIFTS

Map p254 (☎504-609-2429; www.soponola.com; 629 N Carrollton Ave; ⏰10am-6pm Tue-Sat) A warm welcome is the first thing you notice at SoPo, which stands for Southern Posh. Boutique women's wear, which is found upstairs, and gifts with Southern flair are the focus.

TUBBY & COOS — BOOKS

Map p254 (☎504-598-5536; www.tubbyandcoos.com; 631 N Carrollton Ave; 10am-7pm Thu-Tue; 📶) Haven't found the droids you were looking for? Then stop by this self-proclaimed 'geeky' bookstore where books and movies loved by nerds take the spotlight. *Game of Thrones, Dr Who, Star Wars* – the gang is all here. The slogan for the store's Dungeons & Dating trivia night is boss. Eat snacks. Meet nerds. Play trivia.

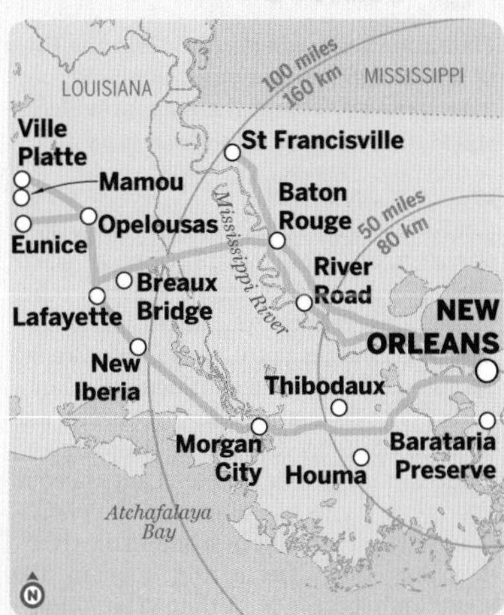

Day Trips from New Orleans

River Road Plantations p160

Graceful antebellum mansions with elaborate gardens, majestic live oaks and clustered slave shanties offer a glimpse into a foreign but not-too-distant past.

St Francisville p161

Antiques, birds and ghost stories, plus a few plantations, make a fine trip. And that's without mentioning the museum at the 18,000-acre penitentiary in Angola.

Lafayette & Breaux Bridge p163

Join the party – or the *fais-do-do* (Cajun dance) – in Lafayette and Breaux Bridge, where Cajun dance halls and crawfish boils keep things lively. And the food? It's serious business around here.

Cajun Prairie p167

Suit up for dancing and a lot of great music in the prairielands, where a young wave of fiddlers and accordion players keep Cajun and zydeco music relevant – and fun.

Down the Bayou p169

Swamps, alligators and oil. And a whole lot of Cajun culture. Soak it all in – and enjoy fresh seafood – on a road trip that's best done slow.

River Road Plantations

Explore

Plantations dot River Road, which follows the Mississippi as it winds it's way past New Orleans. In the past (and to be fair, even today), people visited these homes for their architecture and the moonlight-and-magnolia narrative that was built around them. An increasing number of visitors find this story to be one told in bad taste; at the least, they want the accompanying story of the slave labor that built and maintained the area's plantations. Some of the places we list delve into that history, while others give it a cursory reference.

Note that River Road is actually two roads lining the west and east banks of the Mississippi River. Looking at a map, the east bank is the area above the river and the west bank is the area below the river. 'Downriver' means heading southeast, as the river flows toward New Orleans. 'Upriver' means northwest, against the river's flow toward Baton Rouge. River Road has various route names along the way, yet few of the towns you pass through will display any signage to indicate the change in route numbers. Sound confusing? It's not – just follow the sinuous levees.

The Best

➡**Sight** Laura Plantation (p160)

➡**Place to Eat** Wayne Jacob's Smokehouse (p161)

Top Tip

Bridges are not that numerous on this part of the Mississippi River. Several plantations are on the west bank, so plot your itinerary carefully and allow extra time for travel.

Getting There & Away

➡**Direction** Northwest

➡**Travel time** From three hours to all day depending on stops.

➡**Car** Take I-10 west to I-310, exit at Destrehan and follow River Road (alternately called Hwy 44) northwest from there.

SIGHTS

Plantation tours offer a peak into the lives of antebellum plantation owners and, perhaps more so than in the past, provide insights into the hard lives of slaves as well.

LAURA PLANTATION HISTORIC SITE

(☎888-799-7690, 225-265-7690; www.lauraplantation.com; 2247 Hwy 18, Vacherie; adult/child $20/6; ⏲10am-4pm) Where other plantations reflect the tastes of Anglo-America, Laura is a rare example of a Creole-operated, West Indies-influenced manor house. The blue-and-yellow property was built in 1805 by Guillaume Duparc and named for his granddaughter, Laura Locoul. Four generations of women ran the plantation, and the tour – the best one on the river – describes their fascinating role in the operation's success. More than 12 buildings – slave cabins, barns, sugar-processing stations and the like – still stand.

More than 5000 pages of plantation documents, including Laura's diary, provide firsthand details about the plantation life of women, children and slaves.

WHITNEY PLANTATION HISTORIC SITE

(☎225-265-3300; http://whitneyplantation.com; 5099 Highway 18, Wallace, LA; adult/child under 12yr/student $22/free/15; ⏲9:30am-4:30pm Wed-Mon, tours 10am-3pm) The Whitney is the first plantation in Louisiana that focuses on the history and realities of slavery. Visitors are given a historical tour into the world of the German American Haydel family and their slaves, but the visit emphasizes the lived experience of the latter group. In addition to a tour that focuses on the appalling living conditions slaves toiled under, the property is speckled with memorials and monuments to the area's slave population.

DESTREHAN PLANTATION HISTORIC SITE

(☎877-453-2095; www.destrehanplantation.org; 13034 Hwy 48; adult/child under 7yr/7-17yr $18/free/7; ⏲9am-4pm) Destrehan, the oldest plantation home remaining in the lower Mississippi Valley, was originally established for indigo production. Antoine Robert Robin DeLongy commissioned the original French Colonial–style mansion in 1787, which uses *bousillage* (mud- and straw-filled) walls supported by cypress timbers. The house features a distinctive African-style hipped roof, no doubt the inspiration of the plantation's builder, who was partially of African descent. Viewing the historical-documents room that contains original Louisiana Purchase–era artifacts is a highlight.

When DeLongy's daughter, Celeste, married Jean Noel Destrehan, they added the present Greek-revival facade. Destrehan was part of a tribunal, held on the property, that tried and convicted slaves involved in a revolt just upriver in 1811. Costumed docents lead tours through the graceful home where the pirate Jean Lafitte was once a guest. Possible demonstrations include making *bousillage*, cooking in a hearth and learning African American herbal remedies.

EATING

WAYNE JACOB'S SMOKEHOUSE & RESTAURANT CAJUN $

(☎985-652-9990; www.wjsmokehouse.com; 769 W 5th St, LaPlace; mains $7-18; ⏰9am-2pm Mon, to 5pm Tue & Wed, to 8:30pm Thu & Fri, to 1pm Sat, 10:30am-2pm Sun) This is the place to stop on your way upriver. LaPlace is known for producing fantastic andouille sausages, and Wayne Jacob's smokes up some of the best. Po'boys, red beans and rice, and Cajun comfort food fill out the menu and portions are generous. There's also a long list of daily specials.

But whatever you choose, make sure to include an order of the smoky chicken and andouille gumbo. It's some of the best we had in southern Louisiana. An amazing array of sausages are for sale in back.

St Francisville

Explore

Tranquil St Francisville retains nearly 150 of its original 18th- and 19th-century houses and buildings. That includes the lodging place of the town's most famous (temporary) resident, John James Audubon, who lived a few months at Oakley Plantation. He returned frequently to sketch avian species in the surrounding woodlands for *The Birds of America*.

This area wasn't part of the 1803 Louisiana Purchase, it stayed with the Spanish-controlled Florida territory until 1810. Cotton plantations sprang up from the 1800s into the early 1900s, followed by the town itself.

In the morning, pick up a walking-tour brochure at the visitor center and stroll past historic homes nearby. There should be enough time to then visit two of the town's plantations. For variety, tour one plantation, then drive 25 miles to the penitentiary museum at Angola.

The Best

➡**Sight** Louisiana State Penitentiary Museum (p162)

➡**Nature** Mary Ann Brown Preserve (p162)

➡**Place to Eat** Magnolia Café (p163)

Top Tip

Pretty day? Pack a lunch for Rosedown Plantation. There are a few picnic tables near the visitor center.

Getting There & Away

➡**Direction** Northwest

➡**Travel time** Two hours

➡**Car** Follow I-10 west from New Orleans to Baton Rouge. Take US 110 and Hwy 61 north from there.

Need to Know

➡**Area Code** ☎225

➡**Location** 113 miles northwest of New Orleans

➡**Tourist office** (☎800-789-4221, 225-635-4224; www.stfrancisville.us; 11757 Ferdinand St; ⏰9am-5pm Mon-Sat, from 9:30am Sun)

SIGHTS

OAKLEY PLANTATION & AUDUBON STATE HISTORIC SITE HISTORIC SITE

(☎225-635-3739; https://audubonstatehistoricsite.wordpress.com; 11788 Hwy 965; adult/student/senior $8/4/6; ⏰9am-5pm Tue-Sat; Ⓟ) Oakley is the spot where artist John James Audubon spent his tenure, arriving in 1821 to tutor the owner's daughter. Though his assignment lasted only 3½ months (and his room was pretty spartan), he and his assistant finished 32 paintings of birds found in the plantation's surrounding forest. Several original Audubon prints hang from the walls. The building was built in the Federal style, which gives it a more austere, understated aesthetic compared to nearby properties.

Tours are refreshingly free of the obsession with cutlery and homeware minutiae that characterizes other plantation experiences. The 100-acre grounds include a lovely herb and vegetable garden, two 1840s slave cabins, a kitchen with brick hearths still in working order and a barn. The half-mile wooded Cardinal Trail is great for bird-watching.

MARY ANN BROWN PRESERVE NATURE RESERVE

(☎225-338-1040; www.nature.org; 13515 Hwy 965; ⏲sunrise-sunset) Operated by the Nature Conservancy, the 110-acre Mary Ann Brown Preserve takes in some of the beech woodlands, dark wetlands and low, clay-soil hill country of the Tunica uplands. A 2-mile series of trails and boardwalks crosses the woods, the same trees that painter John James Audubon tramped around when he began work on *Birds of America*.

TUNICA FALLS WATERFALL

(☎225-635-4221; tourism@stfrancisville.us) Tunica Falls, which is technically called Clark Creek Nature Area, is about 30 minutes away from St Francisville. The pleasant, hilly trails wind you past lovely waterfalls. Crude maps can be found at the visitor center and also at the general store in Pond, MS (at Hwys 24 and 969), the town in which you park, where the trailhead is located.

ROSEDOWN PLANTATION HISTORIC SITE HISTORIC SITE

(☎225-635-3332; www.crt.state.la.us; 12501 Hwy 10; adult/student $10/4; ⏲9am-5pm) Get your cameras out for the corridor of live oaks fronting this lovely plantation home. Commissioned by Daniel and Martha Turnbull, the 1835 cypress-and-cedar house still contains many original mid-19th-century furnishings. Note the frighteningly narrow and well-worn circular stairwell used by slaves – they had to carry water and wood upstairs while maintaining their balance. Outside, the formal gardens have been meticulously restored based on Margaret's garden diaries. Be warned: Rosedown is a major stop on the tour-bus circuit.

LA STATE PENITENTIARY MUSEUM AT ANGOLA

At the end of LA 66, about 25 miles northwest of St Martinsville, sits an 18,000-acre plot of farmland surrounded on three sides by the Mississippi River. The place goes by several names. Angola. The Farm. The Louisiana State Penitentiary. There are more than 5100 prisoners incarcerated here, and for some reason, they have become a tourism attraction.

While we find it morally sticky to visit a prison in the state with the highest incarceration rate in the country, said prison system is also an important element of the modern Louisiana story. The small but fascinating **Louisiana State Penitentiary Museum** (☎225-655-2592; www.angolamuseum.org; Angola; admission free; ⏲8am-4:30pm Mon-Fri, til 4pm Sat, & 11am-4pm Sun in Oct) , located just outside the gates of Angola, displays artifacts from the prison, which had its origins on the site in the 1880s. Visitors can walk inside a tiny prison cell, look at a lethal array of prison-made weapons, and ogle a denim shirt worn by George Clooney while filming scenes from the movie *Out of Sight* (1998). Scenes from *Dead Man Walking* (1995) and *Monsters Ball* (2001) were also filmed here. The most disturbing display is Gruesome Gertie, the electric chair used to execute 86 people in Angola between 1941 and 1991.

Prison Enterprises oversees crop production on the grounds, and prisoners grow and cultivate much of their own food. Jellies produced here are for sale in the museum's gift shop along with T-shirts reading 'Angola: A Gated Community.' The penitentiary is also known for its annual **rodeo** (www.angolarodeo.com), marketed as 'The Wildest Show in the South.' Every Sunday during the month of October inmates rope and ride in various events that are open to the public. At some point, a monkey rides a dog while incarcerated men shovel out livestock feces; frankly, we can't imagine a darker, more surreal take on the human condition.

For more background on the state's prison system, read the excellent Times-Picayune series *Louisiana Incarcerated* at www.nola.com/prisons, which won a prestigious Sidney Award for investigative journalism from the Hillman Foundation.

MYRTLES PLANTATION HISTORIC BUILDING

(☎800-809-0565, 225-635-6277; www.myrtlesplantation.com; 7747 US Hwy 61 N; day adult/child tours $10/7, night tours $12; ⌚9am-5pm, tours 6pm, 7pm & 8pm Fri & Sat; P) Owners and docents alike perpetuate the idea that Myrtles is one of the 'most haunted houses in America.' And hey, this place is certifiably creepy. Tours do not seem to be quite as architecturally and historically informative as other plantation tours in the region, but paint a vivid picture of life during the plantation era. Mystery tours, offered Friday and Saturday evenings, are geared toward ghost stories while daytime tours focus on details about the house and its furnishings.

Brave visitors can opt to spend the night in one of the B&B rooms (from $175 per night) in the main house (c 1796). It's possibly your best chance for spotting a specter among the Carrera marble mantels and gold-leaf furnishings.

EATING

Though there are a few places to eat in St Francisville, restaurants are not the highlight of the town.

MAGNOLIA CAFÉ CAFE $

(☎225-635-6528; www.themagnoliacafe.net; 5687 Commerce St; mains $7-13; ⌚10am-4pm daily, to 9pm Thu & Sat, to 10pm Fri) A purple-and-yellow-painted pig greets guests outside the entrance of this colorful old house where you can order fresh salads and sandwiches; try the spicy shrimp po'boy. Daily specials include Louisiana dishes and there's live music some Friday evenings.

BIRDMAN COFFEE & BOOKS CAFE $

(☎225-635-3665; 5687 Commerce St; mains $5-6.50; ⌚7am-5pm Tue-Fri, 8am-2pm Sat & Sun; wi-fi) Don't plan on lingering over homemade cookies and wi-fi first thing; this coffee shop is busy, busy in the morning. Return in the afternoon and peruse the few used books at a more leisurely pace.

SLEEPING

St Francisville has a whole host of historic lodgings. Check out www.stfrancisville.us.

★SHADETREE INN BED AND BREAKFAST B&B $$

(☎225-635-6116; www.shadetreeinn.com; cnr Royal & Ferdinand Sts; r incl breakfast from $145; P ❄ wi-fi) Sidled up against the historic district and a bird sanctuary, this super-cozy B&B has a gorgeous flower-strewn, hammock-hung courtyard and spacious, upscale rustic rooms. A deluxe continental breakfast can be served in your room and is included along with a bottle of wine or champagne.

3-V TOURIST COURT HISTORIC INN $$

(☎225-721-7003; www.themagnoliacafe.net/magnolia3vtouristcourts.html; 5687 Commerce St; 1-/2-bed cabins $75/125; P ❄ wi-fi) These 1920s motor court cabins are spare but homey with kitchenettes, refrigerators and microwaves; the small bathrooms are clean and well lit. Walk across the gravel drive and you're at Magnolia Cafe; the rest of the old town is just beyond.

Lafayette & Breaux Bridge

Explore

The Cajun heartland in and around Lafayette is truly a place apart, with dance halls and crawfish boils on the one hand, and an arts and eating scene that's hipper and more creative than outsiders often expect.

If you're planning to visit several towns, including those in the Cajun prairie, then Lafayette – known as the Hub City – makes a good home base. Visit the Acadian Cultural Center and a living history site in Lafayette in the morning, then head to Breaux Bridge for crawfish, a swamp tour and a dance hall band. If you spend the night, drive south to the Tabasco factory and Shadows-on-the-Teche in New Iberia on your way back to New Orleans via Hwy 90 the next morning. I-10 borders the north side of Lafayette; Hwy 90 runs north–south bisecting it.

The Best

➡**Sight** Vermilionville (p164)
➡**Place to Eat** French Press (p165)
➡**Place to Drink** Blue Moon Saloon (p166)

Top Tip

Find weekly live-band listings for the region in the **Times of Acadiana** (www.timesofacadiana.com) newspaper and online at www.arnb.org/louisiana.php.

Getting There & Away

➡ **Direction** Northwest

➡ **Travel time** 2½ hours

➡ **Car** Follow I-10 west all the way from New Orleans to Lafayette.

Need to Know

➡ **Area Code** ☎337

➡ **Location** 135 miles northwest of New Orleans

➡ **Tourist office** (☎800-346-1958; www.lafayettetravel.com; 1400 NW Evangeline Thruway; 8:30am-5pm Mon-Fri, from 9am Sat & Sun)

SIGHTS & ACTIVITIES

Lafayette

Lafayette, the largest city in Cajun country, is the self-proclaimed capital of French Louisiana. For a city of relatively small size, Lafayette is brimming with restaurants – it claims to have the most per capita in the country. Throw in a few music venues, a strong arts scene and a general Louisiana appreciation of the good things in life, and you've got a city worth exploring.

ACADIAN CULTURAL CENTER MUSEUM

(☎337-232-0789; www.nps.gov/jela; 501 Fisher Rd; 9am-4:30pm Tue-Fri, 8:30am-noon Sat; P) Part of the multi-site Jean Lafitte National Park, the Acadian Cultural Center is a good place to learn about Cajun history and traditions. Interpretive exhibits trace *Le Grand Dérangement* and spotlight food and music. In the spring, summer and fall, rangers lead narrated boat rides (adult/child/senior $12/8/10), which describe the life of trappers and traders.

VERMILIONVILLE VILLAGE

(☎337-233-4077; www.vermilionville.org; 300 Fisher Rd; adult/student $10/6; 10am-4pm Tue-Sun) Well-informed costumed guides bring history to life by taking you through a 19th-century Cajun village. Among the dozen or so buildings on view are homes dating from 1795 to 1860. Bands perform in the barn; there are cooking demonstrations; and in spring and fall you can take boat tours on the bayou. There's also a restaurant – La Cuisine de Maman (aka Mama's Kitchen) – that serves Cajun and Creole dishes.

The organisation behind the village is committed to preserving the cultural and natural resources of Bayou Vermilionville. The village is located next to the Acadian Cultural Center.

Breaux Bridge

The sign on the namesake drawbridge in downtown Breaux Bridge welcomes you to the 'Crawfish Capital,' a title bestowed on the town by the state legislature in 1959. Since then, the town of 7500 has hosted an annual **Crawfish Festival** (www.bbcrawfest.com; May) in the first complete weekend in May. Breaux Bridge is adjacent to Lafayette, to the point that it feels almost like an extension of that city,

Swampy Lake Martin is 5 miles south of Breaux Bridge and several operators run two-hour water tours through the cypress and moss-filled waters. Alligators abound. If you can, try to ride with the owner of the company rather than an assistant; you may have a more informative trip.

CAJUN COUNTRY SWAMP TOURS TOUR

(☎337-319-0010; www.cajuncountryswamptours.com; adult/child $20/10; daily by appointment) Butch Guchereau, born and raised in the Bayou Teche area, offers two-hour eco-minded tours on quiet crawfish skiffs.

CHAMPAGNE'S SWAMP TOURS TOUR

(☎337-230-4068; www.champagnesswamptours.com; adult/child $20/10; daily by appointment) Guides who can speak both French and English lead these two-hour tours. If you want to see an alligator, they'll do their darndest to find one for you.

WORTH A DETOUR

NEW IBERIA

Settled by the Spanish in 1779, New Iberia prospered on the sugarcane of surrounding plantations. Today the town's best-known native son is mystery writer James Lee Burke, whose page-turning detective Dave Robicheaux novels take place in and around New Iberia.

A top attraction is **Shadows on the Teche** (☎337-369-6446; www.shadowsontheteche.org; 317 E Main St, New Iberia; adult/senior/student $10/8/6.50; ⏰9am-5pm Mon-Sat, last tour 4:15pm; 👪), a grand Greek-revival plantation house on the banks of the bayou. The home stayed in the Weeks family from construction in 1831 until it was willed to the National Society for Historic Preservation in 1958. More than 17,000 papers describing the most minute details of the house's history were left in the attic, making this one of the most well-documented historic plantations in Louisiana. Tours begin 15 minutes after the hour.

Outside town is the region's best-known destination, the **McIlhenny Tabasco Factory** (☎337-365-8173; www.tabasco.com; admission free; ⏰tours 9am-4pm), which sits on Avery Island. Driving here feels a bit like entering Oz. After paying the man in the tiny booth (admission $1) and waiting for the gate to lift, you drive onto the island. Which isn't really an island. It's a salt dome that extends 8 miles below the surface. The salt mined here goes into the Tabasco sauces, as do locally grown peppers. The mixture ferments in oak barrels before it's mixed with vinegar, strained and bottled. You'll get a few tiny bottles, in several flavors, after the short tour. At the gift shop, try free samples of Tabasco-spiced chili, jalapeno ice cream and just about any Tabasco-imprinted item you can imagine.

In 1890 Tabasco founder EA McIlhenny started a bird sanctuary on the island. At **Jungle Gardens** (☎337-369-6243; http://junglegardens.org; adult/child $8/5; ⏰9am-5pm) you can drive or walk through 250 acres of moss-covered live oaks and subtropical jungle flora. There's an amazing array of waterbirds (especially snowy egrets, which nest here in astounding numbers) as well as turtles and alligators.

James Lee Burke's fictional detective Dave Robicheaux likes to drop by **Victor's Cafeteria** (☎337-369-9924; 109 E Main St; mains $5-14; ⏰6am-2pm Mon-Fri, to 10am Sat, to 2pm Sun), and so do his fans. Get in line at the counter of this laid-back little landmark to order favorites such as gumbo and fried shrimp, and home-style Cajun standards. Note the limited hours; enter on the right.

Just down the street from Shadows-on-the-Teche, **Clementine Dining & Spirits** (☎337-560-1007; http://clementinedowntown.com; 113 E Main St; mains $17-28; ⏰11am-2pm & 4-9pm Tue-Thu, to 10pm Fri, 6-10pm Sat, closed Sun & Mon) serves seafood, chicken and steak dishes as well as Louisiana favorites such as shrimp po'boys and oysters Rockefeller.

EATING

Lafayette loves to eat. In the compact city center, you can't walk without tripping on a good restaurant, and in general this city takes a decidedly indulgent attitude towards gastronomy.

Entertainment almost always goes with eating in Lafayette, which is good for families especially; restaurant–dance halls are nonsmoking and all ages are welcome.

★ **FRENCH PRESS** CAJUN $

(☎337-233-9449; www.thefrenchpresslafayette.com; 214 E Vermilion St, Lafayette; mains $6-15; ⏰7am-2pm Tue-Fri, 9am-2pm Sat & Sun) This place triggers plate envy. Every dish looks delicious as it's carried past. Should I have ordered the Cajun Benedict? I hear it's the best thing on the menu. Maybe the Acadian breakfast sandwich. Or maybe the Sweet Baby Breesus! Here it is. Three biscuits with bacon, fried boudin balls and Steen's cane syrup. And a cauldron of cheese grits. Oh man.

Inside a former print shop – those are typeface drawers on the wall – this new-on-the-scene restaurant also serves gourmet sandwiches and a short menu of seafood and savory meats for dinner. People like to linger and chat on weekends, so if you don't want to wait, come at 9am or 1pm.

ARTMOSPHERE AMERICAN $

(☎337-233-3331; www.artmosphere.co; 902 Johnston St, Lafayette; mains under $10; ⌚11am-2am Mon-Sat, to midnight Sun; ☑) Your place if you're keen for vegan/vegetarian food, or even just a hookah. There's a lovely selection of beer on offer, and live music every night. The crowd largely consists of the student and artist set.

OLD TYME GROCERY CAFE $

(☎337-235-8165; www.oldetymegrocery.com; 218 W St Mary St, Lafayette; meals $5-9; ⌚8am-10pm Mon-Fri, 9am-7pm Sat) The shrimp po'boy here sets a good standard for the rest of Louisiana. Step inside this busy but helpful grocery, order at the counter, grab a bag of Spicy Cajun Zapp's chips and order up! Settle in at the cozy dining room off the side or go back to your hotel room and chow down. We're hungry now at the memory.

TACO SISTERS MEXICAN $

(☎337-234-8226; www.tacosisters.com; 407 Johnston St, at Vermilion St, Lafayette; mains $3-10; ⌚6am-6pm Mon-Fri, 8am-3pm Sat) Opened by Molly and Katy Richard, the namesake sisters, this mango-colored taco shack serves juicy tacos and burritos with a Cajun kick. Everything's housemade and fresh, from the smoked fish to the marinated chicken and the salad dressing. Order at the first window, pay at the second, and if you drop a tip in the jar they'll ring a bell.

CAFÉ DES AMIS CAJUN $$

(☎337-332-5273; www.cafedesamis.com; 140 E Bridge St, Breaux Bridge; mains $17-26; ⌚11am-9pm Tue-Thu, from 7:30am Fri & Sat, 8am-2pm Sun) Well-known local restaurateur Dickie Breaux does things right at this longtime local fave in a 1920s downtown storefront. The beignets are crisp and light, and spicy barbecued shrimp never tasted so good. Friday mornings you can sit under the pressed-tin ceiling and hear French spoken. Saturday mornings, the place is full to capacity for the zydeco breakfast featuring live bands.

BLUE DOG CAFE CAJUN $$

(☎337-237-0005; www.bluedogcafe.com; 1211 W Pinhook Rd, Lafayette; mains lunch $8-12, dinner $12-22, brunch $23; ⌚11am-2pm & 5-9pm Mon-Thu, to 10pm Fri & Sat, 10:30am-2pm Sun) Make reservations if you hope to enjoy the live jazz and Cajun music brunch; any given Sunday, the line stretches out the door by 10:30am. Enjoy bayou bisque with seafood, crawfish étouffée over rice, pork grillades (thin, browned strips with gravy) and cornbread dressing. Late Louisiana artist George Rodrigue's artwork is still displayed here. There's live music Thursday through Saturday evenings.

☆ ENTERTAINMENT

If you get the chance to stay overnight in the area, there are some great live-music options.

BLUE MOON SALOON LIVE MUSIC

(☎337-234-2422; www.bluemoonpresents.com; 215 E Convent St, Lafayette; cover $5-8; ⌚5pm-2am Tue-Sun) Dang, we love this place. And if the Lost Bayou Ramblers are fiddlin' it up on a Saturday night, well, you'll find us sipping a beer, hanging on the dance floor and howling at the blue moon. Anyway, the employees are happy, the patrons are happy, the musicians are happy, the dancers are happy. So c'mon cher, let's *fais-do-do*.

ATCHAFALAYA CLUB LIVE MUSIC

(☎337-228-7512; http://patsfishermanswharf.com/atchafalaya.html; ⌚8pm-late Fri & Sat, 6-10pm Sun) Shuffling its feet beside Pat's Fisherman's Wharf in Henderson, the Atchafalaya Club hosts a great variety of Cajun bands. The Foret Tradition regularly belts out mean swamp pop, and you might see the talented Lost Pine Boys, now familiar from HBO's *Treme*. Henderson is 8 miles east of Breaux Bridge.

ARTMOSPHERE LIVE MUSIC

(☎337-233-3331; www.artmosphere.co; 902 Johnston St, Lafayette; ⌚10am-2am Mon-Sat, til midnight Sun) Graffiti, hookahs, hipsters and an edgy line-up of acts; it's more punk rock bohemain than bayou Cajun dance hall, but it's a lot of fun, and there's good Mexican food to boot.

LA POUSSIERE LIVE MUSIC

(☎337-332-1721; www.lapoussiere.com; 1301 Grandpoint Hwy, Breaux Bridge; ⌚7-11pm Sat, 3-7pm Sun) Cajun club La Poussiere doesn't serve food, just drinks and dance. Live bands play Saturdays and Sundays – cover charge and show times depends on who's playing.

RANDOL'S DANCE

(☎337-981-7080; www.randols.com; 2320 Kaliste Saloom Rd, Lafayette; ⏰5-10pm Sun-Thu, to 10:30pm Fri & Sat) Dishes such as crab cake au gratin are quite tasty, but the nightly live Cajun tunes are the why-go. Regulars are always scooting around the floor; sit on the bench around the dance floor (separated from the tables by some awkward plexiglass) and you *will* be asked out onto the floor.

SLEEPING

Chain motels and hotels crowd Hwy 90, south of the intersection with I-10.

★BLUE MOON GUEST HOUSE GUESTHOUSE $

(☎337-234-2422, 877-766-2583; http://bluemoonpresents.com; 215 E Convent St, Lafayette; dm $18, r $70-90; P ❄ @ 📶) Not for the faint-of-heart, perfect for the fun lovin', this tidy old home includes admission to Lafayette's popular down-home music venue, which is basically on a covered patio in the back of the house. The friendly owners, full kitchen and camaraderie among guests create a casual hangout environment. Prices skyrocket during festival time. Located on a side street in downtown Lafayette; dorms are mixed gender.

BAYOU CABINS CABINS $

(☎337-332-6158; www.bayoucabins.com; 100 W Mills Ave, Breaux Bridge; cabins $70-150) Welcome to the bayou! Each of the 12 cabins (one of them is a duplex) on the Bayou Teche is unique. Cabin 1 has 1949 newspapers as wallpaper (aka insulation) and cabin 6 has a '50s theme complete with Elvis. After check-in, guests are welcomed by hosts Rocky and Lisa Sonnier with Cajun hospitality and a homemade platter of boudin, cracklin' and head cheese.

A full, hot breakfast is served at 9am. At night, Christmas lights twinkle from the cabin fronts, a festive backdrop if you bring home a few pounds of spicy crawfish to devour on the front porch.

JULIET HOTEL $$

(☎337-261-2225; www.juliethotel.com; 800 Girard Jefferson, Lafayette; r from $129) Twenty upscale neutral rooms – with custom-made linens – occupy the former Le Parisienne department store in downtown Lafayette. Look for the lion's-head fountain gracing the curvaceous pool.

Cajun Prairie

Explore

North of I-10 in central Louisiana the bayous and swamps give way to grasslands and prairies. The main attraction in the region's sleepy towns – Opelousas, Eunice and Mamou – is music. The best time to visit all three communities is Saturday, taking in a live show at Fred's Lounge in Mamou followed by a Cajun jam at the Savoy Music Center in Eunice. Spend the afternoon in area museums, then dance to zydeco in Opelousas.

Opelousas is 24 miles north of Lafayette via Hwy 49. Eunice is 20 miles west of Opelousas via Hwy 190 and Mamou is 11 miles north of Eunice. You can loop back to Lafayette taking LA 13 south to the I-10 or swinging north to Ville Platte, home of a top-notch music store, and return via Opelousas.

The Best

➡ **Place to Eat** Ruby's Café (p168), Eunice

➡ **Place for Live Music** Fred's Lounge (p169), Mamou

Top Tip

There are four museums in Eunice, but all of them are closed on Mondays. To learn more about Cajun culture and hear live music, aim for a Saturday visit.

Getting There & Away

➡ **Direction** Northwest

➡ **Travel Time** Three hours

➡ **Car** Head west out of New Orleans on I-10; at Lafayette, turn north on I-49.

Need to Know

➡ **Area Code** ☎337

➡ **Location** 155 miles northwest of New Orleans

➡ **Tourist office** (☎337-457-2565; www.eunicechamber.com; 200 S CC Dusan St, Eunice; ⏰9am-3pm Mon-Fri)

SIGHTS

CAJUN MUSIC HALL OF FAME & MUSEUM MUSEUM

(☎337-457-6534; www.cajunfrenchmusic.org; 230 S CC Duson Dr, Eunice; ⏰9am-5pm Tue-Sat) FREE Showcasing Cajun instruments and other musical memorabilia, this hall of fame in Eunice is worth a peek. Zydeco fans will be out of luck – Cajun music is the sole focus here.

PRAIRIE ACADIAN CULTURAL CENTER CULTURAL CENTER

(☎337-457-8499; www.nps.gov/jela; 250 West Park Ave, Eunice; ⏰9:30am-4:30pm Wed-Fri, to 6pm Sat) FREE This cultural center has interpretive exhibits about the history and traditions of the prairie Acadians and regular events, such as live Cajun music at 6pm on Saturdays and a traditional quilting circle at 3pm on Wednesdays.

FLOYD'S RECORD SHOP MUSIC

(☎337-363-2138, 800-738-8668; www.floydsrecordshop.com; 434 E Main St, Ville Platte; ⏰8:30am-4:30pm Mon-Sat) A good way to round out your musical tour of the prairie is to stop by this record shop in Ville Platte, 14 miles northeast of Mamou. In 1957 Floyd Solieau left his DJ job to start both the record shop and Flat Tire Music. The shop, still in the family, is a cultural icon and an excellent resource for all things Cajun – CDs, instruments, books and souvenirs. Through the years, under various label names, Floyd has waxed records for dozens of French-language Cajun and swamp pop legends.

EATING

RUBY'S CAFÉ CAFE **$$**

(☎337-550-7665; 123 S 2nd St, Eunice; mains $9-23; ⏰6am-2pm Mon-Fri, 5-9pm Wed & Thu, to 10pm Fri & Sat) Ruby's does a decent line in plate lunches served in a '50s diner setting. Of course, this is a '50s diner on the Cajun prairie, so mains include fried alligator, gumbo and buckets of crawfish. The seafood platter is a glorious overindulgence in all things battered and fried. On weekend nights, this spot (of course) becomes a Cajun dance hall.

ENTERTAINMENT

Opelousas is the epicenter of Louisiana zydeco culture. You haven't heard the soul-and funk-mixed Acadian music till you've experienced it at Richard's Club (built in 1947) just west of town. Long a top venue in the state, Richard's has had several incarnations, most recently as Miller's Zydeco Hall of Fame, which opened in mid-2012. If you're overnighting in the area, there are a few good options for live music.

LIBERTY THEATER THEATER

(☎337-457-6577; www.eunice-la.com/index.php/things-to-do/liberty-schedule; 200 Park Ave, Eunice; admission $5) It's kind of like the Cajun version of the *Grand Ole Opry* show in Nashville. But at the Liberty Theater, built in 1924, locals dance to a variety of bands who play for the Saturday-night radio broadcast *Rendez-vous des Cajuns*. The live musical variety show is broadcast on local radio stations every Saturday from 6pm.

SAVOY MUSIC CENTER LIVE MUSIC

(☎337-457-9563; www.savoymusiccenter.com; Hwy 190, Eunice; ⏰9am-5pm Tue-Fri, 9am-noon Sat) On Saturday mornings 3 miles east of town, this accordion factory and shop hosts a Cajun-music jam session at 9am that lasts about three hours. Musician Marc Savoy and his guitarist wife, Ann, often join in as well as son Wilson, a member of four-time Grammy nominee the Pine Leaf Boys. Look for the huge Savoy Music Company sign west of the Cajun Campground – and a long line of parked cars on Saturday mornings.

SLIM'S Y-KI-KI LIVE MUSIC

(☎337-942-6242; www.slimsykiki.com; 182 N Main St, Opelousas; ⏰7pm-late Fri & Sat) Slim's is a hotbed of zydeco activity in town, a down-and-dirty nightclub with low ceilings, a smoky atmosphere and some seriously hot Afro-Creole zydeco rhythms. Listen for big names such as Chris Ardoin and Lil Nate.

ZYDECO HALL OF FAME LIVE MUSIC

(11154 Hwy 190, Opelousas) This spot began as part of a circuit of clubs that welcomed African American musicians – such as Fats Domino – to play during pre-1960s segregation. Back then, owner Richard Eddie gave a start to many a 'French la-la' band, as he called the emerging zydeco sound. Tight crowds and oven-hot conditions add to the rough appeal. The exact performance

THE TAO OF FRED'S

On Saturday mornings you can listen to a local Cajun radio broadcast on KVPI 1050AM starting at 9:05am. The show broadcasts from **Fred's Lounge** (420 6th St, Mamou; ⌚8am-2pm Sat) in Mamou, 10 miles north of Eunice on Hwy 190. The town's main drag, Sixth St, is a ragtag collection of slow businesses and boarded storefronts, but this little backwater attracts regulars from around the state for Fred's Saturday-morning show. Live traditional Cajun bands play upbeat two-steps and accordion-filled waltzes before a jovial crowd getting awfully merry during breakfast hours. The small brick saloon ain't much to look at, but it has hosted all the greats. In the 1950s the Courir de Mardi Gras started up here again, and radio broadcasts begun in 1967 helped fuel the Cajun revival.

So what's the scene at Fred's? On a Saturday morning people are drinking by 9:10am, dancing by 9:15am and smoking cigarettes like it's 1965. Alfred 'Fred' Tate purchased this bar in 1946 and turned it into a Cajun gathering place. Today the lounge is only open during the Saturday-morning concerts, but Fred's still packs them in.

Doors open at 8:15am, but locals don't arrive until the broadcast starts, just after 9am. The white-haired gents and the ladies in their long prairie skirts and ballet-like dance slippers are the most fun to watch. Longtime manager and bartender Tante Sue was known for swigging shots of cinnamon schnapps from a hip flask. Today the party rolls on beneath a big banner printed in her honor: *Laissez les bons temps rouler* (Let the good times roll).

schedule can be hard to determine; check the hall's Facebook page for details.

Down the Bayou

Explore

The maze of bayous and swamps arching southwest of New Orleans – 'down the bayou,' as locals say – is where the first Cajuns settled. Their traditional lifestyle is still in evidence in small part, though now it's mostly older folks who speak French and make a living from fishing the waterways. The best way to experience this culture is to take a swamp tour and afterwards pull up a big plate of fresh-caught crawfish.

In the morning, drive straight to Morgan city for the 10am tour at the Rig Museum. Here you'll experience the modern face of Cajun culture: largely tied to natural resource extraction and the myriad contracting careers and firms that surround this enormous industry. It's a good reminder that for all the gator-gumbo clichés, the Cajuns are savvy business people; whatever you feel about oil and gas, these resources have been a financial windfall for Cajun folks.

Stop in Houma for a swamp tour or drive to Thibodaux, where you can learn about Cajun culture in the wetlands region and pull off the road for a look at well-preserved slave cabins, stark reminders of the South's past. If you only have a half-day for the bayou region, head south to the Barataria Preserve, where wooden walkways meander through the swamp.

The Best

➡**Sight** Rig Museum (p170), Morgan City

➡**Place to Eat** Rita Mae's Kitchen (p171), Morgan City

Top Tip

Wear walking shoes to the Rig Museum. You'll climb at least 26 steep steps and do a fair bit of walking around the rig, inside and out.

Getting There & Away

➡**Direction** Southwest of Morgan City

➡**Travel time** 1½ hours

➡**Car** To get to Houma, take I-10 west to I-310, cross the Mississippi River and follow Hwy 90 west 22 miles. Take LA 182 south at exit 210 into town. Thibodaux is 20 miles northwest of Houma on Hwy 24. To Morgan City, follow Hwy 90 west for 60 miles.

Need to Know

➡**Area Code** 985

➡**Location** 60 miles southwest of Morgan City

➡**Tourist office Houma** (985-868-2732; cnr Hwy 90 & St Charles St, Houma; 8am-4pm); **Thibodaux** (985-446-1187; 318 E Bayou Rd, Thibodaux; 8:30am-4:30pm Mon-Fri)

The tour stops inside dorms, the kitchen and the rec area, and then winds outside to the actual drill site. Questions are encouraged, and you will learn a lot about life on a floating rig and how it all works. In fact, Big Charlie is still used as a training facility. Be forewarned: the tour may not always be 100% politically correct (environmentalists and feminists beware), but it is 100% interesting.

SIGHTS & ACTIVITIES

Morgan City

RIG MUSEUM MUSEUM

(985-384-3744; www.rigmuseum.com; 111 1st St, Morgan City; adult/child/senior $5/3.50/4; tours 10am & 2pm Mon-Sat) If you want to get a firsthand look at what it really means when American politicians say 'Drill Baby Drill,' take the 90-minute guided tour at the International Petroleum Museum and Exposition (aka Rig Museum). This informative tour winds up, down and around Big Charlie, the first ever offshore drilling rig. It was completed in 1954, eight years after it was first proposed by creator AJ Laborde of Marksville, LA.

Houma

Numerous bodies of water (Bayou Black, Little Bayou Black, the Intracoastal Waterway and Bayou Terrebonne) wend their way through the city center of Houma, a town of 30,000 people. The city itself offers little of interest to travelers, save functioning as a place for the swamp-tour-bound to stop and eat. Reservations are advised for all tours.

★**LOUISIANA LOST LAND TOURS** ECOTOUR

(504-400-5920; http://lostlandstours.org; tours from $90) Get in touch with the folks at Lost Land Tours in New Orleans to learn about exploring this area by boat. Guides are committed to teaching paddlers about the fragile environmental wonderland that is the extensive wetlands of South Louisiana; tours are led by Pulitzer Prize-winning journalist Bob Marshall.

WORTH A DETOUR

BARATARIA PRESERVE

Wanna take a walk on the wild side? Below New Orleans, the Mississippi River flows 90 miles to the bird's-foot-shaped delta, where river pilots board ships entering from the Gulf. The 20,000-acre **Barataria Preserve** (504-689-3690; www.nps.gov/jela/barataria-preserve.htm; 6588 Barataria Blvd, Crown Point; visitor center 9am-5pm) FREE, a unit of southern Louisiana's Jean Lafitte National Historic Park, offers hiking trips into the swamp. It's a good introduction to the wetlands environment. Though this is not a pristine wilderness (as canals and other structures offer evidence of human activity), wild animals and plants are still abundant. Even a brief walk on the boardwalks that wend their way through the swamp will yield sightings of gators and egrets.

If you have several hours and want to see a variety of landscapes, walk or drive about 1 mile from the visitor center to the trailhead for the Bayou Coquille Trail and the Marsh Overlook Trail. Bring your phone to hear the free audio tour. Ranger-led wetlands walks are offered Wednesday to Sunday at 10am. Stop by the visitor center to see where the walk will start. Gates to trailhead parking lots are open 7am to 5pm. If arriving before or after those times, park outside the gates. For information about canoeing, also call or stop by the visitor center. Some waterways may be impassable due to heavy vegetation growth.

To reach the preserve, take Business Hwy 90 across the Greater New Orleans Bridge to the Westbank Expressway and turn south on Barataria Blvd (Hwy 45) to Hwy 3134, which leads to the national-park entrance.

ANNIE MILLER'S SON'S SWAMP & MARSH TOURS TOUR

(☎985-868-4758; www.annie-miller.com; 3718 Southdown Mandalay Rd, Houma; adult/child $15/10; 👪) Eight miles west of Houma, this is run by the son of a local storytelling legend. He, like his mom before him, has been feeding chicken drumsticks to the alligators for so long that the swamp critters rise from the muck to take a bite when they hear the motor.

CAJUN MAN'S SWAMP CRUISE CRUISE

(☎985-868-4625; www.cajunman.com; Hwy 182, off Hwy 90; adult/child $25/15) Black Guidry entertains passengers with an accordion while piloting them through a scenic slice of Bayou Black. The launch is 10 miles west of downtown Houma.

WETLAND TOURS ECOTOUR

(☎985-851-7578; www.wetlandtours.com; Janet Lynn Lane; per adult/child $50/30) Captain Wendy Billiot's eco-oriented Wetland Tours cruise across a swampland lake near the coast (four-person minimum). She also offers angling charters that specialize in teaching women and children (and men!) to fish. Call or email for reservations and half- and full-day charter prices.

Thibodaux

Positioned at the confluence of Bayous Lafourche and Terrebonne, Thibodaux (ti-buh-dough; population 14,400) became the parish seat at a time when water travel was preeminent.

COURTHOUSE HISTORIC BUILDING

(cnr 2nd & Green Sts) The copper-domed courthouse was built in 1855 and remains a testament to Thibodaux's glory days, now long past. It's this history that holds the interest for visitors here.

LAUREL VALLEY VILLAGE HISTORIC SITE

(☎985-446-7456; Hwy 308; admission by donation; ⏲10am-3pm Tue-Fri, from 11am Sat & Sun) Among the cane fields, about 2 miles east of town on Hwy 308, this is one of the best-preserved assemblages of sugar-plantation slave structures in Louisiana. Overall, some 60 structures (c 1755 and later) survive here, including the old general store and a school house.

WETLANDS CAJUN CULTURAL CENTER CULTURAL CENTER

(☎985-448-1375; www.nps.gov/jela; 314 St Mary St; ⏲9am-7pm Mon & Tue, to 5pm Wed-Fri; 👪🐾) FREE Exhibits at Thibodaux's Wetlands Cajun Cultural Center cover virtually every aspect of Cajun life in the wetlands, from music to the environmental impacts of trapping and oil exploration. Visitors learn about 'the time of shame,' from 1916 to 1968, when the Louisiana Board of Education discouraged the use of Cajun French. Cajun musicians jam at the center from 5pm to 7pm on Monday evenings.

EATING

RITA MAE'S KITCHEN AMERICAN, CAJUN $

(☎985-384-3550; www.morgancitymainstreet.com/ritamaeskitchen.htm; 711 Federal Ave, Morgan City; mains $5-18; ⏲8am-10pm Mon-Sat, to 5pm Sun) Rita Mae's comes recommended up, down and around the bayou. In a small house near the Hwy 90 overpass, this little cottage serves up comfort food like grandma used to make, but maybe just a little bit better. Come for omelets in the morning or fill up on juicy burgers, po'boys, fried chicken and red beans and rice later in the day.

LEJEUNE'S BAKERY $

(☎337-276-5690; www.lejeunesbakery.com; 1510 Main St/Hwy 182, Jeanerette; mains $3-5; ⏲7am until the bread runs out) For a quick but satisfying snack between Morgan City and New Iberia, swing off Hwy 90 at Jeanerette and drive though the small downtown to Lejeune's. If the red light is on that means it still has French bread available for sale. Trust us when we say people from Louisiana will fight over this bread: it's that good.

The LeJeune family has been operating the bakery since 1884 and still uses the same recipes!

FREMIN'S CAJUN $$

(☎985-449-0333; www.fremins.net; 402 W Third St, Thibodaux; mains $11-26; ⏲11am-2pm Tue-Fri, 5-9pm Tue-Thu, to 10pm Fri & Sat) Located in a building dating from 1878 in downtown Thibodaux, Gilded Age Fremin's serves traditional Italian pastas as well as seafood and steaks. A few dishes, such as the crawfish tortellini carbonara, have a hint of Cajun flair. At lunch, look for po'boys, burgers and sandwiches plus a few steaks.

Sleeping

Where you stay in New Orleans depends largely on why you've come here. You can shell out some cash for top accommodations and play the whole time in the French Quarter, or experience the softer (but still fun) side of the city via one of its many quirky B&Bs. There are many options on offer; the city's one weakness is a lack of backpacker hostels.

Hotels

New Orleans hotels come in all the standard shapes and sizes. Most commonly you'll find either large purpose-built properties or cozier lodgings in older buildings. Figuring out which is which by an establishment's name alone is impossible (an 'inn' here might have five rooms or 500), so read reviews carefully. The two areas where you'll find large hotels are the French Quarter and the CBD; in the latter in particular, you'll find more modern accommodation geared at the convention crowd. Boutique hotels tend to crop up in the CBD and art-gallery heavy Warehouse District.

B&Bs

For charm, you can't beat the Crescent City's hundreds of B&Bs, which are housed in everything from colorful Creole cottages to stately town houses and megamansions. B&Bs provide intimate surroundings, interesting architecture and, in many cases, a peaceful courtyard in which to escape the maddening crowds. The complimentary morning meal at B&Bs is almost always a continental breakfast, although in a city with this many great breakfast spots, there's no need to settle for juice and toast. Each of the city's residential neighborhoods is burgeoning with B&Bs and guesthouses; there's a particularly large glut in Fabourg Marigny and the Bywater.

Longer-Term Rentals

Even if you're staying for just a week or less, renting an apartment is an option in the French Quarter, Faubourg Marigny and the Garden districts. Live in the lap of luxury at corporate digs or keep costs down by buying groceries and using a kitchen at more basic options. Independent owners list places for rent at **Airbnb** (airbnb.com) and **Vacation Rentals by Owner** (www.vrbo.com).

Room Rates & Seasons

Lodgings in New Orleans generally charge by room, rather than per person. The city is peculiar in that it's busy during the shoulder seasons of spring and fall (February through May and September through November) and slow during the summer months (due to seriously oppressive heat from June through August).

Rates usually drop like a stone from June until August. Most hectic and high-priced times are Mardi Gras (February or March), Jazz Fest (late April to early May) and other holidays and festivals. At these times rates can triple or more, and you may find places requiring three-night (or more) minimum stays. We list prices for high spring and fall. If you're arriving for Jazz Fest, book at one of the mansions-turned-B&B in Mid-City.

Parking

Parking can seriously add to your bottom line (an extra $17 to $40 per night) if staying in the Quarter or the CBD. Parking in other neighborhoods is usually free; street parking is rarely an issue in the Garden District, Uptown, Mid-City, the Marigny or the Bywater. If you like your car accessible in a dedicated, on-site lot, look for the parking icon in our reviews.

Lonely Planet's Top Choices

Audubon Cottages (p177) Gorgeous, deceptively spacious cottages in the French Quarter.

Soniat House (p177) Quintessential French Quarter historic hotel.

Columns Hotel (p185) Sip a mint julep in this Southern mansion.

Auld Sweet Olive Bed & Breakfast (p179) Hip yet cozy B&B in the heart of bohemian action.

Best by Budget

$

Bywater Bed & Breakfast (p179) Occupies the Golden Mean between funky and cozy.

India House Hostel (p186) Well-run hostel with a fun clientele.

Lookout Inn of New Orleans (p179) Wonderfully weird outpost in Bohemian Bywater.

$$

Auld Sweet Olive Bed & Breakfast (p179) Tropical decor infuses this wonderful Creole home.

La Belle Esplanade (p186) Gorgeous historical home managed by an original New Orleans character.

Lafitte Guest House (p175) Historical building converted into a central, fun hotel.

$$$

Audubon Cottages (p177) Gorgeous Creole suites in the French Quarter.

Soniat House (p177) One of the finest boutique properties in the Quarter.

Roosevelt New Orleans (p183) Legendary retreat with a block-long lobby and Sazerac Bar.

Best for Families

Prytania Park Hotel (p184) Lower Garden District at your family's fingertips.

Hampton Inn St Charles Ave (p185) Within easy distance of the zoo and Audubon Park.

Dauphine Orleans (p178) Boutique-hotel style with family-friendly amenities.

Best Historic Stays

Hotel Monteleone (p177) Has hosted some of the nation's top literary luminaries.

Gentry Quarters (p176) Sleep in the Quarter in a classic Creole cottage.

Soniat House (p177) Antique elegance permeates every level of this hotel.

Best Contemporary Cool

Loft 523 (p183) One of the few local hotels that fits the contemporary boutique label.

W French Quarter (p178) Chic and sophisticated blend of historic and modern.

Loews New Orleans Hotel (p183) Waterfront flash and chic amenities.

Best B&Bs

Bywater Bed & Breakfast (p179) Eccentric house decked out with bohemian folk art.

Ashton's Bed & Breakfast (p186) An elegant B&B dripping with historical accents.

Maison de Macarty (p180) Old World elegance in the artsy enclave of the Bywater.

NEED TO KNOW

Price Ranges

In our listings the following indicate the price of an en suite double room in high season.

$	less than $100
$$	$100 to $250
$$$	over $250

Reservations

➡ Conventions can fill the city any time.

➡ You'll almost always get a better rate by booking ahead.

➡ For Mardi Gras or Jazz Fest, reserve rooms six months to a year in advance.

➡ For last-day hotel bookings at reduced rates contact New Orleans Welcome Center (p224).

Online Resources

New Orleans Online (www.neworleansonline.com/book)

Louisiana Bed & Breakfast Association (www.louisianabandb.com)

New Orleans Hotels (www.bestneworleanshotels.com)

Lonely Planet (http://www.lonelyplanet.com/usa/new-orleans/hotels)

Gay Stays

Note that all properties we list are GLBT-friendly. New Orleans is a tolerant town.

Air-conditioning

All accommodations listed have air con. You'd melt in summer without it.

Where to Stay

Neighborhood	For	Against
French Quarter	Centrally located, so no need for a car, especially if you're staying in the Quarter. High competition means high standards of accommodation.	Touristy and loud, sometimes bordering on obnoxious. If driving, it is difficult to find parking and maneuver in the narrow streets.
Faubourg Marigny & Bywater	Cozy, independently owned guesthouses and B&Bs. Some have an authentic bohemian vibe going; all are gay-friendly. Low-key, but close to some great live music.	Small properties means inconsistent access to major modern amenities such as 24-hour room service. Less privacy than larger hotels.
CBD & Warehouse District	Best area for modern amenities. Many hotels here have excellent attached bars and restaurants. Many family-friendly spots.	The least quintessentially 'New Orleans' part of New Orleans. Many hotels are boring, convention-style places. Parking can be expensive. Potentially far from French Quarter *and* Uptown.
Garden, Lower Garden & Central City	Charming B&Bs set in wonderful historic homes, plus a few larger hotels on St Charles Ave. Walking distance to Magazine St shopping.	Not for folks who need funkier edges to their accommodation. Having a car really helps if you stay out here.
Uptown & Riverbend	Posh hotels and smaller (but just as opulent) guesthouses for those needing beauty and quiet. Within striking (sometimes walking) distance of the most exciting restaurants in the city.	Far from French Quarter and Marigny, so having a car is recommended.
Mid-City & the Tremé	Smaller guesthouses with character in beautiful historic neighborhoods far from the French Quarter's bustle.	You need a car out here. Sights and activities are scattered around rather than centralized. No larger hotels and their reams of amenities.

French Quarter

If you are looking for the historic flavor of the Old Quarter, here is a general rule of thumb: the further away you stay from the CBD, the better. Bourbon St, of course, is party central. The Lower Quarter is more residential, with guesthouses and smaller hotels, and staying down there is just as convenient. Large hotels cluster around Iberville and Canal Sts.

LAFITTE GUEST HOUSE BOUTIQUE HOTEL **$$**
Map p238 (504-581-2678; www.lafitteguesthouse.com; 1003 Bourbon St; r incl breakfast $195-260;) This elegant three-story 1849 Creole town house is at the quieter end of Bourbon St. The guest rooms are lavishly furnished in period style, although the antique washbasins and fireplaces seem an odd contrast to flat-screen TVs. Many rooms have private balconies. Lafitte's Blacksmith Shop, one of the street's more welcoming (and some say haunted) taverns, is on the opposite corner.

OLIVIER HOUSE HOTEL **$$**
Map p238 (504-525-8456; www.olivierhouse.com; 828 Toulouse St; r from $139, 1-/2-bedroom ste from $179/199;) The main house was built in 1838 by Marie Anne Bienvenu Olivier, a wealthy planter's widow, and is an uncommon beauty with Greek-revival touches. Rooms range from the relatively economical to the elaborate, with balconies and kitchens; most have furnishings evoking the early 19th century. The main courtyard is lush with trees and flowers. A second courtyard has a small pool.

HOTEL ROYAL BOUTIQUE HOTEL **$$**
Map p238 (504-524-3900, 800-650-3323; www.frenchquarterhotelgroup.com/hotel-royal.html; 1006 Royal St; r from $159;) Lace-like ironwork balconies, gas lanterns and decorative topiaries – everything an 1833 New Orleans home should be. Inside, renowned architect and designer Lee Ledbetter has infused each of the individually decorated guest quarters with subtle, softly contemporary touches. A modern dark-wood four-poster bed and chocolate linens contrast nicely with the rough, white-plaster walls and plantation shutters in the king suite.

HOTEL PROVINCIAL HOTEL **$$**
Map p238 (504-581-4995, 800-535-7922; www.hotelprovincial.com; 1024 Chartres St; r incl breakfast from $169, ste from $249;) Behind its stately stucco facade, this hotel fills much of the block with a series of finely restored buildings and a large parking area. The best rooms have high ceilings and open onto the interior courtyards. Others can be cramped and dark. Decor ranges from commercial standard to ornately historic. The back courtyard is a revelation, as is its lovely pool.

BIENVILLE HOUSE HOTEL BOUTIQUE HOTEL **$$**
Map p238 (504-529-2345, 800-535-9603; www.bienvillehouse.com; 320 Dectaur St; r from $140, ste from $250;) The Bienville is the definition of a well-executed historic French Quarter hotel. The wrought-iron balconies that ring the tiled lobby give way to a lovely courtyard with swimming pool; interior period design matches the promise of the Federal-meets-French-Creole exterior. Rooms are pretty, and a good size for the Quarter, which tends to offer rooms on the small side.

HOTEL VILLA CONVENTO HOTEL **$$**
Map p238 (504-522-1793; www.villaconvento.com; 616 Ursulines Ave; r from $179;) Classic New Orleans, the Villa occupies an 1833 town house in the residential part of the Lower Quarter, complete with a three-story red-brick facade and wrought-iron balconies. Out back in the annex (probably former servants' quarters) are more rooms, all with traditional decor, from comfy quilts to lacy canopies. Prices for budget doubles fall to as little as $99 when demand dwindles.

LE RICHELIEU HOTEL **$$**
Map p238 (504-529-2492, 800-535-9653; www.lerichelieuhotel.com; 1234 Chartres St; r from $155;) Le Richelieu's red-brick walls once housed a macaroni factory, but extensive reconstruction in the early 1960s converted it into a good-value hotel. Spacious rooms are decorated with standard synthetic floral spreads, but the price includes parking (a big plus); you're within an easy walk of Frenchmen St; and there's a pool. Prices drop precipitously in the slow summer season.

INN ON URSULINES HOTEL **$$**
Map p238 (504-525-8509; www.frenchquarterguesthouses.com; 708 Ursulines Ave; r from $208;) This Spanish-era Creole cottage is one of the oldest buildings in the French Quarter. It's located in the laid-back Lower

Quarter, and despite its historical roots, hosts some tastefully modern rooms. Those located in front are a short step up from the sidewalk, perhaps too close to the neighborhood's stream of yammering late-night pedestrians. Those out back are much quieter.

HISTORIC FRENCH MARKET INN HOTEL **$$**
Map p238 (☎888-626-2725; www.frenchmarketinn.com; 501 Decatur St; r from $140; P ❄ ☎) You hardly have to stumble out of bed to get a daiquiri on this busy block of Decatur, and you're not far from aromatic coffee at iconic Café du Monde. A good budget choice, this hotel has pleasant rooms with crisp linens, although not much daylight (consider it a boon if you get in late). Hidden within the complex is a pleasant courtyard.

BOURBON ORLEANS HOTEL HOTEL **$$**
Map p238 (☎504-523-2222, 800-521-5338; www.bourbonorleans.com; 717 Orleans Ave; r from $134; P ❄ ☎) A polished-marble classic whose gray exteriors and white trim are almost as stately as the grand foyer, it 's combined of several buildings, mostly dating from the early 1830s. Most streetside rooms have access to the classic wrought-iron balconies. (Bourbon St, needless to say, can get noisy.) Traditional rooms feature especially comfortable beds and ergonomic desks, but note that standard rooms set a new standard for smallness.

PRINCE CONTI HOTEL HOTEL **$$**
Map p238 (☎888-626-4319; www.princecontihotel.com; 830 Conti St; r/ste from $130/210; ❄ ☎) The three floors of this 19th-century structure house a glut of guest rooms decorated with early 20th-century-style furnishings and a general sense of dignified understatement. The lobby and parlor areas might have been plucked from a Jane Austen novel, but otherwise the property is suffuse with modern amenities such as turn-down service and cable TV.

CHATEAU HOTEL HOTEL **$$**
Map p238 (☎504-524-9636; www.chateauhotel.com; 1001 Chartres St; r $130-200; ❄ ☎) Nothing is cookie-cutter here; rooms range in size and have varying floral motifs. Many feature wrought-iron beds, which echo streetside balcony details. Though they're on the smallish side, we'd opt for courtyard rooms, which are cool and open up to a pool. In the late spring and summer low season, rates can fall as low as $99 per night.

GENTRY QUARTERS B&B **$$**
Map p238 (☎504-525-4433; www.gentryhouse.com; 1031 St Ann St; r incl breakfast from $155; ❄ ☎) This charming old Creole house contains five homey rooms with kitchenettes. Modest but comfortable furnishings give the rooms a lived-in feel, while linens and towels are fresh and clean. Most rooms open onto a lush garden patio, where you might be visited by two friendly dachshunds. Some rooms are large enough for families. There's a two-night minimum.

HOTEL ST MARIE HOTEL **$$**
Map p238 (☎504-561-8951, 888-626-4812; www.hotelstmarie.com; 827 Toulouse St; r incl breakfast from $140; ❄ ☎) The St Marie was built to look historic from the outside, but is up-to-date on the inside. Its best feature is its inviting courtyard, which has a swimming pool and umbrella-covered tables amid lush plantings. The neocolonial guest rooms are comfortable and well appointed, and their spacious dimensions do the trick. Just around the corner is Bourbon St at its most extreme.

BIDDING FOR A BED

When maximizing quality while minimizing price is your aim, websites such as **Hotwire** (www.hotwire.com) and **Priceline** (www.priceline.com) are an excellent gamble. They don't let you see the property name before you commit to paying, but you can choose the neighborhood, star level and amenities before you either bid or buy at up to 50% off the advertised rate. The drawbacks: you can't change your mind (they're nonrefundable) and nonsmoking rooms can't be guaranteed. Still, if you're flexible, the system works.

Splashing out can be more affordable too if you find a chichi package auction on **Luxury Link** (www.luxurylink.com). Occasionally there are 'mystery name' properties but quite often the hotels are identified and described (with gorgeous photos to ogle) so you know what you're gambling on.

WESTIN NEW ORLEANS AT CANAL PLACE HOTEL $$

Map p238 (504-566-7006; www.westinneworleanscanalplace.com; 100 Iberville St; r from $180;) At 29 stories high, the Westin has some of the city's best views of the Mississippi River. Watching the parade of freighters, tankers and barges in the wee hours beats TV. Rooms are large and modern, with good desks and signature 'heavenly beds,' as well as small sitting areas. There's a rooftop pool that, needless to say, has more good views.

SAINT HOTEL $$

Map p238 (504-522-5400; www.thesainthotelneworleans.com; 931 Canal St; r from $210, ste from $760;) Modern New Orleans hotels have to balance the needs of those who want some historic preservation versus those who don't like a place to feel too stodgy. The Saint pulls off this balance nicely, with clean duo-chromatic color schemes (white walls, dark wood floors) offset with little azure accents – quite contemporary, yet alleviated by a historic property's elegance throughout.

NINE-O-FIVE ROYAL HOTEL HOTEL $$

Map p238 (504-523-0219; www.905royalhotel.com; 905 Royal St; r from $165, ste from $295;) On a particularly scenic block, the Nine-O-Five eschews the usual Nola shtick and opts for the timeless comfort you'd expect to find if this house belonged to a dignified aunt. Front rooms with balconies are the choice for those who want to survey always entertaining Royal St, but for seclusion, get a room off the cute courtyard out back.

COURTYARD NEW ORLEANS DOWNTOWN HOTEL $$

Map p238 (504-523-2400; www.ibervillesuites.com; 910 Iberville St; r from $189;) Promotional rates can be a real bargain at this property, located near the heart of the Bourbon St madness. Discounts can be very attractive, but the trade off is you sleep in surroundings that don't exactly drip with historical character. Still, some guests will enjoy the modern furnishings and geometric designs that infuse the linens and bathroom.

INN ON ST PETER HOTEL $$

Map p238 (504-524-9232; www.frenchquarterguesthouses.com; 1005 St Peter St; r from $187;) This inn is located in a 19th-century treasure built during the Spanish Colonial period. Wraparound iron balconies and a lovely facade conceal rooms with surprising character – a carved bed here, exposed brick there. The St Peter is a little beyond tourist central, which has advantages (quiet) and disadvantages (you might want to take a cab home).

CORNSTALK HOTEL B&B $$

Map p238 (504-523-1515; www.cornstalkhotel.com; 915 Royal St; r $169-269;) The Cornstalk is known more for its exterior than its interior, which makes sense once you see its famous maize-bedecked gates. Pass through the cast-iron fence and into a plush, antiqued B&B where the serenity sweeps away the whirl of the busy streets outside. Gem-like rooms are all luxurious and clean – carpets are given the once-over monthly. Limited parking.

★AUDUBON COTTAGES HOTEL $$$

Map p238 (504-561-5858; www.auduboncottages.com; 509 Dauphine St; cottages from $700;) At the Audubon Cottages, you get to sleep in one of seven immaculately restored historical buildings, ranging from two-bedroom suites with private courtyards and walk-in showers to former slave quarters once used as a studio by John James Audubon. You'll have your own saltwater pool, attentive staff and the satisfaction of having privacy and quiet within the Quarter.

★SONIAT HOUSE BOUTIQUE HOTEL $$$

Map p238 (504-522-0570, 800-544-8808; www.soniathouse.com; 1133 Chartres St; r from $245, ste from $425;) The three houses that make up this hotel in the Lower Quarter epitomize Creole elegance at its unassuming best. You enter via a cool loggia into a courtyard filled with ferns and a trickling fountain. Some rooms open onto the courtyard, while winding stairways lead to elegant upstairs quarters. Singular attention has been paid to art and antiques throughout.

HOTEL MONTELEONE HOTEL $$$

Map p238 (504-523-3341, 866-338-4684; www.hotelmonteleone.com; 214 Royal St; r from $290;) Perhaps the city's most venerable hotel, the Monteleone is also the Quarter's largest. Not long after it was built, preservationists put a stop to building on this scale below Iberville St. Since its inception in 1866, the hotel has lodged literary luminaries including William Faulkner,

Truman Capote and Rebecca Wells. Rooms exude an old-world appeal with French toile and chandeliers.

W FRENCH QUARTER HOTEL **$$$**

Map p238 (☎504-581-1200; www.whotels.com; 316 Chartres St; r from $349, ste from $499; P ❄ @ ≋) Like all W hotels, this one wears its style on its trendy sleeve. Where the French Quarter is colonial charm, this is all palatial grandeur, even if it feels a little understated. Rooms vary, but all boast contemporary sleekness. The best are airy spaces opening onto an inner patio. Ponder the pool's azure waters or just enjoy a breeze.

DAUPHINE ORLEANS HOTEL **$$$**

Map p238 (☎504-586-1800, 800-521-7111; www.dauphineorleans.com; 415 Dauphine St; r incl breakfast from $299; P ❄ ☜ ≋) Through a lush courtyard sits bright-yellow Creole cottage-style rooms with exterior access (once part of a carriage house). Request one of these, or one of the rooms with exposed cypress beams and brick across the road in the former home of merchant Herman Howard. Other rooms have less character, but similar appointments, including earthy color schemes and high thread-count sheets. The bar was once an infamous brothel.

RITZ-CARLTON NEW ORLEANS HOTEL **$$$**

Map p238 (☎800-542-8680, 504-524-1331; www.ritzcarlton.com; 921 Canal St; r from $280; ❄) Sip tea surrounded by neoclassical antiques and French fabrics; dip into a magnolia-scented aromatherapy bath; or retire to the library cigar club. An ample number of smiling staff wait to attend, whether you're ready for turn-down service or need a complimentary shoe shine. The solid wood floors, tall beds and brick fireplaces would fit in at an English manor house.

HAUNTED HOTELS

An eerily cold 14th-floor hallway leads to a vision of children playing; cafe doors open and shut on their own; despite the bar being locked, guests see a patron who isn't there... Andrea Thornton, Director of Sales & Marketing at the **Hotel Monteleone** (p177), had heard dozens of first-hand accounts of supernatural sightings when she decided investigation was in order. In 2003 the hotel invited the International Society of Paranormal Research (ISPR) to come spend several days, during which they identified 12 disparate spirits on the property, one a former employee named 'Red.' And, indeed, hotel records showed that an engineer who went by the nickname Red worked at the hotel in the 1950s.

Hearing or seeing children is the most common of the mischievous-but-benign activities people experience in the historic hotel. Numerous guests have reported seeing a little boy in a striped suit (aged about three) in room 1462. Speculation is that it's Maurice, son of Josephine and Jacques Begere, looking for his parents. While Maurice was in the hotel being watched by a nanny, his father was thrown from a coach and died instantly; his mother passed a year later.

In a town with such a strife-torn history – slavery, war, fever, flood – hauntings (if they exist) are hardly a surprise. And the Monteleone is far from the only hotel in the Quarter to report sightings. Among others, ghostbusters might want to check out the following:

Bourbon Orleans Hotel (p176) Once an orphanage and an African American convent; children have been seen and heard playing on the 6th floor.

Dauphine Orleans (p178) Bottles appear rearranged at May Bailey's bar, site of a once-infamous brothel, and moans and sounds of beds moving at night have been reported.

Hotel Provincial (p175) Building 5 was constructed on the site of a Civil War hospital; guests report sometimes gruesome visions of wounded soldiers and bloody sheets.

Lafitte Guest House (p175) 'Marie,' a little girl who died of yellow fever, is said to appear in the mirror in room 21, where her mother stayed.

Le Pavillon (p183) Apparitions materialize bedside in this 1907 hotel, where the ISPR identified at least four resident spirits.

OMNI ROYAL ORLEANS HOTEL $$$

Map p238 (504-529-5333; www.omnihotels.com; 621 St Louis St; r from $269;) The Omni Royal is hard to miss; its massive structure was actually the centerpoint of a preservation battle during its construction. Everything here screams opulence and grandeur, from the marble-tiled lobby ringed with enormous statues to the heated rooftop pool to the dignified rooms that combine a bit of historical furnishing with handsome frilliness. Pets are welcome.

ROYAL SONESTA HOTEL $$$

Map p238 (504-586-0300; www.sonesta.com/royalneworleans; 300 Bourbon St; r from $249;) Don't the doormen look fancy in their blue royal-guard-look tux and tails? Most times of year this hotel exudes a gracious charm, but the location is ground zero for Bourbon St excesses (staff grease pillars to keep revelers from climbing to the balconies). Still, the nearly 500 rooms provide classy retreats from the strip clubs and cover bands.

ASTOR CROWNE PLAZA HOTEL $$$

Map p238 (504-962-0500; www.astorneworleans.com; 739 Canal St; r/ste from $253/426;) An $11 million renovation buys you some stylish design details. Look for stacked silver bubble lamps and tall-tufted headboards with pops of russet orange in a primarily neutral color scheme. Business is this 638-room hotel's primary pleasure, but tourists, too, will enjoy the grand lobby, pool terrace and Dickie Brennan's Seafood Bar.

Faubourg Marigny & Bywater

Across Esplanade Ave from the Quarter, the grid-defying street pattern in the Marigny and Bywater is speckled with colorful cottages, many of which have been converted into homey, reasonable-priced B&Bs. Savvy night owls feel the pull of the lively Frenchmen St scene. It's possible to walk to the Quarter from either neighborhood, but if you're heading back to the Bywater at night, you'll probably want to cab it.

BYWATER BED & BREAKFAST B&B $

Map p242 (504-944-8438; www.bywaterbnb.com; 1026 Clouet St; r without bath $100;) This is what happens when you fall through the rabbit hole and Wonderland is a B&B. This spot is popular with lesbians (it's owned by a lesbian couple), but welcomes everyone. It's about as homey and laid-back as it gets. Expect to stay in what amounts to a folk-art gallery with a bit of historical heritage and a hallucinogenic vibe.

LOOKOUT INN OF NEW ORLEANS GUESTHOUSE $

off Map p242 (504-947-8188; http://lookoutneworleans.com; 833 Poland Ave; r $99;) This cozy little inn is located way at the end of the Bywater, a few blocks' walk from some excellent bars and restaurants. Four funky suites are individually appointed; your room may feature Elvis, dragons, a zebra-print sofa sleeper or Spanish-mission style furnishings. There's a mini-pool and a hot tub if you need a soak.

LIONS INN B&B B&B $

Map p242 (504-945-2339; www.lionsinn.com; 2517 Chartres St; d $90-135;) On a quiet Marigny block, the Lions Inn is a bright, friendly place suitable for gays and straights. Nine simply furnished guest rooms have splashes of vibrant color and no fussy antiques. Jump into the swimming pool and Jacuzzi or use one of the free bicycles to peddle the five blocks to the edge of the Quarter.

BURGUNDY B&B $

Map p242 (504-261-9477; http://theburgundy.com; 2513 Burgundy St; r incl breakfast $90-130;) This vibrant red-and-white 1890s double shotgun house is a fine B&B that's located on the quieter residential edge of the Marigny. You're within a quick walk of local nightlife and the music scene on St Claude Ave. Four color-coded rooms (red, green, blue and coral) surround an attractive courtyard, parlor, library and sitting area.

★AULD SWEET OLIVE BED & BREAKFAST B&B $$

Map p242 (504-947-4332; www.sweetolive.com; 2460 N Rampart St; r incl breakfast from $150;) The Krewe de Vieux parade goes right by this grand B&B. Even if you don't come during the pre-Lenten season, you can see parade regalia such as the co-owner's King Endymion costume on display. The house itself is similarly theatrical, once owned by a set designer and mural artist. Individual rooms are suffused with decorative touches – faux wood and magnolia blooms.

PIERRE COULON GUEST HOUSE GUESTHOUSE **$$**

Map p242 (504-250-0965; www.pierrecoulonguesthouse.com; 714 Spain St; r 1-2 person incl breakfast $150, 3/4 person $225/300;) This guesthouse is located in a gorgeous Creole cottage that feels like the home of an eclectic professor. The property manages to blend a sense of historic coziness with a funky edge, and is within walking distance of the Marigny's finest bars and restaurants. A lovely outdoor courtyard is perfect for an afternoon of lazy reading.

DAUPHINE HOUSE B&B **$$**

Map p242 (504-940-0943; www.dauphinehouse.com; 1830 Dauphine St; r $125;) The Dauphine only has two rooms, but it's actually a pretty big house, a classic Creole Esplanade Ridge–style mansion that happens to be located in Faubourg Marigny. The rooms are quite plush and the place puts us in mind of a luxurious house of sinful fun and good times. Which is pretty much what New Orleans is, right?

COLLINWOOD HOUSE B&B **$$**

Map p242 (504-301-4353; www.collinwoodhouse.com; 2408 Dauphine St; r $120-225;) This off-violet colored Creole mansion conceals rooms that wouldn't be out of place in a BBC period drama about lords, manors, upstairs-downstairs style romances, tweed and gin. We love the Shogun Room, partly modeled after an imperial Japanese sweet; and the Continental Room, which looks perfect for a rendezvous with an aristocrat.

HOTEL PARKING BLUES

Overnight hotel parking can run as high as $44 per night in the CBD, an amount that can do serious damage to your budget. If convenience isn't that important to you, compare prices at one of the many public parking lots and garages on Poydras St or its offshoots. It's still expensive but you're likely to save from $10 to $20 per night and probably won't have to walk more than a few blocks. On Saturday nights you can try parking on the street – read the signage, but street parking is typically free on Sundays. Just don't leave valuables in sight or stay in one street spot longer than 24 hours.

LA BOHEME DE MARIGNY B&B **$$**

Map p242 (504-598-6544; www.flipkey.com; 735 Touro St; cottage from $500;) You can probably figure by the name that this is a pretty funky spot. It's also an excellent accommodation option if you're traveling with a group and need to split an entire property. This classic Creole cottage has three bedrooms and is suffused with charm and exposed brick; you'll feel as if you're staying in a folk-art museum.

B&W COURTYARDS B&B **$$**

Map p242 (504-324-0474, 800-585-5731; www.bandwcourtyards.com; 2425 Chartres St; r incl breakfast $159-179;) The B&W is tastefully bohemian, but it also has the right amount of historical accents. There are six highly individualized rooms; our favorite is the Peach Blossom, which has a 'Far East comes to New Orleans' vibe that's quite attractive, like a classy set for a Chinese martial-arts movie built into a Marigny home. Service is friendly and unobtrusive.

LAMOTHE HOUSE B&B **$$**

Map p242 (504-947-1161; www.frenchquarterguesthouses.com; 621 Esplanade Ave; r from $187; P) Lovely, oak-shaded Esplanade Ave is a prime jumping-off point for prowling Frenchmen St and the Lower Quarter. Guest rooms here are furnished with antiques that you may feel guilty about bumping into, and thick curtains keep out the sun when you're sleeping off a big night. If you're determined to revive early, take a dip in the pool after your continental breakfast.

MAISON DE MACARTY B&B **$$**

Map p242 (504-267-1564; www.maisonmacarty.com; 3820 Burgundy St; r/ste from $150/225;) This 19th-century ruby-red Bywater mansion conceals a surprising number of historical heritage rooms. The interior is stuffed with all kinds of cozy antiques; it's not as crazy funky as the average Bywater property, but not as dowdy as guesthouses in other neighborhoods. There's a pool out back, and you're a 10-minute bike ride from the Quarter.

BALCONY GUEST HOUSE GUESTHOUSE **$$**

Map p242 (504-945-4425; www.balconyguesthouse.com; 2483 Royal St; r from $118;) The Balcony is owned by the sort of fun-loving bohemians that make the Marigny area so special. The interior is filled with *objects d'art* from around the world, and rooms seamlessly blend the tropical aesthetics of Indochina and south Louisiana. The eponymous balcony overlooks one of the most charming intersections in the city, adjacent to good bars and coffee shops.

FRENCHMEN HOTEL HOTEL **$$**

Map p242 (☎800-831-1781; www.frenchmenhotel.com; 417 Frenchmen St; r incl breakfast from $120; P ❄ 📶 ≋) The three thoroughly refurbished 1850s houses that comprise this smart hotel are clustered around a courtyard with a swimming pool and Jacuzzi. High ceilings, balconies and some rustic exposed brick are remnant from the buildings' more elegant past. Mix-and-match furnishings have limited antique appeal. The real selling point is the hotel's proximity to everything that Frenchmen St has to offer. Concierge service is an upscale touch for a bargain hotel.

CRESCENT CITY GUESTHOUSE B&B **$$**

Map p242 (☎504-944-8722; www.crescentcitygh.com; 612 Marigny St; r from $110; P ❄ 📶) This laid-back B&B is a great choice for those who want peace and quiet but don't feel like surrendering the option of walking into the French Quarter, or onto Frenchmen St. The rooms are simple but cozy, and the owner is a very friendly treasure trove of New Orleans knowledge. The back garden is a great spot to chill with a book.

ROYAL STREET COURTYARD B&B **$$**

Map p242 (☎504-943-6818; www.royalstcourtyard.com; 2438 Royal St; r incl breakfast $110-150, ste $250; ❄) This attractive guesthouse has clean, comfortable rooms that could use an update; but while the interior of the place is a little old fashioned, the beds do the trick. It's got a prime location; the rooms come with a continental breakfast; and there's a hot tub out in the back, which is always a plus. No kids under 16.

MELROSE MANSION B&B **$$$**

Map p242 (☎504-944-2255; www.melrosemansion.com; 937 Esplanade Ave; ste weekdays/weekends from $180/300; ❄ 📶 ≋) An exquisite 1884 Victorian mansion, Melrose stands out even among its stately neighbors. This is a retreat for the well heeled and for honeymooners. Rooms are luxurious, airy spaces, with high ceilings and large French windows. Fastidiously polished antique furnishings include four-poster beds, cast-iron lamps and comfortable reading chairs in every room.

CBD & Warehouse District

The hotels in the CBD tend to be modern behemoths and posh high-rises catering to those with business-expense accounts. Even the Warehouse District, despite its artistic leanings, mostly accommodates the convention set. Prices do plummet, however, when occupancy is low. There are far more big-name chain hotels in these neighborhoods than we could possibly mention, so if you have a loyalty-point fave, look it up online.

★LE PAVILLON HISTORIC HOTEL **$$**

Map p244 (☎504-581-3111; www.lepavillon.com; 833 Poydras Ave; r $179-279, ste from $695; P ❄ 📶 ≋) Le Pavillon exudes an old-school *joie de vivre* that's easy to love. Fluted columns support the porte cochere off the alabaster facade, and the doorman wears white gloves and a top hat (and somehow doesn't look ridiculous). Both private and public spaces are redolent with historic portraits, magnificent chandeliers, marble floors and heavy drapery.

At the same time, it has a sense of fun, best exemplified by the nightly serving of peanut-butter-and-jelly sandwiches in the lobby at 10pm. Rates are unexpectedly low for a hotel of this quality, and during slow periods Le Pavillon offers some astounding deals. Breakfast buffet is famously good. Parking is $39 per night.

DRURY INN & SUITES HOTEL **$$**

Map p244 (☎504-529-7800; www.druryhotels.com; 820 Poydras St; r incl breakfast $129-170, ste $139-195; P @ 📶 ≋ 🐾) They had us at 'Three free alcoholic drinks.' And the included light dinner. And the helpful tips, along with a local map, that they gave us at check-in. The Drury Inn embraces New Orleans' fun-loving, welcoming spirit and that's why we love it. The red-and-gold decorated rooms are stylish, comfy and come with 37in flat screens, pillow-top mattresses, and a microwave and refrigerator.

The free drinks are served nightly at 5:30pm along with light fare such as hot dogs and baked potatoes. Hot breakfasts are complimentary, too, and there's a guest laundry. Check the online eSaver rate for the best price. Parking is $25 per night. Pet fee is $10 per day.

COUNTRY INN & SUITES HOTEL $$

Map p244 (☎504-324-5400; www.countryinns.com; 315 Magazine St; r incl breakfast $169-199, ste $219-239; P @ ☎) The exterior of this 155-room hotel looks a bit uninspiring, but step inside and this ugly duckling morphs into a boutique swan. The hotel encompasses seven historic downtown buildings dating from the 1800s. Period touches – exposed beams, red brick, an ivy-covered courtyard – add character to this incarnation of the national chain.

Because of the hotel's unusual structure, each room is slightly different in form and appearance, but all come with microwaves and refrigerators. Guests can enjoy a hot buffet breakfast in the morning and cookies in the afternoon. There's a helpful front desk. Parking is $33 per night.

HAMPTON INN NEW ORLEANS DOWNTOWN HOTEL $$

Map p244 (☎504-529-9990; www.neworleanshamptoninns.com; 226 Carondelet St; r incl breakfast $169-219; P @ ☎) Rooms are spacious, and the workout room gets a thumbs up at this Hampton Inn, which is located on the upper floors of the Carondelet Building (considered the Crescent City's first skyscraper). Per Hampton protocol, there's a complimentary breakfast buffet. The location is just two blocks from the Quarter and around the corner from a streetcar. Floors are accessed with the room key. Parking is $34 per night

AIRPORT ACCOMMODATIONS

Lots of flights out of New Orleans depart at the crack of dawn. Not an easy schedule if you've been tempted to make a full night of it in the French Quarter during your last hours in the Big Easy. Nervous or conscientious types might opt for staying as near the tarmac as possible. Many hotels near the airport offer 24-hour free shuttle services that take just a few minutes to reach the terminals. These hotels include the following:

Country Inn & Suites – Airport (☎504-305-1501; 1501 Veterans Memorial Hwy, Kenner; r incl breakfast $96, ste $102-172; ❄ @ ☎) One mile from Louis Armstrong New Orleans International Airport.

Doubletree (☎504-467-3111 800-222-8733; www.doubletree.com; 2150 Veterans Memorial Hwy, Kenner; r $119-129, ste $199; ❄ @ ☎ ≋) Two miles from the New Orleans International Airport. Parking is $6 per day.

Hilton (☎504-469-5000 800-872-5914; www.hilton.com; 901 Airline Dr, Kenner; r $129; ❄ @ ☎ ≋) Sits across the street from the New Orleans International Airport. Wi-fi is $14.95 per day.

HOTEL MODERN HOTEL $$

Map p244 (☎504-962-0900; www.thehotelmodern.com; 936 St Charles Ave; r $129-159, ste $259-459; P ❄ @ ☎ 🐾) The eye-catching Hotel Modern isn't exactly a 'hidden gem,' but if you want welcoming, reasonably priced accommodations near the Arts District and the National WWII Museum, this hip number is a great choice. Rooms are spartan, and the smallest can feel cramped, but all come with mini-fridge, Keurig coffeemaker and desk. Look for monochromatic accent walls, clean lines and an old book or two for whimsy.

There's an on-site restaurant as well as a dark and sultry cocktail lounge, Bellocq. Check the Hotel Tonight app for rates as low as $85. Valet parking is $30 per day and self-parking is $10 per day. There are a few free public spots along Lee Circle – nab one in the late afternoon.

LAFAYETTE HOTEL HOTEL $$

Map p244 (☎504-524-4441; www.lafayettehotelneworleans.com; 600 St Charles Ave; r $179-197, ste $215-233; P ☎ 🐾) Pleasant and small, this 1916 hotel is steps from Lafayette Sq and within easy walking distance of the Julia Row arts district and the National WWII Museum. Surrounding blocks have a classic feel that's generally lacking in the modern CBD. The 44 rooms are furnished with dark wood, antiques and king-size beds. Walls are painted in rich, classic colors; bathrooms are roomy and finished in marble.

Lafayette Sq was the center of the American St Mary neighborhood, developed after the Louisiana Purchase. Parking is $31 per night; wi-fi is $5 per night (but not usually assessed). There is a one-time nonrefundable $50 fee for pets. Some rooms were under renovation at press time.

EMBASSY SUITES HOTEL HOTEL $$

Map p244 (☎504-525-1993; www.embassyneworleans.com; 315 Julia St; r incl breakfast $189-

639; P @ ≋ ≋) Great for an annual group getaway, every room here is a large suite, and no two are exactly the same. Most have balconies; higher floors have views of the city and the river. Adjoining historic loft-building rooms, in what was once a cotton warehouse, have tall ceilings and exposed brick walls. Complimentary cocktails are served between 5:30pm and 7:30pm.

Beyond the rooms, the architecture astonishes with vast size and a cacophony of angles, but the eccentric design grows on you. The soaring atrium is indeed impressive. Parking is $35; wi-fi is $13 per night or free if you sign up for the Hilton HHonors program.

LA QUINTA INN & SUITES DOWNTOWN — HOTEL $$

Map p244 (504-598-9977; www.lq.com; 301 Camp St; r incl breakfast $179, ste $219; P @ ≋ ≋ 🐾) This shiny high-rise with its stylish rooms is not necessarily what you'd expect from the mid-level La Quinta hotel chain. Rooms are downright modern with flat-screen TVs, oversize graphic art and green throws on triple-sheeted beds. An outdoor pool, laundry facilities and continental breakfast all add to the value, and it's just a few blocks from the Quarter. Parking is $26 per night.

INTERNATIONAL HOUSE — BOUTIQUE HOTEL $$

Map p244 (504-553-9550; www.ihhotel.com; 221 Camp St; r $159-299, penthouses $679-979; @ ≋) Lavish rooms at this boutique crash-pad offer an array of amenities, from marble desks to iHome stereos to two-headed showers. Should the budget allow, go for the penthouse rooms and their sweeping terraces. Be aware that 11th-floor 'Rockstar' rooms are windowless and may come with a pull-chain hatch that leads to the roof – or perhaps a parallel New Orleans?

The fashionable Loa bar sits amid soaring columns and plush tufted ottomans. There's even an iMac for those who want to check their email. Parking costs $39 per night.

LOFT 523 — BOUTIQUE HOTEL $$

Map p244 (504-200-6523; www.loft523.com; 523 Gravier St; r $209-239; @ ≋) If you've ever wondered what it would be like to sleep inside a piece of modern art, now's your chance. Top design magazines have recognized the industrial-minimalist style of the 18 rooms, where whirligig-shaped fans circle over low-lying Mondo beds. If you're looking for style, privacy and a free-standing half-egg tub – this is the place.

For drinks and posh lounging, guests have access to the mod, London-inspired Gravier Social Club beside the lobby. Since International House is a sister property, you share their fitness center. Parking costs $39 per night, and there's a $200 flat fee for pets. The front door is so hip it's invisible, but look close and you'll find it between the Omni and Lucky Dogs.

★ ROOSEVELT NEW ORLEANS — HOTEL $$$

Map p244 (504-648-1200; www.therooseveltneworleans.com; 123 Baronne St; r from $269, ste from $329; P @ ≋ ≋) The majestic, block-long lobby harks back to the early 20th century, a golden age of opulent hotels and grand retreats. Swish rooms have classical details, but the spa, John Besh restaurant, storied Sazerac Bar and swanky new jazz lounge are at least half the reason to stay. The rooftop pool is pretty swell, too. It's an easy walk to the French Quarter.

Known originally as the Grunewald, the hotel was the city's elite establishment when it opened in 1893. In the 1930s its bar was frequented by governor Huey Long. A meticulous $145 million renovation saw it reopen its doors in 2009 as part of the Waldorf-Astoria Collection. Parking costs $44 per night. Wi-fi is $15 per day, but it's free in the lobby.

LOEWS NEW ORLEANS HOTEL — HOTEL $$$

Map p244 (504-595-3300; www.loewshotels.com; 300 Poydras St; r $259-299, ste $459; P @ ≋ ≋ 🐾) They say the enormous windows were installed so that steamship executives, who once occupied the building, could watch their ships on the Mississippi. Big views are just part of the fun at this snazzy hotel. The breeziness starts in the lobby with upbeat, eye-catching photos of New Orleans. The 285 elegantly modern rooms are larger than average. All are on the 11th floor and above, many with superb river views.

There's an indoor lap pool and health center, plus a noted spa. The Swizzle Stick bar off the lobby regularly hosts live jazz. Loews is pet-friendly and charges a $100 pet cleaning fee, plus $25 per day. Parking is $39 per night.

WINDSOR COURT HOTEL — HOTEL $$$

(504-523-6000; www.windsorcourthotel.com; 300 Gravier St; r $295, ste $345-555; P ≋ ≋) The sparkling lobby, with its portraits of noblemen and their Brittany spaniels, could double as a drawing room in the real Windsor Court. Revamped guest rooms are painted 'robin's egg' blue, and come with Italian marble bathrooms, toile with aristocratic prints, butler's pantries and Frette linens. There's also a 4500ft spa.

Unwind in the clubby confines of the Polo Club Lounge or return to the lobby for a craft cocktail at the Cocktail Lounge. Parking is $36 per night.

Garden, Lower Garden & Central City

Stately Greek-revival town houses front leafy lanes in the lower district, and as you move northwest, the houses only get more elaborate. Both historic Garden District neighborhoods are largely residential today, but you're in luck: there are a few inns, hotels, and B&Bs from which to choose. B&Bs may have a two-night minimum stay requirement on event weekends.

★GARDEN DISTRICT B&B B&B $

Map p248 (☎504-895-4302; www.gardendistrictbedandbreakfast.com; 2418 Magazine St; ste incl breakfast from $95; ❄@) This inviting B&B is a great budget option and our favorite spot for an extended stay. The private four-suite town house is like your own character-filled efficiency apartment. Each spacious room (most sleep three) has a separate entrance, kitchenette and table seating plus brick walls, tall ceilings and homey antiques such as a 1950s (nonworking) stove. Fresh-made breads, wrapped to go, and fruit are set out every morning.

Rooms are stocked with coffee and cereal, and juice and yogurt are in your mini-fridge. The Patio Suite includes a wonderful little private courtyard. The innkeeper provides loads of local restaurant info, and respects guests' privacy. Close to the Irish Channel and within walking distance of good Magazine St shopping.

CAMP BOW WOW

Pets aren't allowed at most B&Bs, so for travelers who like to bring Fido on the road, local B&B owners recommend **Camp Bow Wow** (☎504-891-3647; www.campbowwow.com; 2731 Tchoupitoulas St; per dog per night $42), a daytime and overnight 'camp' for dogs. Once boarded, your dog will enjoy exercise, play areas and campfire treats. Anxious owners can watch their dogs on the doggie web cam. Woof woof!

Reduced price per dog if you board more than one. Owners and pets must complete a short interview before your canine will be allowed to board. The Camp Bow Wow folks want to make sure your dog plays well with others and is up-to-date with shots.

PRYTANIA PARK HOTEL HOTEL $

Map p248 (☎504-524-0427; www.prytaniaparkhotel.com; 1525 Prytania St; r/ste incl breakfast from $79/129; P❄📶) Prytania Park is one of the best deals going. Basic rooms can run as low as $79 to $99 on weekends, depending on what's going on in town. Older fixtures and quirky features (well-worn exterior hallways with unattractive views, for example) may not impress more-particular travelers.

Kids will get a kick out of the loft rooms that come with a spiral staircase. Complimentary parking is available in a guarded lot behind the property. The hotel is one block from the St Charles Ave streetcar and within walking distance of the WWII Museum. Check for last-minute reservations.

TERRELL HOUSE B&B $$

Map p248 (☎504-247-0560; www.terrellhouse.com; 1441 Magazine St; r incl breakfast $185-275; 📶) Southern hospitality is what impresses most at this stately 1858 Georgian-revival house with cast-iron galleries, a spacious courtyard and exquisite touches. Original art adds to the freshness of the simple but tasteful carriage-house rooms. Think high-thread-count linens, colorful spreads and clean-lined wooden or iron beds. Suites in the main house are more antique in nature, with period furnishings, silk draperies and Oriental rugs.

Common rooms are galleries filled with art, antiques and potted plants. Other amenities include in-room minifridges stocked with soda and bottled water. Breakfast menu sounds divine. Owner Linda O'Brien is a warm host who's on top of the details. No children under 12.

GREEN HOUSE INN B&B $$

Map p248 (☎504-525-1333; www.thegreenhouseinn.com; 1212 Magazine St; r incl breakfast $169-199, ste $269; P@🛜🏊🐾) The house's striking color – a tropical rubber-tree green – certainly stands out on a still-gentrifying section of Magazine St, near the Warehouse District. Things stay green within the landscaped pool and garden (clothing optional), which is surrounded by palms and exotic blooms. Though named primarily for flowers, the guest rooms are far from delicate, with clean-lines, hardwood floors, exposed brick and some nautical-themed decor.

Continental breakfast is available. Booking ahead is preferred, and walk-ups are not accepted. There's a $25 one-time fee for pets.

HOTEL INDIGO HOTEL $$$

Map p248 (☎504-522-3650; www.neworleansindie.com; 2203 St Charles Ave; r from $239; P❄@🛜🐾) Hotel Indigo, we like your finger-popping style. In the guestrooms, New Orleans-themed photographic murals root you firmly in the city while bright pillows and bold prints add an artsy sense of fun. The hotel, which opened in 2013, is steps from the St Charles streetcar line, and the big-windowed lobby overlooks Mardi Gras parades and the Rock-n-Roll Marathon route.

Skip the restaurant breakfast in the morning and take an invigorating walk to a local coffee shop or bacon-and-eggs joint. Parking is $23 per day, and pets $50 per stay. We had no problems with free public parking along Jackson Ave.

Uptown & Riverbend

For the most part, Uptown and Riverbend step it up in the style department; grittier neighborhoods are further off the beaten path. Streetcars clank by the historic mansions, manicured gardens and parks that line leafy St Charles Ave. There are a handful of lovely places to stay in this part of town.

★PARK VIEW GUEST HOUSE B&B $$

Map p250 (☎504-861-7564; www.parkviewguesthouse.com; 7004 St Charles Ave; r incl breakfast $189-229; @🛜) The breakfasts are amazing (oh, those cheese grits) at this well-appointed three-story inn, where everyone seems glad to see you. Beside Audubon Park, this ornate wooden masterpiece was built in 1884 to impress people attending the World Cotton Exchange Exposition. The 21 rooms and guest lounge are heavy with solid wood antiques, and the wraparound verandah overlooking the park and St Charles Ave is lovely.

Tulane and Loyola Universities are just blocks away – many of the hotel's frequent guests are visiting parents. Complimentary wine is served in the afternoon and there's a computer for guest use.

HAMPTON INN ST CHARLES AVENUE HOTEL $$

Map p250 (☎504-899-9990; www.hamptoninn.hilton.com; 3626 St Charles Ave; r incl breakfast $199-219, ste $249; P@🛜🏊) Sits beside St Charles Ave, just across from the streetcar line, but manages to feel quiet and subdued. Floors are accessible only by keycards, which adds a layer of personal security, and there's free parking in a dedicated lot for guests directly behind the hotel. Nondescript mid-size rooms come with flat screens, gold-flecked green carpets and lots of counter space in the bathroom.

Weekends book up fast; make reservations well before your arrival date.

CHIMES B&B $$

Map p250 (☎504-899-2621; www.chimesneworleans.com; 1146 Constantinople St; r incl breakfast $158-198; @🛜) Five pleasant little rooms here each have outstanding individual touches, such as a floating staircase made from 4in-thick cypress slabs, or a sunken stone tub. Rooms surround a lovely patio and gardens, creating a courtyard community of sorts. Breakfast consists of fresh-baked goods and local Community Coffee. Eight namesake chimes hang on the front porch of the main house.

Chimes is located in a quiet residential neighborhood, but is quite close to Magazine St. Two- or three-night minimum stay required on weekends, depending on the season.

COLUMNS HOTEL HISTORIC HOTEL $$

Map p250 (☎504-899-9308; www.thecolumns.com; 3811 St Charles Ave; r incl breakfast Fri-Sun from $170, Mon-Thu from $130 ; ❄🛜) This white-porched Southern manse, built in 1883, is a snapshot from the past. Fortunately, that past doesn't take itself too seriously. A magnificent mahogany staircase climbs past a stained-glass window to the 20 rooms, ranging from smallish doubles to the two-room Pretty Baby Suite (named for the 1970s Louis Malle film shot here). The environs are not exactly posh, but they are well loved.

Elaborate marble fireplaces, richly carved armoires and claw-foot tubs are among the highlights. To absorb the late-night revelry, take a front room on the 2nd floor. A lavish hot breakfast is included. Guests enter through the columned front verandah and continue past two wood-paneled parlors that double as a bar-cafe.

Mid-City & the Tremé

There's not a whole lot going on sleeping-wise out here, but what's available is nice: historical homes converted into B&Bs and guesthouses that cost a fraction of the rates you'll find in the French Quarter. It's an ideal area to stay in for Jazz Fest – the Fair Grounds are only a short walk away.

INDIA HOUSE HOSTEL HOSTEL **$**

Map p254 (504-821-1904; www.indiahousehostel.com; 124 S Lopez St; dm/d $20/55;) This colorful place is larger than it looks. Half a block off Canal St in Mid-City, the hostel is a mini-complex of subtropically themed good times. The grounds include an above-ground pool, a cabana-like patio and three well-worn old houses used for sleeping. And the ambience? India House has the sort of free-spirited party atmosphere that got you into backpacking in the first place.

Bunk beds include linen and tax. Guests can use the washer and dryer, and log onto the internet. Children not permitted.

★LA BELLE ESPLANADE B&B **$$**

Map p254 (504-301-1424; www.labelleesplanade.com; 2216 Esplanade Ave; r incl breakfast $179-209;) A little quirky, a little saucy, and the co-owner wears a jaunty fedora – a devil-may-care touch that ties the whole colorful shebang together. Furnishings in the five themed suites vary, but look for chunky headboards, plush chairs, Gibson Girl portraits and claw-foot tubs. Bright, monochromatic walls keep it all pretention-free. Savor crawfish pie and other tasty Southern fare for breakfast.

There's a small Museum of Curiosities in the entryway; the fedora-wearing co-owner writes a very amusing blog for the B&B's website; and the place is a ten-minute walk from the Jazz Fest grounds.

DEGAS HOUSE HISTORIC HOTEL **$$**

Map p254 (504-821-5009; www.degashouse.com; 2306 Esplanade Ave; r/ste incl breakfast from $199/300;) Edgar Degas, the famed French Impressionist, lived in this 1852 Italianate house when visiting his mother's family in the early 1870s. Rooms recall his time here through period furnishings and reproductions of his work. The suites have balconies and fireplaces, while the less expensive garret rooms are cramped top-floor quarters that once housed the Degas family's servants.

Stays include a hot breakfast. During his stay Degas produced the city's most famous painting, *The Cotton Exchange in New Orleans*. Easels, of course, are available.

ASHTON'S BED & BREAKFAST B&B **$$**

Map p254 (504-942-7048, 800-725-4131; www.ashtonsbb.com; 2023 Esplanade Ave; r incl breakfast from $209-239;) Looking at the detailed plaster ceilings, the ornate stained glass and the crisp paint and trim at this wonderful mansion, it's very hard to imagine it had a 60ft hole in the front of it after Hurricane Katrina. Nothing to worry about, though; innkeepers Patrick and Karma Ashton have meticulously restored this 1861 Greek-revival building. Luxe furnishings include half-tester canopy beds and claw-foot tubs.

A hot Creole breakfast and complimentary refreshments throughout the day are included. Ashton's is well situated if you're in town for Jazz Fest. Festive decorations – such as fancy pumps from the Muses parade (Karma is a member) – fill the home before Mardi Gras.

HH WHITNEY HOUSE B&B **$$**

Map p254 (504-948-9448; www.hhwhitney.com; 1923 Esplanade Ave; r incl breakfast $125-175, ste $195;) Common areas are not as spiffy as those in other B&Bs in the neighborhood, but this 19th-century Italianate house is a convenient choice if you're attending Jazz Fest. There are five rooms over two floors; each has its own style, but all include vintage furniture and antique embellishments. The back garden is a nice spot to lounge under the shade of leafy oaks.

If you're a *Gone with the Wind* fan, there's an entire suite themed for Scarlett O'Hara, complete with Vivien Leigh portrait.

Understand New Orleans

NEW ORLEANS TODAY 188

Changing demographics are altering New Orleans, even as Louisiana slips into the sea.

HISTORY 190

How one of the oldest ports in America became jazz's birthplace, a modern innovation hub and an all-hours funkstorm.

PEOPLE OF NEW ORLEANS 202

Learn the folkways and quirks of the distinctive cast of characters that makes up one of America's most idiosyncratic cities.

ARCHITECTURE 205

How to recognize the architectural dress donned by this distinctive grand dame.

MUSIC 210

The music makes New Orleans, but just how did New Orleans make the music?

ENVIRONMENT 213

New Orleans is shaped by, and constantly shaping, its surrounding wetlands.

New Orleans Today

New Orleans has entered a phase of oddly measured confidence buttressed by insecurity. New bars, restaurants and revitalized neighborhoods have given the city a hipness cachet among visitors that hasn't been present for decades. On the flip side, changes have been accompanied by wariness from locals. Better, they say, to be uniquely New Orleanian than hip. Which raises the question: a decade removed from Katrina, can the city's character continue to weather such change?

Best on Film

A Streetcar Named Desire (1951) Classic Nola drama, with Marlon Brando and Vivien Leigh.

Down by Law (1986) Jim Jarmusch, Tom Waits, Roberto Benigni, a prison break and a swamp.

King Creole (1958) Elvis hits up the old sleazy Quarter.

New Orleans Exposed (2005) Shoestring documentary offering a harrowing look at Big Easy housing projects.

Abbott & Costello Go to Mars (1953) The comic duo thinks they're going to Mars, end up at Mardi Gras and never realize they haven't left Earth.

Best in Print

Bienville's Dilemma (Richard Campanella; 2008) Definitive guide to the city's physical and cultural geography.

A Confederacy of Dunces (John Kennedy Toole; 1980) Quintessential New Orleans picaresque novel.

Nine Lives (Dan Baum; 2009) Nine oral histories form a cross-section of modern New Orleans.

New Orleans Noir (2007) Short stories explore the city's dark side.

The Awakening (Kate Chopin; 1899) Love, tragedy and gender roles; one of the first American novels written from a woman's perspective.

A Smoking Ban Smoking Gun?

New Orleans has enacted a smoking ban in indoor businesses from April 2015. This is the sort of public health policy the rest of the world cottoned on to over a decade ago, but New Orleans is proudly and stubbornly protective of its vices. As such, there has been a fascinating backlash, with opponents taking the position that the health of the city's soul is improved by something that is unhealthy to its lungs.

If that seems like a lot to swallow (or inhale, as it were), consider this observation, once made by a visitor: 'New Orleans is a place where you can drink outside and smoke inside.' Essentially, people don't want to lose a cheeky embrace of sin. Scratch the surface and you find many of those who oppose the ban are less prosmoking, and more against the idea of anyone in a position of power proclaiming what's best for everyone. You can stop New Orleanians from smoking indoors, but you'll never stomp their anti-authority attitude.

C'mon, Hear the Noise

In recent years, an increasing number of famous bars, music venues and street musicians have been told to turn down their music by the New Orleans police. To say this was surprising would be a huge understatement: even the most puritan locals were shocked that the city of New Orleans was enforcing a previously rarely enforced noise ordinance in the live-music capital of the world.

After an outcry, the city council commissioned a report that recommended a French Quarter noise limit of between 90 and 100 decibels, measured at a venue's open doors and windows, but this level is disputed by the Vieux Carré Property Owners Residents and Associates (VCPORA), a French Quarter neighborhood group, which wants the cap at 70 decibels – the sound of a radio in your living room. The sound report urged the city to, above all else, be consistent with its enforcement of noise laws. Whether that consistency trends towards letting the music play, or turning it down to indoor levels, remains to be seen.

The 'G' Word

New Orleans has ever been a city of immigrants, but the latest wave of newcomers has been met with no small amount of tension. Ironically, said newcomers are domestic transplants, made up in large part by young professionals from other parts of the country, attracted by a perceived sense of place and 'authenticity' present in New Orleans' crumbling streets, rich food, vibrant street culture and peeling architecture.

The city is, in other words, dealing with gentrification, like many cities in America. The cost of living is being driven up, and some disgruntled locals believe the gentrification-generation does not respect the city's traditions or customs. Not so, say others, pointing out that newcomers often fight hardest for preserving heritage architecture, while older locals have moved to suburbs. However the debate plays out, there is no doubt gentrifiers have made an impact on New Orleans. But then, so has each fresh set of arrivals (French, Spanish, Americans, Jews, Germans, Irish, Vietnamese, Hondurans). Historically, this city changes her newcomers, rather than the other way around.

Louisiana Land Loss

It doesn't matter how much New Orleans changes or resists change if the city has no dry ground to sit on. Louisiana is experiencing the fastest rate of land loss in the world. Roughly 25 to 35 square miles of wetlands vanish underwater per year. At this rate, New Orleans could be a new Atlantis in a century.

The culprit? Coastal erosion, saltwater intrusion, decreased sediment deposits due to dams, canals and levees, oil and gas excavation that cause the land to lose structural integrity, and rising sea levels caused by climate change. Addressing all of these issues will require a comprehensive strategy, but Louisiana is a very conservative state that takes a dim view of environmentalism. New Orleans, on the other hand, skews to the political Left, and land loss has become a major priority for her citizens. The situation has been primed for a showdown between the city and the state, and in a larger sense, Louisiana and the Gulf of Mexico.

if New Orleans were 100 people

60 would be African American
30 would be White
5 would be Hispanic
3 would be Asian
2 would be mixed race

Hurricane Katrina

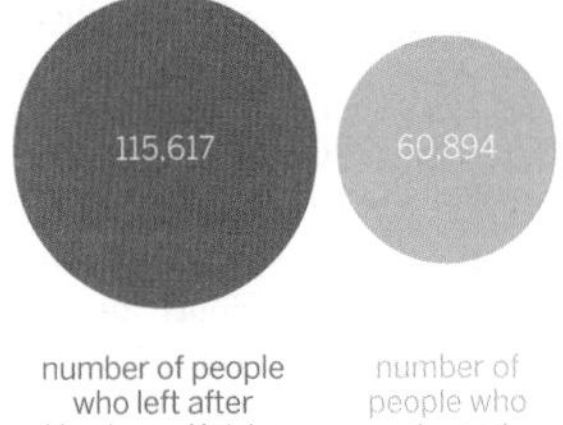

number of people who left after Hurricane Katrina

number of people who returned

population per sq mile

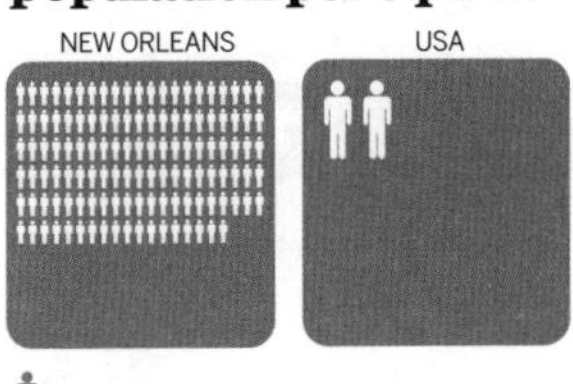

History

New Orleans has ever been a place for exiles and seekers: French aristocrats and frontiersfolk; rebel slaves, defeated slaveowners and mixed-race children of uncertain status; American explorers, Spanish merchants and Jewish refugees; prostitutes and nuns; musicians, artists, homosexuals and, recently, those seeking to rebuild and revitalize an almost-drowned city.

The Quality of Creole

Throughout all of this history, New Orleans' population has exemplified the quality of Creole: a racial, religious, transnational, linguistic mix of settlers who forged a unique identity, a sum of many parts into a greater whole. Many aspects of New Orleans' culture today – street names, food, Mardi Gras – suggest a profound influence left behind by the French and Spanish, who took turns governing this city before the USA absorbed it. It is equally significant that African culture, often with Caribbean influences, has always held a stronger sway here than elsewhere in the US.

Early settlers planned a canal to link the Mississippi River to Bayou St John and, eventually, Lake Pontchartrain. The proposed canal was never built, but after the Louisiana Purchase its location – Canal St – became the border between the French Quarter and the American Sector, where Americans settled in what is now Uptown.

Being a major capital of the South has determined many events in New Orleans' history and contributes to its character today, but it is important to note that while this city is geographically Southern, culturally it has always been a place apart. New Orleans has its back to the South and its mouth to the sea, and much of its population has arrived via the latter: international immigrants and refugees and, after 2005, do-gooders and entrepreneurs looking to rebuild.

By North American standards, New Orleans is an old city, and the depth of its history has always been cherished by locals. Even the painful elements of its history – slavery, disease and segregation – have all played a part in shaping one of the most distinct regional identities in the USA.

TIMELINE

Pre-European Contact

Louisiana is populated by thousands of members of the First Nations, who live in villages and large towns in the Gulf Coast region and northern prairies.

AD 1000

The Morgan Effigy, a human death figure carved from a deer antler, is fashioned somewhere near Pecan Island in southwest Louisiana.

1600s

European explorers search for the entrance to the Mississippi River. Control of this access point would essentially provide command of the interior of the North American continent.

Native Inhabitants

Louisiana was well settled and cultivated by the time of European arrival. Contrary to the myth of hunter-gatherers living in a state of harmony with the forest, local Native Americans significantly transformed their environment with roads, trade networks and substantial infrastructure. They were, however, susceptible to European diseases; the germs brought by early explorers wiped out thousands of Native Americans. Ironically, by the time the French arrived with the goal of colonization, the region had probably reverted to something like a state of nature due to the massive deaths caused by introduced diseases.

After AD 1700, Europeans documented numerous direct contacts with local tribes. A confederation known collectively as the Muskogeans lived north of Lake Pontchartrain and occasionally settled along the banks of the Mississippi River. The Houma nation thrived in isolated coastal bayous from Terrebonne to Lafourche up until the 1940s, when oil exploration began in southern Louisiana and disturbed their way of life.

Andrew Jackson won a one-sided victory at the Battle of New Orleans in 1815, where there were nearly 900 British losses versus 13 US. Ironically, the battle began after the USA and Britain had agreed to end the war. But the victory put a lid on British designs for the Louisiana Territory.

French & Spanish New Orleans

Europeans knew control of the mouth of the Mississippi equaled control of the interior of the continent, but the Mississippi eluded ships on the Gulf until 1699, when Canadian-born Pierre Le Moyne, Sieur d'Iberville, and his younger brother Jean-Baptiste Le Moyne, Sieur de Bienville, located the muddy outflow. They encamped 40 miles downriver from present-day New Orleans on the eve of Mardi Gras and, knowing their countrymen would be celebrating the pre-Lenten holiday, christened the small spit of land Pointe de Mardi Gras. With a Native American guide, Iberville and Bienville sailed upstream, pausing to note the narrow portage to Lake Pontchartrain along Bayou St John in what would later become New Orleans.

Iberville died in 1706, but Bienville remained in Louisiana to found Nouvelle Orléans – named in honor of the Duc d'Orléans (Duke of Orléans) – in 1718. Bienville chose a patch of relatively high ground beside the Bayou St John, which connected the Mississippi to Lake Pontchartrain, thereby offering more direct access to the Gulf of Mexico. Factoring in the site's strategic position, Bienville's party decided to overlook the hazards of perennial flooding and mosquito-borne diseases. Engineer Adrien de Pauger's severe grid plan, drawn in 1722, still delineates the French Quarter today.

1690s

French fur traders establish small villages and forts in the south Louisiana bayous, paving the way for the eventual settlement of New Orleans.

1718

Jean-Baptiste Le Moyne de Bienville founds Nouvelle Orléans. The city is founded in its current location for its strategic position controlling the mouth of the Mississippi River.

1750s

French Cajuns begin to arrive in southern Louisiana following the British conquest of Canada. The area they settle becomes known as (and is still referred to as) Acadiana.

1762

France hands Louisiana Territory, which has proven to be unprofitable, over to Spain in exchange for an alliance in its wars in Europe.

While the evidence is contested, the accepted wisdom in New Orleans is that the African musical traditions kept alive inside Congo Sq served as a base for jazz and later forms of homegrown black music.

From the start, the objective was to populate Louisiana and make a productive commercial port, but Bienville's original group of 30 ex-convicts, six carpenters and four Canadians struggled against floods and yellow-fever epidemics. The colony, in the meantime, was promoted as heaven on earth to unsuspecting French, Germans and Swiss, who began arriving in New Orleans by the shipload. To augment these numbers, convicts and prostitutes were freed from French jails if they agreed to relocate to Louisiana.

The colony was not a tremendous economic success, and women were in short supply. To increase the female population, the Ursuline nuns brought young, marriageable girls with them in 1728. They were known as 'casket girls' because they packed their belongings in casket-shaped boxes. New Orleans was already establishing itself as, and gaining a reputation for being, a loosely civilized outpost. Looking about her, one recently arrived nun commented that 'the devil here has a very large empire.'

In a secret treaty, one year before the Seven Years' War (1756–63) ended, France handed the unprofitable Louisiana Territory to King Charles III of Spain in return for an ally in its war against England. But the 'Frenchness' of New Orleans was little affected for the duration of Spain's control. Spain sent only a small garrison and few financial resources. The main enduring impact left by the Spanish was the architecture of the Quarter. After fires decimated the French Quarter in 1788 and 1794, much of it was rebuilt by the Spanish. Consequently, the quaint Old Quarter with plastered facades we know today is not French, as its name would suggest, but predominantly Spanish in style.

The Spanish sensed they might eventually have to fight the expansion-minded Americans to retain control of the lower Mississippi. So they jumped at Napoleon Bonaparte's offer to retake control of Louisiana in 1800.

Antebellum Prosperity

While Napoleon Bonaparte was waging war in Europe, the US was expanding westward into the Ohio River Valley. Napoleon needed cash to finance his wars, and US President Thomas Jefferson coveted control of the Mississippi. The deal seemed natural, but nevertheless the US minister in Paris, Robert Livingston, was astonished by Bonaparte's offer to sell Louisiana Territory – an act that would double the USA's national domain – at a price of $15 million.

Little cheer arose from the Creole community, who figured the Americans' Protestant beliefs, support for English common law and puritan work ethic jarred with the Catholic Creole way of life. In 1808 the territorial legislature sought to preserve Creole culture by adopting elements of

1768

Creole and German conspirators try to prevent Louisiana from falling into Spanish hands during the Rebellion of 1768; the uprising is squashed and its leaders executed.

1788

On Good Friday, the Great New Orleans fire destroys 856 buildings, which are replaced with Spanish-style construction that characterizes the French Quarter to this day.

1791

Following the slave revolution in Haiti, the arrival of French-speaking migrants, black and white, doubles New Orleans' population and adds a veneer of Caribbean culture.

1803

Napoleon reclaims Louisiana, then sells the territory – which encompasses almost the entire drainage area of the Mississippi River – to the US for $15 million, doubling the nation's size.

Spanish and French law, a legacy that has uniquely persisted in Louisiana to this day, to the abiding frustration of many a Tulane law student.

New Orleans grew quickly under US control, becoming the fourth-wealthiest city in the world and the second-largest port in the USA by the 1830s. The city's population grew as well, and spilled beyond the borders of the French Quarter. Also in the 1830s, Samuel Jarvis Peters bought plantation land upriver from the French Quarter to build a distinctly American section. That plot, beginning with today's CBD, was separated from the Creole Quarter by broad Canal St. Peters married into a Creole family and epitomized the American entrepreneur operating within the Creole host community.

Developers further transformed the 15 riverbank plantations into the lush American suburbs that are now part of Uptown New Orleans. Creole families that benefited from the city's flourishing economy built their opulent homes along Esplanade Ave, from the Quarter to Bayou St John. While the wealthy chose the highest ground, immigrants and blacks expanded into low-lying wetlands.

The late 1850s saw the revival of Carnival. The old Creole tradition, now propelled by Americans, hit the streets of New Orleans as a much grander affair than ever before. Americans also assumed control of the municipal government in 1852, further illustrating the erosion of Creole influence in New Orleans.

Slaves & Free People of Color

From the beginning, people of African descent were an important part of the city's population; many households in New Orleans included a few slaves. Equally significant, though, was the city's considerable number of blacks who were free in the antebellum period.

The French brought some 1300 African slaves to New Orleans in the city's first decade. In 1724 French Louisianans adopted the Code Noir (Black Code), a document that restricted the social position of blacks, but also addressed some of the needs of slaves (abused slaves could legally sue their masters) and accorded certain privileges to free persons of color. Although the import of slaves became illegal in the USA in 1807, slavery itself remained legal, and thanks to smugglers like Jean Lafitte, by the mid-19th century New Orleans had become the largest slave-trading center in the country.

Slaves in French and Spanish Louisiana were allowed to retain more of their African culture than slaves in other parts of the USA. Drumming and dancing were permitted during nonworking hours, and from the 1740s free blacks and slaves were allowed to congregate at Congo Sq, initially called Place des Negres. Immense crowds, including tourists

Affairs between races were socially accepted in old New Orleans, but interracial marriages were not. Plaçage was a cultural institution whereby white Creole men 'kept' light-skinned black women, providing them with a handsome wardrobe and a cottage in the Vieux Carré, and supported any resulting children.

1808

As American settlers move into Creole New Orleans, the territorial legislature officially adopts elements of Spanish and French law to preserve its cultural identity.

1811

The German Coast Uprising, the largest slave revolt in US history, occurs near New Orleans. Two white men and 95 slaves are killed during the fighting.

1815

General Andrew Jackson defeats the British in Chalmette, just outside the city, at the battle of New Orleans. The battle occurs after the War of 1812 has technically ended.

1820s

New Orleans becomes the second-largest immigrant hub in the USA. Many immigrants come from Germany and Ireland; those from the latter often settle in the area now known as the 'Irish Channel.'

from the East Coast and Europe, showed up to witness complicated polyrhythmic drumming and dances, which, by European standards, were considered highly exotic and suggestive.

Voodoo is an authentic part of New Orleans life, but isn't the touristy version of the religion hawked in the French Quarter. If you want to visit an authentic spell shop, stop by F&F Botanica in Mid-City.

Long before the Civil War, New Orleans had the South's largest population of free blacks. In Creole New Orleans they were known as *les gens de couleur libre* – free people of color. Throughout the 18th and 19th centuries, it was not uncommon for slaves to be granted their freedom after years of loyal service. Sometimes the mixed offspring of slaves and owners were granted their freedom. Skilled slaves were often allowed to hire themselves out, working jobs on the side until they were able to earn enough money to buy their freedom. The Code Noir permitted free blacks to own property and conduct business.

Free blacks identified with Creole culture, speaking French and attending Mass. Trained musicianship was prized among many families, and orchestras of free black musicians regularly performed at wealthy Creole balls. The free blacks of New Orleans were considered a highly cultured class who probably enjoyed a higher quality of life than blacks anywhere else in the US (and even many whites). They were often well educated, and some owned land and slaves of their own. But they didn't share all the rights and privileges of white Creoles and Americans: they could not vote or serve in juries, and while going about their business were sometimes required to show identification in order to prove that they were not slaves.

Subtle gradations of color led to a complex class structure in which those with the least African blood tended to enjoy the greatest privileges (octoroons, for instance, who were in theory one-eighth black, rated higher than quadroons, who were one-quarter black).

A Demographic Gumbo

The Creoles could only loosely be defined as being of French descent. The progeny of unions between French Creoles and Native Americans or blacks also considered themselves Creole. Still, while the multicultural stew's constituent parts were not necessarily French, they became French in character after exposure to the city. Early German immigrants, for example, frequently Gallicized their names and spoke French within a generation.

Ironically the group that did not assimilate to the French city was French Acadians. The Acadians (forest-dwellers), former residents of Canada, were deported by the British from Nova Scotia in 1755 after refusing to pledge allegiance to England. Aboard unseaworthy ships they headed south, but the largely illiterate, Catholic peasants were unwanted in the American colonies. Francophile New Orleans seemed a

1828

The first synagogue in the city opens for services. New Orleans Jews are a mixture of Spanish, Alsatian and Germanic groups, giving the community a unique cultural makeup.

1830s

Marie Laveau markets herself as the Voodoo Queen of New Orleans, popularizing the religion among the upper class and linking it to the city's public identity.

1840

Antoine's opens for business. The restaurant is still open today, the oldest family restaurant in America, and its kitchen is supposedly responsible for dishes such as oysters Rockefeller.

1853

A yellow-fever epidemic claims the lives of almost 8000 citizens, or 10% of the city's population. Eventually the outbreak is traced to mosquito-borne transmission.

natural home, but even here the citified Creoles regarded them as country trash. So the Acadians, now dubbing themselves Cajuns, fanned out into the upland prairies of western Louisiana, where they were able to resume their lifestyle of raising livestock.

Other former-French subjects arrived from St Domingue (now Haiti). The slave revolt there in 1791 established St Domingue as the second independent nation in the Americas and first black republic in the world. Following those revolts, thousands of slaveholders fled with their 'property' (slaves) to Louisiana, where slave and master bolstered French-speaking Creole traditions. Thousands of former slaves also relocated from St Domingue to New Orleans as free people of color. This influx doubled the city's population and injected an indelible trace of Caribbean culture that remains in evidence to this day. Their most obvious contribution was the practice of voodoo, which became popular in New Orleans during the 19th century.

As the Civil War approached, nearly half of the city's population was foreign born. Most were from Ireland, Germany or France. The Irish, in particular, took grueling, often hazardous work building levees and digging canals. They settled the low-rent sector between the Garden District and the docks, still known as the Irish Channel.

Despite the Napoleonic Code's mandate for Jewish expulsion, trade practices led to tolerance of Jewish merchants. Alsatian Jews augmented the small Jewish community in New Orleans, and by 1828 they had established a synagogue. Judah Touro, whose estate was valued at $4 million upon his death in 1854, funded orphanages and hospitals that would serve Jews and Christians alike.

Union Occupation

As cosmopolitan as New Orleans was, it was also a slave city in a slave state, and it was over this very issue that the nation hurtled toward civil war. On January 26, 1861, Louisiana became the sixth state to secede from the Union, and on March 21 the state joined the Confederacy – but not for long. The Union captured New Orleans in April 1862 and held it till the end of the war.

Major Benjamin Butler, nicknamed 'Beast,' oversaw a strict occupation, but is also credited with giving the Quarter a much-needed clean-up, building orphanages, improving the school system and putting thousands of unemployed – both white and black – to work. But he didn't stay in New Orleans long enough to implement Abraham Lincoln's plans for 'reconstructing' the city. Those plans, blueprints for the Reconstruction of the South that followed the war, went into effect in December 1863, a year after Butler returned to the North.

'Beast' Butler decreed that any woman who insulted a Union officer would be treated as a 'woman of the town plying her avocation' – ie, a prostitute. Toilet bowls around New Orleans were soon imprinted with Butler's visage.

1857

The Mistick Krewe of Comus launches modern Mardi Gras with a torch-lit night parade. Eventually, hundreds of other 'krewes' will add their imprint to the celebration.

1860s

French instruction in New Orleans schools is abolished in 1862. A statewide ban on French education is implemented in 1868, limiting French cultural influence.

1862

New Orleans is occupied by the Union for the duration of the Civil War. Many citizens resent the Northern presence, setting the stage for a difficult postwar reconstruction period.

1870s

The 'White League' is formed in post–Civil War years as an often-violent backlash against the election of black politicians and the presence of Northern government officials.

Reconstruction

White-supremacist groups appeared throughout the South following Reconstruction. In New Orleans, organizations called the Knights of the White Camellia and the Crescent City Democratic Club initiated a reign of terror that targeted blacks and claimed several hundred lives during a particularly bloody few weeks in 1874.

The 'Free State of Louisiana,' which included only occupied parts of the state, was re-admitted to the Union in 1862. Slavery was abolished and the right to vote was extended to a few select blacks. But the move to extend suffrage to all black men, in 1863, sparked a bloody riot that ended with 36 casualties. All but two were black.

At the war's end Louisiana's state constitution was redrawn. Full suffrage was granted to blacks, but the same rights were denied to former Confederate soldiers and rebel sympathizers. Emboldened, blacks challenged discrimination laws, such as those forbidding them from riding 'white' streetcars, and racial skirmishes regularly flared up around town.

In the 1870s the White League was formed with the twin purposes of ousting what it considered to be an 'Africanized' government (elected in part by new black voters) and ridding the state government of Northerners and Reconstructionists. By all appearances, the White League was arming itself for an all-out war. Police and the state militia attempted to block a shipment of guns in 1874, and after an ensuing 'battle,' the Reconstructionist governor William Pitt Kellogg was ousted from office for five days. Federal troops entered the city to restore order.

Although Reconstruction officially ended in 1877, New Orleans remained at war with itself for many decades afterwards. Many of the civil liberties that blacks supposedly gained after the Civil War were reversed by what became known as Jim Crow law, which reinforced and in some ways increased segregation and inequality between blacks and whites.

Civil Rights

With its educated class of black Creoles, New Orleans was a natural setting for the early Civil Rights movement. In 1896 a New Orleans man named Homer Plessy, whose one-eighth African lineage subjected him to Jim Crow restrictions, challenged Louisiana's segregation laws in the landmark *Plessy v Ferguson* case. Although Plessy's case exposed the arbitrary nature of Jim Crow, the US Supreme Court interpreted the Constitution as providing for political, not social, equality and ruled to uphold 'separate but equal' statutes. Separate buses, water fountains, bathrooms, eating places and courtroom Bibles became fixtures of the landscape. 'Separate but equal' remained the law of the land until the Plessy case was overturned by *Brown v the Board of Education* in 1954. Congress passed the Civil Rights Act in 1964.

1880s

Mardi Gras 'Indians' appear – black New Orleanians dressed in stylized Native American costume, a supposed respectful nod to Indian tribes that resisted white conquest.

1884

New Orleans hosts the World's Fair in what is now Audubon Park. Although the state treasurer steals most of the event's funding, this marks the beginning of the city's tourism industry.

1895–1905

Buddy Bolden, who will eventually go insane and die in relative obscurity, reigns as the first 'King of Jazz.' His music influences generations of performers.

1896

Homer Plessy, an octoroon (one-eighth black), challenges New Orleans' segregation laws. Subsequently, discrimination remains legal under the 'separate but equal' clause.

Into the 20th Century

As the 20th century dawned, manufacturing, shipping, trade and banking all resumed, but New Orleans did not enjoy the prosperity of its antebellum period. Nonetheless, the turn of the century was a formative period: this was when the city morphed from an industrial port into a cultural beacon.

A new musical style was brewing in the city. Called 'jass' and later jazz, the music married black Creole musicianship to African American rhythms. It also benefited from a proliferation of brass and wind instruments that accompanied the emergence of marching bands during the war years. As jazz spread worldwide, the music became a signature of New Orleans, much as impressionist painting had become synonymous with Paris.

In the 1930s oil companies began dredging canals and laying a massive pipe infrastructure throughout the bayou region to the southwest of New Orleans. The project brought a new source of wealth to New Orleans' CBD, where national oil companies opened their offices, but not without significant environmental impact.

New Orleans was inundated with military troops and personnel during WWII. German U-boats sank many Allied ships in the Gulf of Mexico, but New Orleans was never directly threatened. With war came manufacturing jobs. Airplane parts and Higgins boats, used for shuttling troops and supplies to the beach during the Normandy invasion, were built in New Orleans. For the duration of the war Mardi Gras was canceled.

Andrew Higgins, a New Orleans–based industrialist, was the inventor of the Higgins Boat. Originally designed to transport goods across marshy Louisiana, the boat was converted into the famed LCPV: the 'Landing Craft, Personnel, Vehicle' that brought Allied soldiers to shore from the Pacific theater to Sicily and Normandy.

Changing Demographics

The demographics of the city were changing. During the 'white flight' years, chiefly after WWII, black residents moved out of the rural South and into the cities of the North as well as Southern cities such as New Orleans. Desegregation laws finally brought an end to Jim Crow legislation, but traditions shaped by racism were not so easily reversed. In 1960, as schools were desegregated, federal marshals had to escort black schoolchildren to their classrooms to protect them from white protestors.

Most whites responded to integration by relocating to suburbs such as Metairie and the Northshore (Slidell, Mandeville, Covington and other towns). Their children were plucked from public schools and enrolled in private academies; the tragic irony is that formerly all-white public schools became nearly all black.

1897

Storyville, New Orleans' infamous red-light district, is established. The music played in the best 'clubs' helps popularize jazz with out-of-town visitors (ie customers).

1901

Louis Armstrong is born on August 4. He will be sent to reform school and have a storied career, becoming one of New Orleans' most famous musical icons.

1905

A yellow-fever outbreak prompts a huge public health response: all standing water is drained, sealed or oiled. The disease is effectively banished from the city.

1906

The muffuletta sandwich is invented at Central Grocery. Along with gumbo, po'boys, jambalaya and red beans and rice, this will become one of the signature dishes of the city.

Paul Prudhomme gained international renown while working at Commander's Palace in the Garden District, and then his own K-Paul's, which opened in 1979 in the French Quarter. Prudhomme's promotion of Louisiana food was a major engine for tourism growth in New Orleans in the 1980s.

New Orleans' cityscape also changed during the postwar years. A new elevated freeway was constructed above Claiborne Ave and ran through black neighborhoods, largely so white citizens who fled town after desegregation could commute to work easily. The side effect of placing a highway through a major African American commercial district was not hard to predict: businesses shuttered, the economy suffered, and the income gap widened and deepened.

That doesn't mean development was placed on hold during the 1970s. High-rise office buildings and hotels shot up around the CBD, and in the mid-1970s the Louisiana Superdome opened.

In 1978 New Orleans elected its first black mayor, Ernest 'Dutch' Morial. Morial, a Democrat, appointed blacks and women to many city posts during his two terms in office and was both loved and hated for his abrasive fights with the City Council. His tenure ended in 1986, and in 1994 his son, Marc Morial, was elected mayor and then reelected in 1998. In 2001 the younger Morial attempted to pass a referendum permitting him to run for a third term, but the city electorate turned him down. Another African American, businessman Ray Nagin, became mayor in 2002, serving until 2010.

Preservation & Tourism

During the first few decades of the 20th century, the French Quarter was an old and crumbling district, with almost all of its buildings dating from before the Civil War, heavily populated by large families of working-class immigrants and blacks. The issue of preservation arose as prominent citizens began to recognize the architectural value of the French Quarter. The Vieux Carré Commission was founded in 1936 to regulate exterior modifications made to the historic buildings. Gentrification began to take its course as wealthy New Orleanians began to purchase property in the French Quarter, driving up the value of real estate. A similar process took place in neighborhoods such as the Garden District and Faubourg Marigny.

As New Orleans accentuated its antiquity, tourism increased. Bourbon St became oriented toward the tourist trade, with souvenir shops and touristy bars opening up along the street. To accommodate the tourist influx, large-scale hotels were built in the heart of the French Quarter in traditional architectural styles. As the oil boom of the 1970s went bust in the 1980s, tourism became the rock of the local economy. Conventioneers and vacationers regularly outnumbered locals on the weekend, spending cash and spilling beer, primarily in the French Quarter.

Tourist dollars meant job opportunities for locals, and also helped prop up some of the city's specialty industries, particularly the food scene.

1917

The Department of the Navy shuts down Storyville – the red-light district – despite the protests of Mayor Martin Behrman.

1927

During the Great Mississippi Flood, the levee is dynamited in St Bernard Parish, flooding poorer residents' homes to divert water and protect the wealthy in New Orleans.

1936

Vieux Carré Commission is founded to regulate changes to French Quarter exteriors. The Quarter remains to this day one of the oldest preserved neighborhoods in the USA.

1955

Fats Domino records 'Ain't That a Shame.' Along with Dave Bartholomew, Domino helps generate the 'New Orleans Sound' that defines local music in the mid-20th century.

Katrina

Occupying a low-lying, drained swamp that sits on a hurricane-prone coast, New Orleans has long lived in fear of the one powerful storm that could wipe out the city. On the morning of Saturday August 28, 2005, Hurricane Katrina prepared to lay claim to that title. The storm had just cut a path of destruction across Florida – killing seven people – when it spilled into the warm Gulf of Mexico. It quickly recharged from its trip across land, and morphed from a dangerous Category Three storm into a Category Five monster, the deadliest designation on the Saffir-Simpson Scale of hurricane strength. Computer models predicted a direct hit on New Orleans.

Mayor Ray Nagin ordered a mandatory evacuation, the first in the city's history. Four out of five residents left the greater New Orleans metropolitan area. Nearly 200,000 stayed behind. The holdouts included those who could not find transportation, people who thought the predictions too dire, and those who wanted to protect their homes and stores from looters.

The storm weakened to a Category Three before making landfall near the Louisiana–Mississippi line just before midnight. As the sun rose Monday morning, it was clear Katrina's winds had caused extensive damage – blowing out windows, tearing large sections of the Superdome's roof, and knocking over trees and telephone poles. Yet a sense that it could have been much worse prevailed.

Storm Surge

But while house-flattening winds are the most celebrated feature of hurricanes, in this case the most deadly aspect was the storm surge, the rising tide of water driven inland by the gales. Katrina's winds pushed water from the Gulf of Mexico up the Mississippi River, into Lake Pontchartrain, and through the canals that lace the city. The levees built to protect the city did not hold. A torrent of water from the Industrial Canal washed away the Lower Ninth Ward; in neighborhoods such as Lakeview and Gentilly, houses were submerged when the 17th St and London Ave Canals gave way.

In all, four-fifths of the city was submerged in a toxic soup of salt and fresh water, gasoline, chemicals, human waste and floating bodies. The massive pumps that clear the city after rainy days couldn't process the volume of water, which rose as high as 15ft in parts of the city, and remained for weeks. Stranded residents found little time to escape. They moved from the 1st floor to the 2nd floor, then the attic. Some drowned there; those lucky enough to find tools to hack through the roof got out, or used cans of paint to dash out crude appeals for help.

The well-to-do sections of New Orleans on higher ground near the Mississippi River (the 'Sliver by the River') were largely spared Katrina's floodwaters. New Orleans is a basin whose edge (the high part) is the Mississippi River, which did not break the levees. Water overflowed via Lake Pontchartrain and canals.

1960

Federal marshals escort black children into desegregated schools. In the following years, 'white flight' into the suburbs will leave city schools with few white students.

1965

Hurricane Betsy, the billion-dollar hurricane, batters the Big Easy. Improvements to the levee system made following the disaster fail to protect the city in 2005.

1970

Jazz Fest is held for the first time, beginning its long history as a gathering of a few hundred fans celebrating the city's unique musical heritage.

1978

New Orleans' first black mayor, Ernest 'Dutch' Morial, is elected. Despite lingering racial tensions, a dynasty is established: his son, Marc Morial, is elected mayor in 1994 and '98.

The 'Sliver By the River' – Uptown, the Garden district, the French Quarter and parts of the Marigny and Bywater – survived unscathed. Elsewhere, New Orleans reverted to a Hobbesian state of nature. Looters broke into stores, taking necessities such as food and medication, along with luxuries like DVDs and flat-screen TVs. Around 26,000 people took shelter at the Superdome, in increasingly squalid conditions, while others took ad hoc shelter in the Convention Center. Some attempted to walk out of the city across a bridge into neighboring Jefferson Parish, only to find their way blocked by police. Officials said evacuees were not allowed out of the city because the neighboring areas didn't have sufficient facilities to aid them, but also claimed they feared the lawlessness taking hold in New Orleans would accompany the refugees.

Oh, When the Saints...

Pundits, geophysicists and even then–House Speaker Dennis Hastert (who claimed that rebuilding a city that lies below sea level 'doesn't make sense to me,' before backtracking) seriously debated writing off New Orleans as a lost cause. The city, they said, was – by dint of its geography – not worth rebuilding.

Native wags – such as journalist Chris Rose, a columnist for the *Times-Picayune* and author of post-Katrina memoir *1 Dead in Attic* – have suggested the USA has always distrusted this strange little city with a habit of marching to its own beat (often enough, during a Second Line (p158) following a jazz funeral).

Yet millions of Americans and thousands of New Orleanians rose to the challenge. They waded into basements in 100°F-plus weather and slopped out trash, rubble and corpses; they mowed lawns, planted gardens and fixed each other's roofs, sometimes using discarded pieces of swept-away flooring. They celebrated small victories with what beer they could scrape together, and these impromptu parties became their own building blocks of reconstruction, the cultural component of rebirth in a city where enjoying life is as integral as cement.

By 2010 new restaurants and bars were popping up with happy frequency, and the arts scene in particular has turned the town into something of a Southern Left Bank for the 21st century. Young entrepreneurs, attracted by low rents and the city's undeniable culture, are flooding into the city. When the Saints, the local NFL franchise, won the Superbowl in 2010 during Carnival season, the city collectively lost its mind. There was no happier place on Earth.

Alliances between escaped African slaves and Native Americans were not uncommon. Early French settlers also sometimes married Native American women. Today, some 19,000 Louisianans identify themselves as Native American; most are culturally and racially mixed.

1987

The Saints post their first winning season since joining the NFL in 1967; it proves to be their last for many years, earning the team the nickname 'Aints'.

2002

Long-shot Ray Nagin becomes major of New Orleans. Nagin vows to clean up the city, but his term in office has its share of scandals.

2005

The storm surge following Hurricane Katrina floods 80% of New Orleans. The city is evacuated, although thousands who could not or did not leave linger in the city for days.

2007

Republican Bobby Jindal is elected governor of Louisiana, the first Indian American governor of a US state; many consider him an up-and-coming star of the Republican Party.

Rebuild, Reform, Relocate

Determination to reconstruct, a flourishing in the food and arts worlds, and the winning of the Superbowl is the bright side of the rebuilding story. The other perspective? Well, that requires some background on the relationship between New Orleans and the state of Louisiana. The former, since the 1970s, has been largely African American and liberal; the latter, in terms of politics, increasingly conservative.

Many New Orleanian institutions were lost post-Katrina, but of particular note are Charity Hospital, a public teaching hospital, and the city's public school system.

Charity Hospital is being replaced by an enormous medical center. The public school system has already been shuttered; former Orleans Parish public schools have all been replaced by a charter school system (charter schools receive public funding but operate independently of a local school board). A lottery system determines placement in local charters. Teachers were replaced by young, often white individuals enrolled in programs like Teach for America.

Many felt all of the above was an attack on the city's African American population, a way of using a weather-related disaster to further the political goal of stomping out public schools and hospitals. The opposing view was that the above institutions were seriously compromised even before Katrina and in serious need of reform. How one feels on these issues can spark some very contentious debate in New Orleans; while it is true that the public schools, for example, had enormous performance issues, was this attributable to teaching quality or poverty or a combination of both factors? Either way, Charity and the school system were largely staffed by (and served) African Americans, and the loss of these two institutions gutted the local African American middle class.

In the meantime, the neighborhoods of New Orleans are being reshaped by gentrification. Attracted by heritage architecture and culture, young, middle-to-upper-class transplants have moved into New Orleans, bringing both new businesses and economic opportunities – and a concurrent rise in the cost of living. The impact is truly double edged; young families are now pushing strollers through once blighted neighborhoods, but it remains to be seen if this prosperity will extend to the city's poorest and most disenfranchised.

New Orleans History Reads

- *Bienville's Dilemma* (Richard Campanella)
- *Rising Tide: The Great Mississippi Flood of 1927 and How It Changed America* (John M Barry)
- *Storyville* (Al Rose)
- *The Free People of Color of New Orleans* (Mary Gehman)
- *New Orleans: An Illustrated History* (John R Kemp)
- *Breach of Faith* (Jed Horne)

Feb–Mar 2010

The Saints win the Superbowl, Mardi Gras happens and Mitch Landrieu is elected mayor, the first white mayor to win a broad portion of the African American vote.

Apr–Sept 2010

The Deepwater Horizon oil spill pumps 4.9 million barrels of oil into the Gulf of Mexico, becoming the largest, costliest environmental disaster in American history.

2011

The census reveals the population of New Orleans has shrunk by 29% since 2000. A corresponding increase in population is noted in some suburbs.

2014–15

The city of New Orleans begins enforcing a noise ordinance and passes a smoking ban; both moves create considerable outcry on either side of the issue.

People of New Orleans

Ask someone to describe the demographics of New Orleans, and the 'gumbo analogy' – that is to say, a bunch of different ingredients simmered together into something greater than their individual parts – is often invoked. And while we are wary of repeating clichés, that gumbo diagram works (it helps that allusions to food pretty much always go down well in this city). French, Spanish, Africans, Caribbeans, Germans, Jews, Irish, Vietnamese, Hondurans – and perhaps most exotic of all, Americans – all come here and turn out New Orleanian.

The Quality of Creole

The term 'Creole' refers to people of mixed ancestry in most of the post-French Colonial world. The implication is often that a Creole is mixed race, but this isn't necessarily the case in Louisiana, although it can be. Long story short: Louisiana Creole usually refers to the descendants of the original European colonists who settled this area. Because of the shifting political status of the Louisiana colony (French, then Spanish, then French again), those Europeans were most often from France and Spain.

After the Louisiana Purchase in 1803, New Orleans was absorbed into the USA. Unsurprisingly, there was tension between the largely protestant Anglo Americans and Catholic Creole New Orleanians. The latter found the former uncouth and boring; the former considered Louisianans feckless and indolent, proving tired regional clichés stretch back centuries.

New Orleans has a habit of digesting her settlers and turning them into her own, though. Successive waves of immigration into New Orleans added layers to the city's demographic, but the original Creole city teased something quintessentially New Orleanian - ie commitment to fun, food and music - out of each new slice of the population pie.

Take the Italians, who suffused local foodways and musicality with muffuletta sandwiches and crooners like Louis Prima. In a similar vein, the Vietnamese have brought both food and a penchant for festivals; the Vietnamese New Year (Tet) is now a major celebration point for New Orleanians of all creeds and colors. Creole implies mixture, and mixing is something this town excels at, even if it doesn't always do so easily.

Voodoo & Louisiana

If you're a Christian, imagine if the majority of the world discussed your faith through these terms: 'They believe a dead man was brought back to life, and if you drink his blood and eat his body, you can live forever.' The description is technically accurate, but it misses so much context, background and lived experience that it becomes insulting. It reduces a complex belief system to a sensationalistic cliché.

Such is the struggle practitioners of voodoo endure on a daily basis. To a voodoo follower, theirs is a religion like any other. The traditions and source of their faith may seem outlandish to a nonbeliever, but what religion doesn't sound a little weird to someone who doesn't practice it? And even as their religion is stereotyped as a source of witchcraft and sorcery, it is simultaneously commercialized, forming the marketing slogan of dozens of tours, T-shirts and store fronts.

Voodoo as a faith comes from West Africa. It is a belief system that stresses ancestor worship and the presence of the divine via a pantheon of spirits and deities. Slaves from Africa and the Caribbean brought voodoo to Louisiana, where it melded with Roman Catholicism. One faith stressed saints and angels, the other ancestor spirits and supernatural forces; all came under the rubric of voodoo. Hoodoo are the magical implements popularly associated with voodoo, but how much magic they provide and their import to daily worship is often exaggerated (to use the same Christian comparison, many would find it insulting to call a rosary or crucifix a magic talisman).

The most well known voodoo practitioner was Marie Laveau, a 19th-century mixed race woman who married a Haitian free person of color. The legends surrounding Laveau are legion, but she is popularly associated with leading voodoo rituals near Bayou St John and providing magic spells for high-class New Orleans women. It's a fair bet much of this folklore was sensationalized by the popular press of the time; stories of magic brown-skinned women performing devilish rituals sold newspapers and magazines, at least more so than a sober recording of a religion that mixed Western Christianity and African ancestor worship.

Yat-itude

Native New Orleanians are affectionately deemed 'Yats' for their accents; their way of saying hello is the stereotypical, 'Where yat?'

It's an accent that feels closer to Brooklyn than the American South, one formed by a Creole population living in isolation from the rest of North America for decades. Sadly, the yat brogue is, like many regional accents in the USA, a fading thing. It's also a white thing; local African Americans have their own accent, a syrup-y slow drawl that is distinctive from other iterations of Black American English. You may hear someone speaking Yat in New Orleans, but you may find it easier to hear the dialect in neighboring St Bernard Parish, which has absorbed much of the city's working-class white population.

Other yat terms:

Awrite	Alright
Berl	Boil
Bra	A man with whom you are friends, or, a male sibling
Catlick	A Christian denomination led by the Pope
Da, Dat, Dis, Dem	The, That, This, Them
Dawlin'	A woman
Earl	Car juice
Ersta	A bivalve mollusk
Laginiappe	Pronounced 'lan-yap.' A little extra, like when the baker throws in another cookie.
Mirliton	Pronounced 'mel-ee-tawn.' A squash, also known as a chayote, that's pretty great when stuffed with seafood.
Praline	That delicious, sugary baked good? It's a prah-leen.
Turlet	Where one goes to the bathroom
YaMomInEm	Your family

The Cajuns

While many people feel the terms Cajun and Creole are interchangeable, they refer to two very different populations. The Creoles are the largely urbanized descendants of 18th-century French and Spanish colonists. The Cajuns descend from Francophone refugees who fled the maritime provinces of Canada after it was conquered by Britain during the Seven Years'/French and Indian War in the 18th century. This exile was known as *Le Grand Dérangement.*

The maritime provinces (New Brunswick, Prince Edward Island and Nova Scotia) were, under French rule, known as *Acadie,* and the refugees deemed themselves Acadians. A homeless population of Acadians searched for decades for a place to settle until seven boatloads of exiles arrived in New Orleans in 1785. The settlers spread out into the Louisiana countryside and mixed with early German peasant farmers, Isleños (Canary Islanders) and Americans. By the early 19th century some 3000 to 4000 Acadians, or Cajuns as they became known, lived in southern Louisiana. Some occupied the swamplands, where they eked out a living based on fishing and trapping, while others farmed rice.

Cajun culture is distinct within Louisiana. Older Cajuns still speak a distinct dialect of French, and the Cajun Mardi Gras, or *Courir de Mardi Gras,* is its own celebration, a ritual that involves medieval costuming and a drunken scrum over a runaway chicken (see the documentary *Dance for a Chicken* for more background).

Architecture

New Orleans has the most distinctive cityscape in the USA. This sense of place is directly attributable to its great quantity of historic homes, and the cohesion of so many of its neighborhoods. The French Quarter and Garden District have long been considered exemplars of New Orleans architecture, but send the Tremé, the Marigny or the Irish Channel to another city, and they would stand out as treasure troves of history and heritage.

Cross-section of a City

There are 158 sites in Orleans Parish listed on the National Register of Historic Places. While we stress that there's more to the city's architecture than the French Quarter and Garden District, those neighborhoods *do* nicely illustrate the pronounced difference between the two 'sectors' of New Orleans: Creole and American. It's worth noting that there is

Above: A Creole Townhouse

no perfect split between the two sides of the city; Creole cottages can be found Uptown, and shotgun houses pack the Bywater and Marigny.

The Quarter and Creole *faubourgs* (Marigny, Bywater and the Tremé) downriver from Canal St are densely packed with stuccoed brick structures built in various architectural styles and housing types that are rarely found in other US cities. This is where you'll find a glut of candy-colored Euro-Caribbean buildings that seem transplanted into North America.

Cross Canal St and you'll find the wide lots and luxuriant houses of the Garden District more closely resemble upscale homes found throughout the South. This is big mansion territory, but you'll also find thousands of shotgun houses lining these blocks. As one heads up the river into the heart of the Garden District and Uptown, the displays of wealth intensify to the point of near-gaudiness, although the effect scales back a little closer to Tulane and Loyola Universities.

It is worth noting that for all of the city's preservation credentials, fire, rot, hurricanes and redevelopment have all taken their toll on the city's historical building stock. Currently roughly 25 buildings only survive intact from the French and Spanish Colonial age; good examples include the Ursuline Convent, Presbytère and Cabildo.

Gallier Hall, once the City Hall building for New Orleans, marks the epitome of Greek revival pomp and circumstance. It overlooks Lafayette Sq and is used for civic functions today.

French Colonial Houses

Surviving structures from the French period are rare. New Orleans was a French colony only from 1718 until the Spanish takeover in 1762, and twice during the Spanish period fires destroyed much of the town. Only one French Quarter building, the Ursuline Convent, remains from the French period. The convent was built for the climate of French Canada, but the French recognized Caribbean design was more appropriate in New Orleans.

Madame John's Legacy, at 628 Dumaine St, is a good example of a French Caribbean home. Marked by a steep hipped roof, casement windows and batten shutters, it possesses galleries – covered porches – that help keep the house cool in summer. These galleries served to shade rooms from direct light and rainfall.

Out on Bayou St John, the Pitot House, home of the city's first mayor, is another signature French Colonial compound. A huge 2nd-floor wraparound balcony essentially served as the house's living space during the summer months. Furniture would be moved outdoors (even the beds), and residents would take advantage of the breeze to cool themselves off from the summer swelter. This practice of moving a living space into the outdoors (to say nothing of a focus on gardens and fountains) has roots in North Africa, from where the idea spread to Spain, and later this French Spanish colony.

If you head outside of the city, the Laura Plantation, located an hour west of New Orleans, is an excellent example of a French Creole plantation. The raised main house (along with much of the rest of the compound) was built by highly skilled slaves who undoubtedly imported some West African building techniques into the design.

Spanish Colonial Houses

During the Spanish period, adjacent buildings were designed to rub shoulders, with no space between, which created the continuous facade of the French Quarter. While some cottages were built during this time, the signature home of the period is the two-story town house, with commercial space on the ground floor and residential quarters upstairs. While properties were adjacent on the street, there was usually an open area behind the lot, and this space was converted into a well-

A classic example of Creole Architecture

shaded, private courtyard, used like a family room. Arches, tiled roofs and balconies with ornate wrought-iron railings became common.

Creole Town Houses

Very few buildings survive from the Spanish Colonial period, and not all the survivors reflect the Spanish style. But the Creoles of New Orleans appreciated Spanish architecture and regularly applied its key elements (especially the courtyard, carriageway and loggia) to French Quarter town houses. Most surviving examples date from the American period. An especially elaborate, three-story example of the Creole town house, with key Spanish elements, is Napoleon House.

Creole town houses are most common by far within the French Quarter, where they make up much of the area's residential and commercial stock. A few survive within the CBD and Warehouse District, although many of these have been rebuilt or renovated in such a manner that they are no longer true examples of the style.

Perhaps the most distinctive element of a Creole town house, particularly those within the French Quarter, is the balconies. Made from wrought iron, and often wrapped around corners, said balconies were valuable slices of living space during the intense heat of the summer months. Residents would spend so much time on their balconies, dividers would be built between adjoining balconies. In some places, you may see 'Romeo Spikes' – wickedly sharp points meant to prevent potential suitors from shimmying up a balcony pole to a waiting lady love.

Creole and Spanish town houses share many similarities, and many of the Quarter homes built after the fires of 1788 and 1794 share elements of both styles.

The French Quarter is also called the Maghreb Quarter. Packed town houses are built Spanish-style, with outdoor space reserved for private courtyards and public balconies. This in turn is a North African tradition, inherited from the Muslim conquest of Spain. In Morocco, houses built in this style are called *riads*.

A center hall house on Esplanade Ave (p149)

Creole Cottages

The most basic historical structure in New Orleans is also one of its most iconic, and particularly obvious as you head downriver from Canal St. The largest concentration of freestanding Creole cottages is found throughout the French Quarter, the Tremé, Faubourg Marigny and Bywater.

Essentially, a Creole cottage is a square, divided into four smaller squares; while this is the simplest version of the structure, it is one that can be found across the city, but in very few other places in the USA, barring a few other Gulf of Mexico communities.

True Creole cottages are one-and-a-half story buildings. They feature high gabled, sharply sloping roofs and, sometimes, full covered front porches (airy spaces that are crucial during the summer months). With that said, urban Creole cottages, which you are likely to encounter within the French Quarter, Tremé and Faubourg Marigny, generally lack a porch. Either way, Creole cottages lack hallways or corridors and are generally built to the edge of the property line – in other words, they lack anything like a front yard.

The front of the house usually has two casement doors, sometimes four. These openings are often shuttered to shield the interior space from sidewalk traffic, which can be passing within inches away. The airy floor plan has four interconnected chambers, each with an opening (a door or window) to the side of the house. These openings allow for a degree of air flow, providing another cooling mechanism against the heat.

Shotgun Houses

During the latter half of the 19th century, the inexpensive shotgun became a popular single-family dwelling. The name supposedly suggests a bullet could be fired from front to back through the open doorways of all of the rooms, but in truth only the most basic shotgun has doors lined up so perfectly. It's also worth noting that some historians believe the name may derive from a West African word; at the least this style of home is not indigenous to New Orleans, as shotgun homes can be found throughout much of the Caribbean.

The standard 'single-shotgun' house is a row of rooms with doors leading from one to the next. As there is no hall, you pass through each room to traverse the house. Shotguns are freestanding, with narrow spaces along either side. Windows on both sides and high ceilings encourage cross-ventilation and keep the rooms cool. The narrow style of home is a good fit for an urban space; while shotguns are detached housing, they can be clustered together in high density.

'Double-shotguns' are duplexes, with mirror-image halves traditionally forming two homes. Many double-shotguns have been converted into large single homes; it's almost a New Orleanian real-estate cliché for someone to buy a double-shotgun, rent out one half, and then knock down the center wall and create a large single home once they're ready to start a family.

Other variations upon the shotgun formula include 'camel-backs,' which have a 2nd floor above the back of the house, and sidehall homes, which have a corridor appended to the stacked squares of the shotgun.

Briquette-entre-poteaux, where brick fills the spaces between vertical and diagonal posts, was common to French Colonial houses. This style endured during the Spanish period. It is visible where stucco was cleared to expose the exterior walls of Lafitte's Blacksmith Shop in the French Quarter.

Greek Revival

Perhaps no style symbolizes the wealth and showiness of mid-19th-century America than Greek revival architecture. The genre, readily recognizable for its tall columns, was inspired by classics such as the Parthenon. Greek revival houses can be found along St Charles Ave in Uptown and in the Garden District. A nice example is the raised villa at 2127 Prytania St.

Five-Bay Center Hall Houses

The one-and-a-half-story center hall house became common with the arrival of more Anglo-Americans to New Orleans after the Louisiana Purchase in 1803. The raised center hall house, found in the Garden District and Uptown, became the most usual type; it stands on a pier foundation 2ft to 8ft above ground, and its columned front gallery spans the entire width of the house.

Double Gallery Houses

Double gallery houses were built throughout the 19th century (most commonly between 1820 and 1850) on Esplanade Ridge and the upriver side of Canal, primarily in Uptown and the Lower Garden and Garden Districts (these neighborhoods were considered 'suburbs' at the time). Double Gallery homes were built by those seeking space. These two-story houses are set back from the property line and feature a two-story gallery, or porch, framed and supported by columns. The front door is usually set to one side.

Today, many double gallery homes are split into multiple units, with the owners occupying one floor and renters another (usually with separate entrances). Other double gallery residences have been split into separate condo units.

Italianate Style

The Italianate style, inspired by Tuscan villas, gained popularity after the Civil War. Segmental arches, frequently used over doors and windows, and the decorative box-like parapets over galleries are commonly identified as Italianate features.

Music

New Orleans without music is like Washington without politics: inconceivable. In this city of appetites, music feeds the soul. The city's history can be traced in its music. The French and their Creole descendants gave the city two opera companies before any other US city had one. Meanwhile, slaves and free persons of color preserved African music in Congo Sq. These influences came together when French-speaking black Creoles livened up European dance tunes by adding African rhythms. From there, jazz was an inevitability.

The Rise & Fall (& Rise) of Jazz

Above A street jazz procession in the French Quarter, marking the passing of a local jazz musician

A proliferation of brass instruments after the Civil War led to a brass instrument craze that spread throughout the South and the Midwest. Many of the musicians, white and black, learned to play music without learning to read it. Instead they operated by ear and by memory. Improvisation became the default baseline for playing music.

One of the most problematic figures in jazz history is Charles 'Buddy' Bolden, New Orleans' first 'King of Jazz.' Some said Bolden 'broke his heart' when he performed, while others mused that he would 'blow his brains out' by playing so loudly.

Successors to Bolden included Joe 'King' Oliver, whose Creole Jazz Band found a receptive audience in Chicago. Oliver was soon overshadowed by his protégé, Louis Armstrong; working together, Oliver and Armstrong made many seminal jazz recordings, including 'Dippermouth Blues.'

Although jazz went into decline for several decades, the genre has experienced a renaissance since the 1980s. In 1982 then 19-year-old Wynton Marsalis stormed onto the scene followed by his older brother Branford. Other musicians, who were studying with Wynton and Branford's father, Ellis Marsalis, at the New Orleans Center for the Creative Arts, formed the nucleus of a New Orleans jazz revival.

Brass music is distinct from jazz; it's less improvisational and far more danceable. With that said, many brass bands still play traditional music inspired by marching band arrangements of the 19th century. Others, like the streetwise Rebirth, fuse styles from 'trad' jazz to funk, R&B and modern jazz. Rapping trombone player Trombone Shorty jumps between genres like a frog, sometimes bouncing into hip-hop, R&B and even indie rock.

The 2003 German movie *Schultze Gets the Blues* is the tale of a retired German salt miner and accordion enthusiast who hears zydeco on the radio and embarks on a quest to Louisiana in search of the roots of the music.

R&B & Funk

New Orleans owes its reputation as a breeding ground for piano players to Henry Roeland Byrd – also known as Professor Longhair. His rhythmic rumba and boogie-woogie style of playing propelled him to success with tunes such as 'Tipitina' (for which the legendary nightclub is named) and 'Go to the Mardi Gras.'

In the 1960s R&B and New Orleans fell under the spell of Allen Toussaint, a talented producer who molded songs to suit the talents of New Orleans' artists. The formula worked for Ernie K-Doe, who hit pay dirt with the disgruntled and catchy 'Mother-In-Law,' in 1961.

Aaron Neville, whose soulful falsetto is one of the most instantly recognizable voices in pop music, began working with Toussaint in 1960, when his first hit single, the menacing but pretty 'Over You' was recorded. The association later yielded the gorgeous 'Let's Live.' But 'Tell It Like It Is' (1967), recorded without Toussaint, was the biggest national hit of Neville's career.

His brother Art Neville, a piano player from the Professor Longhair school, heads up the Meters, whose sound molded modern New Orleans funk.

The best radio stations in New Orleans are WTUL, 91.5 FM, and WWOZ, 90.7 FM. The former is Tulane University's radio station and plays an eclectic mix of generally high-quality tunes. 'O-Z,' as it's called, plays local New Orleans music and is a backbone of the city's musical community.

Zydeco

Cajun music is the music of white Cajuns, while zydeco is the music of French-speaking African Americans who share the region. They have plenty in common, but the differences are distinct.

Zydeco ensembles originally comprised a fiddle, diatonic button accordion, guitar and triangle (the metal percussion instrument common to symphony orchestras and kindergarten music classes); the rhythm section usually included a *frottoir,* a metal washboard-like instrument that's worn like armor and played with spoons. The end result is a genre of music that is made for dance accompaniment; the Thursday-night zydeco party at Mid-City Rock & Bowl is not to be missed.

Zydeco, it should be noted, is not a static form of music restricted to country dancehalls. Innovators from Clifton Chenier, the father of

Bounce artist Big Freedia performing at Jazz Fest (p50)

> If you want to listen to bounce music in New Orleans, turn your dial to 102.9 FM and 93.3 FM. It's mainly commercial hip-hop on these stations, but they play local talent, too. Bounce shows also kick off with regularity at Republic and Siberia.

zydeco, to Beau Joques, Buckwheat Zydeco, Terrance Simien and Keith Frank have incorporated the blues, R&B, funk and soul into the zydeco sound. Baton Rouge rapper Lil Boosie uses zydeco music to propel his lyrics on the appropriately named track 'Zydeco' on the mixtape 225/504.

Bounce

While outfits such as No Limit Records and Partners-N-Crime and artists like Lil' Wayne and Dee-1 represent New Orleans in the hip-hop world, bounce is the defining sound of young black New Orleans. It's a high-speed genre distinct to the city that involves drum-machine driven beats, call-and-response, sexualized lyrics and extremely raunchy dancing. Shows are led by DJs, who play a role similar to a selector at a Jamaican dancehall concert.

The genre was invented in the early 1990s, when bounce became the default dance music in many New Orleans clubs, with DJs calling out over the hyperquick 'Triggerman' rhythm that has been sampled into a thousand-and-one tracks. Then and now, dancers get freaky on the floor and call out wards (subdivisions of the city) and projects (subsidized housing tracts). Pioneers include Juvenile, Soulja Slim, Mia X and DJ Jubilee, whose track 'Get Ready, Ready' is a good introduction to the genre.

External media has dubbed the music of transgender bounce artists including Katey Red, Sissy Nobby and Big Freedia 'sissy bounce' ('sissy' is local slang for gay black people who grew up in poor neighborhoods); while the label has stuck, Katey Red herself has said she simply considers herself a transgender bounce artist.

Environment

New Orleans is shaped by her environment more than most American cities. Consider: while outsiders bemoan the foolishness of placing a city in a low-lying river basin, it was founded precisely here so it could command the mouth of the Mississippi. Nevertheless, the local dance between humans and nature has generally been an uneasy one: do nothing and the land is uninhabitable; impact the land too much and the waters will flood elsewhere.

The Lay of the Watery Land

The first important factor to consider is that New Orleans is surrounded by water. It stands between the Mississippi River, which curls like a devilish snake around much of the city, and Lake Pontchartrain, a large saltwater body connected to the Gulf of Mexico. Swamps and marshes cover much of the remaining area around the city.

The land the city stands on has been wrested from the Mississippi's natural floodplain. The oldest parts of town adhere to the high ground, which is, in fact, made up of natural levees created by the Mississippi depositing soil there during floods. The moniker 'Crescent City' comes from this old footprint on the natural levees, which got its shape by forming along the curve of the river. The high ground in New Orleans is just a few feet above sea level. Much of the rest of the city is below sea level, forming a bowl that obviously remains vulnerable to flooding, despite human-made levees. The city's elevation averages 2ft below sea level. And it is sinking.

Hurricane Katrina hit during the particularly brutal 2005 hurricane season, when a record 27 tropical storms spawned 15 hurricanes. Of the five to make landfall, two (Katrina and Rita) slammed southern Louisiana within a three-week period. Katrina was by far the most destructive, but Rita was actually stronger.

A Dam Headache

The US Army Corps of Engineers built and maintains miles of levees that have kept the Mississippi River on a fixed course for more than a century. You'll see the levee from Jackson Sq, in the French Quarter, as it rises like an evenly graded hill and hides the river from view. That's right: as you walk uphill in New Orleans, you're coming *closer* to the water.

Compounding the difficult geography is the weather. New Orleans sits within the Atlantic hurricane zone, and hurricane season lasts approximately half a year here, from early summer to late fall. Hurricanes cause floods by pushing in water from the Gulf (not, as many assume, the Mississippi). Surging gulf waters run through town via the canal system and can be far more difficult to predict than rising river tides. Storm surges rise like tsunamis, lunging upward as they squeeze through narrow canal passageways. River floods, by contrast, can be observed far upstream, often weeks in advance.

The levee system was extensively updated, repaired and built out after Hurricane Katrina. Hopefully it will stand up to the next storm, but the final test will be whenever a big storm hits, a scenario no one is keen on rushing.

In the travelogue *Bayou Farewell* (2003), author and journalist Mike Tidwell documents the culture, folkways and natural environment of the vast, yet shrinking, Louisiana wetlands. It's one of the better nonfiction literary insights into Cajun culture.

THE BP OIL SPILL

On April 20, 2010, the Deepwater Horizon, an offshore drilling rig owned by Transocean and leased to BP operating in the Gulf of Mexico, exploded after highly pressurized gas expanded into the rig and ignited. Eleven men were killed. Two days later, oil from the underwater Macondo Prospect was spotted seeping into the ocean.

In all, 4.9 million barrels of oil were spilled into the Gulf as a result of the Deepwater disaster, the most expensive in US environmental history. The tourism industry of the Gulf states took a significant hit. Wildlife did worse: oil-slicked animal corpses were found (and continue to be found) on beaches in Grad Isle, south of New Orleans, while reports of lesions, missing eyes and other mutations have been attributed to the chemical dispersants used by BP to clear away oil.

The Gulf of Mexico's tourism and seafood industry seem to have recovered from the spill (helped along by the $7.8 billion settlement BP paid to those who lost livelihoods as a result of the spill), but the long-term impacts remain to be seen. Oil has entered the food chain via zooplankton, which could have biological impacts five or 10 years (or more) down the road. Disturbingly, scientists say they have discovered a 10-million-gallon 'bath mat' of oil that has adhered to the floor of the Gulf of Mexico. How this impacts the ecology of the region has yet to be determined, but one imagines 10 million gallons of oil does not make for a healthy environment.

The Vanishing Coast

If you're still interested in the nitty-gritty government management of the enormous levee and canal system that keeps southeast Louisiana from becoming the Northwest Gulf of Mexico, check out the Southeast Louisiana Flood Protection Authority – East (www.slfpae.com).

Some 30 sq miles of Louisiana coast – an area roughly equivalent to the size of Manhattan – are lost each year due in part to subsidence of the natural floodplains. Erosion is further enhanced by the extensive canal network that's dredged for oil production – Louisiana produces one-fifth of the nation's oil and one-fourth of its natural gas. Oil pipes and rigs are also subject to leaks and spills. In addition, the wakes of shipping traffic wear away the delicate edges of the canals.

Miles of bird refuges – home to more than half of North America's bird species, as well as freshwater homes to Louisiana's treasured crawfish – are disappearing. For New Orleans, the loss of these wetlands makes the city more vulnerable to hurricanes, as the diminishing land buffer enables hurricanes to maintain full strength nearer to the city. For similar reasons, New Orleans will become more vulnerable to storm surges like the one that followed Katrina.

Schoolchildren in Louisiana grow up learning that their state is shaped like a boot, but given the amount of land loss experienced in the last few decades, journalist Brett Anderson has proposed a new map be drawn of the state, one where the iconic boot looks as if it has been slashed with a pair of garden shears. See his story 'Louisiana Loses Its Boot,' on medium.com.

We want to finish on an upbeat note, but the loss of Louisiana's coast has not only continued unabated in recent years – it's gotten worse. This is a conservative state where environmental protection laws are unpopular, especially when the affected industries are oil and shipping. It's easy to paint such industries as villains, but they have provided employment for thousands of residents and helped lift the Cajuns, formerly one of the poorest demographics in the country, out of poverty.

With that said, here's hoping for better news in future. In the meantime, we advise you to see the Louisiana wetlands south of New Orleans now. They may well be underwater in a generation.

Survival Guide

TRANSPORTATION . . 216

ARRIVING IN NEW ORLEANS 216

Louis Armstrong New Orleans International Airport 216

Other Airports. 217

Union Passenger Terminal. 217

GETTING AROUND NEW ORLEANS 217

Bicycle 217

Boat 217

Bus 218

Car & Motorcycle 218

Streetcar 219

Taxi 219

DIRECTORY A–Z 220

Customs Regulations . . . 220

Electricity 220

Emergency 220

Internet Access. 220

Legal Matters 220

Medical Services 221

Money. 222

Opening Hours 222

Post. 222

Public Holidays. 223

Safety. 223

Tax & Refunds. 223

Telephone 224

Toilets. 224

Tourist Information 224

Travelers with Disabilities. 224

Visas. 225

Women Travelers 225

GLOSSARY 226

Transportation

ARRIVING IN NEW ORLEANS

The majority of travelers to New Orleans will arrive by air, landing in Louis Armstrong New Orleans International Airport (MSY) in Kenner, about 13 miles west of downtown. The airport was originally named for aviator John Moisant and was known as Moisant Stock Yards, hence the IATA code.

Another option is to fly into Baton Rouge (BTR), 89 miles north of the city; or Gulfport-Biloxi (GPT), Mississippi, 77 miles east. Neither of these options is as convenient as a direct flight to New Orleans, but they may be cheaper during big events such as Mardi Gras or Jazz Fest.

Many travelers drive or bus to New Orleans, which is located at the crossroads of several major highways. Train travel to New Orleans is easy; the city is served by three Amtrak lines. Although New Orleans is the Queen of the Mississippi, there are just a handful of riverboats – mostly ferries arriving from adjacent suburbs.

Louis Armstrong New Orleans International Airport

New Orleans' **airport** (MSY; ☎504-303-7500; www.flymsy.com; 900 Airline Hwy; 📶) is in the suburb of Kenner, 13 miles (about 30-minutes' drive) west of the city along the I-10 freeway. It's a small airport with only three active concourses, so it's pretty easy to get around. It's not a major hub, so you'll likely connect here through Atlanta, Houston, Dallas, Chicago or Charlotte.

Shuttle

Most visitors take the **Airport Shuttle** (☎866-596-2699; www.airportshuttleneworleans.com; one way/round-trip $20/38) to and from the airport. It offers frequent service between the airport and downtown hotels, although it can be time-consuming, especially if your hotel is the last stop. At the airport, buy tickets from agencies in the baggage-claim area. For your return to the airport, call a day ahead to arrange for a pickup, which you should schedule at least two hours prior to your flight's departure.

Taxi

A taxi ride downtown costs a flat rate of $33 for one or two passengers or $14 per person for three or more passengers.

Car

Rental agencies and cars are housed at a new facility within walking distance of the terminals. Exit at the West Terminal baggage claim. The quickest drive between the airport and downtown is the I-10. Coming from downtown on I-10, take exit 223 for the airport; going to downtown, take exit 234 as the Louisiana Superdome looms before you. Traffic can get very clogged near the Huey Long Bridge.

Bus

If your baggage is not too unwieldy and you're in no hurry, **Jefferson Transit** (☎504-364-3450; www.jeffersontransit.org; adult $2) offers the cheapest ride downtown aboard its E2 Airport Downtown Express. The ride to New Orleans follows city streets and stops approximately every two blocks. On weekdays, until 6:52pm, the bus goes all the way to Tulane and Loyola Ave, at the edge of downtown and the French Quarter; on weekends it will only get you as far as the corner of Tulane St and Carrollton Ave. From there it's a cheap cab ride to the French Quarter, or you can transfer to a **Regional Transit Authority** (RTA; ☎504-248-3900; www.norta.com; fares $1.25 plus 25¢ per transfer) bus. Bus 27 will get you to St Charles Ave in the Garden District; bus 39 follows Tulane Ave to Canal St, just outside the French Quarter. Check the RTA website (www.norta.com/getting-around/getting-to-the-airport.aspx) for more details about public transit to and from the airport from downtown New Orleans.

Other Airports

It's worth checking out the following airports if you plan to rent a car, but probably not otherwise. **Baton Rouge Metropolitan Airport** (BTR; ☎225-355-0333; www.flybtr.com) is 89 miles (and minutes) north of town. **Tiger Airport Shuttle** (☎225-333-8167; www.flybtr.com; $145-175) provides direct service to downtown New Orleans; rates fluctuate based on the time of day. **Gulfport-Biloxi International Airport** (BTR; ☎228-863-5951; www.flygpt.com) is about 77 miles (80 minutes) east of New Orleans; there are five national rental-car agencies on-site.

Union Passenger Terminal

Bus

Greyhound (☎504-525-6075; www.greyhound.com; 1001 Loyola Ave; ⏰5:15am-1pm & 2:30-6pm) buses stop at the **New Orleans Union Passenger Terminal** (☎504-299-1880; 1001 Loyola Ave), which is also known as Union Station. It's seven blocks upriver from Canal St. Greyhound regularly connects to Lafayette, Opelousas and Baton Rouge, plus Clarksdale, MS, and Memphis, TN, en route to essentially every city in continental USA.

Train

Three **Amtrak** (☎800-872-7245) trains serve New Orleans at the **New Orleans Union Passenger Terminal** (☎504-299-1880; 1001 Loyola Ave). The *City of New Orleans* train runs to Memphis, TN; Jackson, MS; and Chicago, IL. Alternatively, the *Crescent Route* serves Birmingham, AL; Atlanta, GA; Washington, DC; and New York City. The *Sunset Limited* connects Los Angeles, CA, with Tucson, AZ and New Orleans.

GETTING AROUND NEW ORLEANS

Bicycle

Cyclists will find New Orleans flat and relatively compact; however, heavy traffic, potholes, narrow roads and unsafe neighborhoods present some negatives to cycling, and fat tires are a near necessity. Oppressive summer heat and humidity also discourage a lot of cyclists.

All ferries offer free transportation for bicycles. Buses are now equipped with bike racks. Only folding bicycles are permitted on streetcars.

Bicycles can be hired around town.

American Bicycle Rental Co (☎504-324-8257; www.amebrc.com; 325 Burgundy St; per day $36; ⏰9am-5pm)

Bicycle Michael's (☎504-945-9505; www.bicyclemichaels.com; 622 Frenchmen St; per day from $35; ⏰10am-7pm Mon & Tues, Thu-Sat, to 5pm Sun)

Bike Nola (☎504-858-2273; www.bikenola.net; 1209 Decatur St; per day $40; ⏰8am-8pm Sun-Thu, to 10pm Fri & Sat)

Boat

Ferry

The cheapest way to cruise the Mississippi River is aboard the **Canal Street Ferry** (www.nolaferries.com; per person $2; ⏰6am-9:45pm Mon-Fri, 10:45am-8pm Sat, 10:45am-6pm Sun), which operates between Canal St and the West Bank community of Algiers. The ferry is open to pedestrians and cyclists (no cars). Have exact change for the fare. Change will not be given, and you cannot pay in advance for the return trip.

Riverboat

Visitors to New Orleans during Mark Twain's time arrived by boat via the Mississippi River, but the days of paddle steamboats plying the Big Muddy are now over. One exception? An eight-day paddleboat river cruise, with onboard lodging, offered by

CLIMATE CHANGE & TRAVEL

Every form of transport that relies on carbon-based fuel generates CO_2, the main cause of human-induced climate change. Modern travel is dependent on aeroplanes, which might use less fuel per kilometer per person than most cars but travel much greater distances. The altitude at which aircraft emit gases (including CO_2) and particles also contributes to their climate change impact. Many websites offer 'carbon calculators' that allow people to estimate the carbon emissions generated by their journey and, for those who wish to do so, to offset the impact of the greenhouse gases emitted with contributions to portfolios of climate-friendly initiatives throughout the world. Lonely Planet offsets the carbon footprint of all staff and author travel.

American Cruise Lines (☎800-460-4518; www.americancruiselines.com; from $4450), which departs from New Orleans and travels upriver to Baton Rouge, returning with stops at plantations and historic sites. If you're into a short, tourist-oriented sightseeing cruise, short-voyage **riverboats** (☎504-587-1719, 504-529-4567; www.creolequeen.com) still ply the river.

Bus

The **Regional Transit Authority** (RTA; ☎504-248-3900; www.norta.com; fares $1.25 plus 25¢ per transfer) offers bus and streetcar services. Service is decent, but we wouldn't recommend relying solely on public transport during a New Orleans visit, especially if you're staying longer than a few days.

No buses run through the heart of the French Quarter, so most visitors only use them when venturing uptown or out to City Park.

Car & Motorcycle

Driving

Having your own or renting a car in New Orleans can make it much easier to fully experience the entire city, from Faubourg Marigny up to Riverbend, and out along Esplanade Ave. If you are planning to spend most of your time in the French Quarter, though, don't bother. You'll just end up wasting money on parking.

Many city streets, even in posh Uptown, are in an atrocious state, and tires have accordingly short life spans. Navigating tricky left turns through very common four-way intersections can be a hazard. Crossing St Charles Ave, while watching for the streetcar, adds another level of adventure. Although stop signs are set out in residential areas, not everyone obeys them. New Orleanian friendliness can be annoying if people stop their cars in the middle of a narrow street to chat with someone – every New Orleans driver has a story about this incident. New Orleans drivers are also generally terrible at signaling turns.

Visitors from abroad may find it wise to back up their national driver's license with an International Driving Permit, available from their local automobile club.

Parking

Downtown on-street parking is typically for short-term use only. In some parts of town, look for solar-powered parking meters. One meter often serves an entire block, so don't assume parking is free just because there's no meter on the curb immediately beside where you park. There are also all kinds of restrictions to do with street cleaning that limit when you can park on certain streets. Be sure to read all parking signs before leaving your car. Enforcement is particularly efficient in the French Quarter, the CBD and the Warehouse District.

Vehicles parked illegally are frequently towed in the Quarter. If you park your car in a driveway, within 20ft of a corner or crosswalk, within 15ft of a fire hydrant or in restricted areas on a street-sweeping day, you will need to pay to retrieve your car from **Claiborne Auto Pound** (☎504-565-7450; 400 N Claiborne Ave; ⏰7am-1am).

Free street parking is available on many blocks in the Lower Quarter and along Esplanade Ave. Otherwise, there are plenty of commercial lots scattered through downtown and the French Quarter; expect to pay around $25 to $40 per day, and keep in mind that rates skyrocket at night.

Outside the Quarter and downtown, parking is a cinch. There's plenty of street parking and not many restrictions, although you will find parking meters along much of Magazine St. Be careful of street parking during Mardi Gras and Jazz Fest, when police are liable to ticket you for even very minor infractions.

For more details about parking enforcement visit www.nola.gov/dpw/parking.

Rental

Most big car-rental companies can be found in New Orleans. At Louis Armstrong Airport, rental agencies and cars are now within walking distance of the terminals; in years past a short shuttle ride was required. Typically to rent a car you must be at least 25 years of age and hold a major credit card, as well as a valid driver's license.

Rates go up and availability lessens during special events or large conventions. A compact car usually costs $30 to $45 a day or $350 to $420 a week. On top of that, add various fees and taxes and an optional loss/damage waiver (LDW; insurance), usually charged by the day. US citizens who already have auto insurance are probably covered, but should check with their insurance company first.

Agencies in or near the downtown area include the following:

Avis (☎504-523-4317, 800-331-1212; 1317 Canal St)

Budget Rent-a-Car (☎504-565-5600, 800-527-0700; 1317 Canal St)

Hertz (☎504-568-1645, 800-654-3131; 901 Convention Center Blvd)

Streetcar

Streetcars (aka trolleys or trams) have made a comeback in New Orleans, with four lines serving key routes in the city. They are run by the **Regional Transit Authority** (RTA; ☎504-248-3900; www.norta.com; fares $1.25 plus 25¢ per transfer). Fares cost $1.25 – have exact change – or purchase a Jazzy Pass (one-/three-/31-day unlimited rides $3/9/55), which is also good on buses. Jazzy Passes can be purchased from streetcar conductors, bus drivers, in Walgreens drugstores and from ticketing machines at RTA shelters along Canal St. Streetcars run about every 15 to 20 minutes, leaning towards every 30 minutes later at night.

Canal Streetcar Lines

Two slightly different lines follow Canal St to Mid-City. Both run from Harrah's Casino up Canal St. The Cemeteries line (from about 5am to 3:30am) goes to City Park Ave. More useful for tourists is the City Park line (from about 6am to 1am), which heads up a spur on N Carrollton Ave, ending up at the Esplanade Ave entrance to City Park.

Riverfront Streetcar Line

This 2-mile route (operating from about 5:30am to 11:30pm) runs between the French Market, in the lower end of the French Quarter near Esplanade Ave, and the upriver Convention Center, crossing Canal St on the way.

St Charles Avenue Streetcar Line

When the St Charles Ave route opened as the New Orleans & Carrollton Railroad in 1835, it was the nation's 2nd horse-drawn streetcar line. Now it is one of the few streetcars in the US to have survived the automobile era. It runs 24 hours from Carrollton and Claiborne, down Carrollton to St Charles, then via St Charles Ave to Canal & Carondelet.

Loyola-UPT Streetcar Line

This new line picks up Amtrak train and Greyhound bus passengers at Union Passenger Terminal (UPT) on Loyola Ave before continuing to Canal St. It then follows Canal St toward the river, stopping at Harrah's Casino before turning and traveling downriver to the French Market. Runs from 6am to about 11:45pm.

Taxi

If you're traveling alone or at night, taxis are recommended. **United Cabs** (☎504-522-9771; www.unitedcabs.com; ⏰24hr) is the biggest and most reliable company in New Orleans. You might have to call for a pickup, unless you are in a central part of the French Quarter, where it is relatively easy to flag down a passing cab.

Fares within the city start with a $3.50 flag-fall charge for one passenger (plus $1 for each additional passenger). From there it's $2 per mile. New Orleans is small, so don't expect fares to top $20. Don't forget to tip your driver about 15%.

Directory A–Z

Customs Regulations

US Customs and Border Protection (www.cbp.gov) allows a person to bring into the US up to 200 cigarettes duty-free and each person over the age of 21 years to bring in 1L of liquor. Non-US citizens are allowed to enter the USA with $100 worth of gifts from abroad. There are restrictions on bringing fresh fruit and flowers into the country and there is a strict quarantine on animals. If you are carrying $10,000 or more in US and foreign cash, traveler's checks, money orders or the like, you need to declare the excess amount. There is no legal restriction on the amount that may be imported, but undeclared sums in excess of $10,000 may be subject to confiscation.

Electricity

The electrical current in the USA is 110V to 115V, 60Hz AC. Outlets may be suited to flat two-prong (not grounded) or three-prong (grounded) plugs. If your appliance is made for another electrical system, you will need a transformer or adapter; if you didn't bring one along, buy one at any consumer electronics store around town.

Emergency

Ambulance (911)

Fire (911)

National Sexual Assault Hotline (800-656-4673)

Police (Emergency) (911)

Police (Nonemergency) (504-821-2222)

Internet Access

Many hotels offer wi-fi and cable internet access. Wi-fi is available in almost every coffee shop in town, and all branches of the New Orleans public library (www.neworleanspubliclibrary.org).

Legal Matters

Although it may seem that anything goes, New Orleans has its limits. Common tourist-related offenses include underage drinking, drinking outdoors from a bottle rather than from a plastic go cup, teen curfew violations and (most commonly) flaunting of private parts.

For people aged 21 years or more, the legal blood-alcohol limit for driving in Louisiana is 0.08%; however, you can be cited for driving while impaired even when your blood-alcohol content is lower.

The legal drinking age is 21. Curfew laws are strict. In general, anyone 16 years and younger, who is unaccompanied by an adult, must be home by 8pm Sunday through Thursday and by 9pm on Friday and Saturday during the school year, and by 11pm on Friday and Saturday during the summer. The curfew is 8pm year-round in the French Quarter and parts of Faubourg Marigny.

Most bars will offer your drink in a plastic cup, so accept it if you're going to wander off with your drink. Bourbon St flashers rarely get in serious trouble for exposing their private parts, but repeatedly doing so in front of the cops is asking for trouble. Don't grope flashers. That's a no-no and, we hope, rather obvious.

The legal age for gambling is 21, and businesses with gaming devices (usually video poker machines) out in the open are closed to minors. Even cafes with gaming devices are off-limits to minors, unless the games are contained within private rooms or booths.

Medical Services

Excellent medical care is readily available, but the need for medical insurance when visiting anywhere in

PRACTICALITIES

Newspapers & Magazines

Gambit (www.bestofneworleans.com) Weekly publication.

The Times-Picayune (www.nola.com) Three times a week.

New Orleans Magazine (www.myneworleans.com/new-orleans-magazine) Monthly.

The Lens (http://thelensnola.org) Investigative journalism; online only.

Radio

88.3 WRBH Reading radio for the blind.

89.9 WWNO NPR (National Public Radio).

90.7 WWOZ Louisiana music and community radio.

91.5 WTUL Tulane Radio.

93.3 WQUE Hip-hop and R&B.

95.7 WKBU Classic rock.

Smoking

The city has passed a law banning smoking and vaping in bars, restaurants, casinos and hotels, taking effect April 22, 2015. Smoking is still permitted in most outdoor gathering areas, including patios, courtyards and balconies. Smoking is also permitted in parks, except Lafayette Sq and the Cancer Survivors Plaza on Loyola Ave in the CBD.

Time

New Orleans Standard Time is six hours behind GMT/UTC. In US terms, that puts it one hour behind the East Coast and two hours ahead of the West Coast. In early March clocks move ahead one hour for Daylight Saving Time; clocks move back one hour in early November.

Tipping

Tipping is not really optional. In bars and restaurants the waitstaff are paid minimal wages and rely on tips for their livelihoods. The service has to be absolutely appalling before you should consider not tipping. Tip at least 15% of the bill or 20% if the service is good. You needn't tip at fast-food restaurants or self-serve cafeterias.

Taxi drivers expect a 15% tip. If you stay at a top-end hotel, tipping is so common you might get tennis elbow from reaching for your wallet. Hotel porters who carry bags a long way expect $3 to $5, or $1 per bag; smaller services (holding the taxi door open for you) might justify only $1. Valet parking is worth about $2, and is given when your car is returned to you.

the USA cannot be overemphasized. Doctors often expect payment on the spot for services rendered, after which your insurance company may reimburse you. US citizens should check with their insurer before leaving home to see what conditions are covered in their policy.

If you need immediate medical attention and you are in your hotel, your first call should be to the front desk. Some of the larger hotels have agreements with on-call doctors who can make house calls if necessary. In really urgent situations, you can call an ambulance (☎911), which will deliver you to a hospital emergency room.

If you can get to an emergency room, your best bet is the **Tulane University Medical Center** (☎504-988-5263; www.tulanehealthcare.com; 1415 Tulane Ave; ⏲24hr), located in the CBD.

Pharmacies

Nonprescription medications and contraceptives can be purchased in the pharmacy section of drugstores such as **Walgreens** (☎504-525-7263; www.walgreens.com; 619 Decatur St; ⏲8am-midnight, pharmacy 9am-7pm Mon-Fri, to 5pm Sat, 10am-4pm Sun) in the French Quarter. Other branches, and pharmacies such as CVS, are common around the city.

Money

There are three straightforward ways to handle money in the USA: cash; US-dollar traveler's checks; and credit or bank cards, which can be used to withdraw cash from the many automatic teller machines (ATMs) across the country. US dollars are the only accepted currency in New Orleans.

ATMs

With a Visa card, MasterCard or a bank card affiliated with the Plus or Cirrus networks you can easily obtain cash from ATMs all over New Orleans.

Changing Money

Most major currencies and leading brands of traveler's checks are easily exchanged in New Orleans. You will also find various independent exchange bureaus.

When you first arrive at the airport, you can change money at **TravelEx America Business Center** (☎504-465-9647; ⏲7am-7pm) on the 2rd floor of the West Terminal. TravelEx charges a sliding service fee. It also offers travel insurance, photocopy and fax services, emergency cash and wire money transfers. The Western Union section of the office closes at 4:30pm Monday through Friday and 2:30pm Saturday and Sunday.

Whitney National Bank (Louis Armstrong New Orleans International Airport; ⏲9am-5pm Mon-Thu, to 5:30 Fri) on the 2nd floor of the West Terminal also changes money, charging a flat $15 service fee if you don't have an account with them. Other services include cash advances on credit cards, traveler's checks, money orders and ATMs.

Better exchange rates are generally available at banks in the CBD. The main office of **Whitney National Bank** (☎504-586-7272; 228 St Charles Ave; ⏲9am-4:30pm Mon-Thu, to 5pm Fri) buys and sells foreign currency.

Credit & Debit Cards

Major credit cards are widely accepted by car-rental agencies and most hotels, restaurants, gas stations, shops and larger grocery stores. Many smaller restaurants and bars accept cash only. Many recreational and tourist activities can also be paid for by credit card. The most commonly accepted cards are Visa, MasterCard and American Express. Discover and Diners Club cards are also accepted by a large number of businesses.

Traveler's Checks

ATMs and debit cards have nearly rendered traveler's checks obsolete, but if your bank isn't affiliated with one of the common bank networks such as Cirrus or Plus, the old-fashioned way can be pretty handy. Some younger waitstaff and shop clerks might be unsure how to react to them, though.

They're still virtually as good as cash in the USA, and they can be replaced if lost or stolen. Both AmEx and Thomas Cook, two well-known issuers of traveler's checks, have efficient replacement policies.

You'll save yourself trouble and expense if you buy traveler's checks in US dollars.

Opening Hours

New Orleans maintains business hours similar to much of the rest of the USA, except when it comes to bars.

Banks 9am to 5pm Monday to Thursday, 10am to 5:30pm Friday. Some branches are open 9am to noon Saturday.

Bars Usually 5pm until last customer leaves (official closing 2am on weekdays and 3am or 4am on weekends).

Post offices 8:30am to 4:30pm Monday to Friday and 8:30am to noon Saturday.

Restaurants 10am or 11am to 11pm (sometimes with a break from 2pm to 5pm); usually closed Sunday and/or Monday.

Stores 10am to 7pm or 8pm.

Post

New Orleans' **main post office** (701 Loyola Ave; ⏲7:30am-7pm Mon-Fri, 8am-3pm Sat) is near City Hall. There are smaller branches throughout the city, including in the CBD at **Lafayette Sq** (610 S Maestri Place).

There are lots of independent postal shops as well, including the **Royal Mail Service** (☎504-522-8523; www.royalmailnola.org; 828 Royal St) and the **French Quarter Postal Emporium** (☎504-525-6651; www.frenchquarterpostal.net; 1000 Bourbon St; ⏰9am-6pm Mon-Fri, 10am-3pm Sat). These shops will send letters and packages at the same rates as the post office.

Postal Rates

Postal rates have a tendency to increase frequently, but at the time of writing the rates were 49¢ for 1st-class mail within the USA and 34¢ for postcards.

It costs $1.15 to send a postcard or 1oz letter internationally.

The **US Postal Service** (USPS; ☎800-275-8777; www.usps.com) also offers a Priority Mail service, which delivers your letter or package to anywhere in the USA in three days or less. The price is a flat rate of $5.75 for mailing an envelope, regardless of weight or destination. The price for a Priority Mail box starts at $5.95.

Receiving Mail

If you don't want to receive mail at your hotel, you can have mail sent to you at the main post office, marked c/o General Delivery, New Orleans, LA 70112. General Delivery is US terminology for what is known as poste restante internationally. General Delivery mail is only held for 30 days. It's not advisable to try to have mail sent to other post offices in New Orleans.

Sending Mail

If you have the correct postage, you can drop mail weighing less than 13oz into any blue mailbox. To send packages 13oz and more, you must take them to a post office or postal shop.

Public Holidays

Note that when national holidays fall on a weekend, they are often celebrated on the nearest Friday or Monday so that everyone enjoys a three-day weekend. The following are all national holidays.

New Year's Day January 1

Martin Luther King Jr Day Third Monday in January

Presidents' Day Third Monday in February

Memorial Day Last Monday in May

Independence Day July 4

Labor Day First Monday in September

Columbus Day Second Monday in October

Veterans Day November 11

Thanksgiving Fourth Thursday in November

Christmas Day December 25

Safety

New Orleans has an atrocious crime rate, and has one of the worst murder rates in the country. The vast majority of violent crime occurs between parties who already know each other, but tourists are occasionally targeted.

Exercise the caution you would in any US city. The possibility of getting mugged is something to consider even in areas you'd think are safe (eg the Garden District). Solo pedestrians are targeted more often than people walking in groups, and daytime is a better time to be out on foot than nighttime. Avoid entering secluded areas such as cemeteries alone.

Large crowds typically make the French Quarter a secure around-the-clock realm for the visitor. However, if your hotel or vehicle is on the margins of the Quarter, you might want to take a taxi back at night. The CBD and Warehouse District have plenty of activity during weekdays, but they're relatively deserted at night and on weekends. The B&Bs along Esplanade Ridge are close enough to troubled neighborhoods to call for caution at night. In the Quarter, street hustlers frequently approach tourists. Walk away.

Pedestrians crossing the street do not have the right of way and motorists (unless they are from out of state) will not yield. Whether on foot or in a car, be wary before entering an intersection, as New Orleans drivers are notorious for running yellow and even red lights.

To see where crime is occurring before you visit, log on to www.crimemapping.com/map/la/neworleans.

Tax & Refunds

New Orleans' 9% sales tax is tacked onto virtually everything, including meals, groceries and car rentals. For accommodations, room and occupancy taxes add an additional 14.75% to your bill plus $1 to $3 per person, depending on the size of the hotel.

For foreign visitors, some merchants in Louisiana participate in a program called **Louisiana Tax Free Shopping** (www.louisianataxfree.com). Look for the snazzy red-and-blue 'Tax Free' logo in the window or on the sign of the store. Usually these stores specialize in the kinds of impulse purchases people are likely to make while on vacation. In these stores, present a passport to verify you are not a US citizen and request a voucher as you make your purchase. Reimbursement centers are located in the **Downtown Refund Center** (☎504-568-3605; The Outlet Collection at Riverwalk, 500 Port of New Orleans Place; ⏰10am-6pm

Mon-Sat, 11am-6pm Sun) and the **Airport Refund Center** (Terminal C, Louis Armstrong International Airport; ⌚8am-5pm Mon-Fri, 9am-3pm Sat & Sun) in the main ticket lobby in Terminal C at the airport.

Telephone

Phone Codes

AREA CODES

The area code in New Orleans is ☎504. In Thibodaux and Houma it's ☎985; Baton Rouge and surrounds ☎225; and Shreveport and the northern part of the state ☎318.

When dialing a number with a different area code from your own, you must dial ☎1 before the area code. For example, to call a Baton Rouge number from New Orleans, begin by dialing ☎1-225. Note that hotel telephones often have heavy surcharges.

TOLL-FREE CODES

Toll-free numbers start with ☎1-800 or ☎1-888 and allow you to call free within the USA. These numbers are commonly offered by car-rental operators, large hotels and the like. (Note our listings omit the '1,' eg ☎800-000-0000.) Dial ☎411 for local directory assistance, or ☎1 + area code + 555-1212 for long-distance directory information; dial ☎1-800-555-1212 for toll-free number information. Dial ☎0 for the operator.

INTERNATIONAL CODES

If you're calling from abroad, the international country code for the USA (and Canada) is ☎1.

To make an international call from New Orleans, dial ☎011 + country code + area code (dropping the leading 0) + number. For calls to Canada, there's no need to dial the international access code ☎011. For international operator assistance, dial ☎00.

Cell Phones

The USA uses a variety of cell (mobile) phone systems, only one of which is compatible with systems used outside North America: the Global System for Mobile telephones (GSM), which is becoming more commonly available worldwide. Check with your local provider to determine whether your phone will work in New Orleans and if roaming charges will apply.

Fax

Besides hotel fax machines, fax services in the French Quarter include **French Quarter Postal Emporium** (☎504-525-6651; www.frenchquarterpostal.net; 1000 Bourbon St; ⌚9am-6pm Mon-Fri, 10am-3pm Sat). In the CBD there is **Kinko's FedEx Office Center** (☎504-654-1057; www.fedex.com; 555 Canal St; ⌚7am-7pm Mon-Fri, 10am-6pm Sat & Sun).

Phonecards

Phonecards are readily sold at newsstands and pharmacies. They save you the trouble of feeding coins into pay phones, and are often more economical as well.

Toilets

A recording by Benny Grunch, 'Ain't No Place to Pee on Mardi Gras Day,' summarizes the situation in the French Quarter. While tour guides delight in describing the unsanitary waste-disposal practices of the old Creole days, the stench arising from back alleys is actually more recent in origin.

Public rest rooms can be found in the Jackson Brewery mall and in the French Market. Larger hotels often have accessible rest rooms off the lobby, usually near the elevators and pay phones.

Tourist Information

Right next to popular Jackson Sq in the heart of the Quarter, the **New Orleans Welcome Center** (☎504-568-5661; www.crt.state.la.us/tourism; 529 St Ann St; ⌚9am-5pm) in the lower Pontalba Building offers maps, listings of upcoming events and a variety of brochures for sights, restaurants and hotels. The helpful staff can help you find accommodations in a pinch, answer questions and offer advice about New Orleans.

Information kiosks scattered through main tourist areas offer most of the same brochures as the Welcome Center, but their staff tend to be less knowledgeable.

Order or download a Louisiana-wide travel guide online from the **Louisiana Office of Tourism** (www.louisianatravel.com).

In the Tremé, you can pick up a New Orleans map and look at displays about city attractions at the **Basin St Visitors Center** (☎504-293-2600; www.neworleanscvb.com; 501 Basin St; ⌚9am-5pm) inside Basin St Station

Travelers with Disabilities

New Orleans is somewhat lax in this department. Sidewalk curbs rarely have ramps, and many historic public buildings and hotels are not equipped to meet the needs of wheelchair-users. Modern hotels adhere to standards established by the federal Americans with Disabilities Act by providing ramps, elevators and accessible bathrooms.

Red streetcars on the Canal St, Riverfront and Loyola-UPT streetcar lines are accessible to disabled riders. The green streetcars that run along St Charles Ave are protected from changes by the National Register of

Historic Places and have not been made accessible (www.norta.com/Accessibility.aspx). Regional Transit Authority buses offer a lift service; for information about paratransit service (alternative transportation for those who can't ride regular buses), call **RTA Paratransit** (Paratransit queries 504-827-8345, Paratransit scheduling 504-827-7433; www.norta.com).

Visas

Apart from most Canadian citizens and those entering under the Visa Waiver Program, a passport with an official visa is required for most visitors to the USA; contact the US embassy or consulate in your home country for more information about specific requirements. Most applicants have to be interviewed before a visa is granted and all applicants must pay a fee. You'll also have to prove you're not trying to stay in the USA permanently. The US Department of State has useful and up-to-date visa information online at http://travel.state.gov/content/visas/english/visit.html.

If you're staying for 90 days or less you may qualify for the Visa Waiver Program (VWP); at the time of writing, citizens of roughly three-dozen countries were eligible.

Women Travelers

Intoxicated bands of men in the French Quarter and along parade routes are a particular nuisance to females. Otherwise respectable students and professionals can be transformed by New Orleans in ways not particularly flattering. Women in almost any attire are liable to receive lewd comments. Outfits deemed provocative will lead to a continuous barrage of requests to 'show your tits.' This occurs on any Friday or Saturday night, not just during Mardi Gras. Many men assume that any woman wearing impressive strands of beads has acquired them by displaying herself on the street.

Any serious problems encountered should be reported to the police. Abuse hotlines are available, including the **National Sexual Assault Hotline** (800-656-4673) as well as the **Metropolitan Center for Women & Children** (504-837-5400). Both hotlines are available 24 hours.

The New Orleans branch of **Planned Parenthood** (504-897-9200; www.plannedparenthood.org; 4018 Magazine St) provides healthcare services for women, including walk-in pregnancy testing and emergency contraception.

Glossary

banh mi – Vietnamese sandwiches of sliced pork, cucumber, cilantro and other lovelies; locally called a Vietnamese po'boy

beignet – a flat square of dough flash-fried to golden, puffy glory, dusted with powdered sugar and served scorching hot

boudin – a tasty Cajun sausage made with pork, pork liver, cooked rice and spices

bousillage – mud- and straw-filled walls supported by cypress timbers

briquette-entre-poteaux – a style of architecture common to French-colonial houses, where brick fills the spaces between vertical and diagonal posts

Cajun (cuisine) – the rustic cuisine of the countryside

calliope – an organ-like musical instrument fitted with steam whistles; historically played on showboats and in traveling fairs

Creole (cuisine) – the rich, refined cuisine of the city

étouffée – a Cajun or Creole stew of shellfish or chicken served over rice

Fais do do – a Cajun dance party

faubourgs – literally 'suburbs,' although neighborhoods is a more accurate translation in spirit

frottoir – a metal washboard-like instrument that's worn like armor and played with spoons

go cup – a plastic cup given to patrons in bars so they can take their drink with them when they leave

gris-gris – amulets or spell bags

jambalaya – hearty, rice-based dish with any combination of fowl, shellfish or meat (but usually includes ham)

krewes – a deliberate misspelling of 'crews'; organizations or groups of people that create floats and stage festivities during Mardi Gras

migas – scrambled eggs mixed with fried tortilla strips

mudbug – a term for crawfish

muffuletta – a round sesame-crusted loaf spread with a salty olive salad and layered with cheeses and deli meats

plaçage – a cultural institution whereby white men 'kept' light-skinned black women as their mistresses

po'boy – a large sandwich made on French bread and overstuffed with a variety of fillings

Santeria – a Puerto Rican religion related to voodoo

Sazerac – a potent whiskey drink that uses rye as its primary ingredient, with aromatic bitters (including the locally produced Peychaud's), a bit of sugar and a swish of absinthe

snowballs – shaved ice in a paper cup doused liberally with flavored syrup

tasso – a cured, smoked piece of ham

Vieux Carré – alternate term for French Quarter; literally 'Old Square'

zydeco – a style of local music that combines French tunes with Caribbean music and blues

Behind the Scenes

SEND US YOUR FEEDBACK

We love to hear from travelers – your comments keep us on our toes and help make our books better. Our well-traveled team reads every word on what you loved or loathed about this book. Although we cannot reply individually to your submissions, we always guarantee that your feedback goes straight to the appropriate authors, in time for the next edition. Each person who sends us information is thanked in the next edition – the most useful submissions are rewarded with a selection of digital PDF chapters.

Visit **lonelyplanet.com/contact** to submit your updates and suggestions or to ask for help. Our award-winning website also features inspirational travel stories, news and discussions.

Note: We may edit, reproduce and incorporate your comments in Lonely Planet products such as guidebooks, websites and digital products, so let us know if you don't want your comments reproduced or your name acknowledged. For a copy of our privacy policy visit lonelyplanet.com/privacy.

OUR READERS

Many thanks to the travelers who used the last edition and wrote to us with helpful hints, useful advice and interesting anecdotes:

Bryan Banek, Celine Baures, Jonas Juhlin, Heather Monell, Stephanie Simard, Murray Tate, Carah Whaley

AUTHOR THANKS

Amy C Balfour

A very warm thank you to coauthor Adam Karlin and his welcoming family – I had a blast! Big thanks also to Christian and Karen Blessey for showing me the town and introducing me to great people and restaurants. And how do you say August? Thanks also to Rozanne Whalen, Kathlyn Perez, Catherine Moloney, Courtney and Spencer Murphy, Stacy and Jeremy Head, Terance Fowler, Deborah Gerhardt, Charlotte Reid, Jim Dawson and local experts Melissa Smith and Ryan Hughes. Dora Whitaker – thank you for this awesome assignment!

Adam Karlin

Thank you to the Bobellershaws (Mike and Nora), whose generosity of spirit is a model for this entire city, if not the world; Andrew Holbein the Jazzman and Zach the Younger-Man, who both pushed me so hard to be here; Dan Favre and Trish Kelly, for general winning all over the place; and just too many New Orleans people to mention. Thanks also to an extended family that has encompassed and embraced my actual family: AJ, Halle, Matt, Maria, Adrian, Darcy, Molly, Travis, Kate, Paige, Morgan, David, Jonah, Melissa, Rob, Katie, Carin...the list goes on. Thank you Amy Balfour for hanging like a champ; Dora Whitaker for putting me on this passion project of a book; Mom and Dad for letting me live here with their blessings; Gizmo for warming my lap as I write; and most of all Rachel, for her enormous love and support, and my Sanda, whose fresh eyes see the city better than all of us.

ACKNOWLEDGEMENTS

Cover photograph: French Quarter, Danita Delimont Stock/WL.

THIS BOOK

This 7th edition of Lonely Planet's *New Orleans* guidebook was researched and written by Adam Karlin and Amy C Balfour, who also researched and wrote the previous edition. The fifth edition was written and researched by Adam Karlin and Lisa Dunford. This guidebook was produced by the following:

Destination Editor Dora Whitaker
Product Editors Kate Kiely, Martine Power
Senior Cartographer Alison Lyall
Book Designer Mazzy Prinsep
Assisting Editors Victoria Harrison, Susan Paterson, Jeanette Wall
Cover Researcher Campbell McKenzie
Thanks to Larissa Frost, Victoria Harrison, Jouve India, Wayne Murphy, Jeanette Wall, Lauren Wellicome, Tony Wheeler, Tracy Whitmey

Index

See also separate subindexes for:

EATING P232

DRINKING & NIGHTLIFE P233

ENTERTAINMENT P234

SHOPPING P234

SLEEPING P235

1850 House Museum 68

A

A Streetcar Named Desire 97, 129
Acadian Cultural Center (Layfayette) 164
Acadian people 204
Acadiana 191
accommodations 15, 172-86, *see also* Sleeping subindex
  air-conditioning 173
  airport 182
  Bywater 179-81
  CBD 181-4
  Central City 184-5
  Faubourg Marigny 179-81
  French Quarter 175-9
  Garden 184-5
  gay-friendly 45, 173
  Lower Garden 184-5
  Riverbend 185-6
  Uptown 185-6
  Warehouse District 181-4
  websites 176
activities 22-3, *see also* bicycling, walks
African American people 188-9
African American Social Aid & Pleasure (S&P) Clubs 158
air travel 217
airport accommodations 182
Alcee Fortier Park 27, 150
Alex Beard 108
ambulance 220
Amistad Research Center 133
Angola (St Martinsville) 162
Annie Miller's Son's Swamp & Marsh Tours (Houma) 171
antiques 42, 43
Aquarium of the Americas 26, 105
aquariums 107
architecture 21, 205-9
  center hall house 209, **208**
  Creole 6, 207-8, **6**, **205**, **207**
  preservation 198
area codes 224
Armstrong, Louis 211
art galleries 67, *see also individual art galleries*
  Arthur Roger 109
  Lemieux Galleries 109
  Soren Christensen Gallery 109
Arthur Roger 109
arts 39-40, 42, *see also* festivals & events, film, literature, music
Arts District 108
Ashé Cultural Arts Center 121
ATMs 222
Audubon Zoo 26, 132, **26**, **132**

B

Backstreet Cultural Museum 151
Barataria Preserve 26-7, 170
bars 38, *see also* drinking & nightlife
bathrooms 224
Baton Rouge Metropolitan Airport 217
Battle of New Orleans 191
Bayou Boogaloo 23
Bayou Farewell (2003) 213
Bayou St John 118, 152
B&Bs 172, 173
Beauregard-Keyes House 67
beer 35, 38
bicycling 27, 87, 93
Bienville, Sieur de 191
Big Freedia 44, 212, **212**
bird refuges 214
Blaine Kern's Mardi Gras World 106
Blanchard, Terence 57, **54**
boat travel 217-18
Bolden, Charles 'Buddy' 196, 211
Bonaparte, Napoleon 192-3
Boosie, Lil 212
bounce music 212
Bourbon St 175, **98-9**
BP oil spill 214
Breaux Bridge 163-7
Burke, James Lee 165
burlesque 80
bus travel 216-17, 218
business hours 31, 35, 222
Butler, Benjamin 195
Butterfly Garden & Insectarium 26, 104-5, 107, **20**
Byrd, Henry Roeland 211
Bywater, *see* Faubourg Marigny & Bywater

C

Cabildo 62, 118, **62**
Cajun Country Swamp Tours (Breaux Bridge) 164
Cajun Man's Swamp Cruise (Houma) 171
Cajun Mardi Gras 204
Cajun Music Hall of Fame & Museum (Cajun Prairie) 168
Cajun people 204
Cajun Prairie 167-9
Canal St 190
Carnival 22, 193
car travel 29, 216, 218
casket girls 69
Castle-Haley, Oretha 123
CBD & Warehouse District 49, 100-14, **100**, **108**, **244-5**
  accommodations 181-4
  activities 106
  drinking & nightlife 101, 112-13
  entertainment 40, 113-14
  food 101, 109-12
  highlights 100-1, 102-3
  landmarks 105
  shopping 101, 114
  sights 102-3, 104-7
  street parking 104
  transport 101
  walks 108
cell phones 14, 224
cemeteries 118, 119, 151
Central Business District, *see* CBD
Central City, *see* Garden, Lower Garden & Central City
Champagne's Swamp Tours (Breaux Bridge) 164
Chenier, Clifton 211-2
children, travel with 26-7
  accommodation 173
  Audubon Experience 107
City Park 9, 26, 146-7, **3**, **9**, **146**
civil rights movement 123, 196
Civil War Museum 106
classical music 40
climate 15, 217
Clouet Gardens 87
clubs 37
coastal erosion 214
cocktails 12, 23-4, 35, 38, **12**, **34**
Code Noir 193, 194
coffee 38
Colonel Robert Short's House 120
community gardens 126
Congo Sq 157

Sights 000
Map Pages **000**
Photo Pages **000**

Congo Square New World Rhythms Festival 23
Contemporary Arts Center 106
costs 14, 31, 35, 173, 223-4
courses 31
Courthouse (Thibodaux) 171
credit cards 222
Creole architecture 207-8
Creole culture 52-3, 192-3, 194-5, 202
Creole food 20-1
Creole peoples 190
Creole Queen 68
Crescent City Blues & BBQ Festival 25
Crescent Park 13, 87
crime 16, *also see* safety
culture 188-9, 190
currency 14
currency exchange 222
customs regulations 220
cycling 27, 87, 93

D

dance 40
dangers, *see* safety
Decatur St 77, **98**
Dee-1 212
Destrehan Plantation (River Road) 160-1
d'Iberville, Sieur 191
disabilities, travelers with 224-5
Down the Bayou 169-71
drinking & nightlife 12, 34-8, 99, **34**, **36** *see also individual neighborhoods*, Drinking & Nightlife subindex
 costs 35
 gay clubs 45
 opening hours 35
driving, *see* car travel
Dryades St 123

E

electricity 220
emergencies 220
entertainment 39-41, *see also individual neighborhoods*
 costs 40
 free 41
 weekly gigs 40
environment 213-14
environmental issues 189, 214
Esplanade Avenue 149
Essence Music Festival 23
etiquette 17, 28-9
European settlement 191
events, *see* festivals & events

F

Fair Grounds Race Course 149
Farm, the (St Martinsville) 162
Farrow, Daniel **5**
fashion 42, 43
Faubourg Marigny & Bywater 49, 85-97, **85, 242-3**
 accommodations 179-81
 bicycling 87
 cycling tours 93
 drinking & nightlife 86, 92-4
 entertainment 40, 86, 94-6
 food 86, 88-92
 highlights , 11
 shopping 97
 sights 87-8
 tours 88
 transport 86
Faulkner, William 83
ferry travel 217
festivals & events 22-3, *see also* Mardi Gras, Jazz Fest
 children, with 27
 gay 45
 Jazz Fest 50-7
 Mardi Gras 50-7
film 40, 188
fire 220
Floyd's Record Shop (Cajun Prairie) 168
food 13, 30-3, **10**, *see also individual neighborhoods*, Eating subindex
 cooking demonstrations 122
 costs 31
 courses 31
 Creole 20-1
 opening hours 31
Franklin Avenue 99
free people of color 193-4
Freedia, Big 212
French Acadian people 194-5
French Market 65, 73
Frenchmen Art Market 87
Frenchmen Street 87, 99
French Quarter 48, 58-84, **58**, **70**, **238-9**, **28**, **98-9**
 accommodations 175-9
 drinking & nightlife 59, 77-9
 entertainment 40, 80
 food 59, 71-7
 highlights 58-9, 60-4
 pedicabs 82
 shopping 80-4
 sights 59, 60-4, 65-71
 tours 66
 transport 59
 walks 70, **70**
French Quarter Festival 23, **39**
Freret Street 99, 138
Freret Street Market 138
funk music 211

G

galleries, *see* art galleries
Gallery Burguieres 67
Gallery for Fine Photography, A 67
Gallier Hall 104
Gallier House Museum 66-7
Garden, Lower Garden & Central City 12, 49, 115-27, 248-9, **115**, **120**, **12**
 accommodations 184-5
 drinking & nightlife 116, 124-6
 entertainment 40, 126
 food 116, 121-4
 highlights 115-17
 shopping 116, 126-7
 sights 117-21
 transport 116
 walks 120
gay travelers 44-5
Gay Easter Parade 23
gentrification 189, 201
George Schmidt Gallery 109
German Coast Uprising, the 193
Goodrich-Stanley House 119
Grace King House 119
Great New Orleans fire 192
grillades **57**
grits **57**
Gulfport-Biloxi International Airport 217

H

Harouni Gallery 67
Harrah's Casino 107
haunted hotels 178
health 221-2
Hemmerling Gallery of Southern Art 67
Hermann-Grima House 71
Historic New Orleans Collection 65
historic sites 118
Historic Voodoo Museum 68
history 52, 65, 69, 123, 190-201
 architectural preservation 198
 demographics 197-8
 tourism 198
holidays 223
hotels 172
 haunted 178
 parking 180
House of Broel 118-19
House of Dance & Feathers 88
Hurricane Katrina 17, 189, 199-201, 213

I

immigration 202-4
Insectarium 26, 104-5, 107
international codes 224
internet access 220
Irish Channel 118
itineraries 18-19

J

Jackson, Andrew 191
Jackson Square 27, 60, **60**
jambalaya 31, **30**
Jazz Fest 9, 23, 50-7, **3**, **8**, **24**, **54**, **56**, **212**
 food 57
 history 55
 planning 56
jazz music 41, 192, 197, 210-11, **210**
Jean Bragg Gallery of Southern Art 108
Jean Lafitte National Historic Park 69
Joan of Arc Parade 22
Joseph Carroll House 120

Sights 000
Map Pages **000**
Photo Pages **000**

Jungle Gardens (New Iberia) 165

K

Katrina, *see* Hurricane Katrina

L

Labranche buildings 70
Lafayette 163-7
Lafayette Cemetery No 1 117, **117**
Lafitte, Jean 193
land loss 189
language 14
Laura Plantation (River Road) 160
Laurel Valley Village (Thibodaux) 171
Laveau, Marie 150, 194
Le Grand Dérangement 204
Le Musée de f.p.c. 149
Lee Circle 107
legal matters 220-1
Lemieux Galleries 109
lesbian travelers 44-5
Levee Path 134
LGBTIQ travelers 44-5
literature 188
live music 20, 39, 169, 188
Living with Hurricanes: Katrina & Beyond (exhibition) 63, **63**
Livingston, Robert 192
local life 28-9
Louis Armstrong New Orleans International Airport 216
Louis Armstrong Park 152
Louis Armstrong statue 152
Louisiana Children's Museum 27, 107
Louisiana Crawfish Festival 23
Louisiana Lost Land Tours (Houma) 170
Louisiana State Penitentiary Museum (St Martinsville) 162
Lower Bourbon Street 68
Lower Garden District, *see* Garden, Lower Garden & Central City
Lower Ninth Ward 88
Lucky Rose 67

M

Magazine Street 9, 142, **8**
Mahalia Jackson Theater 152
Mardi Gras 6, 22, 29, 50-7, 153, 195, 196, **6**, **17**, **24**, **51**, **53**
  beads 29, **53**
  costume contests 54
  Indian gangs 153
  information 55
Markey Park 88
Marsalis, Branford 211
Marsalis, Ellis 211
Marsalis, Wynton 211
Martin Luther King Jr Day 22
Mary Ann Brown Preserve (St Francisville) 162
McIlhenny Tabasco Factory (New Iberia) 165
McKenna Museum of African American Art 121
medical services 221-2
Mercedes-Benz Superdome 104
Merieult House 65
Metairie Cemetery 150
Michalopoulos Gallery 67
Mid-City & the Tremé 49, 144-58, 186, 254-5, **144**, **254-5**
  accommodations 186
  drinking & nightlife 145, 156
  entertainment 40, 157
  food 152-5
  highlights 144-8
  outdoor activities 145
  shopping 158
  sights 145, 146-52
  transport 145
Mid-Summer Mardi Gras 25
Milton Latter Memorial Library 133
Mississippi River 75, 190, 191, 213
Mississippi riverboats 68
mobile phones 14, 224
money 14, 31, 35, 173, 222
Morgan Effigy, the 190
Morial, Ernest 'Dutch' 198
Mortuary Chapel 151
motorcycle travel 218
Musée Conti Historical Wax Museum 71
museums 21, *see also individual museums*
music 11, 158, *see also individual musicians*
  classical 40
  funk 211
  hip-hop & bounce 41
  jazz 41, 192, 197, 210-11, **210**
  live music 20, 39
  R&B 211
  rock music 41
  zydeco 41, 211-12
music stores 43
Musical Legends Park 71
Myrtles Plantation (St Francisville) 163

N

National WWII Museum 13, 102, **102**
Native Americans 191
neighborhood parades 17
Neville, Aaron 211
Neville, Art 211
new age healing 96
New Iberia 165
New Orleans African American Museum 151
New Orleans Center for Creative Arts 94
New Orleans Cotton Exchange 105
New Orleans Jazz National Historic Park 65-6
New Orleans Pharmacy Museum 71
New Orleans Wine & Food Experience 23
newspapers 221
nightlife, *see* drinking & nightlife, Drinking & Nightlife subindex
Nobby, Sissy 212

O

Oakley Plantation & Audubon State Historic Site (St Francisville) 161
Off Bourbon in the Quarter 99
Ogden Museum of Southern Art 103, **103**
Old Ironworks 88
Old New Orleans Rum Distillery 87
Old US Mint 65
Oliver, Joe 'King' 211
opening hours 35, 222
opera 40
Oretha Castle-Haley Blvd 123
Our Lady of the Rosary Rectory 150

P

pagan rites 52
parades 17, 158
parking 172, 218
  hotels 180
parks & gardens 21, *see also individual parks & gardens*
Parkway Partners 126
pedicabs 82
pharmacies 222
phonecards 224
Pitot House 149
planning
  budgeting 14, 31, 35
  children, travel with 26-7
  festivals & events 22
  first-time visitors 16-17
  gay travelers 45
  itineraries 18-19
  local life 28-9
  New Orleans basics 14-15
  New Orleans neighborhoods 48-9, **237**, **48**
  packing 16
  repeat visitors 13
  travel seasons 15, 22-3
  websites 14
  what to wear 16
  where to stay 174
Plessy, Homer 196
Plessy v Ferguson case 196
Plessy v Ferguson Plaque 88
po'boy 10, 31, **11**
police 220
Ponderosa Stomp musical festival 25
population 189, 202-4
pop-up dining 91
postal services 222-3
Prairie Acadian Cultural Center (Cajun Prairie) 168
Presbytère 63
Preservation Hall 81, **5**
Preservation Hall Jazz Band, the 24
Preservation Resource Center 107
prostitution 69
public holidays 223

R

radio stations 211, 212, 221
R&B 211
Rebellion of 1768 192
reconstruction 196
Red Dress Run 24
Red, Katey 212

rental cars 218
Rig Museum (Morgan City) 170
Rink, the 120
River Road Plantations 160-1
Riverbend, *see* Uptown & Riverbend
riverboats 217-18
Creole Queen 68
Riverwalk 68
Steamboat Natchez 68
Riverfront 69
Riverwalk 68
rodeo (St Francisville) 162
Rodrigue Studio 67
Rosedown Plantation Historic Site (St Francisville) 162
Rosegate 120
Royal Street 64, **64**
Running of the Bulls 23

S

safety 223
Sanctuary 151
Satchmo festival 24
Schultze Gets the Blues 211
Second Lines 17, 158
Seven Years' War 192
sexual assault hotline 220
Shadows on the Teche (New Iberia) 165
shopping 9, 42-3, 223 *see also individual neighborhoods*, Shopping subindex *see also* individual neighborhoods
Shorty, Trombone 211
shotgun houses 208-9
shuttle 216
Sidney Bechet, bust of 152
sissy bounce 212
slavery, abolition of 196
slaves 193-4
smoking 188, 221
Soren Christensen Gallery 109
Southern Decadence festival 24
Southern Food & Beverage Museum 13, 119, 122
souvenirs 42, 43

Sights 000
Map Pages **000**
Photo Pages **000**

St Anthony's Garden 70
St Augustine's Church 151-2
St Charles Avenue **129**
St Charles Avenue Streetcar 10, 128-9, 135, **10, 128-9**
St Claude Avenue 99
St Francisville 161-3
St Joseph's Night 22-3
St Louis Cathedral 61, **3, 61**
St Louis Cemetery No 1 148-9, **148**
St Louis Cemetery No 3 149
Steamboat Natchez 68
Storyville 69, 197
St Patrick's Day 22
St Roch Cemetery 87
St Vincent's Infant Asylum 119
streetcars 128-9, 219, **129**
Super Sunday 23

T

taxes 17, 223-4
taxis 216, 219
telephone services 14, 224
Tennessee Williams Literary Festival 23
Tet 22
theater 40, 41
time 14, 221
tipping 17, 31, 35, 221
toilets 224
tourism 198
tourist information 14, 224
Touro Synagogue 133
tours 66
cemeteries 151
Save Our Cemeteries 119
swamp 164
wetlands & swamps 170, 171
train travel 217
travel to New Orleans 15, 216-17
travel within New Orleans 15, 217-19
traveler's checks 222
Tremé, the *see* Mid-City & the Tremé
Tulane University 133
Tunica Falls (St Francisville) 162
Twelfth Night 52

U

United Fruit Company 105
Upper Bourbon Street 71
Uptown & Riverbend 49, 130-43, 250-1, **130**
accommodations 185-6
drinking & nightlife 131, 139-41
entertainment 40, 141
food 131
highlights 9, 10
shopping 131, 142-3
sights 132-4
transport 131
Ursuline Convent 66, 69
US control 192-3

V

Vermilionville (Lafayette) 164
Vietnamese New Year 22
vintage stores 43
visas 14, 225
voodoo 150, 194, 202-3
Voodoo Spiritual Temple 68

W

walks, *see also* tours
French Quarter 70, **70**
Garden District 12, 120, **120**
Warehouse District, *see* CBD & Warehouse District
Washington Square Park 88
weather 15, 22-3, 213
websites 14, 173
crime 223
gay & lesbian travel 45
Wetlands Cajun Cultural Center (Thibodaux) 171
Wetland Tours (Houma) 171
White League, the 195, 196
White Linen Night 24
Whitney Plantation (River Road) 160
Williams Gallery 65
Williams Research Center 65
Williams, Tennessee 97
wine 35
women travelers 225
Women's Guild of the New Orleans Opera Association 120

Y

Yats 203
yellow fever 197

Z

zydeco 41, 211-12

EATING

13 Monaghan 91

A

Acme Oyster & Seafood House 75
Adolfo's 92
Angeli on Decatur 73, 90
Angelo Brocato 154
Antoine's 77
Arabella Casa Di Pasta 90-1
Arnaud's 77
Artmosphere (Lafayette) 166

B

Ba Chi Canteen 13, 135
Bacchanal 89
Bao & Noodle 91
Bayona 76
Bennachin 72
Birdman Coffee & Books (St Francisville) 163
Blue Dog Cafe (Lafayette) 166
Bon Ton Café 111
Booty's 91
Boucherie 137-8
Bourbon House 77
Brennan's Restaurant 76
Broussard's 77

C

Café Adelaide 110
Café Amelie 73
Café Beignet 74, 76
Café Degas 154
Café des Amis (Breaux Bridge) 166
Café du Monde 76
Café Reconcile 124
Cajun Seafood 155
Cake Café & Bakery 90
Camellia Grill 134-5
Carmo 111
Casamento's 135
Central Grocery 72
Clancy's 137
Clementine Dining & Spirits (New Iberia) 165
Clover Grill 72
Cochon 111
Cochon Butcher 111
Commander's Palace 124

Company Burger, the 138
Coop's Place 71
Coquette 123
Court of Two Sisters 76
Cowbell 138
Creole Creamery 135
Croissant D'Or Patisserie 73

D
Dat Dog 134
Delachaise 136-7
Dickie Brennan's 76
Dis and Dat 153
District: Donuts Sliders Brew 121
Domenica 110
Domilise's Po-Boys 134
Dooky Chase 155
Drago's Seafood Restaurant 110

E
Eat New Orleans 73
Elizabeth's 92
Emeril's 112

F
Fatoush 92
Fiorella's 71-2
Four Calendar Cafe 91
Franklin 92
Fremin's 171
French Market 73
French Press (Lafayette) 165

G
Galatoire's 72
Gautreau's 137
Gene's 91-2
Green Goddess 74-5
Guy's 135
GW Fins 77

H
Hansen's Sno-Bliz 136
Herbsaint 111
High Hat Cafe 138

I
Il Posto 135
Irene's Cuisine 73

J
Jacques-Imo's Café 138
Johnny Sanchez 110
Johnny's Po-Boys 74
Joint 89
Juan's Flying Burrito 123
Junction 90

K
Kebab 90
K-Paul's Louisiana Kitchen 76
Kukhnya 91
Kyoto 136

L
La Divina Gelateria 74
La Petite Grocery 139
Laphet 91
Latitude 29 75
Le Pavillon 110
Lejeune's 171
Lil' Dizzy's 155
Lilette 137
Liuzza's By the Track 154
Lola's 154-5
Lost Love 89

M
Magasin Cafe 137
Magnolia Café (St Francisville) 163
Mahony's Po-Boy Shop 136
Mandina's 155
Mardi Gras Zone 92
Mariza 92
Mat & Naddie's 139
Maurepas Foods 89
Meauxbar 73
Meltdown 89
Midway Pizza 138
Mister Gregory's 74
Mona Lisa 72
MoPho 155
Mother's 109

N
Nola 77
Nonna Mia Café & Pizzeria 155

O
Old Tyme Grocery (Lafayette) 166
Oxalis 92

P
Pagoda Cafe 152-3
Parasol's 122
Parkway Tavern 152
Patois 137
Peche Seafood Grill 13, 111
Piety Street Snoballs 89
Pizza Delicious 13, 88
Pizza Domenica 136
Popeyes 154
Port of Call 71
Purloo 122, 124

R
Rampart Food Store 89-90
Red's Chinese 88-9
Refuel 137
Restaurant August 110
Rita Mae's Kitchen 171
Rock-n-Sake 112
Ruby Slipper 153
Ruby Slipper Downtown 109
Ruby's Café (Cajun Prairie) 168

S
Sake Café Uptown 123
Salt N Pepper 74
Satsuma 91
Satsuma Maple 134
Seed 122
Seoul Shack 91
Slice 121
Slim Goodie's Diner 123
Sneaky Pickle 90
SoBou 13, 76
St James Cheese Co 134
St Roch Market 89
Stanley 74
Stein's Deli 121
Sucré 121-2
Surrey's Juice Bar 121
Sylvain 74

T
Taco Sisters (Lafayette) 166
Tee-Eva's Old-Fashioned Pies & Pralines 135-6
Toup's Meatery 154
Toute de Suite Cafe 106
Tracey's 122
Twelve Mile Limit 154

V
Verti Marte 72
Victor's Cafeteria (New Iberia) 165

W
Wayne Jacob's Smokehouse & Restaurant (River Road) 161
We've Got Soul 91
Who Dat Coffee Cafe & Cafe Nero 89
Whole Foods 136
Willie Mae's Grocery & Deli 136
Willie Mae's Scotch House 155

Y
Yo Mama's 74

DRINKING & NIGHTLIFE

A
Abbey 79-80
AllWays Lounge 95
Avenue Pub 124

B
Balcony Bar 125
Barcadia 113
Bayou Beer Garden 156
Bellocq 113
Big Daddy's Bar 94
BJ's 92-3
Boot 141
Bouligny Tavern 140
Bourbon Pub & Parade 79
Buffa's 93
Bulldog 125

C
Café Lafitte in Exile 78
Cane & Table 78
Capdeville 113
Carousel Bar 78
Chart Room 78
Circle Bar 112
Columns Hotel 139
Cooter Brown's Tavern & Oyster Bar 118, 139-40
Cosimo's 78
Country Club 93
Cure Bar 139, **36**

D
Double Play 80
Dungeon 79

E
Erin Rose 78

F
Fair Grinds 156

Faubourg Wines 93
Finn McCool's 156
Flora Gallery & Coffee Shop 94
F&M's Patio Bar 140
Fred's Lounge 169
French 75 78
Freret Street Publiq House 138, 140

H

Half Moon 125

I

Igor's Lounge 125

J

John 93

K

Kajun's Pub 95
Krewe du Brew 125

L

Lafitte's Blacksmith Shop 70, 78
Latitude 29 13, 78
Le Bon Temps Roulé 140
Loa 112-13
Lost Love 93
Lucy's Retired Surfers Bar 113, 118

M

Markey's 93
Mid-City Yacht Club 156
Mimi's in the Marigny 92
Molly's at the Market 77
Monkey Hill Bar 141
Ms Mae's 140

N

Napoleon House 79
NOLA Brewing 13, 124

O

Oak Wine Bar 141
Old Absinthe House 78-9
Orange Couch 93
Oz 79

P

Pal's 156
Pat O'Brien's 70, 79
Pearl Wine Co 156
Pirate's Alley Cafe 79
Polo Club Lounge 112

R

R Bar 93
Rendezvous 125
Root Squared 125
Rue de la Course 141
Rusty Nail 113

S

Saint Bar & Lounge 125
Sazerac Bar 112
Siberia 95
Snake & Jakes 140
Solo Espresso 93
Spitfire Coffee 78
St Joe's 139
Still Perkin' 126
Sweet Lorraine's 95
Swizzle Stick Bar 112

T

Tonique 77
Treo 156
Tropical Isle 79
Twelve Mile Limit 156

Y

Yuki Izakaya 94

ENTERTAINMENT

AllWays Lounge 95
Apple Barrel 96
Artmosphere (Lafayette) 166
Atchafalaya Club (Henderson) 166
Balcony Music Club 80
Banks Street Bar 157
Blue Moon Saloon (Lafayette) 166
Blue Nile 96
Bullets 157
Café Istanbul 96
Café Negril 96
Candlelight Lounge 157
Checkpoint Charlie 95
Chickie Wah Wah 157
d.b.a. 94
Dragon's Den 96
Fleur de Tease 80
Fountain Lounge 114
Fred's Lounge 169
Gasa Gasa 141
Hi Ho Lounge 94
House of Blues 80
Howlin' Wolf 113
Kajun's Pub 95
La Poussiere (Breaux Bridge) 166
Liberty Theater (Cajun Prairie) 168
Maison 95
Maple Leaf Bar 141
Marigny Opera House 94
Mid-City Rock & Bowl 157
New Movement Theater 94-5
Old Marquer Theatre 96
One Eyed Jacks 80
Palm Court Jazz Café 80
Prytania Theatre 141
Randol's (Lafayette) 167
Republic New Orleans 114
Saenger Theatre 157
Saturn Bar 95
Savoy Music Center (Cajun Prairie) 168
Siberia 95
Slim's Y-Ki-Ki (Cajun Prairie) 168
Snug Harbor 95, **99**
Spotted Cat 94
Sweet Lorraine's 95
Three Muses 96
Tipitina's 141
Vaughan's 95
Zeitgeist 126
Zydeco Hall of Fame (Cajun Prairie) 168-9

SHOPPING

A

Aidan Gill for Men 126
Alex Beard 108
Arcadian Books & Art Prints 82
Ariodante 114
Artisans' Well 96

B

Beckham's Bookstore 82
Berta's & Mina's Antiquities 143
Big Fisherman Seafood 127
Bloomin' Deals 143
Boutique du Vampyre 83
Bywater Bargain Center 97

C

C Collection 143
Central Grocery 84
Centuries 82
Chiwawa Gaga 81
Cole Pratt Gallery 142-3
Collectible Antiques 82
Crescent City Comics 142

D

Dirty Coast 127, 142
Dr Bob's Studio 97

E

Electric Ladyland 97
Euclid Records 97
Exodus 80

F

F&F Botanica Spiritual Supply 158
Faubourg Marigny Book Store 97
Faulkner House Books 70, 83
Feet First 143
Fifi Mahony's 13, 80
Fleur de Paris 83
Fleurty Girl 127
Flora Savage 83
French Market 73
Funky Monkey 126

G

Garden District Bookshop 127
GoGo Jewelry 127
Green Eyed Gator 81
Greg's Antiques 82

H

Hazelnut 142
Hové Parfumeur 84
Humidity Skate Shop 84

I

I.J. Reilly's 97
Island of Salvation Botanica 96

J

James H Cohen & Sons 70, 81
Java House Imports 83
Jim Russell Records 127

Sights 000
Map Pages **000**
Photo Pages **000**

L

Leah's Pralines 84
Librairie Books 82
Louisiana Music Factory 97
Lucullus 82

M

Magazine Antique Mall 127
Maple Street Book Shop 142
Mary Jane's Emporium 84
Maskarade 84
Massey's 158
Meyer the Hatter 114
Moss Antiques 81
MS Rau Antiques 82-3

N

New Orleans Art Supply 97
New Orleans Cajun Store 83
New Orleans Food Co-op 96
New Orleans Music Exchange 127

O

Od Aomo 81
Outlet Collection at Riverwalk 114

P

Peaches Records & Tapes 81
Pelican Coast Clothing Co 143
Pied Nu 143
Potsalot 142

Q

Queork 80

R

REpurposingNOLA Piece by Peace 108

S

Shops at Canal Place 114
Simon of New Orleans 126-7
SoPo 158
Southern Candy Makers 84
Storyville Apparel 127

T

Thomas Mann Gallery I/O 127
Trashy Diva 126
Tubby & Coos 158

Z

Zombie's House of Voodoo 84

SLEEPING

3-V Tourist Court (St Francisville) 163

A

Ashton's Bed & Breakfast 186
Astor Crowne Plaza 179
Audubon Cottages 177
Auld Sweet Olive Bed & Breakfast 179

B

B&W Courtyards 180
Balcony Guest House 180-1
Bayou Cabins (Breaux Bridge) 167
Bienville House Hotel 175
Bourbon Orleans Hotel 176, 178
Burgundy 179
Bywater Bed & Breakfast 179

C

Chateau Hotel 176
Chimes 185
Collinwood House 180
Columns Hotel 185-6
Cornstalk Hotel 70, 177
Country Inn & Suites 182
Courtyard New Orleans Downtown 177
Crescent City Guesthouse 181

D

Dauphine House 180
Dauphine Orleans 178
Degas House 186
Drury Inn & Suites 181

E

Embassy Suites Hotel 182-3

F

Frenchmen Hotel 181

G

Garden District B&B 184
Gentry Quarters 176
Green House Inn 185

H

Hampton Inn New Orleans Downtown 182
Hampton Inn St Charles Avenue 185
HH Whitney House 186
Historic French Market Inn 176
Hotel Indigo 185
Hotel Modern 182
Hotel Monteleone 177-8
Hotel Provincial 175, 178
Hotel Royal 175
Hotel St Marie 176
Hotel Villa Convento 175

I

India House Hostel 186
Inn on St Peter 177
Inn on Ursulines 175-6
International House 183

L

La Belle Esplanade 186
La Boheme de Marigny 180
La Quinta Inn & Suites Downtown 183
Lafayette Hotel 182
Lafitte Guest House 175, 178
Lamothe House 180
Le Pavillon 178
Le Richelieu 175
Lions Inn B&B 179
Loews New Orleans Hotel 183
Loft 523 183
Lookout Inn of New Orleans 179

M

Maison de Macarty 180
Melrose Mansion 181

N

Nine-O-Five Royal Hotel 177

O

Olivier House 175
Omni Royal Orleans 179

P

Park View Guest House 185
Pierre Coulon Guest House 180
Prince Conti Hotel 176
Prytania Park Hotel 184

R

Ritz-Carlton New Orleans 178
Roosevelt New Orleans 183
Royal Sonesta 179
Royal Street Courtyard 181

S

Saint 177
Shadetree Inn Bed & Breakfast (St Francisville) 163
Soniat House 177

T

Terrell House 184

W

W French Quarter 178
Westin New Orleans at Canal Place 177
Windsor Court Hotel 183-4

SPORTS & ACTIVITIES

A Bicycle Named Desire 97
Belladonna Day Spa 119
Canal Street Ferry 106
Confederacy of Cruisers 93
Ninth Ward Rebirth Bike Tours 88
Wild Lotus Yoga 96

New Orleans Maps

Sights

- Beach
- Bird Sanctuary
- Buddhist
- Castle/Palace
- Christian
- Confucian
- Hindu
- Islamic
- Jain
- Jewish
- Monument
- Museum/Gallery/Historic Building
- Ruin
- Shinto
- Sikh
- Taoist
- Winery/Vineyard
- Zoo/Wildlife Sanctuary
- Other Sight

Activities, Courses & Tours

- Bodysurfing
- Diving
- Canoeing/Kayaking
- Course/Tour
- Sento Hot Baths/Onsen
- Skiing
- Snorkeling
- Surfing
- Swimming/Pool
- Walking
- Windsurfing
- Other Activity

Sleeping

- Sleeping
- Camping

Eating

- Eating

Drinking & Nightlife

- Drinking & Nightlife
- Cafe

Entertainment

- Entertainment

Shopping

- Shopping

Information

- Bank
- Embassy/Consulate
- Hospital/Medical
- Internet
- Police
- Post Office
- Telephone
- Toilet
- Tourist Information
- Other Information

Geographic

- Beach
- Hut/Shelter
- Lighthouse
- Lookout
- Mountain/Volcano
- Oasis
- Park
- Pass
- Picnic Area
- Waterfall

Population

- Capital (National)
- Capital (State/Province)
- City/Large Town
- Town/Village

Transport

- Airport
- BART station
- Border crossing
- Boston T station
- Bus
- Cable car/Funicular
- Cycling
- Ferry
- Metro/Muni station
- Monorail
- Parking
- Petrol station
- Subway/SkyTrain station
- Taxi
- Train station/Railway
- Tram
- Underground station
- Other Transport

Note: Not all symbols displayed above appear on the maps in this book

Routes

- Tollway
- Freeway
- Primary
- Secondary
- Tertiary
- Lane
- Unsealed road
- Road under construction
- Plaza/Mall
- Steps
- Tunnel
- Pedestrian overpass
- Walking Tour
- Walking Tour detour
- Path/Walking Trail

Boundaries

- International
- State/Province
- Disputed
- Regional/Suburb
- Marine Park
- Cliff
- Wall

Hydrography

- River, Creek
- Intermittent River
- Canal
- Water
- Dry/Salt/Intermittent Lake
- Reef

Areas

- Airport/Runway
- Beach/Desert
- Cemetery (Christian)
- Cemetery (Other)
- Glacier
- Mudflat
- Park/Forest
- Sight (Building)
- Sportsground
- Swamp/Mangrove

MAP INDEX

1 French Quarter (p238)
2 Faubourg Marigny & Bywater (p242)
3 CBD & Warehouse District (p244)
4 Garden, Lower Garden & Central City (p248)
5 Uptown & Riverbend (p250)
6 Mid-City & the Tremé (p254)

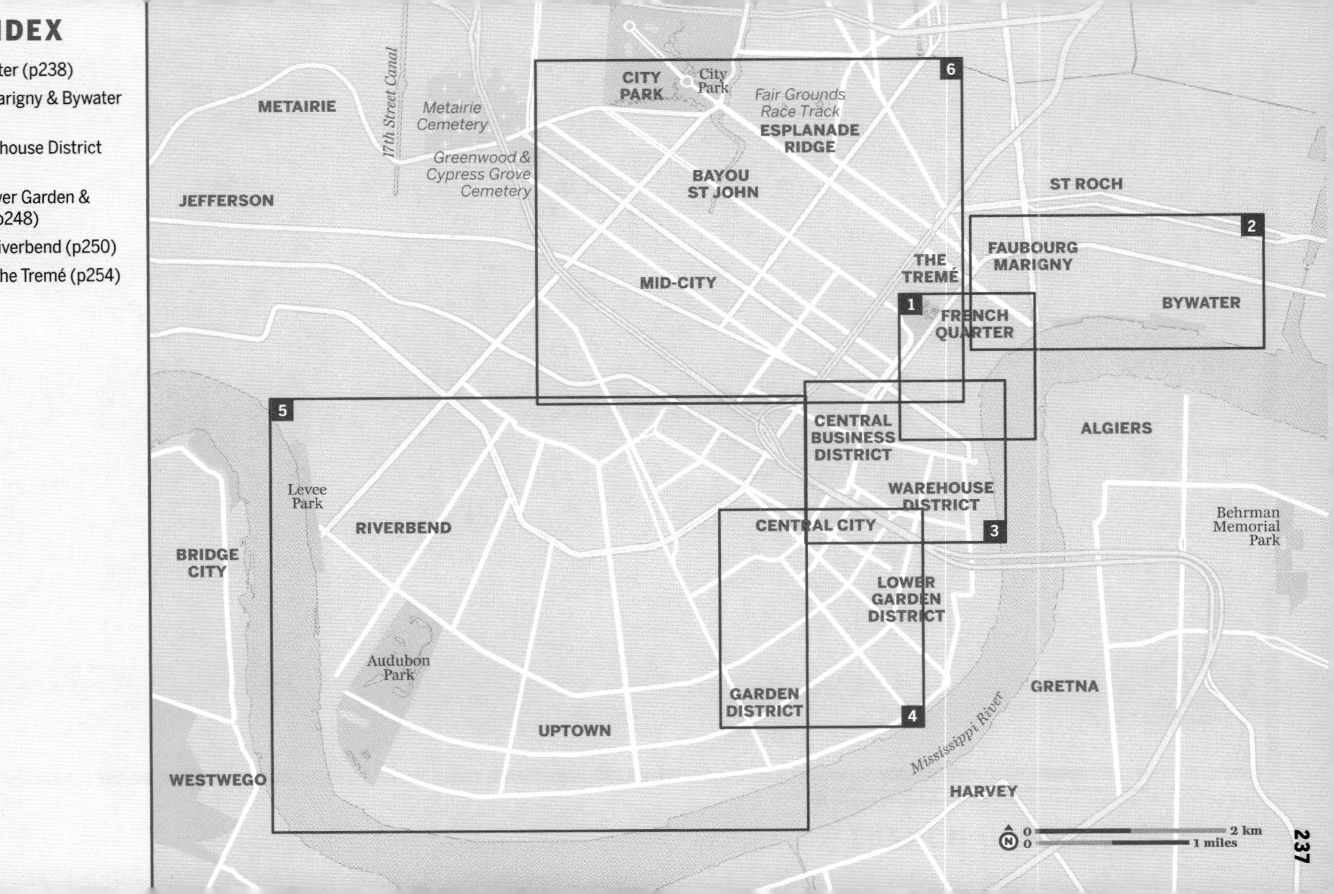

FRENCH QUARTER

Key on p240

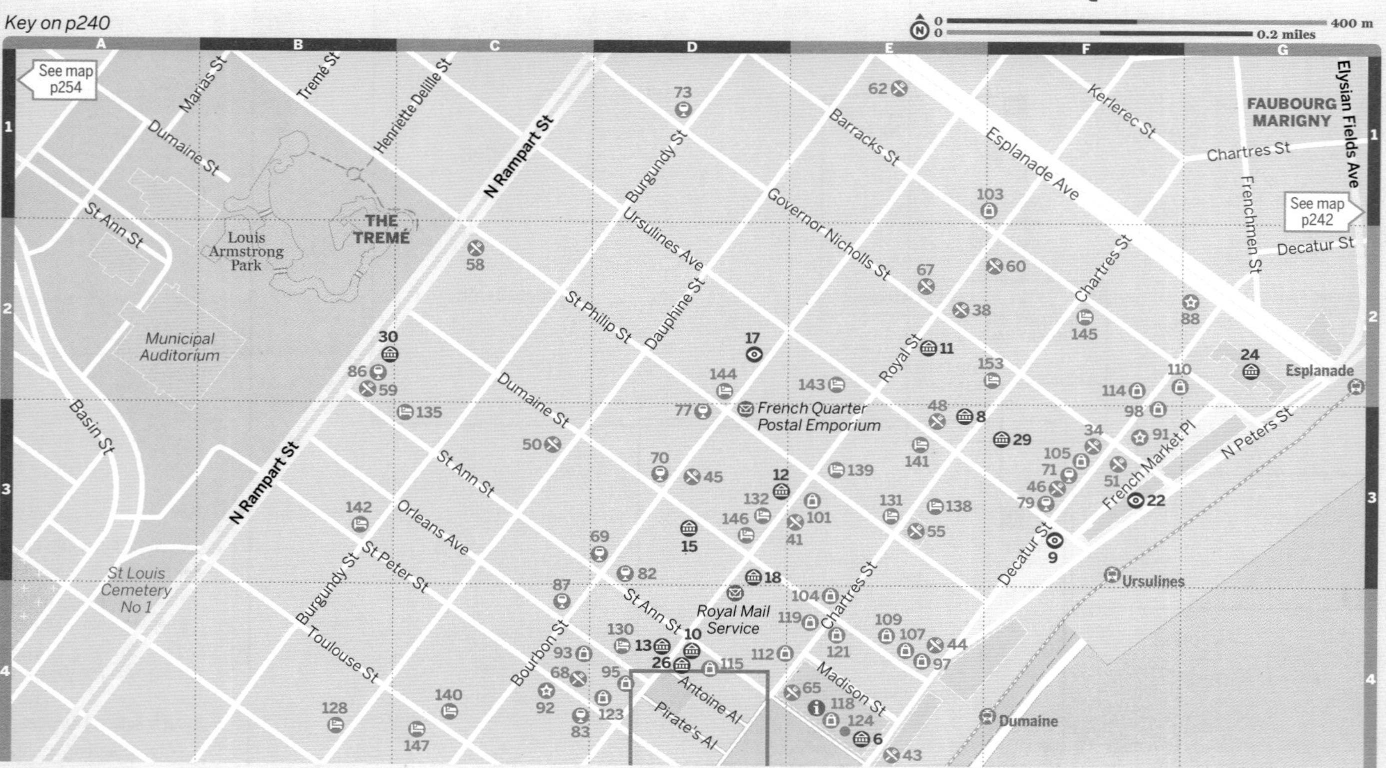

FRENCH QUARTER

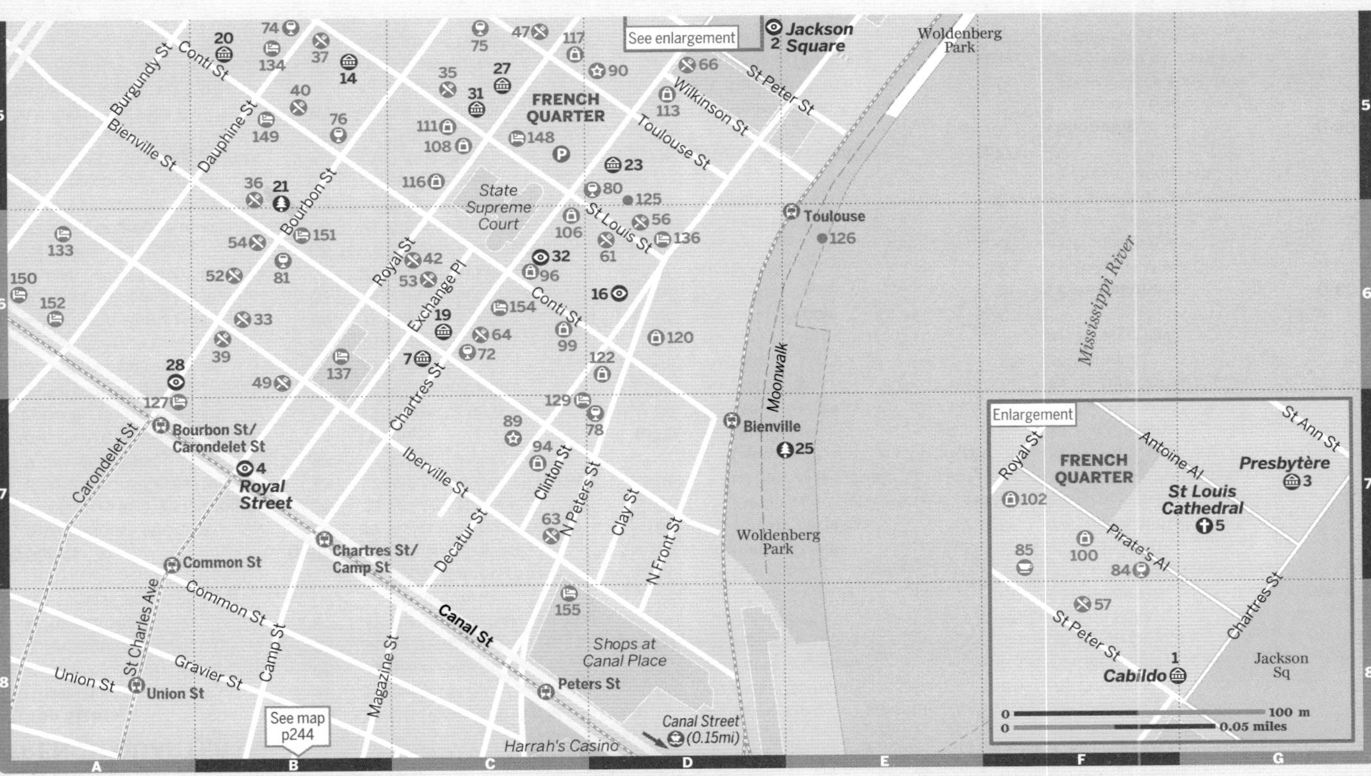

FRENCH QUARTER *Map on p238*

Top Sights (p60)

1 Cabildo F8
2 Jackson Square D5
3 Presbytère G7
4 Royal Street B7
5 St Louis Cathedral G7

Sights (p65)

6 1850 House Museum E4
7 A Gallery for Fine Photography C6
8 Beauregard-Keyes House E3
9 French Market F3
10 Gallery Burguieres D4
11 Gallier House Museum E2
12 Harouni Gallery D3
13 Hemmerling Gallery of Southern Art D4
14 Hermann-Grima House B5
15 Historic Voodoo Museum D3
16 Jean Lafitte National Historic Park D6
17 Lower Bourbon Street D2
18 Lucky Rose D3
19 Michalopoulos Gallery C6
20 Musée Conti Historical Wax Museum B5
21 Musical Legends Park B5
22 New Orleans Jazz National Historic Park F3
23 New Orleans Pharmacy Museum D5
24 Old US Mint G2
25 Riverfront E7
26 Rodrigue Studio D4
27 The Historic New Orleans Collection C5
28 Upper Bourbon Street A6
29 Ursuline Convent F3
30 Voodoo Spiritual Temple B2
31 Williams Gallery C5
32 Williams Research Center C6

Eating (p71)

33 Acme Oyster & Seafood House B6
34 Angeli on Decatur F3
35 Antoine's C5
36 Arnaud's B5
37 Bayona B5
38 Bennachin E2
39 Bourbon House B6
Brennan's Restaurant (see 116)
40 Broussard's B5
41 Café Amelie E3
Café Beignet (see 21)
42 Café Beignet C6
43 Café du Monde E4
44 Central Grocery E4
45 Clover Grill D3
46 Coop's Place F3
47 Court of Two Sisters C5
48 Croissant D'Or Patisserie E3
49 Dickie Brennan's B6
50 Eat New Orleans C3
51 Fiorella's F3
52 Galatoire's B6
53 Green Goddess C6
54 GW Fins B6
55 Irene's Cuisine E3
56 Johnny's Po-Boys D6
K-Paul's Louisiana Kitchen (see 96)
57 La Divina Gelateria F8
Latitude 29 (see 78)
58 Meauxbar C2
59 Mister Gregory's B2
60 Mona Lisa F2
61 Nola D6
62 Port of Call E1
63 Salt N Pepper C7
64 SoBou C6
65 Stanley E4
66 Sylvain D5
67 Verti Marte E2
68 Yo Mama's C4

Drinking & Nightlife (p77)

Abbey (see 105)
69 Bourbon Pub & Parade D3
70 Café Lafitte in Exile D3
71 Cane & Table F3
Carousel Bar (see 137)
72 Chart Room C6
73 Cosimo's D1
74 Double Play B5
75 Dungeon C5
76 Erin Rose B5
French 75 (see 36)
77 Lafitte's Blacksmith Shop D3
78 Latitude 29 D7
79 Molly's at the Market F3
80 Napoleon House D5
81 Old Absinthe House B6
82 Oz D3
83 Pat O'Brien's C4
84 Pirate's Alley Cafe F7
85 Spitfire Coffee F7
86 Tonique B2
87 Tropical Isle C4

Entertainment (p80)

88 Balcony Music Club G2
89 House of Blues C7
90 One Eyed Jacks D5
91 Palm Court Jazz Café F3
92 Preservation Hall C4

Shopping (p80)

93 Arcadian Books & Art Prints C4
94 Beckham's Bookstore C7
95 Boutique du Vampyre D4
Central Grocery (see 44)

96 Centuries C6
97 Chiwawa Gaga E4
98 Collectible Antiques F3
99 Exodus C6
100 Faulkner House Books F7
101 Fifi Mahony's E3
102 Fleur de Paris F7
103 Flora Savage F1
104 Green Eyed Gator E4
105 Greg's Antiques F3
106 Hové Parfumeur C6
107 Humidity Skate Shop E4
108 James H Cohen & Sons C5
109 Java House Imports E4
110 Le Garage F2
111 Leah's Pralines C5
112 Librairie Books D4
113 Lucullus D5
114 Mary Jane's Emporium F2
115 Maskarade D4
116 Moss Antiques C5
117 MS Rau Antiques C5
118 New Orleans Cajun Store E4
119 Od Aomo E4
120 Peaches Records & Tapes D6
121 Queork E4
122 Southern Candy Makers D6
123 Zombie's House of Voodoo D4

Sports & Activities

124 Friends of the Cabildo E4
125 New Orleans School of Cooking D5
126 Steamboat Natchez E6

Sleeping **(p175)**

127 Astor Crowne Plaza A7
128 Audubon Cottages B4
129 Bienville House Hotel C7
130 Bourbon Orleans Hotel D4
131 Chateau Hotel E3
132 Cornstalk Hotel D3
133 Courtyard New Orleans Downtown A6
134 Dauphine Orleans B5
135 Gentry Quarters C3
136 Historic French Market Inn D6
137 Hotel Monteleone B6
138 Hotel Provincial E3
139 Hotel Royal E3
140 Hotel St Marie C4
141 Hotel Villa Convento E3
142 Inn on St Peter B3
143 Inn on Ursulines E2
144 Lafitte Guest House D2
145 Le Richelieu F2
146 Nine-O-Five Royal Hotel D3
147 Olivier House C4
148 Omni Royal Orleans C5
149 Prince Conti Hotel B5
150 Ritz-Carlton New Orleans A6
151 Royal Sonesta B6
152 Saint A6
153 Soniat House F2
154 W French Quarter C6
155 Westin New Orleans at Canal Place C8

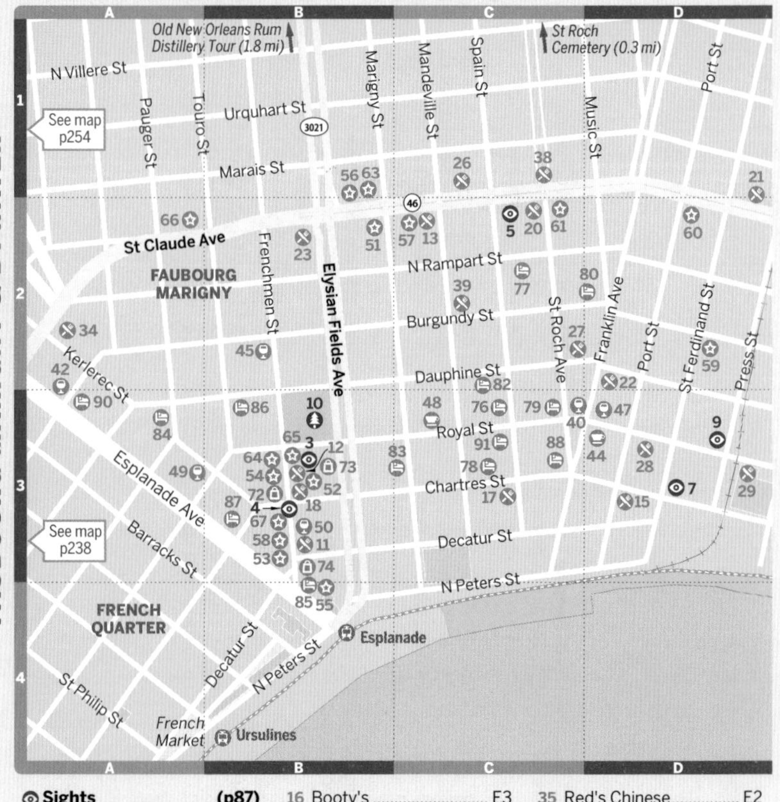

Sights (p87)

1 Clouet Gardens E3
2 Crescent Park F4
3 Frenchmen Art Market B3
4 Frenchmen Street B3
5 Healing Center C2
6 Markey Park F3
7 New Orleans Center for Creative Arts D3
8 Old Ironworks F3
9 Plessy v Ferguson Plaque D3
10 Washington Square Park B3

Eating (p88)

11 13 Monaghan B3
12 Adolfo's B3
13 Arabella Casa Di Pasta C2
14 Bacchanal H4
15 Bao & Noodle D3
16 Booty's E3
17 Cake Café & Bakery C3
18 Dat Dog B3
19 Elizabeth's F4
20 Fatoush C2
21 Four Calendar Cafe D1
22 Franklin D2
23 Gene's B2
24 Joint H4
25 Junction E2
26 Kebab C1
27 Lost Love C2
28 Mardi Gras Zone D3
29 Mariza D3
30 Maurepas Foods F3
31 Meltdown G2
32 Oxalis E3
Piety Street Snoballs .... (see 8)
33 Pizza Delicious F3
34 Rampart Food Store A2
35 Red's Chinese E2
36 Satsuma F3
37 Sneaky Pickle H2
38 St Roch Market C1
39 Who Dat Coffee Cafe & Cafe Nero C2

Drinking & Nightlife (p92)

40 Big Daddy's Bar C3
41 BJ's H3
42 Buffa's A2
43 Country Club E3
Faubourg Wines .... (see 21)
44 Flora Gallery & Coffee Shop D3
45 John B2
46 Markey's E3
47 Mimi's in the Marigny D3
48 Orange Couch C3
49 R Bar A3

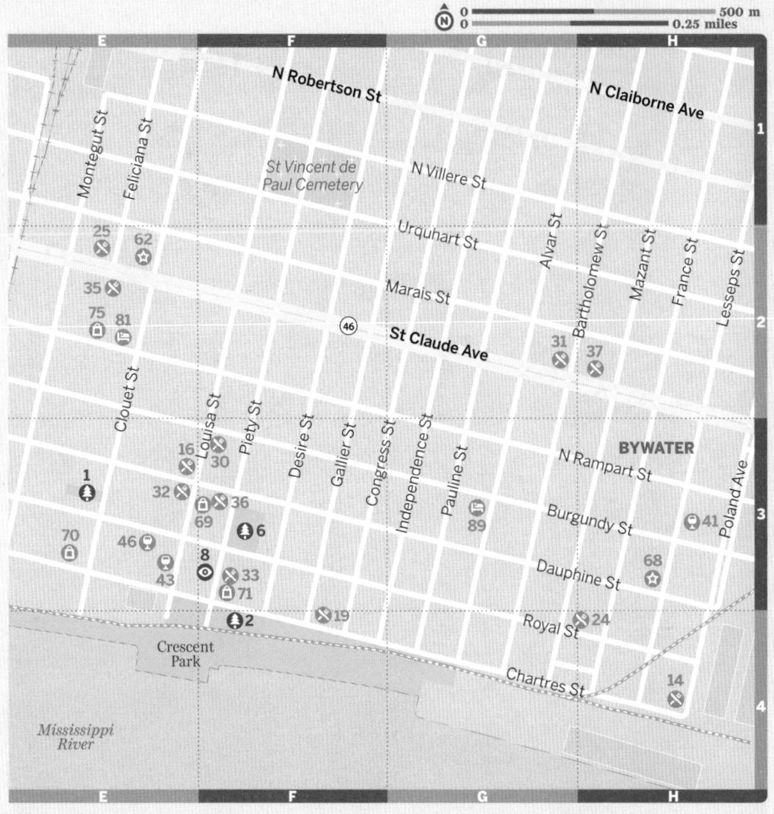

50 Yuki Izakaya B3

Entertainment (p94)

51 AllWays Lounge B2
52 Apple Barrel B3
Blue Nile .... (see 58)
Café Negril .... (see 54)
53 Checkpoint Charlie B3
54 d.b.a. B3
55 Dragon's Den B4
56 Hi Ho Lounge B1
57 Kajun's Pub C2
58 Maison B3
59 Marigny Opera House D2
60 New Movement Theater D2
61 Old Marquer Theatre C2
62 Saturn Bar E2
63 Siberia B1
64 Snug Harbor B3
65 Spotted Cat B3
66 Sweet Lorraine's A2
67 Three Muses B3
68 Vaughan's H3

Shopping (p97)

69 Bywater Bargain Center F3
70 Dr Bob's Studio E3
Electric Ladyland .... (see 64)
71 Euclid Records F3
72 Faubourg Marigny Book Store B3
73 I.J. Reilly's B3
74 Louisiana Music Factory B3
75 New Orleans Art Supply E2

Sports & Activities

A Bicycle Named Desire .... (see 73)
Confederacy of Cruisers .... (see 73)

Sleeping (p179)

76 Pierre Coulon Guest House C3
77 Auld Sweet Olive Bed & Breakfast C2
78 B&W Courtyards C3
79 Balcony Guest House ... C3
80 Burgundy D2
81 Bywater Bed & Breakfast E2
82 Collinwood House C2
83 Crescent City Guesthouse C3
84 Dauphine House A3
85 Frenchmen Hotel B4
86 La Boheme de Marigny B3
87 Lamothe House B3
88 Lions Inn B&B C3
89 Maison de Macarty G3
90 Melrose Mansion A3
91 Royal Street Courtyard C3

Key on p246

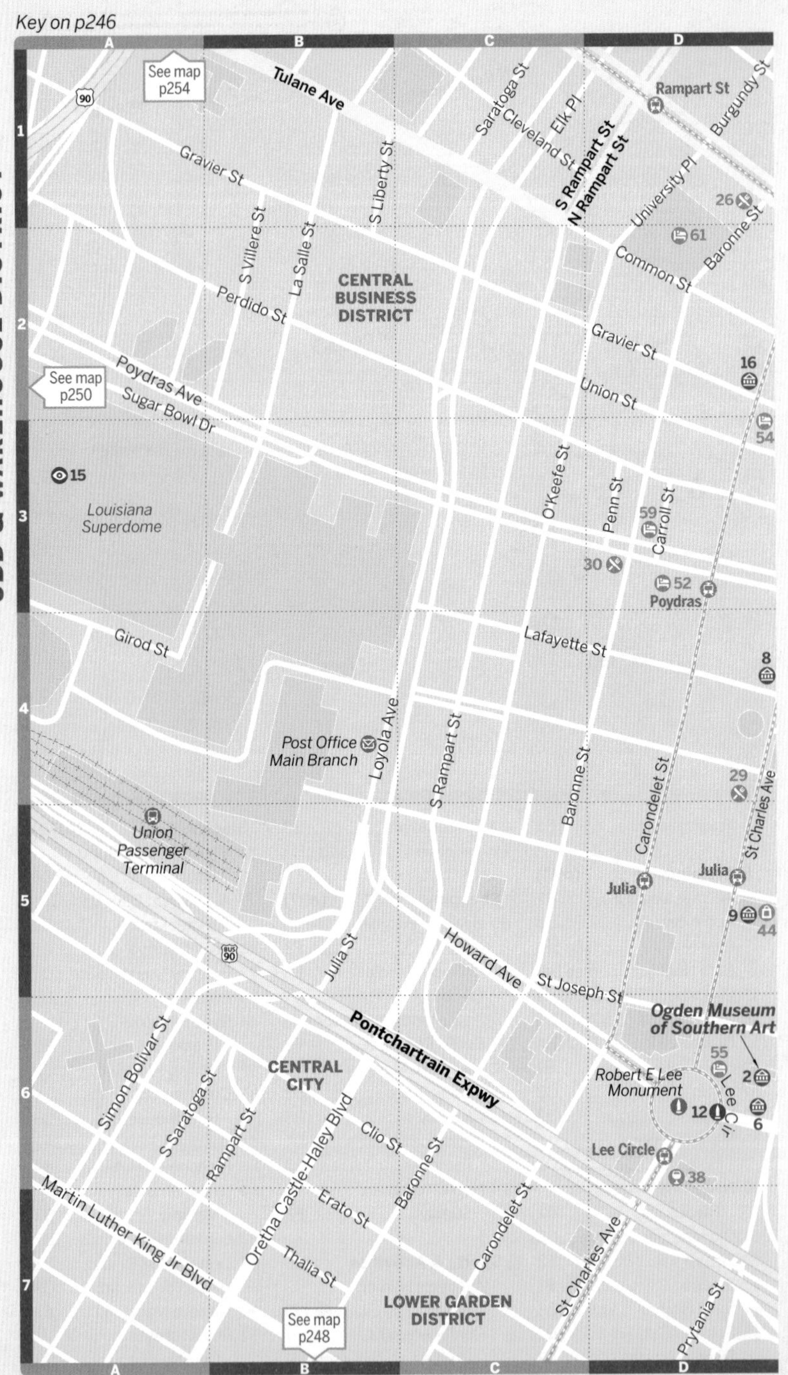

See map p254
See map p250
See map p248
Tulane Ave
Gravier St
Perdido St
Poydras Ave
Sugar Bowl Dr
Girod St
S Villere St
La Salle St
S Liberty St
Saratoga St
Cleveland St
Elk Pl
S Rampart St
N Rampart St
Rampart St
Burgundy St
University Pl
Baronne St
Common St
Union St
O'Keefe St
Penn St
Carroll St
Poydras
Lafayette St
Loyola Ave
Carondelet St
St Charles Ave
Julia
Howard Ave
St Joseph St
Julia St
Pontchartrain Expwy
Ogden Museum of Southern Art
Robert E Lee Monument
Lee Cir
Lee Circle
CENTRAL BUSINESS DISTRICT
Louisiana Superdome
Post Office Main Branch
Union Passenger Terminal
CENTRAL CITY
LOWER GARDEN DISTRICT
Simon Bolivar St
S Saratoga St
Clio St
Erato St
Thalia St
Oretha Castle-Haley Blvd
Martin Luther King Jr Blvd
Prytania St

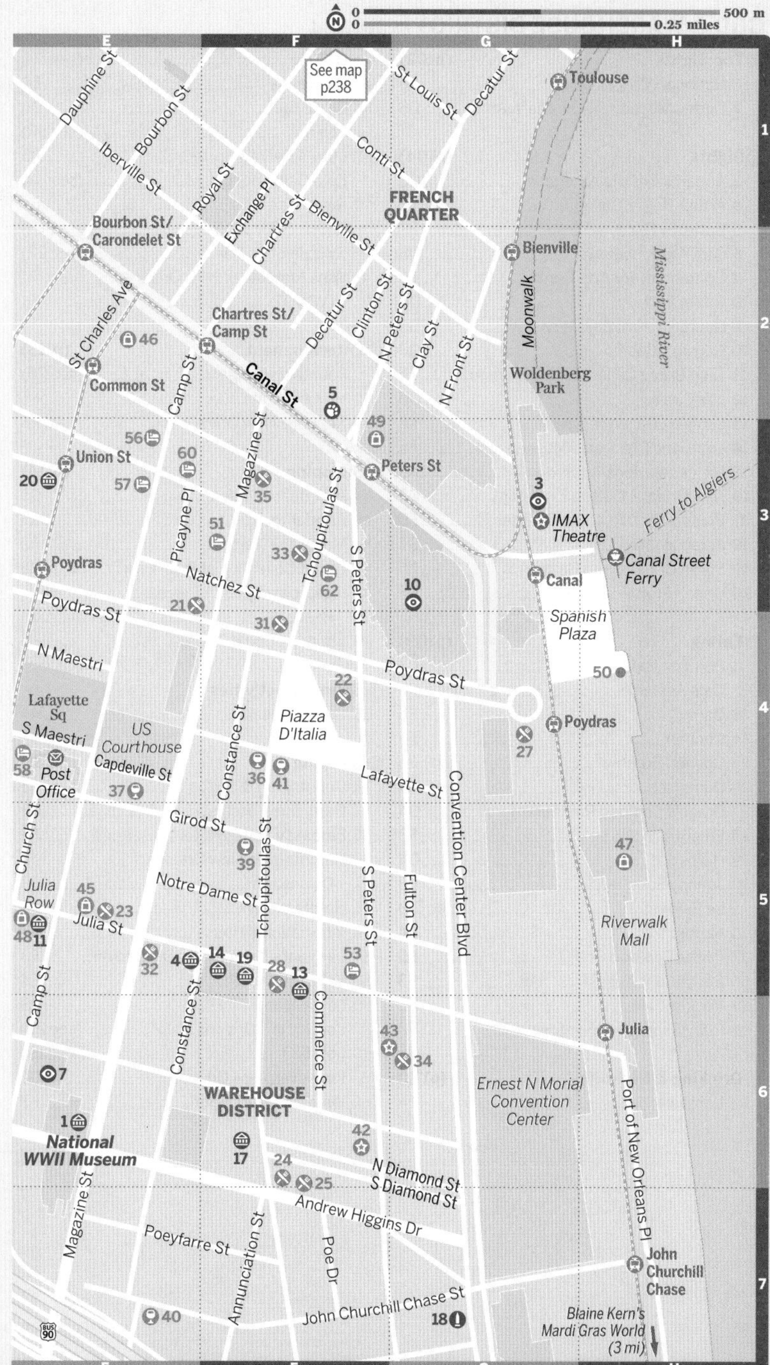

500 m
0.25 miles
See map p238
FRENCH QUARTER
Dauphine St
Bourbon St
Iberville St
Royal St
Exchange Pl
Chartres St
Bienville St
Conti St
St Louis St
Decatur St
Toulouse
Bienville
Bourbon St/ Carondelet St
Chartres St/ Camp St
St Charles Ave
Common St
Canal St
Camp St
Magazine St
Decatur St
Clinton St
N Peters St
Clay St
N Front St
Moonwalk
Woldenberg Park
Mississippi River
Union St
Peters St
Picayne Pl
Tchoupitoulas St
S Peters St
IMAX Theatre
Ferry to Algiers
Canal Street Ferry
Canal
Poydras
Natchez St
Poydras St
Spanish Plaza
N Maestri
Lafayette Sq
S Maestri
US Courthouse
Post Office
Capdeville St
Constance St
Piazza D'Italia
Lafayette St
Convention Center Blvd
Poydras
Girod St
Church St
Julia Row
Julia St
Notre Dame St
Tchoupitoulas St
S Peters St
Fulton St
Riverwalk Mall
Camp St
Constance St
Commerce St
Julia
Ernest N Morial Convention Center
WAREHOUSE DISTRICT
National WWII Museum
N Diamond St
S Diamond St
Andrew Higgins Dr
Port of New Orleans Pl
Magazine St
Poeyfarre St
Annunciation St
Poe Dr
John Churchill Chase
John Churchill Chase St
Blaine Kern's Mardi Gras World (3 mi)
BUS 90

CBD & WAREHOUSE DISTRICT *Map on p244*

Top Sights (p102)
1 National WWII Museum E6
2 Ogden Museum of Southern Art D6

Sights (p104)
3 Aquarium of the Americas G3
4 Arthur Roger Gallery E5
5 Butterfly Garden & Insectarium F2
6 Civil War Museum D6
7 Contemporary Arts Center E6
8 Gallier Hall D4
9 George Schmidt Gallery D5
10 Harrah's Casino G3
11 Jean Bragg Gallery of Southern Art E5
12 Lee Circle D6
13 Lemieux Galleries F5
14 Louisiana Children's Museum F5
15 Mercedes-Benz Superdome A3
16 New Orleans Cotton Exchange D2
17 Preservation Resource Center F6
18 Scrap House G7
19 Soren Christensen Gallery F5
20 United Fruit Company E3

Eating (p109)
21 Bon Ton Café E3
22 Café Adelaide F4
23 Carmo E5
24 Cochon F6
25 Cochon Butcher F6
26 Domenica D1
27 Drago's Seafood Restaurant G4
28 Emeril's F5
29 Herbsaint D4
30 Johnny Sanchez D3
Le Pavillon .... (see 59)
31 Mother's F4
32 Peche Seafood Grill E5
33 Restaurant August F3
34 Rock-n-Sake G6
35 Ruby Slipper – Downtown F3

Drinking & Nightlife (p112)
36 Barcadia F4
Bellocq .... (see 55)
37 Capdeville E4
38 Circle Bar D6
Loa .... (see 56)
39 Lucy's Retired Surfers Bar F5
Polo Club Lounge .... (see 62)
40 Rusty Nail E7
Sazerac Bar .... (see 61)
Swizzle Stick Bar .... (see 22)
41 Wine Institute of New Orleans (WINO) F4

Entertainment (p113)
Fountain Lounge .... (see 26)
42 Howlin' Wolf F6
43 Republic New Orleans F6

Shopping (p114)
44 Alex Beard Studio D5
45 Ariodante E5
46 Meyer the Hatter E2
47 Outlet Collection at Riverwalk H5
48 REpurposingNOLA Piece by Peace E5
49 Shops at Canal Place F3

Sports & Activities
50 Creole Queen H4

Sleeping (p181)
51 Country Inn & Suites F3
52 Drury Inn & Suites D3
53 Embassy Suites Hotel F5
54 Hampton Inn New Orleans Downtown D3
55 Hotel Modern D6
56 International House E3
57 La Quinta Inn & Suites Downtown E3
58 Lafayette Hotel E4
59 Le Pavillon D3
Loews New Orleans Hotel .... (see 22)
60 Loft 523 .... E3
61 Roosevelt New Orleans D2
62 Windsor Court Hotel F3

GARDEN, LOWER GARDEN & CENTRAL CITY *Map on p248*

Top Sights **(p117)**
1 Lafayette Cemetery No 1 ... C6

Sights **(p118)**
2 Ashé Cultural Arts Center ... D2
3 Goodrich-Stanley House ... F3
4 Grace King House ... F4
5 House of Broel ... D4
6 Irish Channel ... D7
7 McKenna Museum of African American Art ... D3
8 Parkway Partners ... E1
9 Southern Food & Beverage Museum ... D2
10 St Vincent's Infant Asylum ... F4

Eating **(p121)**
11 Café Reconcile ... D2
12 Commander's Palace ... C6
13 Coquette ... C7
14 District: Donuts Sliders Brew ... E6
15 Juan's Flying Burrito ... F5
16 Parasol's ... D7
17 Purloo ... D2
18 Sake Café Uptown ... C7
19 Seed ... F2
20 Slice ... E2
21 Slim Goodie's Diner ... B8
22 Stein's Deli ... E6
23 Sucré ... C7
24 Surrey's Juice Bar ... G3
25 Tracey's ... D7

Drinking & Nightlife **(p124)**
26 Avenue Pub ... E3
27 Balcony Bar ... B8
28 Bulldog ... B8
29 Half Moon ... F5
30 Igor's Lounge ... D4
31 Krewe du Brew ... E3
32 Rendezvous ... B8
33 Root Squared ... F5
34 Saint Bar & Lounge ... F5
35 Still Perkin' ... C6

Entertainment **(p126)**
36 Zeitgeist ... D2

Shopping **(p126)**
37 Aidan Gill for Men ... F5
38 Big Fisherman Seafood ... B8
Diaspora Boutique ... (see 2)
39 Fleurty Girl ... B8
40 Funky Monkey ... B8
Garden District Bookshop ... (see 35)
41 GoGo Jewelry ... F6
42 Jim Russell Records ... F5
43 Magazine Antique Mall ... C7
44 New Orleans Music Exchange ... B8
45 Simon of New Orleans ... E6
46 Storyville ... C8
47 Thomas Mann Gallery I/O ... F5
48 Trashy Diva ... F6

Sports & Activities
49 Belladonna Day Spa ... C7

Sleeping **(p184)**
50 Garden District B&B ... D6
51 Green House Inn ... G2
52 Hotel Indigo ... D4
53 Prytania Park Hotel ... F3
54 Terrell House ... G4

GARDEN, LOWER GARDEN & CENTRAL CITY

Key on p247

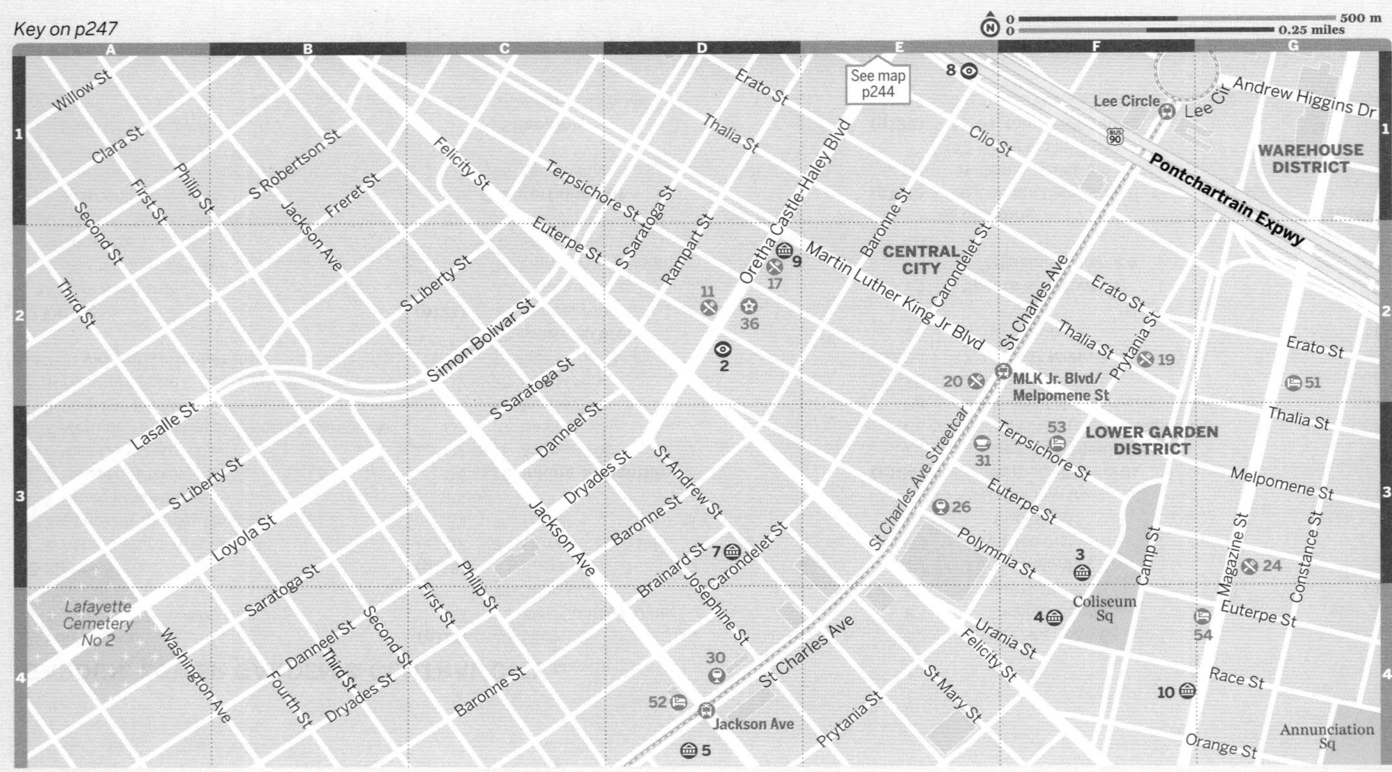

GARDEN, LOWER GARDEN & CENTRAL CITY

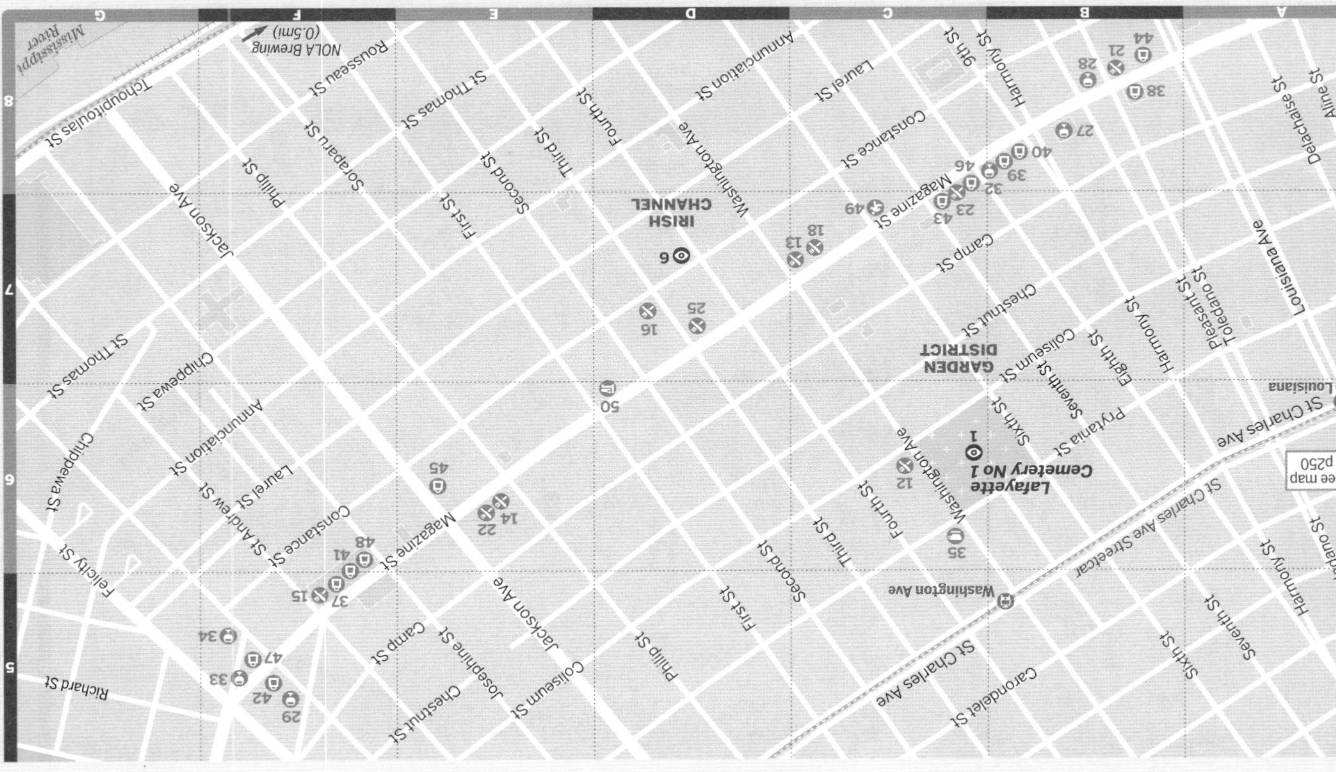

Key on p252

UPTOWN & RIVERBEND
A
B
C
D
1
2
3
4
5
6
7
S Caliborne Ave
S Carrollton Ave
RIVERBEND
Levee Park
Leake Ave
Eagle St
Monroe St
Leonidas St
Joliet St
Cambronne St
Dante St
Dublin St
Short St
Oak St
Neron St
Sycamore St
Panola St
Spruce St
Cohn St
Hickory St
Green St
Birch St
St Mary Cemetery
Carrollton Cemetery
Jeannette St
Fern St
Willow St
Plum St
Burdette St
Adams St
Hillary St
Zimple St
Burthe St
Lowerline St
Pine St
Broadway St
Audubon St
Audubon Blvd
S Claiborne Ave
Versailles Blvd
Hampson St
Maple St
St Charles Ave
Pearl St
Dominican St
Benjamin St
Cherokee St
Millaudon St
Hurst St
Garfield St
Pitt St
Walnut St
Mississippi River
Mississippi River Trail
Broadway
Newcomb Blvd
Tulane University
Loyola University
Tulane University/ Audubon Park & Zoo
Freret St
Ursuline College & Convent
Calhoun St
Palmer Ave
State St
Clara St
Magnolia St
S Robertson St
Nashville Ave
Joseph St
Octavia St
Loyola St
Jefferson Ave
St Charles Ave Streetcar
Nashville
Audubon Park Trail
Audubon Park Golf Course
Exposition Blvd
Prytania St
Henry Clay Ave
Webster St
Eleonore St
Arabella St
Perrier St
Coliseum St
Chestnut St
Camp St
Magazine St
Constance St
Patton St
Laurel St
Annunciation St
Tchoupitoulas St
Leontine St
Valmont St
Bellecastle St
Zoo Ave
East Dr
River Dr
Riverview Dr
Audubon Zoological Gardens
Orleans Parish
Jefferson Parish
1
2
3
4
5
7
9
10
11
12
14
16
20
22
26
31
33
35
36
39
40
41
43
48
49
50
51
52
54
55
56
60
63
66
67
68
72

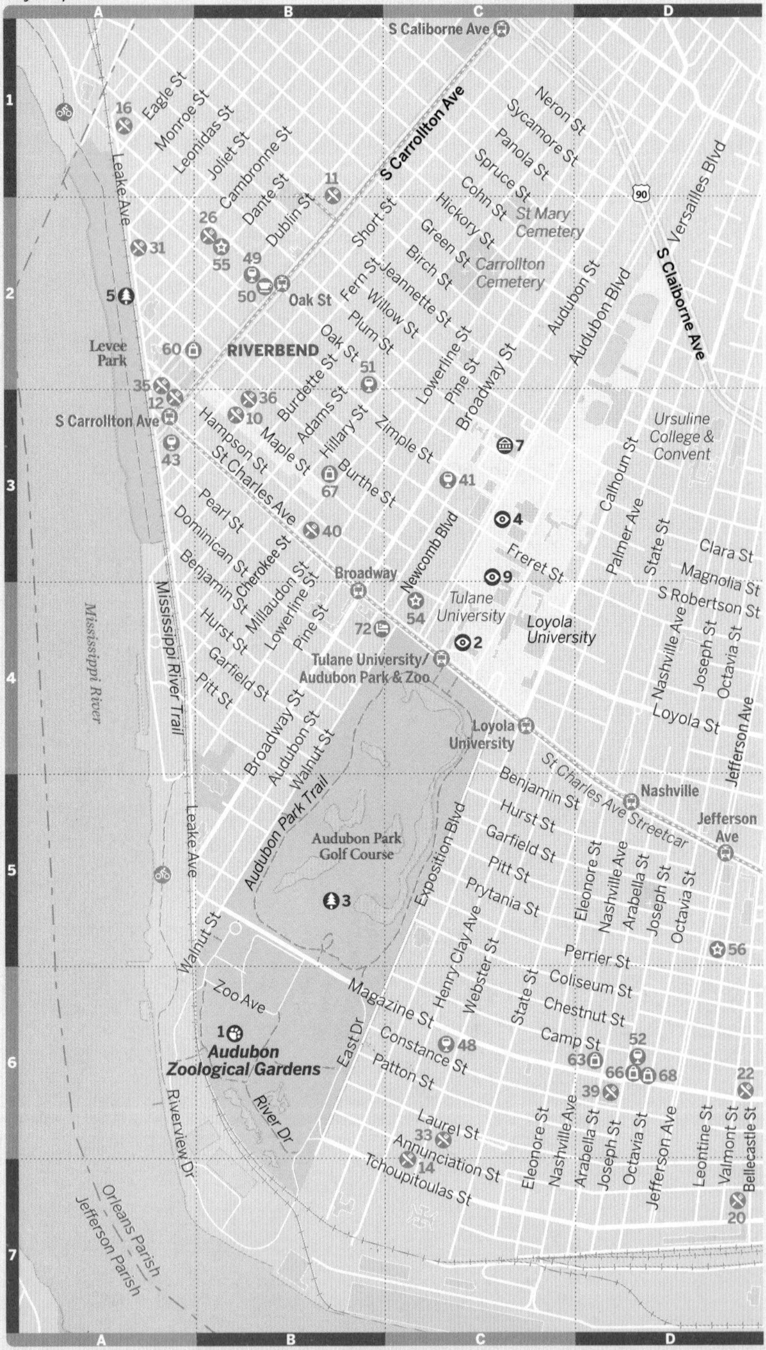

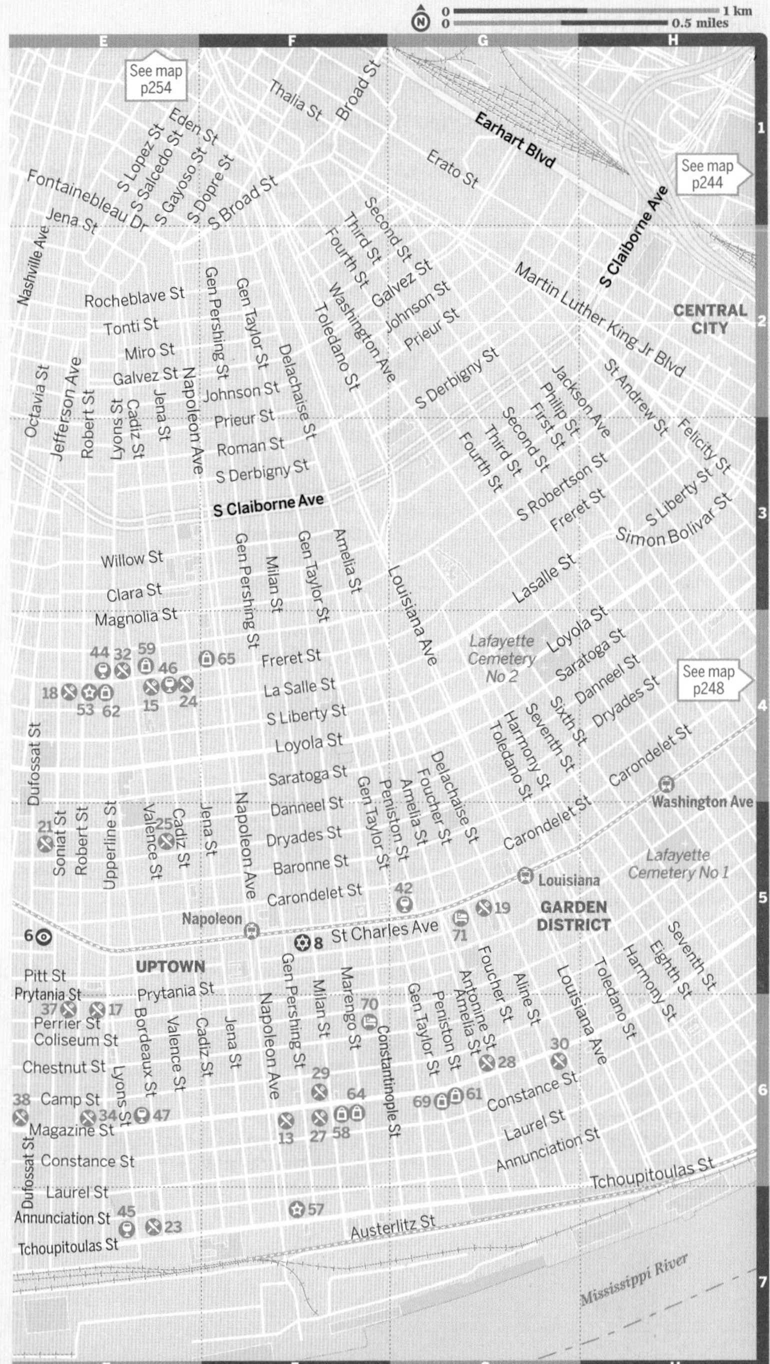

See map p254
See map p244
See map p248
CENTRAL CITY
UPTOWN
GARDEN DISTRICT
Lafayette Cemetery No 2
Lafayette Cemetery No 1
Mississippi River
Napoleon
Louisiana
Washington Ave
St Charles Ave
S Claiborne Ave
Earhart Blvd
Martin Luther King Jr Blvd
Tchoupitoulas St
Magazine St
Napoleon Ave
Louisiana Ave

UPTOWN & RIVERBEND *Map on p250*

Top Sights (p132)
1 Audubon Zoological Gardens ... B6

Sights (p133)
2 Amistad Research Center ... C4
3 Audubon Park ... B5
4 Hogan Jazz Archive ... C3
5 Levee Path ... A2
6 Milton Latter Memorial Library ... E5
7 Newcomb Art Gallery ... C3
Southeastern Architectural Archives ... (see 4)
8 Touro Synagogue ... F5
9 Tulane University ... C3

Eating (p134)
10 Ba Chi Canteen ... B3
11 Boucherie ... B1
12 Camellia Grill ... A3
13 Casamento's ... F6
14 Clancy's ... C7
15 Company Burger ... E4
16 Cowbell ... A1
17 Creole Creamery ... E6
18 Dat Dog ... E4
19 Delachaise ... G5
20 Domilise's Po-Boys ... D7
21 Gautreau's ... E5
22 Guy's ... D6
23 Hansen's Sno-Bliz ... E7
24 High Hat Cafe ... E4
25 Il Posto ... E5
26 Jacques-Imo's Café ... B2
Kyoto ... (see 17)
27 La Petite Grocery ... F6
28 Lilette ... G6
29 Magasin Cafe ... F6
30 Mahony's Po-Boy Shop ... G6
31 Mat & Naddie's ... A2
32 Midway Pizza ... E4
33 Patois ... C6
34 Pizza Domenica ... E6
35 Refuel ... A2
36 Satsuma Maple ... B3
37 St James Cheese Co ... E6
38 Tee-Eva's Old-Fashioned Pies & Pralines ... E6
39 Whole Foods ... D6
40 Willie Mae's Grocery & Deli ... B3

Drinking & Nightlife (p139)
41 Boot ... C3
Bouligny Tavern ... (see 28)
42 Columns Hotel ... G5
43 Cooter Brown's Tavern & Oyster Bar ... A3
44 Cure ... E4
45 F&M's Patio Bar ... E7
46 Freret Street Publiq House ... E4
47 Le Bon Temps Roulé ... E6
48 Monkey Hill Bar ... C6
Ms Mae's ... (see 13)
49 Oak Wine Bar ... B2
50 Rue de la Course ... B2
51 Snake & Jakes ... B2
52 St Joe's ... D6

Entertainment (p141)
53 Gasa Gasa ... E4
54 Lupin Theatre ... C4
55 Maple Leaf Bar ... B2
56 Prytania Theatre ... D5
57 Tipitina's ... F7

Shopping (p142)
58 Berta's & Mina's Antiquities ... F6
59 Bloomin' Deals ... E4
60 C Collection ... A2
61 Cole Pratt Gallery ... G6
62 Crescent City Comics ... E4
63 Dirty Coast ... D6
64 Feet First ... F6
65 Freret Street Market ... F4
66 Hazelnut ... D6
67 Maple Street Book Shop ... B3
68 Pelican Coast Clothing Co ... D6
Pied Nu ... (see 66)
69 Potsalot ... G6

Sleeping (p185)
70 Chimes ... F6
Columns Hotel ... (see 42)
71 Hampton Inn St Charles Avenue ... G5
72 Park View Guest House ... B4

MID-CITY & THE TREMÉ *Map on p254*

Top Sights (p146)

1 City Park ... C1
2 St Louis Cemetery No 1 ... G6

Sights (p149)

3 Alcee Fortier Park ... E2
4 Backstreet Cultural Museum ... H5
5 Botanical Gardens ... C1
6 Carousel Gardens Amusement Park ... B1
7 Congo Square ... H6
8 Esplanade Avenue ... E2
9 Fair Grounds Race Course ... E2
10 Le Musée de f.p.c. ... F3
11 Louis Armstrong Park ... H6
12 Louis Armstrong Statue ... H6
13 Mortuary Chapel ... G6
14 New Orleans African American Museum ... H5
15 New Orleans Museum of Art ... C1
16 Our Lady of the Rosary Rectory ... D2
17 Peristyle ... C1
18 Pitot House ... D2
19 Sanctuary ... D3
20 Singing Oak ... D1
21 St Augustine's Church ... H5
22 St Louis Cemetery No 3 ... E1
23 Sydney & Walda Besthoff Sculpture Garden ... C1

Eating (p152)

24 Angelo Brocato ... B3
25 Café Degas ... E2
26 Cajun Seafood ... H4
27 Dis and Dat ... E6
28 Dooky Chase ... F5
29 Lil' Dizzy's ... H4
30 Liuzza's By the Track ... E2
31 Lola's ... E2
32 Mandina's ... C4
33 MoPho ... B2
34 Morning Call ... C1
Nonna Mia Café & Pizzeria ... (see 25)
35 Pagoda Cafe ... F3
36 Parkway Tavern ... D4
37 Ruby Slipper ... C4
38 Toup's Meatery ... C2
39 Twelve Mile Limit ... B5
40 Willie Mae's Scotch House ... F4

Drinking & Nightlife (p156)

41 Bayou Beer Garden ... D4
42 Fair Grinds ... E2
43 Finn McCool's ... B4
44 Mid-City Yacht Club ... A3
45 Pal's ... E3
46 Pearl Wine Co ... D3
47 Treo ... B5
Twelve Mile Limit ... (see 39)

Entertainment (p157)

48 Banks Street Bar ... A3
49 Bullets ... H2
50 Candlelight Lounge ... G5
51 Chickie Wah Wah ... D5
52 Mahalia Jackson Theater ... H6
53 Saenger Theatre ... G7

Shopping (p158)

54 F&F Botanica Spiritual Supply ... E4
55 Massey's ... C3
56 SoPo ... C3
57 Tubby & Coos ... C3

Sports & Activities

58 City Putt ... B1
59 Wheel Fun Rentals ... D1

Sleeping (p186)

60 Ashton's Bed & Breakfast ... G4
61 Degas House ... F4
62 HH Whitney House ... G4
63 India House Hostel ... D5
64 La Belle Esplanade ... G4

Key on p253

Popp Fountain (1.5 mi)
Delgado Community College
City Park
Victory Ave
Collins Diboll Cir
Big Lake
Fredrichs Ave
LeLong Dr
Bayou Metairie
General Diaz St
Metairie Cemetery (100yd)
City Park & Museum of Art
City Park Ave
St Peter St
Orleans Ave
Toulouse St
Lafitte Ave
Hennessey St
Solomon St
Allard Blvd
Moss St
Delgado Dr
Dumaine St
BAYOU ST JOHN
Helena St
N Anthony St
N Bernadotte St
N St Patrick St
N Olympia St
N Murat St
N Alexander St
Rosedale Dr
David St
Orleans Ave
N Carrollton Ave
Bienville St
Canal St
S St Patrick St
S Olympia St
S Murat St
Cleveland St
Palmyra St
Banks St
Baudin St
D'Hemecourt St
Ulloa St
S Solomon St
S Carrollton Ave
N Carrollton Ave
MID-CITY
Toulouse St
Lafitte Ave
Conti St
Bienville St
Iberville St
N Hagan Ave
N Rendon St
S Cortez St
S Telemachus St
S Genois St
S Clark St
N Jefferson Davis Pkwy
Jefferson Davis Pkwy
S Pierce St
S Scott St
Banks St
S Rendon St
S Lopez St
S Salcedo St
S Gayoso St
S Dupre St
S White St
N Gayoso St
N Dupre St
White St
Broad St
S Broad Ave
Tulane Ave
Mid-City Rock & Bowl (500yd)
Pontchartrain Expwy
Howard Ave
Gravier St
Perdido St
Stroelitz St
Palm St
Edinburgh St
Palmetto St
Euphrosine St
Washington Ave
S Dorgenois St
Earhart Blvd
Clio St
Erato St
See map p250